Nineteenth-Century Chamber Music

ROUTLEDGE STUDIES IN MUSICAL GENRES
R. Larry Todd, General Editor

Nineteenth-Century Chamber Music

ROUTLEDGE STUDIES
IN MUSICAL GENRES

EDITED BY

Stephen E. Hefling

Routledge

New York and London

Published in 2004 by
Routledge
29 West 35th Street
New York, NY 10001
www.routledge-ny.com

Published in Great Britain by
Routledge
11 New Fetter Lane
London EC4P 4EE
www.routledge.co.uk

10 9 8 7 6 5 4 3 2 1

Library of Congress Cataloging-in-Publication Data

Nineteenth-century chamber music/edited by Stephen E. Hefling.
    p.   cm.—(Routledge studies in musical genre)
  Originally published: New York : Schirmer Books, c1998.
  Includes bibliographical references and indexes.
  ISBN 0-415-96650-7 (alk. paper)
    1. Chamber music—19th century—History and criticism.
I. Hefling, Stephen E. II. Series.

ML1104.N56 2003
785'.009'034—dc21   2003047187

Contents

Preface

Chamber music, in the sense that we think of it today, is a concept that crystallized gradually during the course of the nineteenth century. In 1802, shortly after the thirty-year-old Beethoven had boldly staked his claim to the heritage of the Viennese string quartet with the six works of Op. 18, music lexicographer Heinrich Christoph Koch still found it appropriate to define chamber music chiefly from the perspective of its traditionally upper-crust audience:

> Chamber music, in the proper sense of the word, is that music which is only customary at court, and to which, since it is contrived solely for the private entertainment of sovereigns, no one is granted entrance as a listener without special permission. In various courts, however, this expression is also taken to mean the so-called court concerts, which, to be sure, are actually intended only for the court and those associated with it, but at which other people may take part as listeners, isolated, however, in the concert hall from the court.[1]

As several contemporaries confirm, courtly chamber music in Koch's day included not only small genres but concerto and symphony as well. Although the long-standing stylistic categories of church, chamber, and theatrical music had already been substantially blurred, Koch nevertheless offers the distinction that the chamber composer is like "the painter who shades and colors a picture destined to be viewed at close range much more delicately than, for example, a ceiling painting, which is far removed from the eye, and in which these details would not only be lost, but might even weaken the effect of the whole." Displacement of the exclusively aristocratic clientele by larger and more heterogeneous groups of the bourgeoisie had a major impact on all aspects of nineteenth-century art, and chamber music is no exception. In addition, the tensions and interactions between private and public values, amateur and professional players, and, in Koch's simile, delicate canvases versus vast frescos were especially influential—often fruitfully so, yet at times almost to the point of stagnation. The process was gradual and complex.

Inevitably we begin with Beethoven. As Kern Holoman observes in his preface to *The Nineteenth-Century Symphony*, our companion volume in this series, "open this book anywhere, and you are within a few paragraphs of Beethoven."[2] And Beethoven was no less influential in the field of chamber music. Revolutionary though they were, his middle and late quartets were first performed in princely houses and popular restaurant halls before select audiences of perhaps no more than a hundred people.[3] For decades, chamber music had been the domain of skilled and devoted amateurs, both aristocratic and bourgeois. Haydn's hundred-plus baryton trios written explicitly for performance by Prince Nicolaus Esterházy and Schubert's early works for his family's string quartet are diverse cases in point. Beethoven himself had been an able amateur violinist, as was his patron Count Rasumovsky, to whom Beethoven's Op. 59 quartets are dedicated. But in these and later compositions Beethoven makes extraordinary demands that many amateurs could not meet: it was the professional ensemble led by Ignaz Schuppanzigh, first founded in 1804–05 for the express purpose of giving public concerts, that premiered many of them (as well as a few of Schubert's later works). Although Schuppanzigh's initial venture in professional public quartet performance lasted three seasons at most, it was an historic first, as the redoubtable critic and chronicler Eduard Hanslick would note sixty-odd years later.[4] By century's end both the professional quartet and the chamber music hall seating a public audience of several hundred people were regular features of concert life; as was true of the symphony, Beethoven's quartets, trios, and sonatas had become the core of the chamber music repertoire. Nevertheless, private performances, intimate listening, and the involvement of amateurs remained (and remain) fundamental to the living repertoire of chamber music. A decade after Beethoven's death, Gustav Schilling's *Universal-Lexicon* emphasized that the distinguishing characteristic of chamber music in its narrower sense (i.e., as opposed to concert music, which included the orchestra) was that "it was not intended for a large public, but actually only for connoisseurs and amateurs [*Kenner und Liebhaber*]. . . . it was more finely worked out, more difficult, and more artistic, . . . and . . . composers who wrote for the chamber could presume more accomplishment and experience in listening among their audience."[5] Even today Robert Schumann's pithy remark that the four members of a string quartet "constitute their own public" retains a curious validity.[6]

Among the first to struggle with the legacy of Beethoven was Schubert, whose "heavenly lengths" (another of Schumann's memorable phrases) and whose two hundredth anniversary have inspired an unusually long essay by two of our authors—justified, we hope, by the fact that no substantial survey of Schubert's chamber oeuvre has appeared in over twenty-five years. That Schubert regarded Beethoven with both awe and ambivalence now appears reasonably certain, and the achievements of his mature chamber music seem indebted to Beethoven only in general respects. Although he probably heard, and may have been impressed by, several of the late Beethoven quartets, Schubert was by then well on his own path; save for the epic dimensions of the G Major Quartet and C Major Quintet, he does not seem to have responded to the contrasts and complexities of Beethoven's final utterances, which were to become widely known and accepted only during the 1860s and '70s. Moreover, by the mid-1820s the rapidly developing piano had begun to usurp the strings as the vehicle of choice for amateur music-making, a trend that would continue through the century. It may be in part due to this change in taste that Schubert composed—and managed to publish—music for violin-and-piano duo and piano trio during the years that turned out to be his last.

Two chamber music composers well known in their own era but largely neglected in ours are Weber and Spohr, whose musical proclivities "had been essentially determined before they were exposed to the music of Beethoven's second and third periods," as Clive Brown puts it.[7] While Weber's output is not extensive, Spohr's chamber music is impressive both in quality and quantity—the work of an excellent craftsman frequently independent in spirit, as a recent spate of recordings reveals. But unlike Weber and Spohr, who were born in the mid-1780s, both Mendelssohn (b. 1809) and Schumann (b. 1810) felt compelled to take account of Beethoven from early on in their chamber music oeuvre—and late Beethoven at that. During the 1820s Mendelssohn breathed that rarefied musical atmosphere extensively, and his first mature quartet (the A major, Op. 13, of 1827) opens, in the words of R. Larry Todd, with "a powerfully charged sonata-form movement that recaptures the sound world of the opening movement of Beethoven's String Quartet, Op. 132" (p. 188). A dozen years later Schumann, seeking to launch the first quartet project of *his* maturity, studied the late Beethovens "right down to the love and hate contained therein."[8] Brahms's struggles with the Beethovenian heritage are legendary; not until age forty did he complete a quartet that he deemed worthy of publication, and anecdotal evidence suggests that he consigned many more to the fireplace than to the printer.

The vast majority of nineteenth-century French chamber music is all but unknown to English-language readers; accordingly, the fine overview by Joël-Marie Fauquet is especially welcome in this volume. As in Vienna, professionals and amateurs, aristocrats and bourgeoisie, all rubbed shoulders in the sphere of Parisian chamber music at the turn of the century. By about 1830, however, the technical demands of the repertoire and the rise of the public or semipublic concert began to transform the practice of chamber music. Larger audiences prompted the desire for more sound, and Paris was an important center of instrument making: here many of the great Italian string instruments were modernized for greater power, and innovations of the piano builder Erard increased the brilliance of the concert grand. Indeed, during the greater part of the century the piano trio was to be the predominant genre of French chamber music. And the extensive refinement of brass and woodwinds that went hand-in-hand with the experiments in orchestral color of the French Grand Opera completely redefined the role of the winds in chamber music. As in symphonic performances, the repertoire of chamber music concerts came to center on Beethoven, the object of "a French religion," as Leo Schrade put it.[9] Yet there were other influential currents as well. Although it has long been assumed that the renewal of French chamber music took place only in the aftermath of the Franco-Prussian War, Fauquet argues convincingly that "the movement favoring chamber music in France was practically uninterrupted from the eighteenth century on" (p. 302). The story of French chamber music from Cherubini to Debussy is indeed a fascinating one that should be more widely understood.

As is well known, the enormous impact of Liszt and Wagner upon European musical life yielded, on the whole, unfortunate consequences for chamber music. As Gustav Mahler half-humorously summarized the situation in 1893, "We moderns need such a great apparatus in order to express *our* ideas, whether they be great or small."[10] Chamber music did not rank high in the agenda of the moderns, and accordingly during the second half of the century many of the best talents avoided it. Brahms was widely regarded as the quintessential chamber music composer, and he was active in that domain from the Op. 8 trio of 1854 through the Op. 120 clarinet sonatas of 1894. But among those of more progressive inclination were two masters from the Czech lands, Bedřich Smetana and Antonín Dvořák, who did not disdain the field of chamber music; their works are ably surveyed here by Michael Beckerman and his graduate students at the University of California, Santa Barbara. Smetana, a follower of Wagner and Liszt, was also involved in the struggle over nationalist music to a greater extent than his younger compatriot Dvořák. Although Smetana had become a successful and politically influential figure by the 1870s, the onset of syphilis during that decade drew his career to a close before he had completed more than a handful of chamber works. Dvořák, on the other hand, became one of the more prolific chamber composers during the latter half of the century. Following a period of Wagnerian enthusiasm, he reverted to a more traditional style of chamber music during the mid-1870s and garnered the support of both Brahms and Hanslick in Vienna. Like Smetana, Dvořák frequently drew upon the musical accent of his native land, but as Beckerman and colleagues suggest, his motives may have been as much commercial as idealistic: "exotic" music was attractive to both publishers and performers.[11]

Our chronicle concludes with an overview of contrasts and continuities, innovation and preservation, in chamber music at the turn of the twentieth century. Proceeding from observations made by Adorno and

Dahlhaus, John Daverio provides a finely wrought sketch of chamber music's emergence from relative neglect and conservatism to become the "carrier genre" of the New Music during the first decade of the new century. Schoenberg's "air from another planet" in the form of his Second String Quartet, Op. 10, has become the signature piece of the period because, as Daverio writes, it "plays at the border of disparate worlds: tonality and atonality, late Romanticism and Expressionism, nineteenth-century modernism and twentieth-century modernity" (p. 371). The tensions it embodies effectively yield a penetrating critique of inherited suppositions at the moment that the twentieth-century modern emerges (p. 376). Thus chamber music, which in 1802 could be defined as "contrived solely for the private entertainment of sovereigns," had become a primary path to an uncertain future.

—Stephen E. Hefling

Notes

1. Heinrich Christoph Koch, *Musikalisches Lexikon* (Frankfurt, 1802; facs. ed., Hildesheim, 1964), s. v. "Kammermusik."
2. *The Nineteenth-Century Symphony*, ed. D. Kern Holoman (New York, 1997), x.
3. For excellent coverage of the social and musical milieu in Vienna during the period when Beethoven's quartets were first performed, see *The Beethoven Quartet Companion*, ed. Robert Winter and Robert Martin (Berkeley and Los Angeles, 1994).
4. See Robert Winter, "The Quartets in Their First Century," *The Beethoven Quartet Companion*, ed. Winter, 35.
5. Gustav Schilling, comp., *Encyclopädie der gesammten musikalischen Wissenschaften, oder Universal-Lexicon der Tonkunst* (Stuttgart, 1835–38), s. v. "Kammermusik"; cf. also *Handwörterbuch der musikalischen Terminologie*, ed. Hans Heinrich Eggebrecht, s. v. "Kammermusik" by Erich Reimer, 7–12.
6. See below, chap. 5, p. 219 and p. 238, n. 39.
7. Clive Brown, "Weber and Spohr," in *The Nineteenth-Century Symphony*, ed. Holoman, 17–18.
8. See below, chap. 5, p. 215.
9. See below, chap. 7, p. 288.
10. Knud Martner, ed., *Selected Letters of Gustav Mahler*, trans. Eithne Wilkins, Ernst Kaiser, and Bill Hopkins (New York, 1979), no. 112.
11. Regrettably, for practical reasons, a number of other composers generally classified as "nationalists" could not be included in this volume.

Contributors

V. Kofi Agawu is Professor of Music at Princeton University, and has also taught at Yale, Cornell, Kings College, London, and Duke. He has written numerous analytical studies of nineteenth-century works and is the author of *Playing with Signs: A Semiotic Interpretation of Classic Music* (Princeton, 1991) as well as *African Rhythm: A Northern Ewe Perspective* (Cambridge, 1995).

Michael Beckerman is Professor of Music at the University of California, Santa Barbara, and has published widely on Czech music and other topics. His most recent book is *New Worlds of Dvořák: Searching in America for the Composer's Inner Life* (New York, 2003).

Clive Brown is Professor of Applied Musicology at the University of Leeds. He is the author of *A Portrait of Mendelssohn* (New Haven, 2003), and *Classical and Romantic Performing Practice (1750-1900)* (Oxford, 1999). In addition, he has published editions of music by Weber, Spohr, and Beethoven, as well as numerous articles on performance practice and nineteenth-century German opera. An active violinist, he performs Classical and Romantic music using historical instruments and approaches to performance.

The late **John Daverio** was Professor and Chair of Musicology at Boston University. His most recent book is *Crossing Paths: Schubert, Schumann, and Brahms* (Oxford, 2002), and he is also the author of *Robert Schumann: Herald of a "New Poetic Age"* (Oxford, 1997) and *Nineteenth-Century Music and the German Romantic Ideology* (New York, 1993).

Joël-Marie Fauquet is director of research at the Centre National de la Recherche Scientifique in Paris. He is the author of *La grandeur de Bach : L'amour de la musique en France au XIXe siècle* (Paris, 2000) as well as *Les sociétés de musique de chambre à Paris de la Restauration à 1870* (Paris, 1986). Fauquet has also edited the

Correspondance of Edouard Lalo (Paris, 1989) and *Voyage d'un musicien en Italie by Auguste Blondeau* (Paris, 1993), as well as critical editions of music by Lalo and Franck. Currently he is supervising the *Dictionnaire de la musique en France au XIXe siècle* and is preparing a study of César Franck.

Stephen E. Hefling, Professor of Music at Case Western Reserve University, has also taught at Stanford, Yale, and Oberlin. He has published extensively on the music of Mahler, including *Gustav Mahler: Das Lied von der Erde* (Cambridge, 2000), the edited volume *Mahler Studies* (Cambridge, 1997), and an edition of *Das Lied von der Erde* for the Kritische Gesamtausgabe. Also an authority on historical performance practice, Hefling is the author of *Rhythmic Alteration in Seventeenth- and Eighteenth-Century Music: Notes Inégales and Overdotting* (New York, 1993).

Derek Katz is Assistant Professor of Musicology at Lawrence University. He has published articles about Czech music in *Musical Quarterly* and *Hudební veda*, and also writes about music for the *New York Times*. He has contributed to program books for the San Francisco Opera and Lincoln Center, and presented pre-concert lectures at Lincoln Center and Carnegie Hall.

Margaret Notley, who teaches at the University of North Texas, has published on topics such as musical life in turn-of-the-century Vienna and compositional reception of Beethoven in the nineteenth and twentieth centuries.Currently she is finishing a book on late Brahms. For her article "Late-Nineteenth-Century Chamber Music and the Cult of the Classical Adagio" in *19th-Century Music*, Notley received the American Musicological Society's Alfred Einstein Award in 2000.

David S. Tartakoff is Professor of Mathematics at the University of Illinois, Chicago, former conductor of the Northwestern University Philharmonic Orchestra, and chairman of the board of Greenwood, the oldest chamber music summer school in the United States. An avid chamber music player and singer, his greatest musical love has always been Schubert; he and Stephen Hefling have played Schubert's chamber music together countless times.

R. Larry Todd, Professor of Music at Duke University, is the general editor of the Routledge Studies in Musical Genres series, and edited the volume of the series devoted to nineteenth-century piano music. He has written extensively about music of the nineteenth century, focusing especially on Felix Mendelssohn and his sister Fanny Hensel, and is the author of the new biography, *Mendelssohn: A Life in Music* (Oxford, 2003). Among his earlier publications is the edited volume *Schumann and His World* (Princeton, 1994).

Acknowledgments

Special thanks are well overdue to R. Larry Todd, general editor of the Schirmer Repertoires and Genres Series, and to various editors and staff members past and present at Schirmer Books—especially Maribeth Anderson Payne, Jonathan Wiener, and James Hatch—all of whom waited patiently for this volume. The index was prepared by Robert Zolnerzak. Students in chamber music courses at Oberlin College and Case Western Reserve University read portions of the book in manuscript and offered valuable commentary. For permission to reproduce illustrations we are grateful to:

> The Mary Flagler Cary Music Collection in the Pierpont Morgan Library, New York
>
> The Morgan Manuscript Collection in the Pierpont Morgan Library, New York
>
> The Collection of Robert Owen Lehman, on deposit at the Pierpont Morgan Library, New York
>
> The Special Collections Library, Duke University, Durham, North Carolina
>
> The Music Division, Library of Congress, Washington, D. C.

CHAPTER ONE

The Chamber Music of Beethoven

Kofi Agawu

The core of Beethoven's chamber music consists of string quartets, the first of which dates from 1798, the last from the penultimate year of his life, 1826. Like the piano sonatas, the quartets span a considerable portion of his entire composing career and encompass a wide range of compositional techniques and aesthetic choices. Yet the idea of a core repertory is by no means value-free, as if all the chamber music works were submerged in water and the best ones automatically rose to the top. Rather, the core is constructed by the historian or analyst according to specific agenda. For in addition to string quartets, Beethoven wrote string trios, piano trios, a string quintet, another for winds and piano, a septet, an octet, violin sonatas, and cello sonatas. The histories of these works are linked, and there are further linkages to the symphonies, piano concertos, and vocal music. There is, then, no firm chamber music manner, attitude, or stance in Beethoven, one that might ensure that a different "language" was "spoken" in the medium of, say, the string trio from that spoken in the piano sonatas. Beethoven's choice of theme and topic, his layout of periodicity in form, and his construction of tonal narratives: these are ever-present compositional challenges that render the boundaries between genres fluid.

The customary division of Beethoven's development into style periods or manners has proven indispensable to any survey of his works; the present essay is no exception. By the conventional account, a first or early period encompasses the works composed until 1802 and includes sub-periods distinguishing the Bonn years (up to 1792) from the Vienna years. Works written between 1803 and 1812 belong to a middle period, while the third or late period lasts roughly from 1813 to Beethoven's death in 1827. Any periodization is bound to distort historical reality, for lines of influence and affiliation are complexly drawn, while periods of transition are never as fixed as our bald dates suggest. Yet the three-style scheme, promulgated by such nineteenth-century writers as Johann Aloys Schlosser, François-Joseph Fétis, Wilhelm von Lenz, and Alexandre Oulibicheff, and (with some modifications) by such recent writers as Joseph Kerman and Maynard Solomon, has endured in Beethoven criticism. While lending support to the view that Beethoven's composing career is inscribed in his biography, the scheme highlights the different registers that distinguish Beethoven's styles, styles that cannot be conflated into a single homogenous compositional manner without doing considerable violence to the very notions of sameness and difference.[1]

One concrete consequence of the division into style periods is an imbalance in the pattern of distribution of chamber works through Beethoven's career. Consider the violin sonatas. Only one, the four-movement work in G major, Op. 96, composed in 1812, approaches the late period; similarly, only the "Kreutzer" Sonata, Op. 47, composed in 1802–3, belongs to the middle period. The eight other works in this genre are all first-period works. One could of course refine the stylistic grid to capture the different tone in works that mark the transition from the first to the middle period. In that case the "Spring" Sonata, Op. 24, composed 1800–01 and the highly original C Minor Sonata, Op. 30, No.2, composed in 1801–2 and published as part of a set of three, may be seen to lie at the juncture of two contiguous style periods. The point is that with the exception of Op. 96, Beethoven was more or less done with the genre of violin sonata by the time he embarked on the larger projects that encapsulate a middle manner.

A similar imbalance may be observed in the chronology of the string trios, all of which date from before 1800. Again, the Quintet for Piano and Winds, Op. 16, is from 1796, while the String Quintet, Op. 29, was composed in 1801. The balance is only slightly better in the piano trios, in which the "Archduke," Op. 97, Beethoven's final word in that genre, was composed toward the end of the middle period, 1810–11, not during the third period. However, the adumbration of late-period techniques in this work, as well as in the String Quartet in F Minor, Op. 95, should not be underplayed. Only slightly earlier are the two Op. 70 piano trios, both of them unmistakably characteristic of the middle period: powerful, eccentric, and challenging their genre to the limits. All the other piano trios belong to the early period, including several works without opus numbers.

The balance is happiest in what one might be tempted to call the weightiest genres: cello sonata and string quartet. Beethoven wrote two cello sonatas, published as Op. 5 in 1796, but waited a full decade before returning to the genre. The A Major Cello Sonata, Op. 69, composed in 1807–8, is the genre's centerpiece, yet its middle-period categorization is undermined by the heightened lyricism that points ahead to the late style. Finally, two more cello sonatas, one in C, the other in D, were composed in 1815 and published as Op. 102. The overall symmetrical 2–1–2 distribution of these sonatas signals Beethoven's periodic return to the cello sonata genre every ten years or so.

The string quartets, the first nine of which were published in sets, show the clearest stylistic breaks and provide the happiest balance in distribution. First comes the set of six published in Vienna in 1801, numbered Op. 18, that consolidates a Viennese aesthetic, complete with traces of Haydn and especially Mozart. (The A Major Quartet, Op. 18, No. 5, is said to be modeled on Mozart's K. 464).[2] It is a major stylistic jump from Op. 18 to Op. 59, a set of three composed in 1805–6 and nicknamed the "Razumovsky." As we will see, the heroic impetus that found its most characteristic representation in the middle-period symphonies—notably the Third, Fifth, and Sixth—also left traces on the string quartets. Certainly the extraordinary expansiveness of range, texture, color, and form in the first movement of Op. 59, No. 1, marks a new level of intensity in Beethoven's compositional habits. Even the Quartet in E♭, Op. 74, composed in 1809, and the quirky Op. 95 in F Minor, composed the following year, although they reveal a new tone of modesty, concentration, and introspection, actively challenge but do not ultimately invalidate our broad stylistic division. While they may be said to point to the late works, they are finally middle-period works in the same way that the Eighth Symphony, although something of a throwback to an earlier period, remains a middle-period work.

Finally, the last five quartets occupied Beethoven from 1823 to 1826. In fact, apart from Op. 127 in E♭, which was composed in 1823–24, the other four (including the *Grosse Fuge*) were composed in 1825–26 and published during Beethoven's last year. The overall 5–5–6 distribution of the quartets across the early, middle, and late periods respectively, reinforces the view that quartet composition remained central to his creative concerns throughout his life. This is only one of several reasons for building a narrative of Beethoven's chamber music around the quartets.

The Early Chamber Music

If we imagine Beethoven as a child "speaking" a musical language, we can be certain that it was not a "pure" language but a syncretic one, a kind of Creole reflecting German, French, and Italian influences in intonation, syntax, and idiomatic construction. Beethoven's early musical environment included music of earlier eighteenth-century composers (J. S. Bach, Haydn, Gluck, and Mozart), parceled out in a variety of forms and genres, ranging from the public sphere of the symphony, concerto, and opera to the more private sphere of chamber music. His musical influences also included a great many minor composers, whose work he emulated not only as a young composer in Bonn but as an ambitious performer and composer in Vienna. A fuller account of his musical development would acknowledge the traces of these influences, in particular of various national styles, and supplement these with an assessment of the impact of the self-consciously acquired musical knowledge (such as the contrapuntal models and techniques transmitted by Albrechtsberger and Haydn) on his personal musical language. Our task here, however, is not to discuss the formation of this language, information about which is readily available elsewhere,[3] but to identify a few salient features of the early violin sonatas and string quartets that exemplify it. And rather than attempt to deal with the works comprehensively, I shall select aspects of periodicity and topic for comment.[4]

Beethoven's sonatas for violin and piano provide a good lens for observing some of the routines of his early style. Briefly, the Op. 12 and Op. 23 sonatas exemplify a more or less normative adherence to Classical convention. By the time of the "Spring" Sonata, Op. 24, however, disruptive and original features become more apparent. The transitional features of Op. 24 and the works composed around 1800–1802 are consolidated in the Op. 30 sonatas.

One obvious sign of conventional usage is a regular four- or eight-bar phrase structure, in which successive phrases unfold additively. The rondo theme that inaugurates the finale of Op. 12, No. 1, exemplifies this regularity (Example 1.1). Its eight-bar structure is divided into 4 + 4 and incipiently into 2 + 2 + 4. This theme is offered by the pianist to the violinist, who repeats it without modification. Subsequent returns at measures 52 and 119 are free of additional embellishment. The result is a characteristic pattern of balanced, predictable, and ultimately unproblematic exchange between the two instrumental protagonists.

EXAMPLE 1.1.   Ludwig van Beethoven, Violin Sonata in D, Op. 12, No. 1, finale theme.

The closed, eight-bar phrase is, of course, part of the unmarked ordinary syntax of the Classical style. What is noticeable in early Beethoven, however, is the closed nature of some of the basic building blocks, a feature that resists the ongoing, forward dynamism so often associated with his music. In the finale of Op. 12. No.1, phrase succession generally follows an additive rather than a divisive or organic manner. While this tendency may be put to the rondo form itself—the rondo principle prescribes sectionalization—we are a long way yet from the organic and proselike periodicity of later Beethoven.

A similar exposure of seams is evident in the rondo of Op. 12, No. 3, whose theme, quoted in Example 1.2, is an eight-bar folklike tune divided into four-bar halves, the first open, the second closed. Although the rondo theme trades motives with some of the episodic material, it is finally not integrated into a single, prevailing melodic discourse, for all its subsequent appearances have the character of additions, interruptions, or interpolations; they lack the generative capacity of other building blocks.

EXAMPLE 1.2.   Beethoven, Violin Sonata in E♭, Op. 12, No.3, finale theme.

It is possible to speak here of contrast, and to remind ourselves that purposeful contrast was a central feature of Beethoven's work from the very beginning. The period that opens Op. 12, No. 1 (Example 1.3), contains several distinct ideas that, although held together by a broad harmonic sweep, nevertheless retain a somewhat independent profile throughout the movement. First is the full, sonorous D major chord, which establishes the sound of the tonic and the authority of the ensemble. Then comes a series of offbeat arpeggiations designed to test the security of the ensemble and to mark out musical space for each instrument. Next (m. 5) is a smoother, coiling accompaniment figure on the piano, to which the violin responds by beginning a song from its highest note thus far and carrying the musical thought to its lowest register while the piano explores the opposite trajectory and takes on the music's essential voice-leading burden. Then there are the heavily scored, three-note left hand chords (mm. 6ff.), which, literally as well as metaphorically, lie low. The distinctiveness and heterogeneity of musical ideas may recall the practice in Mozart's later works, which elicited complaints from nineteenth-century critics about the overabundance of ideas. Here in early Beethoven, contrast is contained in a 5 + 8 phrase structure, the apparently irregular five-bar portion exhibiting no subsurface linear motion. When in late Beethoven contrast is allowed to determine the very foundations of the musical structure (as in the first movements of Opp. 130 and 132), phrase irregularity and a resultant musical prose become part of the music's basic syntax, although two- and four-bar modules never relinquish their fundamental status.

The squareness of phrase structure, the closed nature of the basic ideas, and the additive approach to form: these hallmarks of Beethoven's early style are reinforced by other factors. The dominance of the piano in these works is indigenous to the genre, as indeed was the case with many of Mozart's violin sonatas, and we will have to wait for the Op. 24 sonata to hear a more equal partnership. Even in a form like theme and variations, which plays an absolutely central role in Beethoven's output, and

EXAMPLE 1.3.   Beethoven, Violin Sonata in D, Op. 12, No.1, mvt. 1, mm. 1–13.

which is used in the middle movement of Op. 12, No. 1, variations follow standard eighteenth-century protocol in being essentially decorative. Beethoven remains faithful to his theme and is not yet ready to probe its essence in the way that he does in the great variation sets of the late works, such as the "Diabelli" Variations, Op. 120, the finale of Op. 111, the second movement of Op. 127, and the third movement of Op. 131.[5]

A certain stiffness and formality of phrase utterance in the Op. 12 sonatas begins to be eroded in the works that Beethoven wrote soon after the turn of the century. At the beginning of Op. 23 in A Minor, the first of Beethoven's minor-key violin sonatas, a new, leaner texture allows the music to breathe more freely, even as it gains momentum from an unbroken succession of eighth notes (Example 1.4). Although the opening period is far from being irregular (its twelve bars are subdivided into 8 + 4, the latter four being a varied and intensified repetition of the preceding four, bringing the period to a decisive end), there are signs here of Beethoven's organicism: the modest harmonic resources, including the four-bar pedal at the beginning; the imitations and contrary motion of the piano material; and the resulting lightness of texture, culminating in right-hand octaves in the last four bars. Everything seems to be held firmly in place by the harmony. Although it shares a $\frac{6}{8}$ meter with the first movement of Op. 12, No. 2, composed two years earlier, the first movement of Op. 23 eschews the charm of Op. 12, No. 2, for a more serious tone, a busy motivic attitude, and an altogether more fluid sense of movement.

The consistent offbeat patterns of the second movement of Op. 23 prepare for Beethoven's scherzo manner, but here the pattern, once established, becomes assuring in its predictability. Predictability is overcome in the scherzo of the next sonata (the "Spring") by an ingenious distribution of phenomenal accents within the prevailing $\frac{3}{4}$ meter to suggest movement out of kilter. In the second movement of Op. 23, the dynamic is further kept open by the pattern of cadential articulation. The piano's first eight bars, articulated as 4 + 4, end in a tonicization of the dominant, a reinforcement of the first four bars, which had ended on V. The violin then

EXAMPLE 1.4.   Beethoven, Violin Sonata in A Minor, Op. 23, mvt. 1, mm. 1–12.

(continued)

8   *The Chamber Music of Beethoven*

EXAMPLE 1.4.   *(continued)*

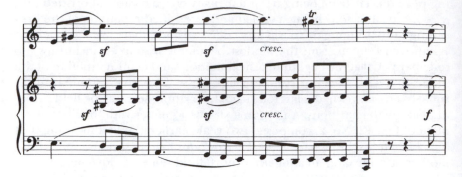

repeats this material verbatim (mm. 9–16). Next comes a second strain of melody, with more harmonic interest. This single eight-bar gesture closes into a full cadence at measures 23–24 (and echoed by the violin at mm. 31–32). Despite the external regularity, therefore, the phrase's deeper sense of direction is kept open.

The tentative gestures of learned style in the first movement of Op. 23 are taken one stage further in the second movement, where, starting at measure 33, a formal announcement suggesting fugato is made. The answer given four bars later by the violin is in the dominant, but is not allowed to run its complete course before the piano interrupts. It turns out that this is but a modest invocation of the learned style in a rhetorical context that does little to mollify the comic aura which often emanates from uses of imitation within the galant style.

Compared to Op. 23, Op. 24 is an altogether more mature, if somewhat uneven, work. One aspect of the first movement reveals a significant departure from the language of the Op. 12 sonatas. In place of an eight-, twelve-, or sixteen-bar opening phrase, Beethoven writes a ten-bar period with subtly hidden seams (Example 1.5). Although a two-bar sequence propels the music to its melodic highpoint, the sense of an additive process is undercut by a harmonic dependency between adjacent subphrases. The phrase expands from the middle; each melodic join is smoothed over by harmonic continuity, making the entire ten-bar phrase a single, indivisible period. When later the two instruments trade roles so the piano now sings the violin's song (m. 11), the earlier phrase is not merely repeated but modified toward its close (mm. 19–20) to initiate a transition.

The sense of an organic discourse in the first movement of Op. 24 meets its first stumbling block in measure 26, where a single note, E♭, appearing apparently from nowhere, disrupts the tonal and periodic ambitions of the earlier music. This, however, is a typical Beethovenian device, familiar also from Haydn: a structural "problem" is introduced and later "solved." But how is the solution effected? How is the problem rationalized? A brief excursion into the realm of harmonic logic is necessary here.

EXAMPLE 1.5. Beethoven, Violin Sonata in F, Op. 24, mvt. 1, mm. 1–10.

From the opening tonic, F, Beethoven heads for the dominant, C. As the bass line sketch in Example 1.6 shows, the transition is in two contiguous and complementary phases. The first, in measures 20–25, is based on a C pedal, suggesting a premature arrival in the dominant key, although the mutual appearance of B naturals and B flats above C suggests being *on* V as well. The second must perform the sense of a transition, and Beethoven chooses G as tonal goal, G being understood as V/V, which will be reached by means of its chromatic lower and upper neighbor notes, A♭ and F♯. And what more logical way to proceed than to approach A♭ from its upper fifth, moving by step down to F♯ before rising to the adjacent G. The E♭ in measure 26 is thus rationalized retrospectively. When it is first heard in measure 26, it seems to have come out of nowhere. Within a few bars, however, it is heard as part of a conventional approach to the dominant of the dominant. Here is a tiny but telling example of Beethoven's

unerring judgment in matters of long- and medium-range harmonic relationships.

EXAMPLE 1.6.   Approach to V in Beethoven, Violin Sonata in F, Op. 24, mvt. 1,
mm. 1–38.

Other harmonic events in this movement continue to reinforce the
novelty and first maturity of the sonatas written around 1800. One is the
striking use of modal interchange (the minor appears in mm. 46, 58, 94,
182). Another is the surprising move to V/VI at the start of the development, a harmony that is usually reserved for the end of a development
section, where it functions as a point of furthest remove, to borrow
Leonard Ratner's phrase.[6] The rhetoric with which Beethoven articulates
this relation in measures 86–89 suggests that he may have overshot his
tonal mark, so to speak, his real goal being B♭ (m. 90) at the start of the
development. Indeed, Beethoven returns to V/VI at the end of the development (mm. 116–23), from which he moves directly to I for the start
of the recapitulation.

A sense of tonal adventure is brought into play here, through which
the listener not only enjoys and savors the thematic ideas but is challenged
by the tonal narrative as well. The deceptive cadence in measures 209–10,
which compels motion to be temporarily halted, then resumed and
brought to a proper conclusion, is among the signs of a narrative impulse
in this movement. Finally, a greater fluidity in the movement of ideas in
the fourth-movement rondo indicates that the interaction between violin
and piano is far from routine or mechanical.

An important exemplar of Beethoven's transition to a new, more individualized middle period is the second of the Op. 30 violin sonatas,
composed in 1802. This C minor work immediately recalls others, including the third of the Op. 1 piano trios (1794–95), the "Pathétique"
Sonata, Op. 13, and the fourth of the Op. 18 string quartets (1798–1800).
These works inhabit a similar sonic and affective environment, drawing
on the inherent chromaticism of the minor mode to convey a deep, sometimes tragic expression. The first movement of Op. 30, No. 2, is compact
and tense, charged and seemingly ready to explode at any time. While
minor explosions do occur later (as at the beginning of the finale), the
work is not consistently volatile or violent.

Consider the cagey manner in which ideas of the opening eight-bar
period are introduced (Example 1.7). First is a descending tonic triad, in
which the E♭ decoration introduces stepwise motion (E♭–F–G) while recapitulating the larger triadic (G–E♭–C) descent in the last three notes of

the gesture. Although tonally closed, this inaugural idea is unsettling, urgently demanding continuation. The "answer" is a subdominant version of the same motive (mm. 3–4). Already, a change in tonal focus is implied without the introduction of a single accidental. Then, taking F as point of departure (m. 5), Beethoven moves stepwise down the scale, first diatonically, then chromatically, closing finally into a half cadence. It is striking how an ostensibly simple opening like this can demonstrate both surface variety and an unwavering sense of tonal direction. With ideas and strategies like these, ideas that compel the listener's attention, we reach toward Beethoven's middle period.

EXAMPLE 1.7.   Beethoven, Violin Sonata in C Minor, Op. 30, No. 2, mvt. 1, mm. 1–8.

The premises outlined at the opening of Op. 30, No. 2, are extended and sometimes modified in the rest of the movement. A separate essay is needed to assess these transformations; here we can do no more than mention a few salient details. The organic thrust of measures 1–8 is reflected in the cumulative thrust of the material of the first key area (mm. 1–24), with its twofold repetition of the perfect cadence in measures 15–16 (at mm. 19–20, 22–23). The second subject (beginning in m. 29) is a march, not a heroic or funeral march, but a jaunty one. This major-mode march is first played by the violin to an eighth-note accompaniment in the piano (mm. 29–36). So stable is the eighth-note figure in the double presentation of the march theme (mm. 29–36 and 37–44) that it begins to draw attention to itself as rhythmic marker, thus reinforcing but also undermining the sense of march. Among numerous ingenious strokes in this movement is the marvelous six-four chord in measure 75, a chord that softens the impact of the tonic to which it leads, pretending at first to deny the resolution of the cadence blatantly prepared in measures 72–74. Such devices of continuity come to the fore in the late style.

The slow and elegant gavotte of the second movement is one of many readily identifiable topics found in the violin sonatas. The march in the first movement, the learned style in the second movement of Op. 23, the dancelike opening movement of Op. 12, No. 2, passages of brilliant, virtuosic display (scattered throughout Op. 24, especially in the outer movements), and moments of meditation that might remind us of the *Empfindsamer* style (as in the slow movement of Op. 30, No. 1): these and numerous other passages, drawn from the thesaurus of conventional eighteenth-century styles, are incorporated into the discourse of the individual works. We will see more clearly the functioning of topics in the string quartets, where the medium encourages such display.

One final detail about the finale of Op. 30, No. 2, will serve as an additional illustration of the kind of long-range hearing that is played out with full conviction in the middle-period works. The main melody is first heard in measures 15–18 (Example 1.8), preceded by an expanded cadence. As heard here, the melody is incomplete; it is as if Beethoven has withheld the complementary four-bar close, as one might hypothesize in the recomposition shown in Example 1.9. No such obvious completion is given when the piano melody is immediately repeated in measure 19, however. When the melody returns in measure 107, transformed from the minor into the parallel major, we expect the appropriate resolution to appear finally. And Beethoven provides the long-awaited completion, but instead of a straightforward completion as imagined in Example 1.9, or as might be done with his own materials (Example 1.10), Beethoven writes a sequential four-bar phrase to which the long-awaited melody functions partly as a local resolution and partly as a global close (Example 1.11). Such long-range melodic connections index a more organic conception of motion than is found in the earliest chamber music works.

Unlike the violin sonata, whose keyboard part is naturally endowed with a fuller, harmonic sound, the string quartet is obliged to create a full sonority by resisting the natural melodic impulse of stringed instruments.

EXAMPLE 1.8.   Main melody of Beethoven, Violin Sonata in C Minor, Op. 30, No. 2, finale.

EXAMPLE 1.9.   Hypothetical completion of the main melody of Beethoven, Violin Sonata in C Minor, Op. 30, No. 2, finale.

EXAMPLE 1.10.   Another hypothetical completion of the main melody of Beethoven, Op. 30, No. 2, finale, using Beethoven's materials.

EXAMPLE 1.11.   Actual completion of the main melody of Beethoven, Violin Sonata in C Minor, Op. 30, No. 2, finale.

Work of this sort confers an immediate seriousness upon the genre. Moreover, the precedents set by Mozart and Haydn amplify the intellectual challenges that the string quartet presented to Beethoven. Deprived of the piano's inherent sonority, the composer must find ways of cultivating a convincing vertical dimension with four stringed instruments. The result is greater scope for the interplay of voices, space, and texture. It would seem that, whereas Beethoven more or less accepted the generic constraints imposed by the violin sonata, he approached the string quartet acknowledging fewer of its inherent limitations, despite the baggage of innovations already provided by Haydn.

The six Op. 18 quartets, Beethoven's first mature essays in that medium, make a neat package, illustrating perhaps more intensively than do the violin sonatas the intellectual force of his compositional strategies. To say that Beethoven probes many of the basic assumptions about eighteenth-century compositional protocol in the string quartets is not to imply that every one of these "experiments" is successful. Still, the six Op. 18 quartets are best approached not as routine statements in a standardized genre but as works self-consciously forging a new style, pressing at the limits of convention. Certainly they adumbrate tendencies developed in later works.

One striking feature of the Op. 18 quartets is the extent to which they use topics, conventional sites of expressive and affective meaning. Like Mozart before him, and to a lesser extent Haydn, Beethoven drew on a variety of musical gestures that carry conventional associations in order to enliven his musical surfaces. Although they derive from the interface between "music" and "society" (including religious ceremony, the hunt of the nobility, peasant life, entertainment, and the dance), topics, once incorporated into a work, take on a structural function, serving to articulate and advance the work's tonal discourse.[7]

Consider, for example, the persistent repeated bass note C at the start of the C Minor Quartet, Op. 18, No. 4. Listeners familiar with bass textures of the period will immediately recognize this as a *Trommelbaß* or drum bass, a motivic pattern that enshrines harmonic stasis even as it contributes tremendous rhythmic energy to this beginning. The accompanying operatic melody is unusually broad-scaled, spanning three full octaves in twelve bars. (Not until the first of the Op. 59 quartets will we encounter a similarly expansive opening gesture.) Consider, too, the divertimento style and stylized musette (evident especially in the drone bass) with which Op. 18, No. 5, opens. Unlike Op. 18, No. 4, with its clear opening theme, Op. 18, No. 5, opens with a set of thematic fragments in the form of the first violin's three *coups d'archet* (mm. 1, 2, and 3). Later the first violin figures (mm. 11ff.) suggest an Italian concerto, complete with an offbeat accompaniment pattern. So saturated is the opening of this quartet with referential figures that a whole world of affect and play is opened up for the listener. Nor is topical play confined to the first key area. The second key area (mm. 25ff.), which begins in the unusual dominant minor, suggests *Sturm und Drang*, while a series of mechanical figures, starting in measure 62 and reminiscent of the divertimento style, help to nail down the cadence in the dominant proper, E major. Furthermore, the core of the development section is occupied by the musette, playing this time in the key of D major, the subdominant. The succession of topics establishes a line of discourse, a sequence of rhetorical stances that provides clues to musical meaning.

The famous "La malinconia" of Op. 18, No. 6, notable for its concentrated and intense expression, suggests fantasia throughout. Precedents for the style evoked here may be found in the *Empfindsamkeit* of C. P. E. Bach. The opening includes a horn call (Example 1.12), a figure associated with greetings as well as farewells. Later, concerto style is invoked by the first violin figures in measures 13–16, while the fugato beginning in measure 21 suggests learned style, one mark of formally acquired skill in the craft of musical composition. Although formal and learned, the passage beginning in measure 21 still retains a strong sense of the improvised and the spontaneous, thus fusing two ostensibly opposed tendencies. Above all the "Malinconia" gropes from harmony to harmony, focusing upon pure voice leading and challenging the listener's sense of harmonic expectation. This is fantasy of a particularly effective sort.[8]

A special place should be reserved for the learned style in the Beethoven quartets, for it is a style that he deploys or invokes with striking effect and in a variety of expressive forms. The lightweight contredanse in the finale of Op. 18, No. 1, is contrasted by a fugato adjoining a more cantabile or singing style. Learned style is not merely intermittent in Op. 18; in at least one case an entire movement, the scherzo of Op. 18, No. 4, is based upon it, together with touches of the sensitive (*Empfind-*

EXAMPLE 1.12.   Beethoven, String Quartet in B♭, Op. 18, No. 6, mvt. 4, "La malinconia," mm. 1–4.

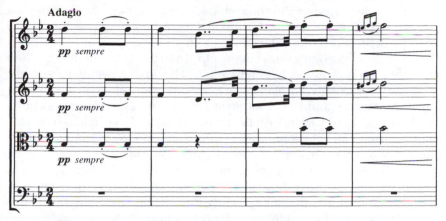

samer) style. This is a new context for a style that would have been simply a way of life for Bach (and to a lesser extent Handel) fifty years earlier; here it takes on a more distinct, even defamiliarized effect. For despite the imitative manner at the beginning, the movement's harmonic and periodic objectives are never lost track of. That is why Beethoven can abandon the imitative procedure in measure 42 (although never the enduring sense of the mechanical) and follow this with a pure circle-of-fifths progression (mm. 44–47, 52–55) in a harmonic rather than a contrapuntal vein before resuming imitative writing in measure 83. It is also why he can incorporate the periodicity of waltz into this ⅜ movement (mm. 103–10) and at the same time enter a dark and mysterious region (mm. 112–21) suggesting the *ombra* topic, thus creating suspense in the manner of Wagner. This is Beethoven at his synthetic best. Within the relative security of an eighteenth-century topical tradition (learned style) punctuated throughout by a sense of the mechanical, Beethoven injects elements of fantasy that suggest a "Romantic" style.

    The foregoing is only the barest sketch of a topical profile for the Op. 18 quartets. We have not mentioned the style of the finale of Op. 18, No. 4, a bourrée in Gypsy style; nor have we discussed the Italian style of ornamentation in the slow movements of Op. 18, No. 2, and Op. 18, No. 1. There is also the arioso style at the end of the third movement of Op. 18, No. 5, the marvelous commedia dell'arte setting in the finale of Op. 18, No. 5, and the march in *alla breve* in measures 45ff. of Op. 18 No. 6. These and dozens of other topics enliven the surfaces of the Op. 18 quartets, conveying a sense of drama in musical gesture.

    The incorporation and speculative treatment of topics in string quartet discourse form only a part of Beethoven's compositional concerns in the Op. 18 set. Equally fundamental are the issues arising from his treatment of form and harmony, purely musical issues that allow us to study

Beethoven's handling of certain premises of Classical tonality. Although we are dealing here with early Beethoven, not the individualized Beethoven of the middle period or the somewhat iconoclastic Beethoven of the late period, it is nevertheless worth thinking about how Beethoven is already exploiting the limits of formal convention.

Consider the outer forms of the Op. 18 string quartets. The quartets use the standard four-movement plan. The first movement, also the weightiest, is usually an *allegro* in a serious vein, often in a duple or quadruple meter, and in sonata form. The second, no less serious in intent, is the slow, reflective, or lyrical movement, and may fall into either a simple ternary form or some variety of sonata form. Next comes the minuet and trio or the scherzo and trio, a lighter, dancelike movement. Finally, an even lighter and quicker-paced movement, often subtending a socially low dance affect, closes off the work. This normal order is sometimes followed and sometimes modified in early Beethoven. For example, the first three of the Op. 18 set all follow this order. Opus 18, No. 4, however, has a scherzolike second movement and a minuet in third place—an excess of dance, so to speak. In Op. 18, No. 5, the order of the middle movements is reversed, the minuet preceding the slow movement. And in Op. 18, No. 6, Beethoven extends the number of movements from four to five, the addition being the fantastic "Malinconia" mentioned earlier, which begins as if it were another slow movement but turns out to be a slow introduction to the finale—this despite its cyclical return later in the finale.

The conventionality of the four-movement form makes it difficult to argue profitably about the effect that violations of movement order have on intermovement balance, except in an ad hoc manner. Still, the case of "La malinconia" suggests a far from normal balance among the elements of Op. 18, No. 6. The first movement is surprisingly square and—as we would say today—unproblematic. The second builds up ornaments almost to a point of excess, while the third—in an apparent transfer of the impulse to experiment from the melodic dimension of movement 2 to the rhythmic dimension of movement 3—presents perhaps the most dramatic rhythmic writing in the entire body of Op. 18 quartets. Finally, the pairing of "La malinconia" with a $\frac{3}{8}$ dance suggests further experimentation; the compound form does not obviously balance out the combined weight of the previous movements. To say that a residual tension persists from this apparent imbalance is not to imply that perfectly balanced, and for that matter, "unified" works of art can avoid such tension; it is rather to point to the essential arbitrariness, or at least illusiveness, of notions of balance and unity.

The individual movements of the Op. 18 quartets exemplify the range of standard late eighteenth-century formal types. The most important of these is, of course, sonata form, which is found in all the first movements of the Op. 18 quartets as well as in the finale of Op. 18, No. 5. Beethoven's periodic structure can be square and predictable, as in the first movement of Op. 18, No. 6, where, in textbook fashion (and strongly reminiscent of the opening movement of the Piano Sonata, Op. 22, also in B♭), he goes from theme group to theme group in a didactic fashion. By contrast, Beethoven can also use sonata form imaginatively, as in the motivically tight first movement of Op. 18, No. 1, where such events as the surprising arrival on A♭ as a way station (mm. 41–42), the beginning of the development on V/VI (as in the first movement of the "Spring" sonata), and the extensive recomposition of the first-key-area material in the recapitulation show a less-than-routine manipulation of the sonata principle.

Also basic to the formal conception of the Op. 18 quartets is the minuet or scherzo with trio, which for Beethoven often provides an avenue for the display of wit in the play of rhythm, harmony, and periodicity. The most interesting of these early scherzos is that of Op. 18, No. 6, which embodies a putative conflict between the notated ¾ meter and a heard ⁶⁄₈, a conflict that some may feel is sustained until the onset of the trio. The first eight bars show the sources of ambiguity: offbeat phrasing, sforzandi on eighth-note upbeats, and repeated notes (Example 1.13).

EXAMPLE 1.13.   Beethoven, String Quartet in B♭, Op. 18, No. 6, Scherzo, mm. 1–8.

A complementary scherzo is that of Op. 18, No. 1, whose eccentricities lie less in the rhythmic or metric realm and more in the harmonic realm. In the first period of the trio, the tonal goal, F, appears only on the very last quarter note. Of the period's sixteen measures, the first four are given to the dominant, the next nine to its upper chromatic neighbor, D♭, and the next two to the dominant again, before the last measure's close on the tonic. This is a way of "problematizing" F as tonic. A similar strategy is used at the start of the scherzo, whose first phrase, lasting ten measures, is divisible into 6 + (2 + 2), and then by twos throughout; it progresses from F to its dominant, C. But because Beethoven uses modulation as premise, the phrase develops a mosaiclike profile, whereby measures 1–2 are "in" F major, measures 3–4 "in" G minor, measures 5–6 "in" A minor (but with a slight change of design), and measures 7–8 and 9–10 "in" C major. The sweep of the bass motion is easily explained as a prolonged F (by stepwise motion through a third, F–G–A) followed by its dominant. But the manner of articulation, the insistence on small two-bar worlds, presents a challenge to our perception of this broader progression.

Other formal types found in the Op. 18 collection include the simple ternary or ABA, as in the second movements of Op. 18, No. 1, and Op. 18, No. 6. The roots of this form in the da capo aria of the Baroque enable ornamentation to come to the fore, especially during the return of the A material. One movement, the third of Op. 18, No. 5, is a variation set. Based on a theme of commonplace character, the first three variations ornament the theme in progressively shorter note values, a standard procedure in eighteenth-century variation protocol. The most sophisticated variation is the fourth, which departs from the theme's harmony and modulates to the mediant instead of to the dominant at the end of the first phrase. Its rich inner-voice writing, infused with chromaticism, points ahead to Brahms. Variation 5 returns to the eighteenth century, reminding us of Boccherini. A long coda in which ♭VI plays a prominent role compensates for the absence of a *minore* variation. A Bach-like sequence in measure 120 is followed by a passage in arioso style marked *poco adagio*, which rounds off the movement.

It would not be an exaggeration to say that the Op. 18 quartets adumbrate just about every significant innovation found in the later quartets. These innovations are distributed in the basic dimensions of form, harmony, periodicity, and topical structure. Before leaving the Op. 18 quartets, however, mention must be made of one of the most ingenious movements among this set, a movement that epitomizes the comic side of Beethoven's language, which is here manifest in an infinite number of allusions to styles, textures, and voice-leading procedures, always with something of an ironic distance, never as a "first language." The finale of Op. 18, No. 5, is simply unparalleled for its invention. Within its *alla breve* pacing, Beethoven constructs a playful country dance, a commedia dell'arte in which rapid shifts of action produce a remarkable stop-and-start quality, conferring on the movement as a whole a sense of theater—

an elemental, improvised theater not staged in any of the other Op. 18 quartets. Beethoven's tongue-in-cheek humor is everywhere apparent. He alludes to species counterpoint pedagogy in the *alla breve* of measures 36–43. He uses an ornamental discant in parallel first-inversion triads (mm. 110–114). There is something of an exotic Gypsy flavor in measures 153–56. Circle-of-fifths progressions are used mechanically (mm. 238–41), and the unusual melodic close on the submediant instead of the tonic reminds us that this is music about music. There is no real harmonic contrast in the movement, except for what is normatively enshrined in the governing sonata form.

The Middle Period Chamber Music

For some time in the nineteenth century, Beethoven's posthumous reputation rested largely on the works of his middle period. Beginning around 1803, he produced in astonishingly rapid succession a series of masterpieces based on a "symphonic ideal": the Third and Fifth Symphonies, the Fourth Piano Concerto, the opera *Fidelio*, the Op. 59 quartets ("Rasumovsky"), the "Ghost" and "Archduke" Trios, the "Waldstein" and "Appassionata" Sonatas, and the "Kreutzer" Sonata. For many ordinary music lovers, these are the Beethovenian works par excellence, the essential Beethoven, staples of the Classical repertoire. This style would appear to be public rather than private, serious rather than comic or lighthearted, grand rather than intimate, loud rather than soft, extroverted rather than introverted. Such broad characterizations are ultimately misleading, however, because they oversimplify the complex profiles of these works, allowing the imprint left by a handful of frequently performed compositions to stand for others.

Joseph Kerman has stressed the influence of the "symphonic ideal" on Beethoven's middle-period works.[9] Within this broad stylistic attitude, however, there is a considerable range of expression. Therefore the idea that Beethoven's early music shows the work of an apprentice or imitator, that the middle music betrays an externalizing impulse resulting in a new, highly individualized voice and the breaking of boundaries: these and other generalizations need to be regarded with skepticism. For the overriding characteristic of the middle-period music is one that we have encountered in the earlier music, one that emerges here in a more intense form: a mixture of creative impulses, some of them conservative or traditional, others innovative or progressive. A survey of the chamber music of this period is therefore obliged to forgo the broad brush of stylistic characterization for a more focused discussion of specific works.

Five works of chamber music other than string quartets may be mentioned. The earliest is the Violin Sonata in A, Op. 47, composed in 1802–3 and dedicated first to the violinist George P. Bridgetower and later to Rodolphe Kreutzer (hence the name "Kreutzer" Sonata). Although the language of most of this work resides squarely within the harmonic limits set by the Op. 30 violin sonatas, the balance between the two instrumental protagonists is redefined, tempering the hegemony of the piano and making of this something of a violin concerto. Mechanical figures associated with Italian virtuoso violin idioms are deployed throughout the first movement not only in the violin part but also in the piano. A contrasting affect is evident in the moving *adagio sostenuto* with which the work opens. Here a bold interchange of mode underlines the timbral difference established in the first eight bars. Also memorable is the hymnlike second subject (beginning in m. 91), a thematic type familiar from such works as the finale of Op. 18, No. 5 (mm. 36–43) and the second subject in the first movement of the Piano Sonata in C, Op. 53 ("Waldstein"). The stop-and-start quality of this movement reflects a more expanded expression of sonata form. A work on such a scale is bound to rely on formulas, and Beethoven uses his share of circle-of-fifths progressions to guide the tonal narrative in the development section.

The two piano trios in D and E♭, Op. 70, composed in 1808, are each strongly marked by contrasts, the first in the thematic realm, the second in the choice of key. (The four movements of the E♭ Trio are in E♭, C, A♭, and E♭ respectively, thus circumscribing a closed tonal plan with a weighting toward the subdominant.) Measures 1–21 of the opening movement of the "Ghost" Trio, Op. 70, No. 1, which make up the opening period, begin with a four-bar passage consisting of a three-octave descending scale played in octaves with registral transferences at every fifth note, thus giving prominence to the interval of a descending fourth. The unexpected appearance of F♮ in measure 5 signals a change of character: it is as if a new character appeared onstage to direct attention to a more lyrical and intimate affect. There are many changes of character in the course of the work, some of them sudden and swift, others more deliberate. As for the tremolo-laden, intensely expressive slow movement in D, nothing in the first movement prepares us for it.

The emerging lyrical impulse that characterizes the first movement of Op. 70, No.1, is even stronger in the Cello Sonata in A Major, Op 69, composed in 1807–8, a fine work based on fairly ordinary musical ideas that are given a memorably "poetic" treatment. The urgency associated with works like the *Eroica* and the Fifth Symphonies is replaced by a more intimate expression. Like its counterpart in the "Kreutzer" Sonata, the first movement of the A Major Cello Sonata begins with the string instrument playing solo. The piano continues the cello idea rather than replying to it, a gesture suggesting that the two instruments belong to a single, larger ensemble. Fermatas halt the motion without disturbing the character of the movement, but once underway it does not stop. The second movement is a scherzo in A minor, memorable for its syncopated principal idea. Then comes a brief *introduzione* marked *adagio cantabile*, which recalls the middle movement of the "Waldstein" Sonata, composed five years earlier. The last movement, in sonata form, is full of rapid figuration, uses a considerable amount of repetition (of cadential figures especially), and is light and lively. If Op. 69 strikes some as antiheroic, or at least nonheroic—which would not be to deny its intermittent heroism—it might serve as a reminder that the heroic is more complexly woven into Beethoven's work than the emphasis on a handful of middle-period works would suggest.

Although the Op. 47 violin sonata, the Op. 70 piano trios, and the Op. 69 cello sonata are all important to their individual genres, pride of place in middle-period Beethoven should be given to the Op. 59 string quartets. Here, and to a considerably greater extent than in the Op. 18 quartets, matters of genre and medium are consigned to the margins in order to focus on purely musical issues such as harmonic and tonal ordering, formal articulation, and rhythmic and metric articulation. And in probing these essential musical features, Beethoven accepts as inevitable a resultant equivocation and an attendant multiplicity of meaning.

For our purposes, we may count five string quartets as middle-period works: the three of Op. 59, in F major, E minor, and C major respectively; the "Harp" Quartet, Op. 74; and the String Quartet in F Minor, Op. 95, the "Serioso." Each of these works is distinct in character. Probably the most compact and concentrated of them is Op. 95, composed in 1810 but not published until 1816. Not by accident does this quartet come at the end of our period, for it is part of the lengthy transition to the works of the late period. Contrasts are extreme in Op. 95, not least in the scherzo, whose first part is based on a mazurka rhythm, the second on a minuet. One might hear a foreshadowing of the scherzo of Op. 127 in this movement. Frequent changes of key and key signature, closed symmetrical sections, and unmediated topics serve to demarcate autonomous sections within the movement. In the sonata-form first movement, too, textures are strongly contrasted. Topics abound: an Italian flavor may be savored in the tentative aria style of measures 13–18; the answer to the closure-laden gesture at the very beginning of the movement is an accompanied recitative (mm. 3–5). The return of the opening motive in measure 6, a half step higher, is marked by a sweet, hymnlike melody. But the cello intrudes twice (mm. 10 and 12), as if to claim its cadenza rights. When finally the aria is allowed to sing through more decisively in the key of D♭ major (mm. 21–28), a sense of calm falls upon the proceedings. But not for long: a deceptive cadence at measures 37–38 disturbs the quietude, bringing back a relative of the opening figure. This is music as drama, as Fred Maus has argued.[10] It demands a new attitude from the listener, an approach that would hear in the unpredictability of the movement's course a heightening of aesthetic pleasure.

This heightening of the demands placed on the listener is one of the hallmarks of Beethoven's middle-period chamber music, and it will be intensified in the late works. Not that the earlier Op. 18 quartets were lacking in imagination, or that they followed a wholly predictable dynamic trajectory. As we have seen, routine enactments of the sonata principle are juxtaposed with more speculative treatments. The appearance of a deci-

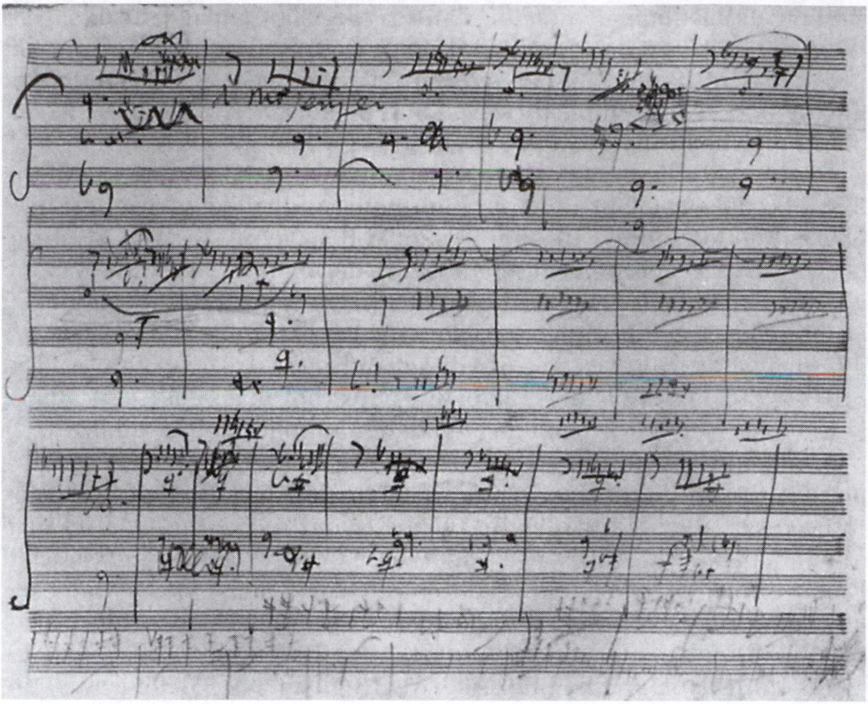

FIGURE 1.1.   Beethoven, String Quartet in F Minor, Op. 95, mvt. 3, sketch for mm. 41ff. Reproduced through courtesy of The Pierpont Morgan Library, New York, Mary Flagler Cary Music Collection, no. 48 (photography: David A. Loggie).

sive work like the first of the Op. 59 set, however, takes this creative process to new heights.

Written around the time of the *Eroica*, the String Quartet, Op. 59, No. 1, is a remarkable consolidation of a new practice: expanded resources, greater ambition and scope in the dynamic trajectory, and a compositional "voice" with greater independence than any that we have encountered so far. The following comments concern the first two movements.

At nearly four hundred measures in $\frac{4}{4}$ time, *allegro*, the first movement of Op. 59, No. 1, epitomizes the broad, fluid, and grand tonal discourse characteristic of Beethoven's middle period. Beethoven appears *not* to be in a hurry. Not that there is any loss of clarity in the tonal goals that serve as linchpins for the movement. But the periodicity is expanded from within—not by the addition of suffixes, as in the early violin sonatas, but by means of an inner growth, an internal phrase expansion. This implies a more organic conception of music, allowing the materials of the music to grow, flower, and bear fruit. Consider the first period of the movement, measures 1–19. The first metrically significant tonic chord occurs at the end of the period, not before, implying an end-orientation rather than a beginning-orientation. This is not to evoke any doubt that we are in F major from the first. Rather, the manner in which F major is defined incorporates some purposeful imprecision, perhaps even impressionism. The second-inversion sound in measures 1–4 produces an ambivalent point of departure, a dual harmonic orientation incorporating dominant and tonic. The persistence of the dyad C/A in second violin and viola in measures 5–7, even where the melodic orientation of the cello has changed, compounds this ambiguity. The shift to dominant harmony in the middle of measure 7 is subtle, almost unrecognized, even though the dominant is absolutely crucial to tonal definition. And the long dwelling on a dominant with its fifth in the bass, in effect a second inversion of the dominant complementing the second inversion of the earlier tonic, intensifies the harmonic elusiveness of the opening period. No wonder the decisive drive to the cadence in measures 16–19, complete with the first violin's whole-note augmentation of the cello's first measure, achieves such a powerful cathartic effect. What is remarkable is that these harmonic ambiguities are achieved without the use of a single chromatic pitch. And the textural as well as registral expansions (from c to f^3) reinforce the goal orientation of the phrase.

There is more to say about this opening period, of course, but what has been said here may serve as an indication of the extraordinary wealth of techniques and materials found in this movement. As far as materials go, Beethoven draws on eighteenth-century topics as he did in the Op. 18 quartets. For example, the angular, broken, improvisatory rhetoric of the passage immediately following the cadence in measure 19 brings to mind the gestures associated with the *Empfindsamkeit* of C. P. E. Bach. At measure 30 a musette, complete with a drone bass, appears, followed in measure 48 by a cadenza. These and many other topics appear in the course of this broad-scaled movement.

Also noteworthy are some of the means by which form is articulated. For example, this is the first instance in Beethoven's quartets in which the first-movement exposition is not formally repeated. At measure 102, after enough activity in the dominant key, several cadences, and an obvious gesture of transition, Beethoven restates the opening four bars as if repeating the exposition. But the "repeat" is quickly cut off and the music veers in other tonal directions—first Bb major, then G minor, and so on. Also striking is Beethoven's denial of some of the expectations built into his materials. For example, the pointillistic passage in Example 1.14 promises a cadence in C. Although the cadence arrives eventually, it does so in the middle of a phrase, whereby its rhythmic effect is considerably weakened. Later, at measures 144–51, the same texture reappears, leading to a long passage that Ratner has described as a parenthesis, a form within a form. Here, at the heart of the development section, Beethoven writes, first, a prelude in fantasia style (mm. 152–84), then a fugato in E♭ minor (mm. 185–210), and finally a postlude or an ending section (mm. 210–22), also marked by fantasy elements and embodying the collapse of learned style. Only after this insertion, this coherent parenthesis, does the composer resume the formal process of development (mm. 223–41).[11]

EXAMPLE 1.14.   Beethoven, String Quartet in F, Op. 59, No. 1, mvt. 1, mm. 85–91.

The recapitulation also introduces some innovations. For example, it reverses the thematic order of the exposition. That is, the broken figures of measures 20ff. open the recapitulation, followed by the first-key material proper at measure 254. By putting the tonally ambiguous opening after other, less ambiguous material, Beethoven recontextualizes the opening of the movement, showing that what was heard previously as a beginning was in fact already *in medias res*. This play with beginning, middle, and ending gestures does not, of course, originate with Beethoven; Haydn frequently indulged in it. Here, however, play occurs in a context in which many of the given procedures of phrase and tonal construction in the Classical style are being interrogated.[12]

Interrogation of a similar sort is found in the second movement of Op. 59, No. 1, a remarkable scherzo in which rhythmic and harmonic/tonal play reach new heights in Beethoven. The form of the movement is ultimately undecidable, for elements that suggest sonata form compete with others suggesting rondo form. What is striking, however, is the almost accidental way in which Beethoven enters new tonal regions, and the crude force with which he gets out of them. To choose just one example of this strategy: after the cadence in F minor at measure 148, the music moves to D♭ major and then through a transitional passage. There is no predicting where we will end up; indeed, the key promised is C minor, because by measures 167–68 Beethoven is on the dominant of C. He overshoots his mark, however, dropping from the note G to F♯ and reinterpreting F♯ as V of B, which key is heard in the subsequent phrase. This is the point of furthest tonal remove in the movement.[13]

The first two movements of Op. 59, No. 1, must surely suggest the power of tonal narratives and undermine our confidence in the value of synoptic analyses of Beethoven's tonal schemes, maplike representations that ignore the shifting and radically contextual meanings of tonal centers. Here tonal innovations are accomplished by the use of the most ordinary materials. The first movement of Op. 59, No.1, for example, develops from a simple rising scale, from which stems the predominantly stepwise motion in the entire movement. The second movement likewise freezes melodic motion at the beginning while developing rhythmic motion—using a sort of mazurka rhythm on a drone. It is this turn to the elemental, this attempt to extract greater and greater musical truths from the most basic materials, that constitutes one of Beethoven's unique accomplishments.

It would require an essay several times the length of this one to point out all striking features in the remaining movements of Op. 59, No.1, as well as in the other Op. 59 quartets. For example, like the scherzo of Op. 59, No. 1, the first movement of Op. 59, No. 2, is a study in rhythmic ambiguity, here an apparent conflict between triple and duple grouping. Of special significance in the second movement is Beethoven's manipulation of pure sonority. The opening choralelike topic enables a concentration on long, slow-moving note values and an abundance of root-position harmonies, and this emphasis is retained even when the topics shift from chorale to aria (m. 17) and march (m. 23). The third and fourth movements serve as a reminder that intramovement balance is sometimes—though not always—a compositional issue for Beethoven. In the third, "Brahmsian" movement, rhythmic experimentation is held in check while cadential reiteration is given stronger accent. Modal coloration in the *thème russe* hints at the archaizing slant forthcoming in some of the late works, most notably in the "Heiliger Dankgesang" of Op. 132, with its Lydian mode and Baroque sequences. And the fact that the finale of Op. 59, No. 2, although in E minor, begins on C (as does the finale of the Fourth Piano Concerto, which is in G major) suggests groping for a new sound to contrast with the predominant E-ness of the work.

Equivocation is more prominent in the third of the Op. 59 quartets, whose first movement, like the beginning of Mozart's "Dissonant" Quartet, begins with a slow, searching, fantasialike passage based on a descending bass. The harmony is at the very least disorienting, but only up to the onset of the *allegro;* once it gets going, the movement eschews traces of ambiguity stemming from the slow introduction, developing its rhetoric by means of neat, regular periods. Here, too, the sense of the past is evident in the divertimento-type construction, although the more self-conscious thematizing of the past does not occur until Beethoven's late quartets. In the second movement the languorous expression of A minor points ahead to

FIGURE 1.2.   Beethoven, Violin Sonata in G, Op. 96, mvt. 1, opening, auto-graph. Reproduced through courtesy of The Pierpont Morgan Library, New York, Morgan Manuscript 16 (photography: David A. Loggie).

Schumann and Mendelssohn, while the third movement, ostensibly a minuet, suppresses bass articulation of strong beats, thus undermining the sense of a cadence. The melodic activity of the cello, the motetlike entries, and the dark, chromatic coda show the range of expressive content that a minuet can sustain. And the fiercely contrapuntal finale, which opens with a formal fugue, develops into a compendium of numerous contrapuntal devices. Meeting that particular obligation does not take away another, namely, the unequivocal establishment of the sound of C as the tonal home of the work. The *Grosse Fuge* will perform a similar function for the Op. 130 quartet.

The sheer length and confident tone of the middle-period chamber music represents, in some respects, a radical departure from, and in other respects a consolidation of, tendencies already implicit in Beethoven's earlier work. Similarly, while the late style offers new perspectives on form, harmony, and periodicity, Beethoven does not make a 180-degree turn from earlier structural principles: an overall coherence can be sensed in Beethoven's chamber music. Yet, as listeners who recall our earliest hearings of Beethoven, we may be unwilling to go along with any interpretative scheme that minimizes the difference in impact between, for example, the first movement of the Bb Quartet, Op. 18, No. 6, and that of a late work in Bb such as Op. 130.

Chamber Music of the Late Period

It is relatively easy to trot out a series of "characteristics" of Beethoven's late style.[14] In the last five string quartets, composed between 1824–26, we can observe straightaway an ongoing concern with form, not only in its outer manifestation but especially in its internal organization. In striking contrast to the constancy and relative stability of the four-movement plan used in earlier quartets, the late quartets experiment with other designs. Only the first and last, Op. 127 and Op. 135, use a Classical four-movement plan, although even here the impact is hardly Classical. Op. 132 is cast in five movements, Op. 130 in six, and Op. 131 in seven. It is of course possible to argue that five-, six-, or seven-movement plans are based on the four-movement scheme, and that they retain the broad sequence of contrasting affect and function inherent in the conventional pattern; departures would then be understood as apparent, not real. This is an argument for the continuity of style and strategy across Beethoven's stylistic periods, an attempt to minimize the radical nature of the last quartets by showing that, in the matter of formal strategy, these works are grounded in a Classical aesthetic.

The argument is at its most plausible when made in connection with the Op. 131 quartet, with its seven movements (the numbering is Beethoven's) of unequal length:[15]

Movements:	1	2	3	4	5	6	7
	Prelude/ slow intro- duction	First move- ment	Intro- duction	Slow move- ment	Scherzo	Slow intro- duction	Finale
Four movement scheme:	1		2		3	4	

By coupling the fugal opening movement with the sonata-form second, in the manner of a slow introduction followed by a well-formed, albeit compressed, *allegro*, we have a compound "first movement." Similarly, the eleven-bar *recitativo accompagnato* that now stands in third position, and which is clearly transitional in function, is easily and plausibly paired with the theme and variations, in the manner of an extended upbeat followed by a prolonged downbeat. This would produce a second movement. Next comes Beethoven's scherzo, which can be renumbered "3" in the new scheme. Finally, as with the earlier 1-2 and 3-4 movement pairs, the beautiful G♯ minor arioso that stands in sixth position may be allied with the great finale, movement 7, to produce a third movement pair, movement no. 4. The order fast-slow-fast-fast of the new scheme (suppressing for now the introductory movements) may thus be compared to the earliest quartets, or to the Op. 59 set, or indeed to Op. 127. While this attempt to normalize late Beethoven may have the advantage of showing the historical embeddedness of his forms, it also has the serious disadvantage of seeming to force Op. 131 into a Procrustean bed.

The argument for a four-movement background scheme in each of the late quartets is harder to sustain against the evidence of the Op. 130 quartet. Here a sequence of six movements of roughly comparable weight (unlike those of Op. 131) takes on the character of a suite, with its succession of self-contained, contrasting dances. Not even the "Cavatina" can be cited to counter the argument that the movements of Op. 130 are comparably weighted, for its weight derives from the intensity and concentration of its expression, not its sixty-six-bar length. On the other hand, the evidence offered by the original finale, the *Grosse Fuge*, which was later detached, published separately (as Op. 133), and replaced by the present finale, undermines the argument about comparable weight. At 741 bars, and marked throughout by a radical self-consciousness in the display of sheer contrapuntal skill, Op. 133 dwarfs everything else in Op. 130. To attempt to collapse Op. 130's six movements into a four-movement plan in order to bring it into line with Classical tradition would be to do the scheme considerable violence.

It is not only in the movement sequence of the late quartets but also in the types of movement that we observe Beethoven's innovations. Fugue, fugatos, and imitative procedures are often cited as hallmarks of the late style. The opening movement of Op. 131, for example, is a fugue based on a subject in the pathetic mode, an affective manner going back at least

a hundred years. But the fugal process is tempered with gestures that derive from the sonata principle. A number of perfect cadences (see, for example, mm. 41–44) inject into this extraordinarily continuous fugue the
formality of cadential articulation more readily associated with sonata
form. Besides, only two areas of the movement pursue the fugal protocol
with some degree of strictness: the opening sixteen bars, where the subject and answer appear in two pairs in the four voices, and measures
93–107, where the same thing happens, only this time the sequence of
voices is modified. Although the long middle section is not free of imitative and learned devices, it is nevertheless improvisational in quality, suggesting a huge fantasia. The crucial feature of Beethoven's late forms is
not their allegiance to a single formal plan—although a number of such
plans are normatively enacted—but rather their playing with the very
idea of a formal plan, incorporating gestures associated with other plans
in a kind of metamusical commentary.

Fugal writing elsewhere is similarly tempered by other influences. A
work as radical as the *Grosse Fuge,* Op. 133, a remarkable and comprehensive compendium of fugal devices, displays in places a style of fugal
writing that betrays a strong galant influence. The second fugue, in G♭
major (mm. 159–232), for example, retains some of the ornamental gestures associated with *Empfindsamkeit* as well as a singsong melodic quality.
The A Minor Quartet, Op. 132, begins with an eight-bar invocation of the
strict style. The procedures here are literally strict: the subject is stated,
introverted, inverted, retrograded, and presented on both tonic and dominant scale degrees (Example 1.15). This eight-bar exposition then serves
as a source of material and technique for the rest of the movement. The
opening four-note idea, G♯–A–F–E (further divisible, if the analyst so desires, into two-note segments that may then be related by transposition,
inversion, and retrogression), permeates the entire movement not only as
a cantus firmus against which a counterpoint is written, but as an element
within the thematic fabric. Thus, although the movement is emphatically
not a fugue—it is, in fact, in sonata form, although the disposition of its
parts is not normative—and although it is not in predominantly fugal
character, it is nevertheless marked throughout by imitative procedures
enshrined in the opening eight bars.

The variation principle is another salient feature of Beethoven's late
forms. Interest in variation does not mark a new impetus in Beethoven:
from the very first, he wrote variation sets not only for keyboard but for a
variety of instrumental genres. The later piano works also have their share
of variations. The Sonata in E Major, Op. 109, for example, finishes with
a hymnlike theme followed by six variations, arranged to progress from
an ornamental, dreamy state (variation 1) to one so engulfed in figuration
that it problematizes the figure-ground duality. The C Minor Sonata,
Op. 111, likewise concludes with a comprehensive set of variations in C
major. Especially remarkable are the "Diabelli" Variations, Op. 120, in
which the theme and the gestalt of the theme are subjected to intricate

EXAMPLE 1.15.   Beethoven, String Quartet in A Minor, Op. 132, mvt. 1, mm. 1–9.

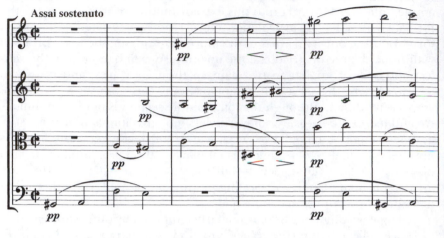

manipulation, an intense probing of essentials. We are here a long way from the ornamental and decorative variations of Haydn or Mozart, or even of earlier Beethoven.[16]

The first of the great variation sets in the late quartets is that of Op. 127, whose second movement, cast in an uncommon $\frac{12}{8}$ meter and marked Adagio, comprises a theme and five variations. To speak of a "theme" here is somewhat problematic, for Beethoven's melody is already ornamented. The listener must abstract a theme out of the theme, a simpler "proto-theme" that will provide a point of reference for one's hearing of the variations. By complicating the premises, Beethoven invites the listener to add to the musical text, to participate actively in establishing its essence. It requires effort to perceive the outlines of the theme in variation 1, for example, for it is imbricated in a web of ornaments and contrapuntal activity in which notions of "theme" and "accompaniment" are seriously undermined. Variation 2, with its mechanical effects reminiscent of clockwork (see also the third movement of Op. 130), is couched in the form of a slow march and marked by busy figuration. The third variation in E major (set up initially as F♭) makes even fewer concessions to the listener. In arioso style, this variation, with its rich harmonies, also only tangentially refers to the periodic layout of the original theme. Only with variation 4, back in A♭ major, do we get something conventional—an ornamental variation in which the distinction between "melody" and "accompaniment" is maintained. Here the theme takes on the character of a grand Italian aria. The fifth variation, beginning in D-flat, is a free gloss on the theme, including an excursion to C♯ minor. Then comes what would have been the sixth variation—a recall of the theme that, however, is presented incompletely. In placing the most conventional last, Beethoven reverses the protocol of his earlier variation sets. It is as though he were testing his listeners' faith in the genre; rewards are reserved for those who persist until the very end.

More far-reaching than the Op. 127 variations is the set that functions as slow movement in Op. 131. Here the theme is square, made up of two repeated eight-bar strains, and avoiding modulation. The theme's profile is clear, based on a recurring archetype found in a number of eighteenth-century works. Unlike the listener to Op. 127, the listener to Op. 131 is given a clearly articulated, symmetrical, and easily digested theme; one does not derive it from a more complicated premise. This grounding allows Beethoven to take greater liberties in subsequent variations. Who would have imagined that a $\frac{2}{4}$, proceeding mainly in quarter notes, could be transformed into a solemn $\frac{9}{4}$ hymn variation, variation 6? Or that a motive derived from the theme could be made the basis of the quasi-canonic third variation, another nod to the strict or learned style? Or that elements of the theme could be incorporated into a fantastic written-out cadenza at the end of the movement? The Op. 131 variations contain both old and new elements, which are easy to follow in places, and radically obscure the theme elsewhere. They represent not so much a "new" concept of variations as a summa of techniques present in earlier Beethoven, some with a stronger accent.

The highly concentrated and laconic variation procedures in Op. 135 provide another perspective on Beethoven's treatment of the genre. Here, in contrast to the breadth and leisurely unfolding of both the Op. 127 and 131 variations, Beethoven concentrates his powers in a short space. The extremely slow tempo—*lento assai*—the singsong melodic line, and the stepwise bass motion all make it difficult to perceive a clear periodicity in the theme. No fanfare accompanies the start of variation 1, whose character approximates that of the theme. Only in variation 4 does the texture breathe, expanding upward in the first violin to reach hitherto unbroached heights and to close on f^2, two octaves up from the note with which the viola announced the variation set.

Particularly salient in the late quartets are various topics, some of which are used as part of the ordinary material of a work, while others are invoked as if on a second level. We have seen in both the Op. 18 and Op. 59 quartets the importance that Beethoven attaches to these conventional signs. In the last quartets, the frequency and significance of topics remains undiminished. Certainly, the strong presence of the past that some listeners have heard in late Beethoven stems in part from the historical weight attached to his materials; this music makes concrete use of elements that are burdened with significance.[17]

A range of affects sustains one of the most common topics found in the late works, namely, the march. The last movement of Op. 131 may remind listeners of early nineteenth-century military-style marches. It is on this parade ground that Beethoven resolves some of the principal tensions accumulated in the preceding movements. One ongoing tension stems from the harmonic rather than the topical process, and it concerns the subdominant or Neapolitan complex that has received tremendous emphasis in the work up until now. To counteract the pull of the subdominant, Beethoven first recapitulates part of the second subject in the key of the Neapolitan, D major (mm. 216ff.) before "correcting" himself by sinking down a half step to the proper key, C♯ major (m. 242). This tonal correction is given profile by the singing melody that provides contrast to the dominant march of the movement, but elements of march are never very far from the surface of the work.

Although infused with fantasy elements, the first movement of Op. 132 harbors a latent march throughout, a march that perhaps becomes most explicit only in the final eleven bars. And although shot through with versions of the four-note motive that announces the learned style of the introductory bars, the movement is topically quite varied. The *alla breve* at the very beginning is interrupted by a cadenza in measures 9–10. A sighing figure in singing style that incorporates a marchlike dotted rhythm emerges in measure 1 as the first and principal theme of the movement. *Empfindsamer* outbursts are heard in measures 18–20. Later, an Italian aria gives profile to the second subject in F major. These topics return several times throughout the movement within the dominant context of the march; as a result, this movement becomes a strong and subtle essay in textural contrast (surpassed, perhaps, only by the first movement of Op. 130). A motivic analysis that ignored the topical dimension would be just as defective as a topical analysis that did not recognize the march as the principal style characteristic of the movement.[18]

The march finale of Op. 131 is notated in $\frac{4}{4}$ and uses much dotted material. The first-movement march of Op. 132 becomes regular after consistently missing a strongly articulated downbeat at the beginning of the movement. But the fourth movement of Op. 132—*Alla marcia, assai vivace* is Beethoven's rubric to the performer—begins in a more disorienting fashion. Dynamic and harmonic accents are deployed in the first four bars to produce countermetrical effects, thus challenging but never completely eroding the sense of march. Eventually the march yields to an unmeasured accompanied recitative, which in turn introduces the waltzlike finale.

Most of the strongly marked contrasts in the late quartets are products of topical differentiation. Op. 130 above all epitomizes contrast as a structural feature. In the first movement, for example, an *adagio* passage that begins as if it might be a slow introduction later returns in ways that enhance its affinities with the principal ideas of the movement. The main *allegro* figure alludes to an archaic canzona style and is initially accompanied by a virtuosic sixteenth-note figure that suggests concerto idiom. It, in turn, is prepared by the recurring *adagio* introduction. Nothing persists for very long in this movement; the design of the musical surface is constantly in flux, maximizing contrasts, enhancing and sometimes challenging the underlying tonal logic. The third movement of Op. 132 features an alternation between chorale (the famous holy song of thanksgiving) and a lively and ornamented dance in $\frac{3}{8}$. And in the first movement of Op. 135, a movement in which topics are understated throughout, a cantus firmus theme in measures 10–14 is interrupted by a cadenzalike gesture, which itself leads to a march—a sequence of topics that recalls the opening movement of Op. 132 (whose fantasialike character, however, is not shared by Op. 135).

Fugues and fugatos, variation form, topics and topical allusions: these mainstays of Beethoven's late style do not, of course, tell the complete story of the late quartets. Another crucial aspect of Beethoven's work is the set of innovations that he introduced in the realm of pitch organization. A whole book is needed to explicate the harmonic logic and rhythmic and timbral innovations of late Beethoven, for the "new" sonorities and apparently irregular meters result from a heightening or intensification of musical rhetoric; they are not inventions of "new" material.

Consider, for example, the scherzo and trio of Op. 135, with their written-out repeats. The first period, with its self-repeating A–G–F motif and syncopated upper voices, proceeds at a typically feverish pace, unfolding a normal sixteen-bar period. As if without warning, an accented E♭ enters at the end of the period (m. 16), and although it could be heard as having been prepared in the previous movement (see mm. 181–85), it is rhetorically extreme: not only is it unintegrated harmonically, but its adherence to an offbeat rhythm suppresses the heard meter, lending the music a momentary sense of disintegration. It is "corrected" to an E♮ in measure 23, enabling the scherzo to resume its normal business. Throughout this movement, and but for the intervention of the disruptive E♭'s, the periods are regular and symmetrical, although they are always on the edge, so to speak, as a result of the syncopation. By contrast, the trio expands its phrase lengths while retaining the singsong character of the scherzo. Beethoven's harmonic innovation in the trio lies in the rising sequence of tonal centers, F–G–A, in which each section is given the appropriate key signature. This succession of whole-tone-related keys, which may be further extended by including the earlier E♭, may be understood as a linear projection of the main motive of the scherzo. Whether or not Beethoven sought to make this link between scherzo and trio is somewhat beside the point. The fact is that this large-scale projection of a melodic fragment indexes the same organicist technique that we have seen in the middle-period works, although the articulation of the keys F, G, and A is such that our sense of the whole is undermined.

Other innovations in harmony and counterpoint may be mentioned briefly. The "Heiliger Dankgesang" of Op. 132 is an example of a "sound" piece, a movement whose primary allegiance is neither to key nor to period structure but to sonority pure and simple. Although nominally exploring the Lydian mode, the chorale portions of this movement are static on the deepest level, revealing no significant large-scale linear motion. The slow material is juxtaposed with the D major dance material, which is by contrast clearly directed, including use of a familiar Baroque descending bass pattern. Each return of material is varied on the surface, encouraging designation of this movement as a "double set of variations."[19] The refusal to act in the slow sections, the suspension of the urgent periodicity found elsewhere, is at once modern and archaic, a throwback to the Renaissance and an anticipation of the twentieth century.

Stasis also breeds continuity, and this becomes evident in places in late Beethoven where resolutions are delayed or dovetailed to ensure a continuity in musical line. One instance is the progression quoted in Example 1.16 from Op. 127, second movement, part of the variation theme itself (see m. 3). Another case, Example 1.17, comes at the end of the set of variations and shows Beethoven prolonging a chord of F♭ major (or E major), which is here functioning as chromatic upper neighbor note to E♭, the dominant. A more colorful example is the first four bars in the third movement of Op. 130 (Example 1.18): Beethoven opts for D♭ major over

EXAMPLE 1.16.   Beethoven, String Quartet in E♭, Op. 127, mvt. 2, mm. 1–5.

Adagio, ma non troppo e molto cantabile

EXAMPLE 1.17. Beethoven, String Quartet in E♭, Op. 127, mvt. 2, mm. 123–25.

EXAMPLE 1.18. Beethoven, String Quartet in B♭ Major, Op. 130, mvt. 3, mm. 1–4.

Andante con moto ma non troppo

B♭ minor, having earlier hinted at the latter in the opening two bars. Note that the B♭♭ of measure 1 would ordinarily go down to A-flat and would thus be comprehensible within a D♭ major chromatic universe. Later, when the ticktock effect is begun by the cello (m. 3), a persistent B♭ (m. 6) ensures that the perceptually dominant D♭ major is not given in "pure" form.

The chamber works surveyed in this essay differ from the public genres of symphony and concerto in the kinds of demands they make on listeners. Chamber music for Beethoven was a forum for experimentation and play, and his numerous works in various genres—string trio, violin sonata, cello sonata, and string quartet—provide ample evidence of such play. Our focus here on the string quartets has been purely pragmatic: the quartets constitute a coherent and consistently challenging body of works. In listening to them, we encounter a range of imaginative solutions to basic compositional problems, problems ranging from the rhetoric of harmony and key through the establishment and disruption of periodicity to the construction of deep and convincing expressive trajectories. Beethoven frequently draws on the commonplaces of eighteenth-century style in the form of topics, partly to invoke an extramusical world and partly to domesticate that world within a purely musical sound environment. Above all, the chamber music of Beethoven provides ample rewards for those who wish to engage the tonal language at an important historical moment and in the hands of one of its most creative exponents.

Notes

1. A straightforward discussion of the "three periods" may be found in Joseph Kerman, *The New Grove Beethoven* (London, 1983), 89–94. Maynard Solomon's view was first set out in "The Creative Periods of Beethoven," *Music Review* 34 (1973): 30–38, and incorporated into his biography, *Beethoven* (New York, 1980). See also his essay "Beethoven: Beyond Classicism," in *The Beethoven Quartet Companion,* ed. Robert Winter and Robert Martin (Berkeley and Los Angeles, 1994). Excerpts from the writings of Schlosser, Fétis, Lenz, and Ulïbïshev (*sic*) on the styles of Beethoven's music may be read in English translation in Ian Bent, *Music Analysis in the Nineteenth Century*, vol. 1 (Cambridge, 1994), 302–29.

2. Concerning the modeling of Op. 18, No. 5, on Mozart's K. 464, see Jeremy Yudkin, "Beethoven's 'Mozart' Quartet," *Journal of the American Musicological Society* 45 (1992): 30–74.

3. The formation of late eighteenth-century musical language is the subject of Leonard G. Ratner's comprehensive study *Classic Music: Expression, Form, and Style* (New York, 1980). See also Charles Rosen, *The Classical Style: Haydn, Mozart, Beethoven* (New York, 1971).

4. Among efficient surveys of Beethoven's life and work, see especially *The Beethoven Compendium*, edited by Barry Cooper (London, 1991). On the quartets, see *The Beethoven Quartet Companion.*

5. For a concise introduction to Beethoven's variation technique as exemplified in a handful of works, see Elaine Sisman, *Haydn and the Classical Variation*

(Cambridge, MA, 1993), 235–62.

6. The point of furthest remove is "a harmonic point in the development section of a sonata form when the harmony begins its return to the tonic. In major-key movements, this point is often V of VI" (Leonard Ratner, *The Beethoven String Quartets: Compositional Strategies and Rhetoric* [Stanford, CA, 1995], 332).

7. On topics, see Ratner, *Classic Music,* and Wye Jamison Allanbrook, *Rhythmic Gesture in Mozart: "Le Nozze di Figaro" and "Don Giovanni"* (Chicago, 1983). See also my *Playing with Signs: A Semiotic Interpretation of Classic Music* (Princeton, NJ, 1991). My discussion of topics below is greatly indebted to Ratner, *The Beethoven String Quartets: Compositional Strategies and Rhetoric.*

8. For a detailed study of "La malinconia," see William J. Mitchell, "Beethoven's La Malinconia from the String Quartet, Opus 18, No. 6," *Music Forum* 3 (1973): 269–80.

9. Kerman, *The New Grove Beethoven,* 110–20.

10. Fred Maus, "Music as Drama," *Music Theory Spectrum* 10 (1988): 56–73.

11. Further discussion along these lines of first-movement form in Op. 59, No. 1, may be found in Ratner, *The Beethoven String Quartets,* 105–16.

12. On aspects of Haydn's manipulation of beginning, middle, and ending gestures, see my *Playing with Signs,* 51–79. See also Janet Levy, "Gesture, Form, and Syntax in Haydn's Music," In *Haydn Studies,* ed. J. Peter Larsen, H. Serwer, and J. Webster (New York, 1981), 355–62.

13. For contrasting perspectives on the form of the second movement of Op. 59, No. 1, see Erwin Ratz, *Einführung in die musikalische Formenlehre,* 2d ed. (Vienna, 1968), and Joseph Kerman, *The Beethoven Quartets* (New York, 1967).

14. As found, for example, in the digest by Kerman in *The New Grove Beethoven.*

15. Op. 131 is the subject of one of Donald C. Tovey's best-known essays, "Some Aspects of Beethoven's Art Forms," in *Essays and Lectures on Music* (Oxford, 1949), 271–97.

16. A detailed study of one set of variations is William Kinderman, *Beethoven's Diabelli Variations* (Oxford, 1987).

17. An exemplary study of the presence of the past in a Beethoven work is Warren Kirkendale, "The 'Great Fugue' Op. 133: Beethoven's 'Art of the Fugue,'" *Acta musicologica* 35 (1963): 14–24.

18. For further elaboration of these comments on the first movement of Op. 132, see my *Playing with Signs,* 110–26.

19. Carl Dahlhaus, *Nineteenth-Century Music,* trans. J. Bradford Robinson (Berkeley and Los Angeles, 1989), 86.

Bibliography

Chua, Daniel. *The Galitzin Quartets.* Princeton, 1995.

Kerman, Joseph. *The Beethoven Quartets.* New York, 1967.

Levy, Janet M. *Beethoven's Compositional Process.* Philadelphia, 1982.

Ratner, Leonard G. *Classic Music: Expression, Form, and Style.* New York, 1980.

———. *The Beethoven String Quartets: Compositional Strategies and Rhetoric.* Stanford, CA, 1995.

Ratz, Erwin. *Einführung in die musikalische Formenlehre.* 2d ed. Vienna, 1968.

Rosen, Charles. *The Classical Style.* London, 1971.

Winter, Robert. *Compositional Origins of Beethoven's Opus 131*. Ann Arbor, MI, 1982.
Winter, Robert, and Robert Martin, eds. *The Beethoven Quartet Companion*. Berkeley
    and Los Angeles, 1994.

CHAPTER TWO

Schubert's Chamber Music

Stephen E. Hefling and
David S. Tartakoff

*For the Music Houseparty, in honor of its fifty-seventh year
and Schubert's two hundredth*

Although Franz Schubert is best known as a master of the lied, chamber music was the genre that, save for one notable hiatus, occupied him most consistently throughout his short career.[1] String quartets dating from 1810 or early 1811 (D. 18–19a) are among the first pieces he is known to have written, while his last completed instrumental work—for many, also his best—is the extraordinary C Major String Quintet, D. 956, finished by early October 1828. Seven weeks later he was dead at the age of thirty-one.

Schubert first became immersed in the rich Viennese heritage of chamber music as the violist of his family's string quartet (his brothers played the violin parts, their father the cello), and according to his brother Ferdinand, he wrote his first quartets when he was ten or eleven. Schubert's teacher Holzer reports the boy learned so quickly during this period that "whenever I wished to impart something new to him, he always knew it already."[2] Accepted as a choirboy into the Imperial Court Chapel in 1808, Schubert was concurrently a student at the Kaiserlich-königliches Stadtkonvikt (Imperial and Royal City Seminary), where both orchestral and chamber works were frequently played.[3] These firsthand experiences vitally influenced his student compositions, which contain numerous reminiscences of Mozart, Haydn, (less frequently) Beethoven, and others; in addition, Schubert's early quartets reveal that he already understood how to write effectively for strings.

The Early Works

Schubert's quartets as a whole fall conveniently into two groups: (1) eleven early works from the years 1810/11 through 1816, which are rarely heard today, and (2) the three quartets from 1824–26—the "Rosamunde" in A Minor (D. 804), "Death and the Maiden" in D Minor (D. 810), and the vast G Major Quartet (D. 887)—which are performed and recorded by nearly every prominent professional quartet. Between these two clusters stands the C Minor *Quartettsatz* of 1820 (D. 703),[4] the head movement of an unfinished quartet, which in its bold design and expressive intensity surpasses all of Schubert's previous instrumental works. The group of early quartets can be further subdivided into: (a) seven compositions of a talented but not yet mature student (D. 18, 94, 32, 36, 46, 68, and 74, composed 1810/11–August 1813), and (b) four works of generally greater poise and import (D. 87 in E♭, Op. 125, No. 1; D. 112 in B♭, Op. 168; D. 173 in G Minor; and D. 353 in E, Op. 125, No. 2), all written between November 1813 and 1816, after he had left the Stadtkonvikt; here the young composer has begun to find his own distinctive voice.

During this period, too, a C minor quartet (D. 103, April 1814, now incomplete) seems to mark a notable advance in Schubert's technical and expressive development, and perhaps something of a personal crisis as well. From the time of the earliest quartets (1810/11–1813) several other movements of chamber music also survive, including a group of six minuets for pairs of oboes, clarinets, horns, bassoons, and trumpet (D. 2d, 1811);[5] an overture in C minor for string quintet (D. 8, June 1811), which Schubert reworked for string quartet (D. 8a, after 12 July 1811); a movement in B♭ for piano trio, entitled "Sonate" (D. 28, July–August 1812); the minuet and finale of a wind octet in F (D. 72, August 1813); and a curious piece in E♭ minor for wind nonet entitled "Franz Schuberts Begräbnis-Feyer [Franz Schubert's Burial Ceremony]" in the composer's own hand (D. 79, 19 September 1813). A number of other works are known to have been lost.

Overall, Schubert's earliest chamber works reveal that he had already absorbed much from the mature Classical style of Haydn and Mozart (although rather less from Beethoven): his gestures are usually effective, ranging in expressivity from conventional elegance to dramatic assertiveness, and he is capable of unusually striking harmonic digressions that nevertheless fit the overall shape and flow of a passage. The minuets of this period, if occasionally a touch stodgy, are fully competent. But although Schubert commands sufficient fluency in spinning out his material to attempt outer movements of ambitious size, he does not demonstrate consistent control of either the fundamental tonal superstructure or the characteristic thematic contrast long since established as normative in sonata-form movements. Whether this is naïve but intentional variation of Classical procedures or merely youthful inadvertence remains unclear; writers such as Einstein, Tovey (implicitly), and Westrup suggest that he lacked the necessary discipline and experience, while Dahlhaus argues that because Schubert's approach to sonata form in the early quartets is essentially monothematic, he sought variety through unusual tonal schemes. What seems certain is that although Schubert's later essays in sonata procedure are frequently original and experimental, particularly as regards tonal structure, he became much more adept at drawing both continuity and dramatic diversity from the traditional archetype.

String Quartet in G Minor/B♭ Major, D. 18

The sole survivor from a group of three quartets "in undecided, shifting keys" written in 1810/11 (although perhaps as early as 1809) is the Quartet in G Minor/B♭ Major, D. 18.[6] While the sequence of four movements (Andante/presto vivace; Menuetto; Andante; Presto) is fairly conventional, only the minuet proceeds in a predictable manner. The work's ominous slow introduction commences in C minor, although it soon seems unlikely that this will be the tonic. (Perhaps Schubert had in mind tonally ambiguous openings such as those in Mozart's "Dissonant" Quartet, K. 465, Beethoven's third "Rasumovsky," Op. 59, or his "Harp" Quartet, Op. 74.) The four-bar motto of the introduction, which will dominate the entire movement, recurs in G minor, D minor, and then B♭: this move to a third-related major mode (mm. 20–21) dissolves the previous tension in a gesture highly characteristic of Schubert. Yet again the theme is interrupted by dramatic chordal outbursts; ultimately the introduction settles on a half cadence and pause in G minor. The ensuing *presto* turns the introductory idea into a theme of rather passionate energy; such a transition suggests the influence of Haydn (the precursor of Schubert's monothematic approach to most of his early quartets).[7] Now G minor is firmly established as the tonic, through pedal point (with crescendo) and full cadence. From this agitated statement emerge tremolos, unison scales, and fanfares in flexible two-bar groupings that could yield a transition, but don't quite; dominant harmony is heard at the double bar, although the music is still clearly in the tonic. Such reluctance to move firmly away from the home key characterizes many of Schubert's early chamber works (and, as Webster observes, several of the later ones as well).[8] The "orchestral" nature of the material following the main theme is readily apparent; not only in the early works but indeed throughout his quartet writing, Schubert adapts the string textures of the larger ensemble for vigorous effects.

The development section of D. 18 opens with the main idea partially inverted, a gesture that seems almost imploring (particularly when doubled by the cello). Schubert could scarcely avoid touching upon G minor at this point, but the full tonic cadence and the succeeding *forte* repetition of the inverted theme in dominant minor generates little momentum. Then an utterly unexpected shift of mode and thinning of texture usher in a canonic treatment of the "motto" idea: the naïve contrast of this episode, while charming, may also strike us today as slightly absurd. The third voice in the canon, moreover (second violin), produces fairly prominent direct octaves. When the fourth entry has had its say, a countermelody in running eighths is placed above the subject.[9] That of course does not alter the D major focus of the "motto," yet merely eight bars after this passage, the movement's reprise is at hand—in D minor. This is probably the earliest of Schubert's numerous ventures in nontonic recapitulation, and compared to more traditional sonata movements, it seems lacking in both preparation and stabilization of the reprise. Equally apparent, however, is that young Schubert's dramatic scheme is to run a course of agitated instability right down to the coda. He has also learned (probably from Mozart and Haydn) that a recapitulation can be dramatically varied and intensified—the dissonant outbursts against the main idea, for example (mm. 149–51) are the movement's most gripping moments; and through energetic spinning out (rather than traditional development) this section doubles the length of the exposition. Harmonically the music veers toward E♭ minor, G♭ major, and F minor, almost as though the tonicity of G minor were somehow fearsome and better avoided. (Such, in far more sophisticated guise, was Mozart's dramatic tactic in the G Minor Symphony, K. 550, one of Schubert's favorite pieces, which he played as a student at the Konvikt;[10] Schubert adopts the procedure in later works as well.) Only at the first ending is the music firmly fixed on the dominant of G minor. Schubert's sixteen-bar coda hardly resolves the accumulated tensions, and with the final recurrence of the motto the movement takes its leave almost where it began. Awkward features notwithstanding, this is an engaging piece, well removed from slavish imitation of eighteenth-century models. Its fresh, experimental nature calls to mind the early Haydn quartets, and its expressive aspirations reveal that Schubert has already felt the dramatic potential of mature Classical instrumental music.

The minuet of D. 18 is a world apart from the bold opening movement—in key (F major), sonority (muted strings), and affect (smoothly linked gestures and somewhat saccharine melodic lines). The asymmetrical seven-bar antecedent-consequent phrase structure sounds thoroughly natural, indicating that Schubert was already at home with such pieces (more so than in the minuets for winds, D. 2d). The ensuing Andante is less successful; although the Haydnesque melodic writing is pleasant, Schubert seems to lose harmonic momentum by again experimenting with asymmetrical (five-bar) phrasing. As the movement unfolds, what would appear to be a binary form (followed by variations) stays in the tonic for the first half, but modulates and closes in the dominant for the second (which is then, asymmetrically, repeated). The Andante concludes rather uncomfortably by rephrasing its opening idea and then simply cadencing in B♭. There follows a finale exuberant in its *buffo* gestures, but lacking integration of content and form, particularly as regards tonal organization. Unlike the opening movement, this one projects no overriding dramatic plan. Midway through is another unexpected, static canonic episode replete with voice-leading problems, and even longer than that of the first movement; there is, however, little development proper. The recapitulation (mm. 141ff.) is greatly curtailed and scarcely manages to restore the tonic before the curtain falls. Still, Schubert's command of gesture, bar-to-bar continuity, rhythmic energy, and local harmonic detail is impressive when the movement is heard and not merely studied. It is not surprising that his family, fellow students, and teachers would be impressed by such a piece from a boy approximately thirteen years old.

String Quartet in D Major, D. 94

The Quartet in D Major, D. 94, is probably the next of Schubert's preserved essays in the genre; today it is believed to date from 1811, or the first half of 1812 at the latest.[11] Stylistically it stands in contrast to the "mixed key" quartet (D. 18) in nearly all respects, yet broadly speaking, many of its charms and shortcomings bring the earlier work to mind. The first movement is lyrical, initially even pastoral. A likely influence is Mozart (e.g., the "Prussian" Quartets in D Major, K. 575, and B♭, K. 589), for like Mozart in many of his "singing allegro" movements, Schubert here pours forth a wealth of flowing, closely related ideas, "any one of which," as Westrup notes, "would prove fruitful in the hands of an experienced composer."[12] The movement mushrooms to the extraordinary length of 371 bars, but Schubert cannot yet shape such abundance into a convincing exposition and draw selectively from it for an effective development. Once again, the chief difficulty is large-scale tonal organization: because the exposition does not fully depart from the tonic, it generates no broad harmonic tension in moving from one group of lovely ideas to another. The development begins with a rather serious and effective dominant prolongation, which Schubert happily dissolves in a manner that seemingly adumbrates his later style; what follows, however, is rambling. A sudden turn to the Neapolitan (m. 148), for example, is arresting but not well timed: its implications of dominant preparation, and therefore reprise, are premature, so Schubert simply sidesteps them. Twenty bars later, for no compelling reason, a seemingly false reprise takes place in C major; but this in fact turns out to be the true reprise, and the ensuing return to D (mm. 191ff.) is awkward at best. As in the earlier quartet, the recapitulation is varied and expanded, yet this time without apparent dramatic goal. The autograph score indicates that Schubert planned, and then cut, a canonic passage in this portion of the movement (following m. 292);[13] by the third recurrence in D of the transitional "fanfare" figure (m. 303), however, one wonders whether additional cuts would have improved the piece.

The slow movement is indeed "an echo of Haydn" (Westrup), but it is also the best-shaped movement encountered thus far.[14] If the minuet recalls Beethoven (Second Symphony) and the trio Mozart (the "Jupiter"), both are well made; and while neither modulates, the third relation between them (D to B♭) is refreshing.[15] Haydn's influence is again apparent in the bubbling finale, an unusual hybrid of sonata and rondo forms. Here

Schubert's penchant for colorful harmonic patches serves the broader scheme to good effect: twice in the exposition he uses extended diversions to the Neapolitan in establishing a structural dominant (F to E, mm. 38–54; B♭ to A, mm. 121–31). Rooted in Haydn and Mozart,[16] this sort of procedure is fundamental to nineteenth-century expansions of tonal space, including Schubert's.

The C Minor Overture, D. 8/8a (1811)

During 1811 and 1812, doubtless influenced by performances at the Stadtkonvikt, Schubert began writing overtures, and not only for orchestra (D. 2a, 4, 12, 26). Overtures for piano (D. 14), string quartet (D. 20), and string quintet (D. 8, also reworked for string quartet, D. 8a) date from this time as well, probably because such "chamber overtures" were more likely to performed (or published) than orchestral ones. Of the three just listed, only one has survived: the C Minor Overture for String Quintet or Quartet (D. 8/8a, June–July 1811), which Schubert wrote for his brother Ferdinand. Not surprisingly, some of its thematic material is closely related to an orchestral model (Cherubini's overture to *Faniska*),[17] and the string parts are treated orchestrally throughout. Like the G minor first movement of the Quartet, D. 18, this piece is dramatic, yet much more so. Most impressive are the harmonic intensity and operatic pathos of the slow introduction: the suspensions, diminished sevenths, long sequential lines, and imploring vocal gestures suggest both passion and technical mastery far beyond that of the quartets composed up to this point. The ensuing *allegro* is motivically dominated by the pickup eighths of the main idea; at first halting, these become urgently energetic, ominously static, and lyrically carefree during the movement's course. Its sonata procedure is unusual but effective: the exposition includes two subsidiary tonal areas (A♭ and F), and a good deal of energy is generated through dominant preparation of F minor. The development is appropriately brief, and for once there is a tonic reprise, although it is subsequently destabilized by moves to the dominant major and, once again, the subdominant (F) minor. Full tonic confirmation is saved for the driving coda, which has a Beethovenian flavor.

The "Sonate" in B♭, D. 28, and the String Quartets in C, D. 32 and B♭, D. 36 (1812–13)

On 28 May 1812 Schubert's mother died, but he continued working apace, possibly to provide a stable focus for his life. On 18 June he began formal studies in counterpoint with court Kapellmeister Antonio Salieri; among his compositions of that summer are a number of keyboard fugues, a *Salve Regina* (D. 27), an orchestral overture (D. 26), and his first work for piano trio, the single-movement "Sonate" in B♭ (D. 28, July–August

1812).[18] Like the opening movement of the D Major Quartet, D. 94, the Sonate is a lengthy piece that introduces a wealth of lyrical ideas. But here the music's elegance and restraint seems almost hyper-Mozartian, and somewhat impersonal—especially in comparison to the impassioned quin-tet-overture of the previous summer. Trying out such contrasting styles was perhaps useful to Schubert in developing his individuality, yet the coolness of the Sonate seems to sidestep more direct personal involvement with the music. Another personal crisis occurred while he was at work on this piece: Schubert's voice broke, bringing to an end his secure activity as a choirboy. Nevertheless, he remained a student at the Konvikt for more than a year. In the fall Schubert turned again to quartet writing, com-pleting a work in C major (D. 32) during October, and beginning another in B♭ (D. 36) that would be finished only the following February. Both re-veal marked gains in the integration of whole and parts, not only within single movements, but also across the span of four. In all probability he was learning more than species counterpoint under Salieri's guidance; as Einstein remarks about the B♭ quartet, "Schubert is developing fast."[19]

The first movements of both quartets are, once again, mono-thematic; in the C Major Quartet this limitation is exploited as an asset. A Presto in ⁶₈ meter, its main idea is dominated by rhythmic triplets and moves in genial two-bar groups that readily expand into a long antecedent-consequent opening. The consequent, however, moves to the subdominant. Now the two-bar units become single-measure pulses, a dominant pedal arrives, the opening idea is expanded, and the music bounces contentedly onward for more than eighty bars: by comparison to the Sonate for piano trio, Schubert has learned quite a bit about both link-age and expansion of material. The exposition's modulation to the dom-inant perhaps arrives a bit late; in the midst of it, however, there occurs a rhetorical *dubitatio*, or moment of doubt—slow-moving chromatic turns that abandon the cheery triplets—which will return in the quartet's fi-nale.[20] The development begins with a pair of diminished-seventh ges-tures (which also return in the finale); two long sequential passages then culminate in dominants of minor tonalities—D, then A—that are never fully realized in the movement. The dominant of A minor (plus the slith-ering *dubitatio*) serves as foil for the tonic recapitulation, which comes as both surprise and mild relief—and which, happily, is effectively curtailed. Nor is the tension of the A minor preparation lost: that is the key of the second movement, a wistful, flowing siciliano that harks back at least to Mozart.[21] The minuet's opening distinctly recalls the first movement; and while the dominant pedal in its second half may seem unoriginal, it cer-tainly keeps matters moving. The delightful trio steps gently into the world of the ländler, one of many charming examples of this dance by Schubert. In the last movement the young composer successfully takes on a delicate compositional problem occasionally found in Mozart and Haydn: minor-to-major transition across the span of a finale. The move-ment is built on a broad scale, but by now Schubert's sense of timing and harmonic tension holds the listener's attention. As in the first movement, the recapitulation of the finale is curtailed; because its principal ideas are closely related, the shift to the major mode seems natural and logical. And Schubert avoids the danger of becoming saccharine through a masterly touch—the reprise of the *dubitatio* idea from the first movement (also present in the finale's exposition), which raises the question of mode once again before the final confirmation of the major. The closing gesture is a Haydnesque transformation of the movement's opening idea.

The B♭ Quartet, D. 36, although different in character, shows a similar level of mastery. Although the monothematic material of the first movement may seem a bit square and repetitive, it provides opportunities for Schubert to deploy the contrapuntal skills he was developing under Salieri. By way of contrast, in the latter part of the development a seemingly innocuous viola ostinato infests the entire texture and precipitates a rushing unison passage of startling intensity. This fades away in an effective extended transition to the recapitulation, the most interesting approach to reprise encountered thus far. While several moments in the first movement seem to recall Haydn, the theme of the slow movement is nearer to Mozart, as Einstein notes;[22] instead of the typical broad Mozartian binary form, however, the structure here is ternary, and each of the three main components is bipartite. It is the modulating middle section, moving unpredictably from tonic minor (B♭) to Neapolitan (C♭) and then to the dominant of G, that displays distinctly Schubertian touches. The D major minuet opens with short-winded, *galant* phrases that sound quite out of date for 1812. In the second half, however, just as it seems the piece can be nothing but prosaic, Schubert makes harmonic detours that reclaim our attention. The trio in B♭ (once again third-related to the minuet) is based on the simplest thematic material; here, too, harmonic shaping provides the music's charm, even in the bridge back to the minuet. The jaunty finale—"hyper-Haydn," one might almost say with Einstein—is self-assured and witty, with a charming lyrical secondary theme. While the movement is essentially a rondo, its long transitional sections suggest sonata-rondo influence and hint at the problem of excessive length posed by several subsequent Schubert finales.

String Quartet in C, D. 46, and fragmentary works (1813)

Less than two weeks later Schubert began another quartet, this time in C (D. 46), that was finished in only five days (3–7 March 1813). The agitated dramatic power of its first movement surpasses all of his previous chamber works; given the recent upheavals in his life—the death of his mother, the onset of puberty, and his father's impending remarriage—one wonders whether the piece projects tensions of his inner world. It opens with an Adagio introduction based on the chromatically inflected descending tetrachord, a traditional symbol of lament Schubert will incorporate into a number of chamber works (Example 2.1). This element, along with the relentlessly driving triplet motive of the Allegro con moto (whose searing appoggiaturas grow directly from the introduction) dominates the entire movement. The exposition is distinctly in C minor (E naturals notwithstanding) until the unexpected modal transformation of the main idea that substitutes for a second theme (mm. 43ff.). But the chromatics never subside entirely, and in the transition to the dominant the triplets again become ominous; here is an early glimpse of the major-minor expressive ambiguity Schubert will deploy so tellingly in many works. The return of the introductory material, which leads both back to the exposition's repeat and onward into the development, confirms that the conflict of the movement's opening has not been overcome. Once underway, the development establishes a strong harmonic focus on the dominant and its relative (mm. 102ff.). Such obsessive thematic concentration upon a single motive, the descending semitone, is remarkable; this feature, along with the overall unrest of the movement, points to the influence of middle-period, minor-mode Beethoven.[23] Like the exposition, the development dissolves into a return of the initial lament; the reprise begins on the dominant, creating strong expectations of closure in C minor; but by bringing back the major-mode transformation of the theme in the dominant, Schubert is able to prolong the issue of modal definition until the movement's close—which makes this reprise his most compelling to date. The final chord is major, but the tensions remain unresolved.

EXAMPLE 2.1.   Franz Schubert, Quartet in C, D. 46 (1813), mm. 1–6: *lamento* tetrachord with chromatic passing tones.

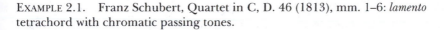

Einstein is surely right in suggesting that this impassioned opening "deserves something better to follow it than the rather sentimental Andante in G after the style of Haydn, and the Minuet in B flat (!) before which the flag of Beethoven's First Symphony flutters all too clearly."[24] But Schubert had already written better examples of both types; perhaps inspiration was lacking here because the composer was in no mood for either singing or dancing. Then comes the finale, which scurries like nothing he had written to this point.[25] The buoyancy persists through the second theme (with its stylized bird calls) into the closing material (mm. 52ff.). But just where the development takes over is nebulous; and by measure 83 it has turned toward C minor—the foreboding key area of the first movement—for a rather rough treatment of the main idea. In the following passages the minor mode grows more prominent as the rhythmic momentum deteriorates into a listless E minor pedal point. Gruff *fortissimo* rebukes in knocking rhythm do not dislodge this despondent reverie, and only as though by chance does the dominant ($^6_5$) of C arrive. As if turning aside from whatever this curious episode might mean, the recapitulation follows without a hitch. An economical movement, as Westrup observes,[26] but also an enigmatic one; it may well reflect Schubert's anguish in view of his father's remarriage.

Between 6 June and 18 August 1813 Schubert completed the outer movements of a quartet in Bb (D. 68), the rest of which is presumably lost. Jagged rhythms and abrupt short phrases in the opening of the first movement again suggest Beethoven—in this case, the Opus 18 quartets rather more than the middle-period "heroic" style.[27] The complex ambivalence of Schubert's relationship to the renowned older master—admiration, yet tinged by the struggle to sing with his own voice—already seems to emerge here:[28] although technically assured, the first twenty-odd bars do not bear the bluntness of their style altogether comfortably. Thereafter an apparently certain move to the dominant is disrupted by a pedal on the dominant of G minor. A brief digression notwithstanding, that harmonic polarity returns, *fortissimo*, with driving triplets throughout the texture: this is the ominous material from the first movement of the previous quartet (D. 46), varied only slightly. It is as well the most unforgettable passage of the present movement, which will recur in both the development and recapitulation, both times pressing toward C minor (just as it had in the earlier work). Its dominant power does not, however, achieve its goal; in both exposition and reprise it yields to a wistfully lyrical second subject. Schubert's voice can be heard here, albeit covered by his Beethovenian commitment to motives from the opening material. But the disruptive force of the triplets is not forgotten: eleven bars before the movement's end they animate a startling three-bar lurch to the Neapolitan, a rupture not dispelled by the forced jubilation of the movement's triple-*forte* close. The finale movement is solid, energetic, and occasionally witty. It contains a striking thematic reminiscence of early Beethoven, plus brusque Beethovenian twists of phrase and harmonic double-backs.[29] Yet it seems simply too long and diffuse. Expanded transitions notwithstanding, this rondo really comprises only two thematic components, which lack sufficient interest and variety for a movement of 466 bars.

On the same day that he finished the Bb Quartet Schubert also completed an Octet for winds in F, D. 72.The piece is scored for the traditional German *Harmoniemusik,* or regimental ensemble, comprising pairs of oboes, clarinets, horns, and bassoons; only the minuet, finale, and part of the opening Allegro (D. 72a) survive. The latter fragment comprises dominant preparation at the end of the development plus the entire recapitulation, which gives a fair idea of the movement's nature: relatively short, light, lyrical, and symmetrical in phrasing.[30] The second half of the minuet contains delightful harmonic touches, and in its second trio the horn writing is warmly Romantic. Rondo and sonata characteristics are combined in the finale, but with none of the complexity found in several of the quartet movements. What is preserved of the work as a whole clearly belongs to the tradition of the informal Austrian divertimento. At the close of the autograph score is a curious inscription, laced with colloquialisms:

> Fine with th' quartet, which was composed by Franzo Schubert, d'rector of the Imperial Chinese Court Chapppul in Nanking, the world-renowned royal residence of His Chinese Majesty. Written in Vienna in a date that I dunno, in some year that on the end has a 3, 'n' a oner at the beginning, 'n' afterwards an eighter 'n' again a oner: meaning 1813.[31]

These lines, although humorous, indicate that young Schubert was not confident of his place in the world, and the same may be said of the E♭ minor wind piece with the rather macabre title "Franz Schubert's Burial Ceremony" dated just one month later (18 September). These weeks must have been a time of turmoil and transition: the quality of Schubert's schoolwork, previously excellent, had fallen off, and he was on notice that if he were to remain at the Konvikt on a special stipend, his marks would have to improve.[32] Instead, he left school by late November and moved to his father's home—a less-than-ideal culmination of his studies.

String Quartet in D, D. 74 (1813)

Meanwhile, four days after the octet was finished (22 August), Schubert was again at work on a D Major string quartet, D. 74. Provided with a special dedication, this one would first be performed on 4 October, his father's name day (i.e., the feast day of the saint for whom he was named). The interval of more than a month was ample time for the younger Franz to write a fine quartet. Yet the result is curiously disappointing, particularly in its first movement—a rambling monothematic piece of more than five hundred measures, lacking any sort of proper development. Opening with a pastoral paraphrase of Haydn, which rolls to a halt after twenty bars, the movement eclectically combines a wide variety of "D major" references and clichés, as Einstein notes.[33] What initially arrests the forward flow is precisely the "knocking" gesture that burst in upon the stagnated development section in the finale of the earlier C Major Quartet, D. 46, composed shortly before Schubert père remarried. In the first movement of this new D Major "Name Day" Quartet, the "knock" motive, banal in itself, recurs compulsively (even for a monothematic movement); its transformation into an ersatz second theme in the dominant (mm. 175ff.) sounds scarcely less than sardonic.[34] Einstein has again cited the source of the slow movement's main theme: the "Prague" Symphony by Mozart, to whom the outer portions of this ternary piece pay homage; the middle section, however, is peculiarly unfocused and unconvincing. Minuet and trio are well shaped, as we would expect. The finale opens with a remarkably close reminiscence of the last movement in Mozart's "Paris" Symphony, as Westrup points out; this is followed by two ideas recalling the finale of the Mozart G Major Quartet, K. 387, and the ensuing secondary theme also sounds distinctly Mozartian in its lyricism. But the remainder of the material seems trite; as in the first movement there is no development section, and the reprise begins in the dominant. In many (though not all) respects the work as a whole is a regression to the level of the previous D Major Quartet, D. 94, written nearly two years earlier. Its dedicatee, however, may have been too challenged by the cello part to notice.[35]

String Quartet in Eb, Op. 125, No. 1, D. 87, and fragmentary works (1813–14)

At the end of October Schubert completed his First Symphony and presumably heard it played by the Konvikt orchestra before he left the school (not later than 23 November).[36] Composing a successful work in this hallowed genre may have coincided with partial resolution of the conflicts Schubert faced in previous months: the schooling issue was being settled, and the decision to return home suggests that he was to some degree prepared to accept his father's remarriage. In any case, the symphony was apparently a turning point in Schubert's maturation, for never again do we encounter in his chamber music the rather disorganized abandon characteristic of the "Name Day" Quartet, D. 74, and several earlier pieces. On the contrary, his next quartet, in Eb, D. 87, dating from November 1813, is his warmest, most inviting, and most polished chamber work to date. Published posthumously (1840) as Op. 125, No. 1, it was for many years the only one of the early quartets to be played with any frequency. Nor is that surprising: each movement is neatly organized and flows effortlessly; a suave, almost Mozartian lyricism pervades the whole, even in the *buffo* finale, whose second theme is invariably hummed by players and listeners alike following a hearing of this quartet. If it lacks the bold strokes found in some earlier works, the Eb Quartet nevertheless shows Schubert solidly in control throughout the cycle of four movements. During the same month he wrote a charming group of minuets and "Deutsche" ("German" dances that are early waltzes) for string quartet (D. 89); these may have been for the family quartet (or friends at the Konvikt) rather than for actual dancing, since the standard dance ensemble of the day comprised two violins plus bass ad libitum, without viola.[37]

Immediately after leaving school Schubert became engrossed in the year-long project of writing his first opera. The so-called Guitar Quartet, D. 96, comes from February 1814, but only the minuet is original Schubert: the rest is his arrangement of a Notturno by Wenzel Matiegka (1773–1830) for flute, viola, and guitar, to which Schubert added a cello part, presumably for his father. Two days before the anniversary of his father's remarriage, Schubert was at work on another quartet in C minor—a key whose dark dramatic associations are already apparent in his earlier chamber music (D. 8, and especially D. 46). Regrettably, only a portion of the first movement now survives, but it is striking music (made accessible in a performing version by Alfred Orel).[38] The hushed introduction, rich in harmonically ambiguous neighbor and passing notes, presents kernels that are subtly transformed to yield all the main components of the ensuing *allegro,* as outlined in Example 2.2. Thus, despite its breadth, the exposition is motivically quite concentrated. The long and rather brooding first theme culminates in a quivering crescendo over a dominant pedal, as though a stormy outburst were imminent. It does not occur here (instead, the theme is repeated), but neither is the expectation fully abandoned: Schubert saves this moment of dramatic intensity for the reprise. The unexpected second theme of the exposition is a genuinely Schubertian moment of lyrical repose. In the closing material we encounter yet again the "knocking" rhythm prominent in two quartets of the previous year; this expands extensively through development-like

EXAMPLE 2.2.   Schubert, Quartet Movement in C Minor, D. 103 (1814): motivic connections.

sequencing and virtuosic passagework (which is clearly indebted to the first-movement coda of Beethoven's "Harp" Quartet, Op. 74). At this juncture a long development could well seem redundant, and Schubert effectively limits it to merely twenty-two measures. Equally effective is the subdominant recapitulation, because the reconfirmation of C minor is planned to take place after the raging episode foreshadowed in the exposition. This climax subsides just as the manuscript breaks off; although Orel's conjectural continuation of the reprise is thoroughly reasonable, it seems likely that Schubert's original conclusion was more powerful. We can only wonder what sort of movements may have followed this impressive opening.

First Maturity (1814–16)

String Quartet in B♭, D. 112 (1814)

Schubert's next quartet, in B♭, D. 112 (posthumously published as Op. 168), was dashed off between 5 and 13 September 1814, in the midst of a remarkable creative period: the first version of his opera *Des Teufels Lustschloß* was finished, and revisions (upon advice of Salieri) were well underway; he had composed his first Mass (D. 105) between May and July; and the following month (October 19) he would write "Gretchen am Spinnrade," the first of his songs universally acknowledged a masterpiece. But the B♭ Quartet is itself a small masterpiece, worthy of many more performances than it receives. The smooth, singing opening is, once again, indebted to Mozart (especially K. 589); but unlike Schubert's earlier D major efforts in this vein (D. 94 and 74), the first movement of the B♭ has firm shape and strong contrasts: a brusque turn from the tonic, although briefly attenuated, precipitates a nervous episode in G minor; when the first violin sings with quiet urgency over the restless triplet accompaniment, the music seems to foreshadow the first movement of "Death and the Maiden," written ten years later. More suddenly than it arrived, this material is transformed into B♭ major, yet the restlessness of the relative minor returns at the end of the section. Then follows a brief but definitive modulation to the dominant, where a "second" theme is derived from earlier lyrical material. Thus we have here an antecedent of Schubert's later "three-key-area" expositions. But the surprises are not over: instead of stock closing gestures, Schubert introduces distinctive jagged rhythms that lead to new twists on the triplet motive from the G minor material; only then do we hear a fairly standard, yet very emphatic, cadential wrap-up in F. If the repeat is taken, the contrast is effective; when the development begins, *pianissimo* in whole notes sinking scalewise down to D♭, the contrast is slightly breathtaking. Now follow two beautifully harmonized episodes based on the second theme: this sort of "development," based on plateaux and repetition, is found in several of Schubert's later chamber works (e.g., the E♭ Piano Trio and the String Quintet). While many critics, including

Gustav Mahler, have found such procedures distinctly uninteresting, Schubert enthusiasts appear to enjoy the charm of the harmonic recolorings.[39] What seems clear is that Schubert largely eschews Beethovenian-style development, even though by now he is thoroughly familiar with it; less than two years after this quartet was written he would complain in his diary of the older master's "eccentricity which unites in indistinguishable confusion, the heroic with the hideous, the hallowed with the Harlequin; which induces transports of frenzy among men instead of transports of delight."[40] These are not his final thoughts on Beethoven (and indeed, one must note that Schubert himself would later write movements more frenzied than delightful); nevertheless, they offer partial insight into the younger man's way of coming to grips with "the tramp of the giant behind," which Brahms, Mahler, and many others also heard across the years of nineteenth century.

"Finished in $4^1/_2$ hours" is the inscription at the close of the first movement. While this music certainly has a fresh, unstudied quality, the claim of such prodigious speed is something of an exaggeration: Schubert had already sketched the movement for string trio. And the ensuing G minor Andante sostenuto opens with a fairly transparent borrowing from the greatest of string trios, Mozart's Divertimento in E♭, K. 563 (second movement: compare especially the minor-mode passage just after the double bar). But it can scarcely be objected that Schubert did not invest the loan well; the movement combines excellent pacing with well-integrated contrasts that constitute worthy homage to the composer who inspired them. Built on a broad binary plan with a reprise in the minor dominant (D minor), the piece comprises three thematic groups. Its somber G minor opening is heard twice, linked by delicate phrase overlap. The second idea interrupts with a leap to E♭ and a sequential ascent; this tension is quickly dispersed, and the theme is lyrically stabilized in B♭. Now in Mozartian manner Schubert spins out flowing ornamental sixteenths, shared among all four parts—a wonderful means of enriching and expanding material scarcely to be found in his earlier slow movements.[41] Particularly pleasing is the way it yields a modulation to F (dominant of the relative) for the third idea: Reed believes this is the moment where Schubert first finds his own distinct lyrical voice.[42] It is in any case a delightfully joyous section, rich in rhythmic independence of the parts. In the reprise the key relations of the three groups are altered—D minor, F major, and E♭ moving to B♭, in which the third idea happily draws to a close. As in the Mozart Divertimento, the main theme returns one last time to close the slow movement, and as in that piece, a striking patch of harmonic color is heard just before the closing cadence. But Schubert's first theme was minor, to which it must return; the *fortissimo* outburst on the Neapolitan is a chilly confirmation of that inevitability.

The minuet, though unexceptional, is very fine, and the serenity of the trio, accompanied pizzicato, is disturbed only in its second half by one recollection of Neapolitan harmony. (Not until the A Minor Quartet of

1824 would Schubert make the minuet genre distinctively his own.) But the madcap finale is altogether original and stunning in the ground it covers during less than four minutes. The dancing rush of eighths, first introduced over sedate dotted halves, soon sweeps all before it; unisons, hemiolas, plus short-lived canons in the brief and witty development all add to the ebullience. That the piece is a miniature sonata form scarcely seems to matter; its elfin lightness in perpetual motion anticipates young Mendelssohn's *Midsummer Night's Dream* Overture and the scherzo of his Octet, Op. 20. As Walter Gray has pointed out, Schubert achieves a new level of maturity in this work. All of the problems he had attacked since his first essay in the genre are successfully solved in the B♭ Quartet—sonata structure, experiments in key relations, variety in recapitulation, and the issue of writing a successful finale.[43]

String Quartets in G Minor, D. 173, and E Major, D. 353 (1815–16)

Only two string quartets date from 1815–16, for Schubert's interest had turned elsewhere. During these years he wrote more than 245 songs (whereas only about 25 survive from before 1814, the year of "Gretchen"); in addition, he completed four symphonies (Nos. 2–5), three Masses (Nos. 2–4), and a variety of smaller-scale works, all the while employed in the vexing position of schoolmaster. Maurice Brown has observed that whereas the songs of this period richly reveal Schubert's musical personality, the instrumental works do so only fitfully.[44] The Quartets in G Minor (D. 173, 1815) and E Major (D. 353, 1816) seem to be cases in point. In neither is Schubert's steadily developing craftsmanship in doubt; on the contrary, many passages show that his counterpoint studies with Salieri (which ended in 1816) have borne good fruit. A number of bold gestures and, especially in the E Major, increasingly complex and differentiated textures suggest cautious absorption of ideas from the "middle" Beethoven quartets (Opp. 59 and 74).[45] Overall, however, these two works do not surpass the B♭ Quartet of 1814. As Einstein notes, the G Minor opens with an obvious transformation of Beethoven's finale to Op. 18, No. 2 (see Example 2.3); this seems strangely bitter, even when the theme is transformed to the major mode at the recapitulation. Nor does the square regularity of the material generate anything like the dramatic sweep of the C minor movement (D. 103) written just over a year earlier. The slow movement of D. 173 has a Mozartian flavor, but it is not Schubert's most impressive writing of this sort; and while the minuet echoes Mozart's great G Minor Symphony, Schubert would pay better homage to that work in the minuet of his Fifth Symphony the following year. The finale is Haydnesque, with strong touches of Hungarian style—an idiom of paramount significance for several of the chamber works Schubert would write between 1824 and 1828.[46] Here, however, the material seems to lack sufficient interest for a movement of such length. The E Major Quartet is noted for the brilliance of its first movement—Italianate brilliance in Einstein's view; but as suggested above, Beethoven may also be an influence, especially in the uncharacteristically concentrated development. The Andante contains some strikingly beautiful modulations, and the ornamental writing is more venturesome than in any of Schubert's earlier chamber works; still, the piece has less charm and immediacy than some earlier slow movements. Mozart is once again the inspiration for the primary theme of the finale (E♭ Symphony, K. 543; F Major Quartet, K. 590); in Westrup's view, "only sour critics would say that it overstays its welcome," yet it can scarcely be denied that the unusual rondo scheme, based on only two thematic components, lacks a certain degree of contrast.[47]

EXAMPLE 2.3.(a).   Beethoven, Quartet in G Major, Op. 18, No. 2, finale (opening).

EXAMPLE 2.3.(b).   Schubert, Quartet in G Minor, D. 173 (1815), mvt. 1 (opening).

Violin Sonatas and String Trios (1816–17)

Apparently Schubert did not return to the string quartet until the end of 1820. During the four-year interval, however, he composed a number of smaller-scale instrumental works plus his first enduringly popular chamber piece, the "Trout" Quintet. From January and February 1816 some thirty-two ländler are preserved—four for two violins (D. 354), the remainder ostensibly for only one violin unaccompanied (D. 355, 370, 374). They may have been performed in several ways, however: many such pieces were published in Vienna at the time, with or without a bass part, which could also be improvised (with harmony) at the keyboard if one were available. Schubert himself arranged several of his violin ländler for piano, which gives us some idea of how he may have improvised accompaniments.[48] And perhaps for small gatherings they were played by violin(s) alone.[49] These ländler are, in any case, *Gebrauchsmusik*—pleasant, but practical, and perhaps still useful for wedding gigs.

The "Sonatinas." During March and April Schubert wrote his first three sonatas for violin and piano, D. 384, 385, and 408. Although the

surviving autographs are clearly headed "Sonate pour pianoforte et violon," the Viennese publisher Diabelli issued them after Schubert's death
as "Sonatinas" (Op. 137, 1836), and as such, inappropriately, they have
long been known. Yet both titles, composer's and publisher's, provide
hints about the place of these works in the history of the genre. By label-
ing the pieces "for pianoforte and violin," Schubert, like Mozart, invokes
the tradition of the accompanied keyboard sonata, in which the violin (or
flute, etc.) plays a subsidiary role. And to be sure, these are the most
Mozartian of Schubert's chamber works. No more than in Mozart's mature sonatas (from about K. 296 on) is the violin dispensable. But neither
instrument is deployed with the brilliance and independence characteristic of Beethoven, nine of whose violin-and-piano sonatas had long been
in print; it is as though (once again) Schubert chooses not to take up this
challenge yet.[50] By the time the three Schubert works were published in
the 1830s, public interest in sonatas of all varieties had diminished considerably; Diabelli probably renamed them "sonatinas" to increase sales
among dilettantes who preferred more approachable sorts of pieces.[51] But
the diminutive title and gracefully simple style of the music itself would
prove problematic to some connoisseurs even into our own century, for
as Schumann observed (in a review of other music), "the sonata style of
1790 is not that of 1840. The demands of form and content have increased
in all respects."[52] Beethoven had become the touchstone.

Taken on their own terms, however, these sonatas are fulfilling fare;
in the first two there is no trace of a certain ungainliness apparent in Schubert's two most recent quartets, and he seems entirely at home in the
Mozartian model. That influence is clearest in the first movement of the
D Major Sonata (D. 384), which seems related to Mozart's E Minor, K. 304,
in several respects: the first theme, *piano,* is based on the repetition of triadic and scalar components; its return (also *piano*) takes place over legato
accompaniment (m. 13; the outburst of *forte* eighths in octaves that separates statements of the theme in the Mozart movement crops up later in
Schubert, mm. 29ff.); and the first theme is treated quasi-canonically (mm.
17ff. and 37ff.). In the development, the gradual buildup of minor-mode
tension and its rapid dispersion during the dominant preparation for the
reprise (mm. 82–101) is a favorite technique of Mozart's.[53] Also notable
here (and in the first movement of the Second Sonata) is a fine sense of
pacing and balance that surely owes much to Mozart's example. But there
are a number of characteristic Schubertian touches in D. 384—specific
harmonic details, for example, of the passage just mentioned,[54] as well as
the exposition's modulation (a surprise deceptive cadence followed by an
augmented sixth yielding V of V [m. 32ff.]). In the ternary second movement the main theme, its embellished return,[55] and the contrasting middle episode in the minor are Mozartian in all but details, as are the
materials of the giguelike finale. Overall, the tone of this work is both elegant and optimistic.

Rather more personal and poignant is the companion Sonata in A Minor, D. 385, which followed almost immediately. Both the rhythm and contour of its quiet opening for piano alone recall a Beethoven theme, and the impetuous leaps for the violin that grow out of it also suggest his influence (mm. 10–18).[56] The smooth transition and flowing second theme in the relative major, however, return to Mozartian lyricism. This leads to a third key area, F major, for cheery closing material delicately laced with reference to chromatic gestures of the opening theme and transition. Transformed to minor for the reprise, this music will of course sound darkly agitated and slightly ironic: while the three-key structure is not to be found in Mozart, such thematic tactics certainly are, in pieces Schubert knew and loved.[57] The development is striking in two respects: (1) It concentrates on a single, simple idea from the exposition's transition (mm. 19–22), rather than the main material; this is a technique Schubert (and later, Brahms) will adopt to good effect in a number of works. And (2) because that simple idea is rich in chromatic passing and neighbor notes, Schubert evolves from it a sense of floating harmonic ambiguity unparalleled in any of his earlier chamber music. Following this, the five-bar dominant preparation of D minor (mm. 72ff.) suggests the onset of a fairly long episode—which turns out to be the reprise, commencing in the subdominant. Development and recapitulation are thereby fused rather than distinguished, and it makes excellent sense to take the indicated repeat of the movement's second half. The second movement is another of Schubert's two-part rondo schemes (ABA′B′A), in which the stately primary material seems to anticipate Mendelssohn; the B sections slowly spin out unusual harmonic progressions involving sequences combined with modal mixture and chromatic alteration, while a seemingly endless pattern of sixteenths flows in one or the other of the instrumental lines. Following Beethoven's example, Schubert expands the sonata to four movements with a minuet—a short yet rather serious interlude before the substantial rondo finale. This is the finest rondo we have yet encountered, as well as an excellent complement to the minor-mode opening movement. Its wistful, unsettled primary material constitutes a self-contained, rounded binary unit in the tonic (A minor), and the inevitability of its return is deployed with dramatic delicacy. The contrasting B episode actually comprises two components—a calmly lyrical double-period melody in F major that leads directly into energetic sequential material beginning in D minor and driven by restless triplets. This Schubert manipulates to raise numerous possibilities (ultimately never fulfilled)—but then, well before expected, the rondo is again at hand. The return of the long episode traverses a different tonal path, but the outcome is the same, and a brief coda brings a resigned close to this superb, subtly balanced movement.

The G Minor Sonata, composed shortly after the first two (D. 408, April 1816), is perhaps the most popular of the set, owing to its starker contrasts and slightly greater demands upon the players. Yet it also seems the most ambivalent as regards the essence of its overall musical statement. We have seen how seriously Schubert takes the tradition of minor-mode severity in earlier works; but here, although the opening portends potent drama, the minor mode ultimately seems something of a distraction. The bold opening gesture of the first movement also concludes it, but in between nothing has been resolved or prolonged: the three-key structure of the exposition (G minor–B♭–E♭) thoroughly loosens the hold of G minor and ushers in pleasantly dancing tunes of little consequence; in the development several opportunities for intensification are brushed aside through slightly bizarre deceptive cadences. Only in the last dozen bars does the piece half-heartedly reclaim its initial tonal and affective identity. The ternary slow movement contains some breathtaking Schubertian modulations in its middle section, but this block of music remains completely detached from the piece's charming yet conservative cornerstones. A minuet bustling with good cheer adds little to the broader picture. And the finale, one of Schubert's shortest, departs from G minor within the first eight bars. The movement concludes in the major, but with none of the tension and subtle preparation that make the best minor-to-major finales of Mozart and Haydn so exciting. Overall, this G Minor Sonata walks away from what Mozart had achieved in this key, yet without opening a more fruitful path.

String Trio in B♭, D. 471 (incomplete). As noted above, Schubert's first effort to write a string trio resulted in the fine B♭ Quartet, D. 112, of September 1814. Two years later he made another attempt, also in the key of B♭ (D. 471), but broke off having written only the first movement and thirty-nine bars of an Andante sostenuto. Why Schubert did not continue remains unclear, for the single completed movement is a gem—the finest to date of his well-balanced, singing sonata-allegros that bear the mantle of Mozart. Thematically, its closest relation is Schubert's earliest fully successful composition of this sort, the first movement of the E♭ Quartet, D. 87 (1813); but as several intervening works (including the first two piano-and-violin sonatas) reveal, his sense of pace and balance has developed considerably.

These qualities, in conjunction with unusually gentle yet playful thematic material, yield a movement of many delights as well as unbroken continuity. The concise development is particularly noteworthy: Motivically it concentrates on four short components of the first, second, and closing themes. Harmonically its focal point (until approaching the reprise) is G minor, first obliquely articulated in the two measures immediately after the double bar. There follows a long sequential ascent involving a good deal of parallel motion plus chromatic inflection (linear intervalic patterns 5–6 and 6–5): this crests in G minor (m. 95), only to descend through more transparent $^6_3$ parallelism to the dominant of G. The prototype for this arch is almost certainly in the development of Mozart's G Minor Symphony, K. 550 (mm. 139–46 [ascent] and 160–65 [descent]), but Schubert has adapted it splendidly to the context at hand: without a single brusque gesture he has gradually brought this intrinsically calm piece to the verge of lament and despair. The singing passage that follows makes another allusion to Mozart in G minor: Pamina's aria "Ach, ich fühl's," sung at the moment "worse than death" when she believes Tamino has abandoned her. As there, this music is moving toward B♭, but full tonicization is yet come; in a delicate transition also inspired by Mozart, Schubert disperses the tension and resolves the entire development into the reprise.[58]

Adagio and Rondo Concertante in F, D. 487. In October 1816, at the urging of his friend Schober, Schubert took his first steps toward greater independence from his father by moving out of the family home. That same month he produced one of his least appealing (and understandably neglected) chamber works: the Adagio and Rondo Concertante in F, D. 487. Scored as a piano quartet, it is really a concerto-like piece for solo piano accompanied by strings, which share significant thematic material only in the Adagio—a rambling, bipartite slow introduction notably lacking in memorable ideas. The ensuing Allegro vivace is an overblown binary structure that presents more than half a dozen long themes, yet entirely lacks the development section one would expect of a sonata form; Schubert's dubbing it "rondo" may have been a private joke. A few passages are so utterly imitative of Mozart as to seem soulless; much of the rest decorates long, empty sequences with the sort of clattering virtuoso piano glitter almost never found in Schubert. The piece was apparently composed for Heinrich Grob, an amateur cellist and the younger brother of the soprano Therese Grob, with whom Schubert was said to be in love at the time. The father of the Grob children having died, Heinrich was (at least nominally) head of the household; whether penniless young Schubert wrote this flashy, rather vulgar piece to impress Therese's protector with his prospects for popular success, or to test Heinrich's sensibilities, or possibly in secret spite of him, remains uncertain. In any case, on only one other occasion did he write chamber music of this sort.

Violin Sonata in A major, D. 574. During the first eight months of 1817 Schubert composed more than three dozen songs and a substantial group of piano sonatas (perhaps as many as half a dozen). In August and September he returned to the two genres of chamber music that had occupied him the previous year—piano-and-violin sonata and string trio—to write what turned out to be his last efforts in both categories. The A Major Sonata, D. 574 (the title "Duo" common today comes again from Diabelli, not Schubert) shows what difference a year can make in the growth of a composer: Gone is the shadow of Mozart, replaced by self-assured Schubert on a broad scale—music that could not be mistaken for that of anyone else. The two instruments are equal partners throughout the work, and while the writing is not virtuosic, it demands professional competence from both players. The opening melodic bass in the piano (which shortly becomes beautiful counterpoint to the entry of the violin) announces the singing nature of the first movement, in which essentially lyrical material is paced in such a manner that interest never lags. A gradual increase in rhythmic diminution spans the entire exposition; the harmonic pulse, which moves in leisurely two-bar groupings at the outset, quickens to single bars during the transition (mm. 29ff.) and increases further during the cadential close of each ensuing thematic period. This activity is projected upon a novel tonal structure: the opening material moves toward the dominant, apparently rather early, only to be displaced by the transition just mentioned, which commences rather surprisingly in the minor dominant (E minor). It leads to a new double-period idea, beginning in G major (mm. 40ff.); as the second statement approaches, an unexpected yet marvelously characteristic modulation to B occurs, which ultimately yields to the dominant for the third thematic idea—a striking twist on the "three-key" scheme found in earlier works. The third theme, a sparkling upward arpeggiation that ends with a leap of a fourth up (or fifth down), is both playful and cheeky; ten bars of smoother closing material then bring the exposition to a calm close. The brief development bears only tangential thematic relation to what precedes it; rather, this section is chiefly a harmonic venture, over a bass line that sinks gradually lower; B minor becomes a focal point (mm. 86–91), then D major (mm. 93–94—major for the moment, but not convincingly so). As the bass reaches its lowest pitch (m. 96), the goal of motion seems uncertain; three bars later a dominant pedal begins to dissolve the tension, and the reprise arrives in another three measures.

Schubert follows this opening with three movements whose character and ordering underscore the cheeriness of the sonata as a whole: two rollicking triple-time pieces flank a flowing, lyrical Andantino (also in three). The second movement, an E major scherzo, arrives *pianissimo* on an insecure $^6_4$ arpeggiation; no sooner is the tonic fully articulated than a dancing sequence toward the dominant has begun. The second half is launched by a favorite Schubertian harmonic move—a major third lower (here to G major) to a tonal center linked by one common tone (b♮). Gradually the energy level subsides, and a G pedal yields to a mock-serious one on C♯, where the main idea of the sonata's finale is surreptitiously introduced; order is restored by very loud chords-plus-arpeggiation on the dominant of E (mm. 53–55), and a rounding of the scherzo follows. The serene C major trio is notable for melodic chromaticism that sounds not at all menacing.[59] In place of a weighty slow movement Schubert writes a light ternary intermezzo in which the first section also comprises three parts. The principal theme establishes a calm, regular one-measure pulse maintained throughout the movement; such *galant* phrases seem to hark nostalgically back to another era. The middle portion of the A section (mm. 9–25) provides exquisitely delicate contrast: in only eighteen measures it traverses the extraordinary course of harmonic centers (each linked by common tone[s]) outlined in Example 2.4; *piano* or *pianissimo* in all but the opening and closing bars, this music drifts effortlessly as though taking place in a dream, unlike anything heard in the earlier chamber works. Such a passage scarcely bears repeating, and in the final section of the movement Schubert makes only veiled reference to it.

EXAMPLE 2.4.   Schubert, Violin Sonata in A, D. 574, mvt. 2, mm. 8–26: harmonic outline.

The finale is a whimsical, scherzolike sonata movement on a tonal plan of three third-related keys (A–C–E); its second group has the character of a trio section, and this music plus that of the E major section remind us that Schubert could and did improvise Deutsche and waltzes endlessly at the piano. The simple development opens with two harmonic plateaus that function as dominant pedals (on C and F), enlivened by motivic gestures from the movement's opening. Subsequently (mm. 142ff.) the same melodic idea is subjected to imitation and inversion in a hushed sequential episode of uncertain tonal destination; but before any serious tension can develop, the dominant of A is at hand, shortly followed by a reprise yet more jovial than the movement's opening. Its conclusion is witty in a Haydnesque manner: the dance is simply called to a halt by all too many of the loud chords with which it began.

String Trio in B♭, D. 581. The B♭ String Trio, in contrast, recalls Brown's observation that Schubert's instrumental works of this period reveal his musical personality only fitfully. There is no questioning either the craftsmanship or the serious intent of this piece, which clearly acknowledges the trio writing of Haydn, Mozart, and the youthful Beethoven, particularly in its treatment of three equal obbligato parts. In that respect alone, it surpasses the earlier first movement of the incomplete work in the same key; yet it lacks that piece's spontaneous lyricism and personal stamp. Westrup's assessment of this trio, while too severe, contains a kernel of truth: "too much like an essay in eighteenth-century style."[60] Nonetheless, it is very good eighteenth-century style, commingled with enough Schubertian touches to warrant more frequent hearings.

Transition: The "Trout" Quintet and the *Quartettsatz* (1819–20)

The "Trout" Quintet, D. 667

By 1818 Schubert was evidently discouraged and depressed by his irksome employment as a teacher in his father's school: fragments of a symphony and two piano sonatas were left incomplete that year, and his production of songs dropped off as well; he wrote no chamber music. In July he left the school and accepted a post as music master to the children of Count Johann Esterházy in Zseliz, some three hundred miles east of Vienna. "I live at last," he wrote to his friend Schober, "and it was high time, otherwise I should have become nothing but a thwarted musician." Yet soon he was lonely for his friends: "Not a soul here has any feeling for true art, or at most the countess now and again."[61] He returned to Vienna that November, but not until the following July did Schubert compose any chamber music. He was then on holiday with his friend the singer Vogl, staying at the home of the wealthy musical amateur Sylvester Paumgartner in Steyr (Upper Austria). "The country round Steyr is inconceivably lovely," Schubert wrote his brother,[62] and the vacation became a joyous interlude of music making and sociability far removed from the frustrations and upheavals of the previous year. Schubert's song "Die Forelle" (The trout) delighted Paumgartner, and at his request Schubert included variations on the lied in a work for the same instrumentation—violin, viola, cello, double bass, and piano—as Hummel's Quintet in E♭, Op. 87.[63] The result was the "Trout" Quintet in A, D. 667, a perennial favorite among chamber music enthusiasts, and (save for the violin sonatas) the earliest of Schubert's chamber works regularly heard today. Like the violin sonata in the same key, the "Trout" is a work of irrepressible good humor. The disposition of its five movements yields effective contrasts, but no overall dramatic progression, for there is no genuine conflict; every cloud is soon dispersed by sunshine. That Schubert manages this without evoking even a trace of boredom is among the work's most remarkable aspects. Much of its bright atmosphere is owing to the treatment of the keyboard part: two other bass instruments in the ensemble free the piano to sparkle in upper-range octave sonorities, first heard in the glittering A major arpeggio with which the "Trout" begins.

In one carefree sweep that simple, unforgettable gesture establishes both mood and prevailing pulse of the first movement: motion in two-bar units is among its principal unifying factors. Another is the motivic concentration of its thematic material, as shown in Example 2.5: neighbor notes (especially lower neighbors, marked "n"), leaps of a fourth (marked "a"), arpeggiation filled in with passing notes, and phrases beginning on the fifth scale degree are prominent features of all the main ideas, which move in a relatively compact melodic range. And a third is the broad, relatively static harmonic-thematic plateaux through which the movement proceeds. It begins with a quiet twenty-four bar exordium (punctuated by the initial flourish), which is closely related to the cheerful main theme but does not yet fully reveal it. The slowly shifting harmonic progression of this passage, shown in Example 2.6, is thoroughly Schubertian, and the drop to the lowered sixth degree almost becomes a leitmotif. At the cadence the sweeping arpeggio returns, articulating most of the harmonic goals in the double-period presentation of the singing primary theme.

The violin dominates the first period, which is closed—a simple I–V–I–IV–I scheme. In the second the piano prevails, and the bubbling

EXAMPLE 2.5.   Schubert, "Trout" Quintet in A, D. 667, mvt. 1: motivic connections.

EXAMPLE 2.6.   Schubert, "Trout" Quintet in A, D. 667, mvt. 1, mm. 1–25: harmonic outline.

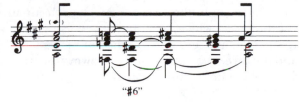

triplets become pervasive, animating the texture all the way to the closing material. Just as the subdominant arrives (m. 50), the music expands into a harmonic digression (still in two-bar units) that shortly ushers in the dominant and the closely related second idea, shared by violin and cello (mm. 64ff.). Both this group and the third unfold in placid, tonic-to-tonic double periods that suggest playful contentment rather than urgency or conflict. As the third theme reaches its second full close (m. 100), the music drifts rather aimlessly through six bars of dominant pedal—but this is a foil: the ensuing *pianissimo* drop of a third to C is exquisite (m. 106), and, as in the introduction, dynamic crescendo and augmented sixth chord reinstate and reinvigorate the structural harmonic center (here the dominant, E). The closing material, replete with snapped arpeggiations (later transformed in the Andante) and exchanges of rippling sixteenths, is the most high-spirited music of the movement, dampened only briefly by yet another third deflection, which quietly recalls the main theme (mm. 136–40). This is pushed aside (for the moment) by an exuberant reconfirmation of the dominant.

The arrival of the development—two bars (again) of gently pulsing vamp, *pianissimo*—is the moment of greatest contrast in the movement, yet the harmonic shift it embodies—to the lowered sixth degree (C)—is long since familiar. Now the main theme returns in three hushed paraphrase statements, for violin, piano, and double bass, cadencing in C, E♭, and B♭ respectively. As the outline of root motion in the development's harmonic scheme (Example 2.7) shows, this inaugurates an arch that continues down to E♭; meanwhile the exposition's triplets surreptitiously animate the texture (in a contour later adopted by the second movement), and the descending sequences grow quieter. Then suddenly, *forte,* main theme and triplet motive, both in octaves, are combined against agitated sixteenth arpeggiations in the piano. Rising sequentially to F minor, this sounds serious; an unexpected third-shift (to A♭) and drop in dynamic level stem the swell, but as Example 2.7 shows, the harmonic motion continues to rise, its tension pressing toward D, the subdominant—whereupon the reprise is at hand. Some critics complain that nontonic recapitulation in the "Trout"—also found in its second and fourth movements—is a cheap labor-saving procedure (in the first movement, for example, the motion from D to A parallels that from A to E in the exposition, requiring no adjustment). Tovey writes scornfully that such "fold-up forms" have nothing in common with the "essentially dramatic" musical symmetry of genuine sonata form.[64] But we have seen Schubert fully capable of writing a tonic recapitulation; that he does not do so in the "Trout" seems perfectly in keeping with the nature of the piece, which, as noted above, is not dramatic, but lyric, even pastoral. Dramatic resolution to the tonic is replaced by more gradual return, and the three thematic groups following the transition from D to A provide ample tonic reaffirmation.

EXAMPLE 2.7.   Schubert, "Trout" Quintet in A, D. 667, mvt. 1, development: outline of tonal motion.

That accomplished, the second movement commences in F: this characteristic third-gesture provides a striking connection, as though we had merely stepped farther and at more leisurely pace into one of the first movement's harmonic diversions. The formal archetype for this Andante is the broad binary slow movement (sonatalike but without development) familiar since Haydn and Mozart; most unusual, however, is the way Schubert treats it. There are three thematic groups plus closing material, cast in four key areas—in the first half, F, F♯ minor, D, and G. The opening section, songlike in melody and design, is a lyrical dialogue between violin and piano, with the viola providing a smoothly undulating accompaniment that is virtually a countermelody. "Andante" is apt: the regular pace established here, reflective but ongoing, bar to bar, prevails throughout the piece. The middle statement of the first idea moves quite simply up to the subdominant (mm. 9ff.), with added triplet ornamentation for the keyboard that becomes increasingly prominent. Imitation between principal parts yields a gently asymmetrical five-bar phrase, a shaping also adopted in the third phrase, which further avoids squareness by incorporating both tonic and subdominant impulses from the previous two statements.

A slightly menacing transition, also five bars, leads through two irregular seventh-chord resolutions to the second group, in F♯ minor, an uneasy semitone above the tonic. Here viola and cello sing exquisitely in the parallel motion of closed-position harmony in the middle register—the genial, sociable *Männerchor* style prominent in later works as well. This tinge of melancholy is dispelled after only eight measures by a move toward D major, which overlaps into the third section of the movement. Now the dotted triadic leaps and contour of the triplets recall, respectively, the closing material and development of the first movement (mm. 114, 167ff.)—but *piano* and more calmly, as though in distant memory. This material begins to move sequentially; the goal is G major, but its arrival is cast in doubt by two shadowy half-diminished sevenths (mm. 45 and 47), and then drawn out through four bars of diminuendo over pedal point. The ensuing close, the quietest moment in the work, just barely maintains the *andante* pace through surface ripple of the dotted figures still reverberating from the third section; these, too, fade away, and the piece comes fully to rest in G, sustained by fermata. And then, a semitone higher, it simply starts over again. Begun in A♭, the same modulatory scheme just followed will lead back to the tonic of F. At this juncture some listeners may feel there is justice in Tovey's charge of "fold-up forms"; others (doubtless the majority) find this naïve, pastoral music too delightful to censure.

The onset of the scherzo creates a bold, ebullient contrast. We first encountered such a scherzo in the A Major Sonata for Violin and Piano, and in certain respects that of the "Trout" is its companion piece. But now, predictably, the structure is fuller, more unified, and even more energetic. The first half is a variant on the traditional double-period format, wherein the antecedent is clearly bound for the dominant (see Example 2.8), but the consequent deflects from that course to C—yet another move to the lowered submediant. Three motivic components unite the movement: the rising fifths and fourths of the opening ("a" and "a'''"); the three repeated quarters, often implicitly followed by a fourth ("b"); and (an expansion of "b") the sweeping downward scale with parallel motion between outer voices ("c"). The latter gesture, expanded, yields the confirmation of C major in the first half of the scherzo (mm. 31ff.) and is prominent in its second half as well. The ubiquitous repeated quarters eventually become a coarse Haydnesque joke for cello and bass just before the rounding off of the scherzo (m. 79), and both quarters and scale find their way into the lilting trio section. Always adept in writing dance movements, Schubert seems supremely confident in this scherzo—a "Beethovenian" movement type that he has now conquered on his own terms. As we shall see, his later chamber music contains additional extraordinary examples of the genre.

EXAMPLE 2.8.   Schubert, "Trout" Quintet in A, D. 667, scherzo, mm. 1–12.

Of the five Schubert chamber works that include a variation movement based on one of his own songs, the "Trout" is the earliest and, save perhaps for "Death and the Maiden," also the finest. The plan of the variations is somewhat unusual, but effective in context: the original form of the song, with the piano's characteristic "empty-downbeat" arpeggiated sextuplets, is saved for the finale; the "Thema" that begins the movement is a more subdued setting for strings alone. Heard thus, four-square over simplest harmonies, the little tune scarcely hints at what Schubert will draw from it. Overall, the first three variations follow the traditional course of successively quicker figuration. But Schubert begins this rhythmic diminution in the accompaniment, enlivening the upper three string parts with sextuplet arpeggiations (adapted from the original piano part of the song) as the piano sounds the theme in upper-range octaves that shimmer with trills and mordents. In the second variation the violin carries on the sextuplets, which now comprise a potpourri of tricky scales, turns, arpeggiations, and slithering chromatics; the violist, meanwhile, calmly enjoys the tune. For the third variation the piano raises the ante to thirty-seconds, again in sparkling high-register octaves (a particularly striking color on the Viennese-style piano of Schubert's day). This provides witty contrast to the theme, now lumbering in bass-and-cello octaves, while the offbeat accompaniment adds to the tongue-in-cheek effect. Tempting it is, indeed, to read these first three variations as a musical compendium of babbling, darting, gliding, and glittering motions inspired by fish and brook.

Variation 4 erupts *fortissimo* and *minore*, raging with *Sturm und Drang*—which lasts for all of four bars, to be shunted aside by the relative major (F) and more quiet fishtailing triplets. Repeated, the blustering outburst seems ridiculous: so much for the traditionally weighty minor-mode variation. By the end of the first half the theme is no longer literally present, which allows for the freest sort of variant yet heard; matters become more serious, and only with a certain wistful reluctance does the second part resume D minor, *pianissimo*, its energy spent. A drop to the lowered submediant (B♭) provides a new beginning for the fifth variation; taking the lead from the previous one, the cello introduces not merely figuration but structural variation of the tune. In the second half a sequential rise (10–8) leads to the distant tonal region of D♭; change of mode then precipitates a slow, quiet fall through the same sequence pattern, now rather chilling in the ambiguity of its goal—which, of course, was really D major after all. And here is the pert little theme, uptempo, unadorned, with its original frisky accompaniment. Schubert spins out the happy moment through written-out repeats, shared by violin and cello, of both the theme's halves; this music could swim along endlessly, and the bubbling sextuplets of the accompaniment ring in the ear well beyond the fermata.

Accordingly, Schubert dispels them: octave E's chime and decay—a call to order almost certain to be heard as a new dominant after the close of the variations. Yet before the listener is fully oriented, a repetitive quickstep march tune enters *pianissimo* over the E pedal, like music to accompany the twirling miniature figurines of a musical clock. This continues, slightly varied by upbeat accent, through *forte* outbursts and a tonal shift to C; the accented pickup motive becomes a sequenced transitional phrase that, as the subdominant is reached, expands into a sweeping second theme (mm. 84ff.). Now the pent-up energy of the march's repetitive two-bar phrases broadens into units of four, and the high-spirited frolic seems destined to last indefinitely. So indeed it will, but the piece requires further molding if its exposition is not to close out fairly soon: Schubert introduces a touch of rhetorical doubt by moving quietly to F♯ minor (m. 108) and sequencing the repetitive eighth-note pattern from the second half of the march. This is the closest approximation of a traditional development passage found in the finale; a dynamic swell accompanies the peak of its harmonic intensity, and then the music subsides quietly back to D major (m. 135). Remaining soft, the head of the march tune in the strings is combined with *dolcissimo* triplets for the piano (which recall both the original "Trout" accompaniment and the violin variation of its theme).

Following a brusque but temporary diversion to B♭ (mm. 155ff.), this material returns, again *piano*, with violin and keyboard exchanging lines. And at last it peals forth in full voice for a dozen bars; the ensuing, rather comical attempt to whisper (mm. 194ff.) calms no one. Nor do three mock-angry arpeggiations, which force another diversion to B♭: this big, jubilant exposition does not conclude, but merely stops, still bristling with vigorous energy. And so, too, the movement—no development section interposes conflict. Rather (as in the work's Andante), the second half mirrors the first, beginning this time in the dominant so as to close in the tonic. Objectors need tell just what wanted developing. The finale, and indeed the entire "Trout," has been set forth not to resolve musical affects—all optimistic in this instance—into others, but to revel in those introduced. Hence the remaining energy when the instruments have become still. As we shall see, Schubert will adopt this same basic approach to the finale in later chamber works that are either decidedly dejected or highly ambivalent in emotional tone.

The Quartettsatz in C minor, D. 703.

The idyll in Steyr came to an end in mid-September 1819, and Schubert returned to his lodgings with the poet Mayrhofer in Vienna. It would be more than a year before he again attempted a work of chamber music, and the intervening months brought many misfortunes. The fragments of an oratorio, *Lazarus*, dated February 1820, were abandoned. In March Schubert was arrested after a night of all-male revelry in the rooms of a friend, Johann Senn, who belonged to a student association that was under police surveillance; it appears Schubert was released, but Senn was detained and permanently exiled from Vienna.[65] Schubert's two theatrical projects of the spring and summer months, *Die Zwillingsbrüder* and *Die Zauberharfe*, were both unsuccessful; the latter, written in a style well beyond the understanding of conservative critics, received some especially nasty notices.[66] That September Schubert evidently gave vent to his scorn and fierce sense of independence in a poem entitled "Der Geist der Welt" (The spirit of the world):

> . . . Thus the Spirit of the World
> Spake: let them but chase
> After dark and far-off goals,
> And with wrangling fill their days;
> . . . Frail and human is their world,
> Godlike understand I all.[67]

Late in November Therese Grob, the neighborhood girl of his childhood with whom Schubert seems to have been in love from mid-1814 until perhaps 1818, was married;[68] this brought closure to the romance (if such it really was), but probably not without residual conflict. And evidently his living arrangement with Mayrhofer was becoming unsatisfactory; by early 1821 Schubert had taken his own lodgings in the same street.

As far as is known, by the end of 1820 Schubert had done no quartet writing for four years. Yet as we have seen, during earlier periods of personal turmoil he had twice written agitated, dramatic quartets in C minor that turned out to be milestones in his chamber music oeuvre: the 1813 Quartet, D. 46, and the now-incomplete quartet movement D. 103, composed just over a year later. Perhaps he sought such catharsis and renewal yet again late in 1820; in any case, it is today generally recognized that the C Minor *Quartettsatz*, D. 703, far surpasses any of Schubert's previous chamber music. As Brown notes, it combines "the lyrical radiance of the 'Trout' Quintet with the dramatic intensity of his finest songs. It is the first of the instrumental masterpieces of the 1820s." Einstein rightly characterizes it as "epoch-making" but also "weird," and notes that "this weird atmosphere is increased by the almost continuous tremolo in the 'accompaniment' or in the theme itself."[69] These and other striking foreground features are wonderfully intertwined with a formal structure that is in many ways characteristic of Schubert's sonata forms during the remainder of his career.[70] And the *Quartettsatz* also contains an unforgettable variant of the sonata paradigm: the elided and reordered reprise withholds the brusquely truncated return of the raging opening, which becomes the movement's parting shot.

That opening is a fourfold sounding of the descending tetrachord (c¹–bb–ab–g), a traditional symbol of lament that Schubert uses in numerous compositions. But here it quakes continuously, not only in articulation, but also through the relentless unsteadiness of the embellishing chromatic lower neighbors: both gestures are ubiquitous, and of paramount significance at manifold levels. Like the onset of a sudden squall, this music sweeps within seconds from a single hushed middle c to a shrieking Neapolitan chord, *ffz* through four octaves: that is the harmonic expansion of the neighbor-note figure, which then collapses through first-violin arpeggiations into a weary cadence. The lamenting tetrachord resumes—now in giguelike eighths, while the tremolo continues to seethe in the viola (mm. 13ff.). The prevalent two-bar groupings recur as well; just as this consequent phrase seems to border on bland repetition, the Neapolitan harmony returns (m. 23), now softer and of smoother contour. Here it functions as pivot to Ab, the new third-related key area of the "double second group" that will be a Schubertian stylistic fingerprint from now on.[71] Yet the anguished, obsessive opening is hardly dispelled, notwithstanding the rich lyricism of the *dolce* new theme: its ascending triadic fifth (mm. 27–28) is but the inversion of the initial tetrachord—and that tetrachord itself answers the fifth at once, *sans* chromatics (mm. 29–30 and 33–34). Recollections of the opening's relentless neighbor notes abound in the accompaniment, and the gigue rhythm bounces disconcertingly onward from the consequent statement of the first theme. Beethoven is the principal precedent for such concentration-*cum*-development already within the exposition, but Schubert deploys it with his own now unmistakable voice.[72]

The cadential shift of mode that closes this material (m. 61) is chilling, if less than unexpected; the ensuing tremolos, wailing scales, and chromatic inflections expand the rage of the movement's initial idea through transitional action that leads right to the dominant of C minor (m. 77)—as though perhaps to precipitate reprise without further argument. But expansion of neighbor-note activity leads (via augmented sixth chord, mm. 83 and 87) to the establishment of G, the major dominant, for the latter part of the double second group.[73] And still there is no genuine contrast: neighbor notes and gigue rhythm abound. The most enticing tune of this section (mm. 105ff.), a linear-intervalic pattern that spins out the descending chromatic tetrachord (g^2–d^2), is severely curtailed by precadential Neapolitan chords in both of its appearances—all of which reinforces the obsessive dominance of the movement's first dozen bars.[74]

In works examined up to this point, the development section is often not Schubert's strongest suit. (Nor would it be, by comparison to Mozart or Beethoven, in most of his subsequent chamber works.) In the *Quartettsatz*, however, limitations become virtues. The ceaselessly regular, repetitive two-bar units characteristic of the entire exposition are not highly malleable. Yet from the perspectives of affect and drama, what is there to develop, or to resolve through reprise, in a piece so fixated on its beginnings? Schubert launches the section following the double bar with a modulatory manifestation of the ubiquitous neighbor-note gesture (G major to Ab). But the thematic material is now by no means fresh, and sequencing does not renew it; even the bit of respite and variety inherent in the Db passage (mm. 157ff.) is quickly quashed by accented neighbors. As Aderhold suggests, there is more saber-rattling than engagement and decisive action in this development. After forty relatively aimless bars, we find the music drifting back toward the dominant via the same augmented sixth (m. 182) that brought it there earlier (mm. 83ff.). And then follows a most masterly stroke: Schubert abandons the premise of conflict resolution. Likely influenced by Haydn's witty false recapitulations, by Beethoven's dramatically altered reprises in *Coriolan* and the first "Rasumovsky" Quartet, and also by his own predilection for nontonic recapitulation, Schubert simply slips into the second theme group through a seemingly innocuous third relation (V/G → Bb, m. 195). This could be the entry into a new developmental diversion; by the time the listener is fully aware of the elision that has taken place (even upon repeated hearings), the course of events leading toward the closing section is fully underway. Those agitated opening bars, which have never really left our awareness, bring the movement to its bitter, inevitable close.[75]

Forty-one bars of a slow movement in Ab survive for this quartet (Example 2.9).[74] Lilting, repetitive, soft, and warmly songlike, its opening seems reminiscent of a lullaby. There are, to be sure, lingering memories of the previous movement in the chromatic neighbors, accented passing notes, and dominant ninths that gently ripple the surface; still, the first twenty bars are a closed segment of exceptional serenity. Change of mode, quickened rhythms, and rather far-ranging modulations indicate increasing agitation; clearly, as Aderhold notes, this Andante opens a new expressive span extending beyond the slow movements of the earlier quartets and foreshadowing the imposing *adagios* of the Octet and String Quintet.[77] But the manuscript breaks off before the nature of the movement's dramatic scheme is fully apparent.

We have no specific clues as to why Schubert abandoned this quartet. In surveying various incomplete works of this period, including the Symphonies in D Major (D. 708A) and E Major (D. 729) sketched and abandoned in 1821, Brian Newbould points to several possible factors, any combination of which may have been influential: compositional obstacles to continuation, problems caused by fast stylistic development during the period 1818–22, distractions (such as interest in other compositional media, or illness), poor prospects of performance, and demoralization in the face of Beethoven's instrumental genius.[78] What seems unlikely in the case of the *Quartettsatz* is that Schubert could have had doubts about the quality of this completed first movement.

EXAMPLE 2.9.   Schubert, *Quartettsatz* in C Minor, D. 703, opening of incomplete mvt 2.

Second Maturity: The Chamber Music of 1824

In any case, for just over three years Schubert wrote no chamber music whatever—an unprecedented hiatus in his output. Numerous songs, two operas never staged during his lifetime, three abandoned symphonies (including the "Unfinished"), completion of the Mass in A♭, a variety of dances for piano, the incidental music for *Rosamunde*, and, notably, the first of the great Müller song cycles, *Die schöne Müllerin*, occupied Schubert from 1821 through 1823. And it was during the latter half of 1822 that Schubert contracted syphilis, which made him intermittently miserable for the next several years and was perhaps a factor in his early death. In a poem entitled "My Prayer," dated 8 May 1823, he writes:

> See, abased in dust and mire,
> Scorched by agonizing fire,
> I in torture go my way,
> Nearing doom's destructive day.[79]

In August of that year he would write to his friend Schober, "Whether I shall ever quite recover I am inclined to doubt"; subsequent letters plus accounts of friends indicate that he was frequently too ill to leave his lodgings and that his mood varied considerably.[80] By mid-February 1824 he was evidently somewhat better and working busily on "quartets and German dances and variations without number."[81] Among the results were three indisputable masterpieces—the String Quartets in A Minor (D. 804, which uses a theme from *Rosamunde* in the slow movement) and D Minor (D. 810, "Death and the Maiden"), plus the Octet (D. 803)—as well as a lesser work, the "Trockne Blumen" Variations (D. 802). But in a notebook entry from the end of March, when all this music lay finished, he writes: "What I produce is due to my understanding of music and to my sorrows." And on the last day of the month he would "wholly pour out my soul" in a well-known letter to his friend Kupelwieser, then in Rome:

> In a word, I feel myself to be the most unhappy and wretched creature in the world. Imagine a man whose health will never be right again, and who in sheer despair over this ever makes things worse and worse, instead of better; imagine a man, I say, whose most brilliant hopes have perished, to whom the felicity of love and friendship have nothing to offer but pain. . . . "My peace is gone, my heart is sore, I shall find it never and nevermore," I may well sing every day now, for each night, on retiring to bed, I hope I may not wake again, and each morning but recalls yesterday's grief.[82]

It is difficult to suppose that the extraordinary music Schubert penned during this period and in his few remaining years remained unaffected by such anguish; as Edward Cone has observed, from the fall of 1822 on "the sense of desolation, even dread, . . . permeates much of his music. . . . a cold wind seems to blow through even some of his sunniest or most placid movements."[83] Moreover, as Jonathan Bellman points out, it was during 1823 that Schubert began to explore the possibilities of the *style hongrois*, the earthy musical accent of the Gypsies—those stereotypically passionate, melancholy, loose-living, impoverished bohemian nomads despised and feared by the German bourgeoisie and upper classes.[84] *Style hongrois* crops up in a number of the later chamber works, among them the Octet, the A Minor Quartet, and the C Major Quintet, as we shall see. Schubert may well have developed a symbolic identification with the Gypsies: he had never made his way into Viennese society as, for example, had Beethoven, and his public successes as a composer were modest and relatively infrequent. Never financially secure, Schubert by all accounts led a rather bohemian life in Vienna, punctuated by late-night revelry and tipsiness whenever there was cause to celebrate. If, as Solomon and others maintain, Schubert was homosexual, it probably made him unwelcome in various circles.[85] Thus it seems not unlikely, as Bellman concludes, that "at his points of lowest psychological ebb, bereft of physical health and emotional support, Schubert's inspiration found voice in the music of a group whose abominable circumstances must have presented an irresistible parallel to his own."[86]

Schubert's incidental music for the play *Rosamunde, Princess of Cypress*, was composed in the fall of 1823 for a production that closed after only two performances; it was his last serious attempt to achieve a success in the Viennese theaters. Yet personal and artistic difficulties notwithstanding, Schubert had ambitious plans for the future. In the same letter to Kupelwieser cited above, he notes that "of songs I have not written many new ones, but have tried my hand at several instrumental works," and after announcing the completion of the two quartets and the Octet, continues: "I want to write another quartet, in fact I intend to pave my way towards grand symphony in that manner.—The latest in Vienna is that Beethoven is to give a concert at which he is to produce his new Symphony. . . . God willing, I too am thinking of giving a similar concert next year."[87] He had, moreover, come to know Ferdinand, Count Troyer, a fine amateur clarinetist in the service of the Archduke Rudolph, and Ignaz Schuppanzigh, the renowned quartet leader and friend of Beethoven's who would participate in several first performances of Schubert's later chamber works.

In January Schubert wrote the Variations for Flute and Piano on "Trockne Blumen" from *Die schöne Müllerin*, presumably for his friend Ferdinand Bogner, professor of flute at the Conservatory in Vienna.[88] The blatant vulgarity of the piece considerably surpasses that of the Adagio and Rondo Concertante (D. 487) of 1816, Schubert's sole previous venture into untrammeled virtuoso glitter. To be sure, as Einstein notes, the rich introduction contains "all manner of mystery and seriousness with unmistakable echoes of 'Der Tod und das Mädchen'"; however, he goes on to suggest that "this Andante should be followed simply by the theme—and nothing else."[89] The theme itself is a lamenting love song in which the protagonist imagines himself buried with the withered flowers given him by the mill maid before she rejected him; the music becomes poignantly ironic in its concluding turn to the bright major mode with the words:

> And when she wanders past the grave mound
> and thinks in her heart: his love was true!
> Then all you little flowers, spring forth, spring forth!
> May has come, and Winter is over.

But Schubert's gaudy variations, overladen with caviarlike diminutions and thundering octaves, overplay the song's irony a hundredfold by making it a travesty of the opera-tune variation set so popular among the rising cult of virtuosi.[90] It is perhaps telling that at the benefit concert given

in January 1829 to raise money for a Schubert gravestone, Bogner chose
not to perform the "Trockne Blumen" Variations, but rather a set of variations by Johann Wilhelm Gabrielsky.[91]

The Octet, D. 803

Two of Schubert's next chamber works manifest the extraordinary level
of variation writing of which he was capable, and all three indicate the
heights to which he was now prepared to rise, on his own terms, in genres hitherto dominated by the increasingly legendary figure of Beethoven.
The Octet came first, completed by 1 March. Whether or not Count von
Troyer actually suggested that it be modeled on Beethoven's ever-popu-
lar Septet, there can be little doubt that Schubert is responding to, and
consciously surpassing, that rather urbane piece. Both works consist of
six movements cast in the same tonal relationships (I–IV–I–V–I–I),
with Andante variations in the middle sandwiched by a minuet as well
as a scherzo (Schubert reverses their order, placing scherzo ahead of minuet). Both call for the same winds (clarinet, horn, bassoon), and Schubert has augmented Beethoven's string complement by adding a second
violin.[92] That additional instrument gives Schubert the possibility of treating the texture both as intimate conversation and like a small orchestra:
he deploys the variety of combinations most skillfully to enliven a work
that lasts about an hour in performance—half again as long as Beethoven's
Septet.

Like Beethoven, Schubert opens with an *adagio* introduction from
which the main subject and other ideas of the ensuing *allegro* will be derived; he even makes his first approach to the dominant (mm. 4–5) by way
of augmented sixth, just as Beethoven had done (mm. 7–8). But therewith
the similarities diminish: Schubert immediately plays his strongest suits—
harmonic color and melodic lyricism—to best advantage, as he will
throughout the Octet, yielding up striking gestures that make the
Beethoven prototype seem pallid by comparison. Schubert's first theme,
built on filled-in arpeggiation over slow harmonic rhythm (like that of the
Septet), extends to a full nineteen bars before arrival of the second period
leading toward the transition, compared to ten measures prior to the parallel gesture in Beethoven. Predictably, the Septet moves to the dominant;
Schubert, however, intersperses an intermediate area, which in this case
vacillates enticingly between relative minor and tonic major. Motives from
the main theme are refashioned into the second subject, which is presented in three varied statements (mm. 50, 61, and 71ff.). As Tovey and
Dahlhaus have observed, such variation techniques, which resemble a meandering commentary on the theme, are a significant factor in Schubert's
idiosyncratic expansion of sonata form.[93] Here they also vaguely raise the
possibility of serious drama in a work that, once the exposition gets underway, seems all brightness and warmth—the world of the "Trout" revisited,
as it were. The arrival of the dominant (m. 90) marks the second part of

the double second group, wherein bubbling sixteenths in the first violin ripple above further dotted rhythms from the main idea. Indeed, by now the movement seems almost monothematic. As in the Septet, the closing section is relatively extensive; characteristically, Schubert's digressions are more colorful and tantalizing.

Beethoven's development section in the Septet is fairly simplistic. There is no motivic working-out; rather, following an inaugural flourish, a single phrase from the closing section (mm. 98ff.) plus one gesture from the transition (mm. 39–40) are linked into two sequential blocks: measures 116–27, moving from C minor to A♭, and measures 128–36, which progress from A♭ to F minor. Three transitional bars then lead to the dominant pedal, over which other ideas are briefly rehearsed, and the reprise is at hand. Schubert proceeds similarly, yet always with a richer harmonic palate: an unexpected transition via diminished seventh and chromatic parallelism brings us to the distant tonal region of F♯ minor (m. 142); then follow two blocks of the second theme (slightly modified) that move from F♯ to B minor, then B to E minor (mm. 142–49, 150–55). Next come two longer parallel units of related material, intensified yet still indecisive (mm. 156–69, 170–82): the broad motion, E minor to D minor, then D minor to C minor, is cut short by a dip to A♭ (m. 183) that brings allusions to the movement's introduction. Another sequence followed by sleight-of-hand (via augmented sixth), and suddenly the introduction actually is at hand (mm. 194ff., but with no indication of "adagio")—a delightful touch of the unexpected ushering in the recapitulatory process. This is curtailed, bringing on the Allegro. Like Beethoven, Schubert sidesteps to the subdominant (mm. 222ff.; cf. m. 172 in the Septet) before recapitulating the second subject. And not surprisingly, he gives the movement a coda far more ebullient than Beethoven's.

The formal procedures of the Octet's first movement are broadly characteristic of Schubert's first movements from this point forth.[94] The three-key (or "double second group") exposition is already familiar. Treatment of the development like a large-scale sequence occurs in several later chamber works, notably the E♭ Piano Trio and the C Major Quintet. And oblique approach to the reprise (perhaps incorporating aspects of the introduction, as in the Quintet) occurs subsequently as well.

No one who has heard the slow movement of the "Unfinished" Symphony could mistake the author of the Octet's Adagio. Already by the second bar both melody and harmony are unmistakably Schubert's. The wistful passing chromatic g♭[1] of that measure, recurring three bars later in the bass, hints vaguely that the pastoral bliss of this movement may not be unbroken; the continuation of this chromatic passing motion, which gives rise to the clarinet's d♭[2] over a diminished seventh in the latter half of measure 6, is more unsettling, as is the harmonic treatment of the melodic high point (m. 9). And all three of these gestures are heard again when, after amorphously overlapping with itself, the melody is repeated in full by the violin, intertwined with an exquisite countermelody in the clarinet (mm.

11–22). These seemingly disruptive, isolated pitches (g♭^{1}, d♭^{2}) are closely akin to what Edward Cone has termed "promissory notes": the possible implications of their deviance from ordinary discourse become fully apparent only later in the piece.[95]

For the moment, however, the music seems to forget them, spinning forth one long lyrical line after another; the bothersome G♭ and D♭ are even temporarily stabilized as the first two moves away from the tonic B♭ (mm. 25ff.). By measure 45 it seems clear that the dominant is the movement's structural goal; although full closure is deliciously delayed (e.g., mm. 60ff.), the expectation of slow-movement binary form is ultimately fulfilled, and after a delightful cadenza for violin joined by clarinet (but note the G♭'s in mm. 69 and 75), the reprise ensues. All is well for the first six bars of the tune, although the transfer of the countermelody to the horn seems both enriching and vaguely portentous. But just as the melodic high point is at hand (m. 86), first bass, then melody go wildly awry. A simple V/IV breaks away as an augmented sixth pressing hard toward D minor (mm. 86–87), which in turn reverts to V$^4_2$ of E♭, *ffz*—a chord that can only be described as horrifying. These are potentially disturbing implications of the chromatic passing motion in the movement's opening bars; the pastoral flow is completely disrupted, and with it the symmetrical binary formal plan.

After an embarrassed silence, the cello quietly brings in the theme in E♭, the harmonic center lingering in the pause following the outburst. And again, crisis ensues at the climactic moment: now the subdominant shift is candidly minor in mode (A♭, m. 104), and the suppressed agitation that barely surfaced in the "promissory notes" becomes overt. The G♭ major episode of the first half (mm. 25ff.) returns, now in minor (mm. 112ff.)— D minor, the first implied goal of the first desperate outburst. Almost magically, the dominant of B♭ begins to emerge from this darkness (mm. 115ff.), and the music seems to resume the course of the movement's first half (cf. mm. 28ff.); when the pedal point material that had ultimately led to closure of the first half returns as dominant of B♭ (m. 123), it seems almost possible that order has been permanently restored. And indeed, everything proceeds as expected, with the addition of delightful—relieving, almost—ornamental dialogue between paired violins and winds.

The cadence (m. 145) brings a quiet codetta, with the main theme radiantly *pianissimo* in the upper strings—until the G♭ reappears, first in passing, then as top voice of a dominant ninth chord; the bass becomes an offbeat muffled sob, pizzicato in lower strings. Again the lilting pulse is destroyed; the effect may be likened to Gretchen's revelation, "sein Kuß!" in Schubert's famous setting from *Faust:* no return to innocence is possible. In the ensuing digression—to D♭—the anguished brokenness intensifies, only to yield in resignation to tonic close. Yet the G♭ stubbornly resists resolution, up until the final two bars. The movement as a whole becomes an unexpectedly powerful drama; in that respect, only the slow movement of the "Unfinished" among Schubert's previous instrumental oeuvre bears comparison. The slow movement of Beethoven's Septet is the product of a different century.[96]

Like portions of the first movement, the scherzo invites comparison to its companion piece in the "Trout" Quintet. The jocular, popular tone and relentlessly driving dotted rhythm are invigorating, while Schubert's gift for harmonic color sweeps aside any possibility of monotony. The instrumentation is most nearly "orchestral" here, while the trio, in contrast, relaxes in smoother rhythms and more transparent scoring. Overall, it is a delightful romp surpassed only, perhaps, by the madcap scherzo of the String Quintet four years hence.

The inventiveness, poise, and sonorous beauty of the Octet's variation movement make it difficult to believe that the same composer had penned the "Trockne Blumen" Variations only weeks earlier. Schubert takes the theme from a love duet in his singspiel of 1815, *Die Freunde von Salamanca;* the text, by his erstwhile friend Mayrhofer, runs thus: "Lying beneath the bright canopy of trees by the silver brook, the shepherd longs for his lovely one and laments in rapturous tones." There is an alluring Viennese sensuousness about this tune that one can nearly taste, as the saying goes, like a fine Riesling wine, and Schubert underscores it directly at the first repeat by the octave doubling of clarinet and violin, a sound distinctly associated with *Heurige,* the wine taverns of Vienna and environs. It is a four-plus-four theme, as is Beethoven's variation theme in the Septet. But whereas Beethoven was satisfied with five fairly conventional variations plus coda, Schubert takes obvious delight in the seemingly endless figurations, dialogues, overlappings, and colorations he can spin forth from his simple song across the span of seven variations that, in addition to the traditional (and in this case, rather exotic) *minore,* also include a wonderfully ethereal reshaping of the material in the flattened submediant (A♭) that would seem to foreshadow Brahms.[97]

The carnival atmosphere of the last variation is the peak of the movement's popular tone; then the ensuing fifteen-bar coda, *più lento* (and nearly a variation in itself), fades the frolic to slumber, rather like the quiet ending of a waltz suite. The minuet that follows is also a rather rustic piece, closer to the domain of the ländler than to the elegance of the court ball. Although it is the least exceptional movement of the Octet, there are many fine touches of instrumental color and harmonic adventure; as Westrup notes, the passage in the second half of the minuet (mm. 23ff.) leading from A♭ to the return of the main theme is particularly striking.[98]

The most unforgettable moment of the entire work is the opening of the finale. Only recollection of the dramatic conflict in the second movement prepares us for the shock of impending peril that this introduction seems to prophesy: tremolos and wailing summonses like lightning in a stormy sky, first on D♭, then on G♭ (not coincidentally, two prominent "promissory" notes in the slow movement),[99] followed by the introduction to the first movement (mm. 11ff.)—music formerly confident and lyrical that is now quaking and fearfully *pianissimo.* The arrival of the dominant in measure 15 brings vague brightness; then the ensuing *allegro* responds with defiant cheerfulness, as though to deny the introduction any significance. Moreover, much of what follows is lowbrow in character, and laced with Gypsy idioms. Trilled dotted rhythms, irregular phrasings, repeated spondees, harmonic parallelism, thumping bass, and overall repetitiousness of the jaunty main theme: all this smacks of *style hongrois,* and many of these features recur in subsequent material. The riotous triplets for violin and clarinet that break out in the second group (mm. 116ff., etc.), which must surely have kept Schuppanzigh and Count von Troyer on their toes, evoke the wildly virtuosic improvisations of Gypsy fiddlers and *tárogató* players.[100]

By the latter part of the exposition (mm. 136, 154ff.) even the viola is swept up in this, and as five distinct rhythmic levels rage over the crude three-note ostinato bass, the music comes to a dizzyingly swirling close in V—only to launch into the mad dance again as the development lurches forward into A♭. Driving and distinctly improvisatory in character, the inner strings, then the cello take the lead; the bizarre sequence in contrary motion of measures 172–78 (muddled by a split-second mixture of mode) is perhaps as close to chaos as anything Schubert ever wrote. On they play through frenzied rising sequences, goal uncertain—and then a feint: the second theme in A, *pp* (m. 203). A descending sequence with diminuendo arrives on a dominant pedal as the texture thins; then a dozen-bar crescendo brings back the full band for the uproarious reprise. We hear it all again (with minor adjustments), music that seems as though it would never cease. Utterly without warning, the introduction returns, now bedecked with Gypsy fiddle flourishes; these do nothing to mollify its severity. The response to this thunderbolt is more defiant than before: faster, and faster still, the coda rages on in the hedonistic dance that rings in the ear well after the piece, far from concluding, has simply ceased.

"Schubert, more than any other composer," writes Westrup of this movement, "seems to have discovered the secret of perpetual motion or at least to have found a way of suggesting that the music is never likely to stop." The finales of the B♭ Quartet (D. 112) and the "Trout" are surely precedents, yet never before had he gone to such extremes. Henceforth he would again, not only in *style hongrois,* but, notably, in tarantella movements. For Westrup, however, the introduction to the Octet's finale is not tortured, confessional, or even sad; "it is sombre, like some of Haydn's introductions, in order that what follows will make a stronger impression by contrast. Its recurrence in the course of the movement can then be interpreted not as a reminder of grief but as a powerful dramatic stroke."[101] Powerful and dramatic it surely is, but in view of all we have reviewed above, it represents more: Schubert, one of the supreme musical ironists, understood that one way to deal with conflict was simply to leave it unresolved. Precisely that was also his fundamental tactic in the three new quartets he was planning to write, two of which were finished in the same month as the Octet.[102] One did not have to be the Promethean hero Beethoven; in face of life-threatening illness, it was enough to be Schubert.

The A Minor Quartet ("Rosamunde"), D. 804

The two quartets of 1824 do not form a complementary pair (as do, for example, the G Minor and C Major Quintets or Symphonies of Mozart): "Death and the Maiden," unprecedented in dimension and dramatic intensity, overshadows the A Minor and indeed seems to look toward grand symphonic style.[103] Yet this should not diminish our appreciation of how extraordinary the A Minor is, and in particular, as Einstein rightly notes, how different it is in style and character from Beethoven—"as far removed as the 'Unfinished' in the symphonic field, and the chamber-music counterpart to the latter."[104] It is a fundamentally lyrical work cast in a satisfying succession of movements. The first, a broad sonata form, and the third, a touching treatment of the age-old minuet, sing of longing, disappointment, and occasionally horror, with no resolution of affective discord. Between them the Andante, based on an entr'acte from *Rosamunde*, is a bucolic interlude (like the scene it introduced in the play),[105] yet is also disrupted by agitation. And the chipper, slightly haughty Hungarian finale, although acknowledging the work's underlying conflict, nevertheless dances away from it.

The quartet opens with the hushed expectancy of a two-bar vamp ("Gretchen am Spinnrade" and Mozart's G Minor Symphony are frequently cited as precedents).[106] Particularly striking is the recurring rhythm ♩. ♫♫ in the lower register that, together with the second violin's ostinato eighths, will quiver through nearly thirty bars of the exposition and the great majority of the development. In addition, the two-bar grouping established here will predominate throughout the movement. As in the first movement of the "Unfinished" Symphony, this exposition is based on two singing themes that are in effect two contrasting lieder.[107] As Einstein notes, the first of these is closely allied in mood to the opening of the quartet's minuet, which opens by quoting Schubert's song "Die Götter Griechenlands" (see Example 2.10), the text of which begins "Lovely world, where are you? / Return once more, fair and flowered age of Nature." But embedded in the triadic head motive of the movement (♩. ♩ | ♩ 𝄾) is a more striking allusion: this same gesture is prominent in Schubert's early ballad "Leichenfantasie" (Funereal fantasy; D. 7, 1811) on a text by Schiller, which is the grim account of a father accompanying the corpse of his dead son to the grave at night for a moonlit burial.[108]

The quartet's lyrical, bittersweet first theme unfolds in open-ended phrases (mm. 3–10, 11–22), the second of which is an expanded variant upon the first made more poignant by inflection of the Neapolitan (m. 19). Then follows a third version, now in major. Einstein suggests that the symbolism of this modal shift is precisely that of "Die Götter Griechenlands," in which "the fairyland of song" (major, fading to minor) is the only re-

EXAMPLE 2.10.   Schubert, "Strophe aus Die Götter Griechenlands," D. 677 (1819), opening.

maining trace of the longed-for lost world.[109] In the quartet, in any case, the major is gruffly quashed by *fortissimo* fragmentation of the theme's tri-adic head motive, back in minor, which trails into wistful bits of solo violin fioratura (mm. 32ff.). This new variant on the main idea picks up momentum only when a feint to the Neapolitan, formerly gentle in its urgency, gives way to a crashing cadence and the fifth version of the theme, raging with loud exchanges of the head motive and triplets laced with chromatic neighbors (46ff.). As is often the case, Schubert moves away from the tonic only late in the game, and then relatively quickly; V of the mediant is established in only four bars as the violin fioratura returns over a general diminuendo.

And there ensues a grand pause. This seemingly facile turn to the second lied, a pastoral pairing of five-bar phrases, is also rather like entering a fantasy realm of song; yet the trills in the second half of the measure and the ostinato eighths of the accompaniment quietly recall what has gone before. Soon the triplets are back (m. 69), their chromatics expanded into anxious ascending bass motion, and the first bar of the new song is even more severely fragmented than had been the head motive of the first. Initially loud, this episode becomes ambivalent in its alternation of *forte* and *piano* (mm. 75ff.). Another evasive shift to very quiet rehearsal of the pastoral lied remains less than fully persuasive, as does the surprise foil of a variant in ♭VI (mm. 91ff.). The exposition closes abruptly in the mediant with *forte* triplets and brusque chords from the agitated, fragmented versions of the main theme.[110]

Sparse imitations on the head motive, *pp*, inaugurate a brief transition to the subdominant for the development proper. It commences, most curiously, with a verbatim return of the movement's first eight bars, including the shady, quaking pedal-point rhythm of the lower voices, absent for the past eighty bars. A false reprise at this juncture is out of the question; rather, in what follows, the main theme gradually yet inexorably unfolds into a distinctly different, unquestionably darker region only hinted at by the agitation of the exposition. The tonality shifts to F minor; as the second violin harps endlessly on the ♭$\hat{6}$–$\hat{5}$ half step against the viola pedal, cello and first violin become enmeshed in a canonic web of the theme's second phrase leading nowhere but louder. At long last there is a tonal shift to C minor, where all elements at play are affectively inverted: that second phrase, originally soft, legato, and consonant, is now staccato, accented, martial, and pitted against itself in imitative suspension figures; the flowing arpeggiation of the accompaniment becomes hammered eighth-note scales in the lower range. Largely static in previous appearances, these materials sequence higher and higher. Just as a cadence into a much-transformed D minor seems at hand, the resolution is shunted by a complete breakdown of motion on a long *fortissimo* diminished seventh, heavily voiced through more than three octaves—followed by silence. And then the very soft, quivering accompaniment from the very first bar: that, we now realize, is the persistent aftershock of this present crisis, already reflected in memory at the beginning of the movement.[111] The song returns—fragmented, disoriented, powerless. The tonal center wanders until at last, beneath a prolonged upper-voice B pedal (mm. 158ff.), the bass slides chromatically down to the dominant of A in preparation for the weary reprise. This reprise alters very little, save for closing in the tonic major, and resolves nothing: brusquely striking down the illusory major mode, the coda seems to reaffirm that the exposition is, so to say, a reaction after the crisis. The horrifying diminished seventh recurs, this time over a dominant pedal, as all motion comes to a halt once again (mm. 289–90). The stormy final four bars are as bitter as the close of the *Quartettsatz*, which also ends in unresolved conflict.

The second movement, a delightful C major Andante, is a welcome contrast. Yet at least in retrospect, it conjures forth dreams of Arcadia never to be realized. Much of the piece seems almost studiously uncomplicated, and one may well wonder with Westrup why Schubert did not write variations on the memorable theme.[112] Evidently that would have yielded too-great complexity for Schubert's pastoral tableau; it is instead a rather loose-knit rondolike structure, ABA′B′. The piece scarcely ventures beyond its tonic-and-dominant foundation except during the latter part of the B′ section, where a brief developmental passage "imposes on the pretty tune a strain which it is hardly able to bear," as Westrup notes. Yet the strain, although short-lived, seems distinctly to recall the anguish of the first movement, whose affective world returns, condensed, in Schubert's unique treatment of minuet and trio. Even the rather reserved Westrup finds here the "suggestion of a world where comfort cannot be expected—the world of a child who is bewildered and suffering." After an ambiguous opening—bass E alone, then hovering $^6_4$, both flicked by lower neighbors—a perceptibly Viennese lilt emerges, more akin to ländler and waltz than to the older minuet. Yet save for one *fp*, the entire first half remains deathly still—all of which puts an ironic twist on the question wordlessly posed by the opening gesture, "Lovely world, where are you?"

The tonic $^5_3$ is barely touched (m. 8) before motion toward the mediant is underway: this is the first in a long circle of third relations that shapes the entire minuet. Although C is major here (mm. 12ff.), it sounds unusually bleak owing to inflections of the lowered-sixth neighbor and to the melodic tritone emphasis (b^1–f^1). Just past the double bar that melodic emphasis becomes more explicitly harmonic in a diminished seventh that yields unpredictably to A♭, sounding first over its dominant pedal (like the movement's opening), then fully tonicized (m. 28). By this point the music has gradually grown warmer and more substantial, even though the symmetrical alternation of *forte* and *piano* harbors a lingering diffidence. Suddenly dynamic and harmonic outrage obliterate this pattern in measure 35: V^7 of A minor arrives via enharmonic reinterpretation (a♭ = g♯) combined with yet another third-descent in the bass (A♭–E♮)—logical, yet devastating: must the tonic pallor return? Structurally, this moment is closely analogous to the crisis point of the first movement; similar, too, are the ensuing near-silence, the drop to the lower register, and the ambiguity of what follows. The E pedal demands A, but its D♯ lower neighbor (note the crucial difference from the opening bar) will not allow of A. Instead follows the arresting plunge to C♯ minor—again through logic of prevailing motion by thirds. And again horrid—bleaker still than the tonic opening it mimics in lower and less resonant pitches of the strings.[113] "Lovely world": this is false reprise of the most gripping kind. The tonic, last in the chain of thirds, comes back in due course, yet without the first theme; rather, an *Abgesang* variant, almost banal in its waltzing gestures, twice phrases out in full cadence. Yet echoes from the opening of the second half linger, and finally only the flickering initial idea provides the close. The ländler elements of the movement seem more at home in the convivial A major trio. Even here the nearly continuous stress of the (typically unaccented) third beat evokes vague unease. Overall, the trio is but a brief diversion from the weighty minuet.

The trio's major-mode brightness and weak-beat accents do, however, provide preparation of sorts for the finale—a freewheeling sonata-rondo based entirely on Gypsy idioms. The frequent drone harmonies and quasi-improvised ritardando, the characteristic spondaic (♩ ♩) and anapestic (♫ ♩) rhythms with accented second beat, and the prominent dotted rhythmic motive ♩. ♫♩ of the primary material are all in *style hongrois;* in the B section (mm. 72–112) the drones and ubiquitous dotted-eighth/sixteenth figures bear the mark of the Rom (while C♯ minor, *pp,* recalls the second half of the minuet); and the third section in the dominant combines two previous dotted patterns with an overlay of flourishing Gypsy triplets (including the rather exotic articulation ♫♫♫), plus the fiddler's temperamental rubato once again (mm. 119–20).[114] The developmental section, beginning in B minor (mm. 175ff.), works the rushing triplets into all four voices through a long series of intensifying sequences (194ff.) landing in F♯ minor and bringing on the now-familiar symbol of crisis, this time twofold: an unexpected harmonic explosion (D$^4_2$) is followed by shocked silence in the upper voices. F♯ minor is restored, but without staying power. The tonic reemerges, hesitantly at first, in what turns out to be a truncated reprise of the primary material (mm. 226ff.; cf. mm. 44ff. in the first section).

The overall nature of this finale is well characterized by Einstein: "It admittedly ends in the major—A major—but in the same Hungarian disguise which Schubert was to use again in *Die Winterreise* in an exactly similar sense: outwardly exuberant and chevaleresque, but—as a number of mysterious phrases suggest—without any real consolation, in spite of the two loud final chords."[115]

The D Minor Quartet ("Death and the Maiden"), D. 810

If "Death and the Maiden" is the most powerfully dramatic of Schubert's chamber works to date, it also poses the most perplexing issues of interpretation. The famous subtitle is not Schubert's, but comes from his already popular song of 1817, "Der Tod und das Mädchen," which provides the theme of the extraordinary slow-movement variations, the centerpiece of the quartet as a whole. Christoph Wolff's fine study of the relation between song and quartet casts considerable light upon the broader contexts of their intertwining. The song (text by Marcus Claudius) is a dialogue in which a terrified maiden is confronted by Death in the traditional guise of a skeleton, just as he is depicted in the frontispiece to the volume from which Schubert took the words (see Figure 2.1). In fashioning his variation theme for the quartet, Schubert ignores the maiden's agitated accompanied recitative style (although this music is influential elsewhere, as we shall see). Rather, he adopts phrases in the solemn, oracular manner associated with Death; the last portion of the theme (mm. 17ff.) originally bore Death's words, "Be of good courage! I am not savage, / You shall rest peacefully in my arms." Thus, the notion of Death as benevolent rather than punitive is one aspect of the work's foundation. Wolff has also shown that, beyond the unusual concentration of the minor mode in all four movements of the quartet (three of them in D minor, the original key of "Death and the Maiden"), there are a number of subtle yet significant motivic links among them, as well as connections with the maiden's portion of the song, which is not used in the variation theme. "This is not to suggest any kind of concrete 'death programme' for the quartet," Wolff writes. "But one has to recognize that Schubert's use of musical topoi and

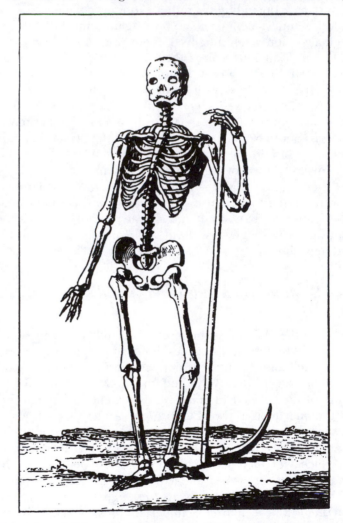

FIGURE 2.1.   *Freund Hain,* frontispiece engraving to Matthias Claudius, *Asmus omnia sua secum portans* (Hamburg, 1775), Schubert's source for the text of "Der Tod und das Mädchen," D. 531. Claudius dedicated the work to Freund Hain: " . . . *he* shall stand as patron saint and household god at the book's front door. . . . Give me your hand, dear *Hain,* and when once and for all you come, do not be harsh with me and my friends."

imagery plays a rather decisive role in this quartet of such enormous and unprecedented dimensions, particularly with respect to the extremely high degree of cyclic coherence. In this way the quartet could be related to the type of 'sinfonia characteristica' as represented in Beethoven's 'Pastoral' Symphony."[116]

Indeed—and consideration of the work's conclusion reveals the broad consistency of its character, just as in the "Pastoral." Although the finale of "Death and the Maiden" has long been recognized as a tarantella (so, too, is the fourth movement of the G Major Quartet), the age-old significance of that topos has been largely ignored. Schilling's 1838 *Universal-Lexicon* of music sums it up thus:

> In the southern lands of Europe and particularly in Italy, most frequently in the region of Taranto (hence the name), there is a large spider called the tarantula. Concerning the bite of this spider, it was said of old that it drove the afflicted person into madness, which would then subside only if one played him a particular music for quite a long time, and this music or melody, which is particularly common in the province of Apulia, is called the tarantella. The persons stung were supposed to dance to this music until they broke out in a heavy sweat and finally collapsed from exhaustion. The whole thing is, however, rightly regarded as a fabrication, or deceitfulness. . . . [117]

The phenomenon of tarantism probably dates from the fifteenth century; beginning in the seventeenth, it was discussed by numerous writers. Although it was widely suspect as a genuine medical malady, the *tarantati* (those who believed themselves ever to have been bitten) resumed their frenzied dancing each year for days on end at the height of the summer heat. Nakedness, drunkenness, erotic arousal, howling, beating, and rolling in the dirt often accompanied the Dionysian "cure," which was never permanent. Many *tarantati* were women, and hints that the annual "carnevaletti" (little carnivals) may have been due to sexual frustration are frequent in the literature. It was believed that the tarantula poison, like the latent syphilis bacterium, could reactivate itself, and that death could follow in hours or days if music and dancing were neglected.[118]

Carl Maria von Weber, whom Schubert knew personally, may have been the first composer to incorporate a tarantella into a concert work: his E Minor Piano Sonata, published in 1823, just before Schubert began his D Minor Quartet. Weber was certainly familiar with the lore of this dance.[119] Schubert almost certainly was as well, for his turn to the trope of tarantism seems transparent: syphilis, which limited sexual activity, could bring madness as well as death. The finale of "Death and the Maiden" is the desperate dance of someone on the threshold of one or both, in contrast to the quartet's slow movement, which grows from music associated with Death as comforter.[120] The finale is a vast sonata-rondo driven by nearly relentless tarantella triplets, and—just as in the first movement of the *Quartettsatz*—the recapitulation of its agitated opening is displaced to the end of the movement (m. 652), yielding a sense of grim inevitability. Even the seeming respite of the second subject, which is major, homophonic, and quasi-chorale in style (mm. 88ff. and 446ff.), eventually succumbs to the rush of triplet motion (e.g., mm. 134ff. and 491ff.). In these latter passages we hear distinct echoes from "Erlkönig"—of the young boy ("Siehst, Vater, du den Erlkönig nicht?"), yet also of the cruelly enticing Elf King himself ("Du liebes Kind, komm, geh mit mir!").[121] And the curious starts and stops in this movement may reflect the fact that periodically the *tarantati* had unwillingly to interrupt their gyrations for practical necessities (such as tuning the instruments).[122] The movement's coda whips up even greater frenzy and brightens momentarily toward D major. Yet ultimately the dancers drop in the three crashing chords of the final minor cadence—if not dead, surely not cured, either.

The work's opening is the most riveting in all of Schubert's chamber music: loud and imperious, then abruptly *pianissimo* and entreating, it introduces two contrasting characters that will occupy much of the movement. So, too, will two other features: the agitated triplets, which seem broadly related to the quaking accompaniment of the Maiden's desperate resistance to Death in the lied, and repeated pitches reminiscent of Death's oracular style, as Wolff has noted (cf., e.g., mm. 7ff. of the first movement and the opening of the second movement). The first fourteen bars of the quartet function as motto and introduction, fusing triplets with the scalewise descending-fifth motive that will become ubiquitous. Yet this introductory constellation of primary material returns (modified) only at the beginning of the coda; its initial function is rather like the ritornello of the lied, which prepares for the dramatic entry of the voice.[123] The core of the movement begins quietly at measure 15, growing higher and louder through two open-ended five-bar phrases. Melodically, they are related to the previous descending fifth (a^1–d^1, mm. 3–4, yields d^1–a^1, mm. 15–19, and d^2–a^2, mm. 20–24); yet they are also the inversion of the traditional descending *lamento* tetrachord, which becomes topical later in the quartet.

Again, however, there is no traditional consequent; the movement seems to begin anew as the first violin resumes its vocal role at measure 25, and the lower parts become more accompanimental. The tortuous chromaticism of measures 32–36 and 38–40 is particularly unsettling (note the contrary motion, first between cello and viola, then violin): these are instances of the so-called omnibus progression, which Schubert likely learned from the Commendatore in *Don Giovanni* and would deploy with uncanny effect in "Der Wegweiser" of *Winterreise:* "Einen Weiser seh' ich stehen unverrückt vor meinem Blick; eine Straße muß ich gehen, die noch keiner ging zurück" (I see a signpost unyielding before my eyes; I must travel a road from which no one ever came back).[124] Out of this rising ambiguity emerges the opening motto, its silences now filled with clattering triplets—as though all we have heard hitherto were a vast antecedent about to be complemented at last. Instead, a descending chromaticized sequence (reversing the previous ascents) withers unexpectedly

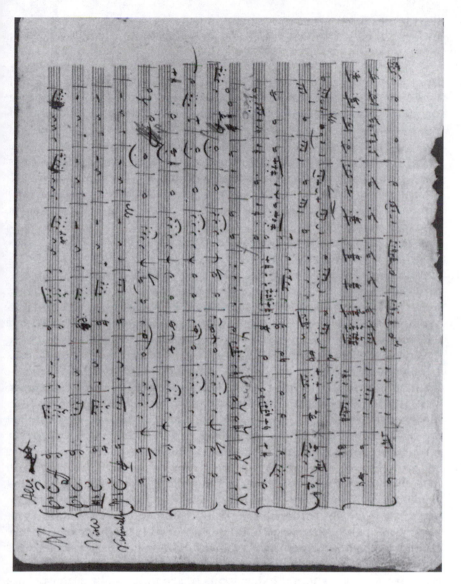

FIGURE 2.2.   Quartet in D Minor, D. 810, mvt. 1, autograph, page 1.
Reproduced through courtesy of The Pierpont Morgan Library, New York,
Mary Flagler Cary Music Collection, no. 72 (photography: David A. Loggie).

into the second group, in the relative (mm. 52ff.); as is so often the case in Mozart, this quick transition from agitation to lyricism is artfully effective, yet leaves much unresolved tension.

And still there are no consequents, but only new beginnings: measures 61ff. present a hurdy-gurdy tune, replete with reedy parallel motion, drone bass, and "short-winded, edgy and repetitive melodic phrases," as Wolff notes.[125] (The hurdy-gurdy is a frequent symbol of death in the iconographic tradition and was also associated with itinerant musicians and beggars; it is as well the instrument played by the "strange old man," the doppelgänger figure at the close of *Winterreise*.) Nor does this music achieve closure; the consequent phrase ending at measure 71 is disrupted, and the ensuing digressions are irresolute. *Forte* cadential elision at measure 83 also launches a long descending sequence of the tune's opening gesture. The triplet accompaniment gives way to driving sixteenths in the first violin—the brusque ornamentation of lamenting chromatic spans (a^2–$g\sharp^2$–$g\flat^2$–$f\sharp^2$; $c\sharp^3$–$c\flat^3$–$b\flat^2$–$b\flat^2$–a^2–$g\sharp^2$) that spiral downward in parallel tenths with the bass; this leads away from F to the minor dominant (m. 90), and the lines are inverted, *fortissimo*.

Quickened sequencing brings further irresolution; diversion to the major mode of the dominant is charming but unconvincing (mm. 101ff.), and suddenly the whole quartet seizes upon the sixteenths, *unisono,* in a desperate retreat to the relative and its rustic lyricism (mm. 112–14). But F is merely a neighbor chord; neither this nor a second attempt to establish it (m. 120) holds ground. Chromaticism sinks back toward V^9 of minor V (m. 128) as first violin and viola play oddly disoriented fragments of the hurdy-gurdy music in hollow octaves. Now follows the only distinct closing in the entire exposition: the jagged *fortissimo* clinching of A minor through seven full measures before the double bar.

Another unexpected lunge by third relation opens the development in C, dominant of F: by now it is clear that there is an urgent need to escape from D minor and its dominant (which must ultimately yield to D). Yet, just as a few bars earlier, the resolute advance does not hold: the dominant seems perilously close at hand by measure 143, and in measure 145 chromatic neighbor tones once again usher in octave fragments of the hurdy-gurdy. Now the dominant ninth is that of F♯—a tritone (*diabolus in musica*) away from where the development sought to make a new beginning.[126] F♯ takes hold furiously in measure 152: triplets from the first group and the jagged fragment of the barrel-organ tune are contrapuntally enmeshed, as they will be throughout much of what follows. Overall, this is one of Schubert's large-scale sequential developments—a dramatic descent from F♯ minor to E minor (mm. 163ff.) to, indeed, the D minor the music so sorely sought to escape (mm. 173ff.). The fiercest outburst thus far in the movement (m. 176) would negate D through gnashing dissonance (making it a secondary dominant ninth), which launches a rapid chromatic sequence replete with scorching cross-relations and neighbor-note clashes.[127] Yet all the sound and fury brings on the dominant of D nonetheless (mm. 182–86). With hushed expectancy the hurdy-gurdy rhythms drone in cello and viola. Now follows the most explicit reference to the Maiden's terrified pleading in the lied: the *sotto voce* first violin line of measures 188–91, with its prominent augmented second (a^1–$b\flat^1$–$c\sharp^2$–d^2) explicitly recalls the contour of her first utterance, "Away, oh, away, go, savage Death!" (cf. Example 2.11).[128] Higher and louder it rises, becoming almost a shriek by the time the reprise arrives, *fortissimo,* with the pounding version of the main theme from measures 41ff. of the exposition.

The recapitulation is curtailed, and needs to be: as noted, the coda is the culmination of this opening movement, as well as its second moment of hushed expectancy. Twice sounds the previous effort to pull away from D minor through dominant-ninth transformation (mm. 303 and 307; cf. 176)—the second weaker than the first. The unexpected *più mosso* at first

EXAMPLE 2.11.   Schubert, "Der Tod und das Mädchen," D. 531 (1817), mm. 1–14.

quotes measures 15–19: Could the entire drama begin anew? Or might the movement vanish, like the Erlkönig and the child, quietly into the nocturnal echo of galloping triplets? There is resistance in the sudden drop to ♭VI at measure 316 (the key of the second group in the recapitulation); predictably, ♭VI gives way to V, but the motivic chromatic rise from D to A is underway and soars into the shrill wail that had been stifled by the inevitable D minor of the reprise. So, too, here (mm. 324–26). But the entreating vocal gesture of the movement's introductory bars returns, twice inflecting the minor Neapolitan—a frequent sonic symbol of pathos—to no avail. The pacing of the final tonic chords prepares for the hushed oracular style of the Andante to follow.

As Wolff suggests, the relation between first and second movements in this quartet closely parallels the dialogue in the song: first comes the Maiden's terror and resistance, then follow Death's assurances that he is a comforter—at least as regards the theme per se of the slow movement. But in the ensuing variations, the conflict seems to emerge again, and it is not difficult to associate the roles of Death and the Maiden with the voices of cello and first violin, respectively.[129] The first variation brings back the repeated-note triplet accompaniment so prominent in the first movement, over which the first violin spins forth operatic cantilena laced with pathetic sighing motives. In the second variation the cello sings the theme, only slightly varied, in its persuasively lyrical tenor range. But the upper voices remain unconsoled: the first violin trembles in leaping off-beat sixteenths, the second violin takes up the dotted hurdy-gurdy rhythm from the first movement, and the viola, clocklike, ticks off a diminution of the theme's treading dactylic rhythm (♩ ♩ ♩ → ♪⁷ ♫) in static octaves and repeated notes. This pattern is further diminished into a heavy gallop (♫ ♫) for the entire quartet in the third variation; after four bars, the inner voices quietly maintain the driving rhythm while first violin and cello enter into a hushed dialogue. In the second half of the variation their discourse becomes a heated exchange of raging rolled chords.[130] The prissy *pianissimo* that interrupts this is surely ironic, for the variation ends with the gallop pounding louder than *fortissimo* in the extreme ranges of the quartet.

The fourth variation is an abrupt and ethereal transformation in all respects: major mode, very soft dynamics, the theme in smooth contours and original rhythmic values, the cello and first violin both in high tessitura, and the accompanying triplets languid and legato. Gülke regards this as something almost akin to "a delicate portrait of the Maiden";[131] whether or not that be the case, he correctly notes that the essential style of this variation carries over into the next and is there gradually yet powerfully overcome. The minor mode and the quaking of the second variation return, first quietly in the triplets of the cello, then more agitatedly in the sixteenths of the first violin, and the whole grows ominously louder over the unyielding pedal point. In the second half the cello seizes the lead as all other voices tremble above; at the movement's high point (mm. 137–40) the extraordinary rhythmic clashes and the first violin's desperate wailing up to a♭³ and g³ suggest crisis and disintegration.¹³² The slow dynamic and rhythmic diminuendo over the next twenty bars marks the ebb of all energy and resistance. The coda is celestial: major at last, and almost devoid of substance. Its closing bars echo the word "schlafen" ("sleep") for listeners familiar with Schubert's song; if Death has won, he is here a comforter, as promised in the lied.

The scherzo is derived from a German Dance for piano (D. 790, No. 5) that Schubert had written in May 1823, when the symptoms of his syphilis had become so severe that he would shortly be hospitalized.¹³³ In reworking it for the quartet, he resumes the fierce energy level of the first movement and incorporates touches of Hungarian exoticism by making the syncopation (adopted from the German Dance) nearly relentless and adding wide-interval downbeat grace notes. Two versions of the descending tetrachord constitute the bass line of the scherzo's first eight bars: the first of these (mm. 1–4) is the inversion of the Maiden's first utterance in the song (also heard in first violin just before the reprise of the first movement: see Example 2.11 above); the second (mm. 5–8) is the traditional chromatic *lamento,* which is transferred to the first violin at the double bar (m. 23). There are as well frequent pitch repetitions in both melody and accompaniment, a marked feature of the song (and variation theme) also transformed in aspects of the first movement, as noted above.¹³⁴ The trio, in tonic major, seems bright and singing—yet its entire first phrase remains a vapid *pianissimo,* and both dotted rhythms and pitch repetitions linger from the scherzo. Overall, the trio's lyrical charms seem only to underscore the severity of the scherzo at the da capo. Therewith the stage is set for the ensuing tarantella.

The "Arpeggione" Sonata, D. 821

In his despairing letter to Kupelwieser of 31 March 1824, cited earlier, Schubert indicated that he had completed two quartets and wanted to write another. The manuscript of the D Minor (although currently incomplete) is dated March 1824; curiously, however, the work was apparently not performed until 1 February 1826. Schuppanzigh (to whom Schubert had planned to dedicate the whole of Op. 29) reportedly disapproved of the new quartet: "My dear fellow, this is no good, leave it alone; stick to your songs!"¹³⁵ Such criticism may well have been a discouraging setback; yet it seems rather reactionary coming from the violinist who would lead premieres of Beethoven's first three "late" quartets (Opp. 127, 132, and 130) during 1825 and 1826. By then, however, as Solomon observes, "Beethoven's greatness had long since become an article of faith in several leading European countries";¹³⁶ Schubert's status was far less compelling. In any case, only in June 1826 did Schubert turn to the third quartet of the originally projected set. His final chamber work of 1824, composed in November, was a sonata for a new instrument, the arpeggione, and piano (D. 821). Precisely why Schubert used the term "arpeggione" remains open to conjecture, but an instrument close to what he had in mind, variously called "guitarre-violoncell," "bowed guitar," or "guitarre d'amour," had been invented in Vienna by one G. Staufer in 1823. This was a six-string, fretted instrument, larger than a guitar but smaller than a cello, held between the knees and played with a bow (or pizzicato). Music for this bowed guitar was generally notated in the treble clef, an octave above sounding pitch; a contemporary report describes its tone as "of magic beauty resembling in the high register the sound of an oboe, in the lower one that of a bassethorn."[137]

The A Minor Sonata Schubert created for this instrument (and possibly for the performer Vincenz Schuster) is a mixture of naïveté and sophistication, of virtuoso flutter and poignancy, that differs from any other of his chamber works. Obviously he seeks a lighter vein than that of the year's two quartets, yet cannot altogether shake their seriousness. Although one might detect occasional echoes of the A Major Violin Sonata (D. 574), there is no return to that sunny landscape, or to the popular cheer and uproarious dancing of the Octet. Rather, all three movements seem wistfully ambivalent, and as in later works by Schumann or Brahms, it is as though the ambivalence were to be lived with rather than overcome. Schubert forgoes his expansive three-key first-movement exposition in favor of the more economical and traditional tonic-relative scheme. The haunting first theme, shared in antecedent and expanded consequent by piano and arpeggione respectively, is self-contained; to it is appended a nine-bar tag (mm. 22–30) that also fades out in the tonic, followed by silence. A rapid transition follows like the sudden afterthought that breaks off a daydream, and when C is fully confirmed (m. 40), all-too-predictable passagework bubbles forth. This reaches the height of its triumphant triviality only to be countered by a touching recall of lyricism (mm. 63ff.), which brings the exposition to a rather unexpectedly reflective close.

The development, although brief by Schubert's standards, is not simple. At a stroke we find ourselves in the pastoral key of F, where the first theme is transformed to the major in bright piano octaves with cheery pizzicato accompaniment in the arpeggione. This won't do, of course, as both parts seem to acknowledge after merely five bars: at measure 79 they join spontaneously a transition to D minor. When this is complete (m. 87), the trivial passagework returns, rather grim in its agitation. Sequencing leads back to F major once again (m. 101), which quickly becomes F minor. Now the left hand of the piano takes up those seemingly trivial neighbor-note sixteenths, and these, decorating a steady bass descent, bring on the dominant of A. This pedal passage becomes the impotent high point of the development, and of the movement as a whole; the reluctance of the arpeggione to accept the inevitable return to tonic is prolonged through nine seemingly improvisatory measures as the piano sits quietly yet unrelentingly on the dominant seventh. Predictably, the reprise brings back the frivolous second group in the tonic major, but not without touches of anguish in the transition thereto. And such a movement must needs have a coda (mm. 188ff.), which turns out to be a poignant variant on the seemingly insignificant tag to the first group. (Thereby we realize why it was then closed off in the tonic.) Two loud, brusque chords conclude the proceedings.

The slow movement, a little gem *sui generis*, is the epitome of the sonata's ambivalence. Its opening, which echoes bygone serenity of Mozart and Beethoven,[138] unfolds a rounded three-part song (mm. 1–11, 12–19, 20–33); one would expect a middle section followed by return of this flowing lyricism. Not at all: with the shift to minor (m. 34) the accompanying eighths become fixated and dissonant. Rather like an unpleasant recollection, this passes fairly quickly, and somewhat surprisingly, the major mode returns at the end of the phrase (mm. 39–41). This passage recurs again, slightly intensified; the outcome is the same. Now the pulsing eighths vanish entirely (mm. 49ff.), and motion is reduced to full-bar units; the progression is I–♭VI–Neapolitan–V, *piano*, with a rising fifth in the arpeggione line. This is music we have heard before: it is the last gesture, delicately transformed, of the coda in the first movement of "Death and the Maiden" (mm. 326ff.); as there, it recurs *pianissimo* an octave lower, but now with chromatic expansion in the bass. The major mode and reflective pace mark this as a quiet recollection of the past, rather than present-time drama as in the quartet; accordingly, it does not seem out of place for the arpeggione to lapse into a musing cadenza that gradually ushers in the sonata's finale.

That movement opens with a warm, folkish tune Brahms might have written thirty years later, and we sense at once the beginning of a rondo: so, too, it is, although not without complications. Like the transition in the first movement, the finale's two couplets (D minor, mm. 53ff.; E major, mm. 189ff.) are introduced without transition, following notable silences. The first of these clearly recalls both the "trivial" passagework of the first movement and the D minor treatment of it in the development. But the second seems rather like an ephemeral world apart—and eventually it yields to a reprise of the first couplet, now in tonic minor (m. 276). The movement draws to a close with a slightly modified return of the rondo. Yet the two final tonic chords (recalling the end of the first movement) maintain the sonata's ambivalence to the last: the first is *fortissimo* and affirmative, the second *piano* and irresolute. And thus concludes Schubert's most productive chamber music year.

Experimentation: The G Major Quartet, and Music for Violin and Piano (1826–27)

During 1825 and the first half of 1826 Schubert was chiefly occupied with songs and compositions for piano, including two complete sonatas (D. 845 and 850) and an unfinished third (D. 840). And it is virtually certain that in 1825 he achieved his goal of progressing from chamber music to a "grand symphony," the "Great" C Major (D. 944).[139] A number of publications appeared in these months, and Schubert's reputation grew steadily. Very likely all of these events buoyed his confidence sufficiently for him to put aside Schuppanzigh's criticisms of "Death and the Maiden" and resume composing chamber music. On the other hand, Schubert's personal circumstances were often unhappy. The Schober-Schubert circle of friends had been dwindling since 1824 owing to absence, illness, and conflict. And in the spring of 1826 Schubert's finances were in such a state that vacationing with his friends was impossible; by the end of May he was bored, lonely, and "not working at all."[140] Then in June he took up his most idiosyncratic chamber work, the huge G Major Quartet, D. 887, finishing the full score in only ten days (20–30 June).

The G Major Quartet, D. 887

Performance of the G Major Quartet requires about fifty-three minutes—fourteen more than "Death and the Maiden." To be sure, Schubert had sampled Beethoven's astonishing expansions of both symphony and quartet during the two years since completion of his own A Minor and D Minor Quartets.[141] But length alone is not the issue, and the influence of Beethoven still less so: within a fairly standard four-movement format Schubert has found his own manner of pressing the quartet idiom beyond its previous capacities. The relentless exertion and endurance demanded of all four players, particularly in the outer movements, is part and parcel of the work's essence.

So, too, is the affective ambivalence that, apparent particularly in the finales of the 1824 chamber music, is here further intensified through the restless device of seemingly ceaseless changes of mode, which occupy the outer movements from the introductory gesture to the codetta of the finale. There can be little doubt about the intended symbolism: Schubert had made the major-to-minor transformation central to the drama of infatuation and rejection in *Die schöne Müllerin*, his 1824 song cycle on poems of unrequited love and suicide by Müller, and modal juxtaposition becomes more explicitly identified with past happiness (major) and present pain (minor) in the *Winterreise* cycle of 1827 (also on poetry by Müller). Yet in the quartet, modal ambiguity becomes normative, occasionally to the point of irony in the Romantic sense—the constant alternation of thought and counterthought, self-creation and self-destruction—in short, dialectic, but without distinct teleology.[142]

Carl Dahlhaus, developing ideas set forth by Theodor Adorno, rightly observes that the quartet's first movement is epic, even novelistic, in scope and tone. It is a movement that unfolds through remembrance, "which turns from later events back to earlier ones," rather than through goal consciousness, "which presses on from earlier to later,"—and therein lies one of its chief differences from Beethoven. Yet Dahlhaus also points to the music's seemingly incongruous agitation, manifest chiefly in the feverish tremolos and triplets present in more than half its bars, which "hardly seems suited to the idea of epic composure"; the same can be said of the ubiquitous modal ambivalence. This interplay of opposites—surface agitation and epic recollection—is apparent from the outset. As Dahlhaus further observes, there is no "theme proper" in the first group; rather, it comprises a sequence of five thematic variants on interrelated kernels— measures 1–14, 15–23, 24–32, 33–53, and 54–63—which are rather like a meandering commentary or a series of expanding circles that proceed from a central idea not explicitly stated at the outset. The first of these segments (mm. 1–14) is clearly introductory in character: the major-minor juxtaposition grows ex nihilo, leading to jagged declamations and a brief echo. These plus half-step gestures and brief arpeggiations are the crucial motivic elements, related, as Dahlhaus puts it, "in the way that images of recollection overlap with one another."[143]

The second variant (15–23) expands the semitone motion into the *lamento* bass (G–F♯–F♮–E–E♭–D), a symbol by now commonplace in Schubert's chamber oeuvre. As Dahlhaus points out, the sequence of root motion in this linear intervalic pattern—G–D, F–C, E♭ . . . , which is also the basis of the next two variant segments—suggests the possibility of infinite motion, or perhaps even regression, in the descending flat direction. Such a sense of limitless continuation and timeless recollection informs much of the movement; indeed, at many points in the quartet it seems that only forced return to formal boundaries prevents the music from spiraling beyond its orbit.[146] One such passage in the first movement is the fourth variant of the first group, which begins to expand upon previously heard kernels: in measures 47–48 the motivic chromatic descent of the bass (C♯–C♮) is combined with contrary motion in the upper voice (a^2–$a\sharp^2$), which yields an augmented sixth. Prolonged throughout measures 49–50, this sonority becomes the dominant seventh of F, which pulls powerfully away from the centrality of G. Through the logic of half-step continuation, the chord is forcibly resolved (as an augmented sixth) to G^6 in measure 51, and the cadence in G of measure 54 launches the sequential meandering once again. This time the music ends up on the dominant of B (F♯, a motivic semitone away from G), which seems to prepare for a second subject in the mediant major. Through such moves musical logic is united with an unhurried manner of expression that is broadly nonteleological.

As Gülke notes, the ensuing second theme is the most inwardly circular in character that Schubert ever wrote.[145] The melodic line immediately reverses the G–F♯ contour of the previous modulation and undulates stepwise through the tetrachord e^1–a^1 for the entire first phrase; only gradually does its reclusive range expand. And B major remains unrealized; instead, the dominant of D is activated (A, a third away from F♯), then chromatically deflected to E minor (m. 67). The music circles back on itself, hints at return to tonic (m. 72), suggests the dominant of B again (73), and at length settles into the dominant (D, mm. 75–77), which ultimately turns out to be the structural secondary key area of the exposition. Thus the movement has woven its way around a circle of third-related key areas—G, B, and D. Now the second theme is repeated, varied, extended, and decorated with quaking triplets in three broad restatements that expand upon the circular third relations and semitone motion inherent in the theme itself, as follows: D → D minor → V/G (mm. 77–109); V/Bb → Bb → V/Bμ (mm. 110–41); V/D → D (mm. 142–68). Through such ongoing variation and seemingly boundless circularity, the dynamism of the Beethovenian sonata form dissolves in ways to be appropriated later in the century by Bruckner, Mahler, and to some extent, Brahms.[146]

Schubert's large-scale sequencing of the second theme resembles his usual tactics in development sections. And he proceeds thus in this development as well, concentrating now on blocks of the first group. The overall result, as Dahlhaus notes, is that the movement as a whole resembles a double variation set almost as much as a sonata form.[147] Just before the first ending (mm. 168–69), the last two bars launch a slithering chromatic bass descent leading back to G for the repeat; beginning at the second ending this extends *sans but précis* through a circle of major thirds comprising key areas rehearsed by the second theme—Bb, F♯, D, and again Bb, which ushers in a shimmering Eb episode of the first variant from the first thematic group (mm. 180–89; cf. mm. 15ff.). The entire process is renewed from the pitch level of Eb, bringing on the first-group episode (with countermelody) up a semitone, in E (mm. 201–9). A motivic modal shift to E minor (m. 210) inaugurates two sequential blocks drawn from the movement's introductory phrase; both modulate (via motivic intervals) up two semitones and then drop a major third (e → F [m. 218] → f♯ [m. 221] → d [mm. 225ff.], and similarly beginning from A minor in m. 234). Thereby the music arrives in the tonic minor; as though in protest, the fourth variant from the first group ascends over the inversion of the *lamento* bass (d–eb–eμ–f–f♯–g, mm. 255–61). But this has nowhere near the fierce energy of the tonic avoidance in "Death and the Maiden," and the futility of the gesture is already apparent at its high point (mm. 268–69). Nothing new or substantive has been accomplished in this development, which, in retrospect, does not seriously raise any such expectations.

The reprise commences (m. 278) in wistful resignation, reversing the major-to-minor conflict of the introductory bars, yet utterly without implication of resolution—a moment of "overpowering pathos" in Tovey's view.[148] Ambivalence, as symbolized by modal mixture, has indeed become normative. The bittersweet poise of reflective memory is maintained throughout the first three variants of the first group; these are the calmest bars of the widely spiraling movement. The energy of the exposition resumes with the fourth variant (m. 310), and from there on the recapitulation follows a fairly predictable course. (Notable variants include reduction of the second theme's appearances from four to three, and the lyrical cello countermelody woven into two of them [mm. 344 and 389ff.].) Recurrence of the chromatic passage that led to the second ending (mm. 415ff.; cf. m. 168) once again touches off the circle of thirds that opened the development, as though similar wide-ranging peregrinations might ensue. Were the music to unfold as it had there, the emphatic E♭ of measures 423ff. must lead to A♭ and thence downward in the flat direction—a course several times interrupted during the exposition's first group. Here again, reinterpretation by means of augmented sixth is made to restore tonic centrality (mm. 426–27; cf. mm. 49–51). Nevertheless, the major-minor ambiguity rampant throughout the movement continues down to its final bars.

And that ambivalence yields a startling link to the second movement: B♮, the most recent modal inflection of the G triad, launches the Andante *in medias res,* rather like the momentary interruption of an ongoing dream; *fzp* in all four voices, it turns out to be the single-pitch dominant of E minor.[149] The course of events continues in a rich melody for cello, delicately commented upon by the three upper voices (a texture recalling the treatment of the second theme in the reprise of the first movement). Yet the melodic stress of the seventh (a♮¹) over the dominant that inaugurates both of these paired phrases (mm. 3 and 7, and the *pp* repetitions in mm. 11 and 15) lends them the concluding, cadential character of an *Abgesang,* the rounding-off of a larger period. What, one wonders, was the music preceding that dominant-unison *sforzando?* Meanwhile (mm. 19ff.) the cello, maintaining the lead, moves away toward C, while the upper parts become eerily static: C then yields via familiar-sounding half step to the dominant of E minor, and shortly we realize our first glimpse of music leading up to the ominous *sforzando* unison. What follows vacillates wistfully between C and E minor and rounds off the short song form in its tonic.

The movement as a whole is a rondolike juxtaposition of contrasting blocks that may be sketched out as in Table 2.1. The shocking B sections abruptly drop a semitone and shift from somnolent quiescence to nightmarish horror in merely four bars—a contrast more violent than any other in Schubert's chamber oeuvre.[150] Utterly bloodcurdling are the unison shrieks of violin and viola, fixated on a rising minor third that becomes irrationally dissonant, incapable of yielding to resolution until the chromaticism recedes, at least temporarily (see Example 2.12). The tremolos, the initial tritone harmonic juxtaposition with emphasis of the diminished seventh (G minor–c♯°7, mm. 52–53), and the shrill calls themselves all echo the demonic realm of the Wolf's Glen in *Der Freischütz.*[151] The first B episode is in G minor: perhaps this, then, is the grim recollection beneath the surface of the first movement's major-minor ambivalence. The second arrives a semitone lower (F♯ minor), thereby composing out the long-familiar chromatic motive. As the primary material returns, tonally knocked off center (B minor, mm. 82ff.), the quaking pulse from the preceding fearful outbursts lingers on in lower and middle voices. Yet like a recurrent nightmare, B returns, now in D minor (mm. 120ff.); this time, however, the resolution is temporarily major (mm. 139ff.), and the closing phrases of the primary material itself (*a²″*) are softened by the sweetness of major after the tonic center is restored (mm. 175ff., *dolce*). The final appearance of the stern

TABLE 2.1. G Major String Quartet, D. 887, Second Movement, Outline of Form.

m.	1	19	32	40	60	82	98	111	120	140	155	167	175	183	196	204	212
	A			**B**		**A'**			**B'**			**A"**					**Coda**
	a^1	b	a^2	c	c	$a^{1'}$	b'	$a^{2''}$	c	b"	b"	$a^{1''}$	$a^{2''}$	b"	$a^{2''}$	a^2	
										(canon)	(canon)			(canon)			
tonal plan	e	C–V/e	(C)–e	g	f♯(→V/b)	b	G–V/b	(G)–b	d	D; →V/e	D; →V/e	e	E	C–V/e	E	(C)–e	**e–E**

dominant *sforzando* that had opened the movement (m. 194) is answered by this same bright transformation, yielding a stronger hint of the serene repose that may have preceded the music's rather abrupt rise to consciousness; thence, anyway, it seems to return in the concluding four bars of tonic major. But this peaceful conclusion in no sense resolves the movement's conflicts. Rather, as in sleep and dreaming, the kaleidoscopic shifting of affects and images has temporarily come to rest.

EXAMPLE 2.12.   Schubert, Quartet in G, D. 887 (1826), mvt. 2, mm. 52–59: harmonic outline.

The scurrying nocturnal scherzo is most notable for its fixation on pitch repetition (recalling the tremolos of the two preceding movements), semitone neighbor notes (particularly ♮6̂–5̂) and static two-bar units that do not build longer phrases. This music is much akin to Mendelssohn, and one wonders whether Schubert may have had in mind a *Walpurgisnacht* scene, as did Mendelssohn in the famous scherzo of his Octet (composed in 1825, but not published until 1830; neither composer would have known the specific work in question of the other).[152] The trio, in G major, at first recalls the lyrical cello solos of the second and first movements; here, however, the simplistic repetitiveness and insubstantial texture sound almost childishly naïve and thus gently ironic. The trio's second half broadens into a flowing ländler, also rather too idyllic for credence; like the trio of the A Minor Quartet, this one seems to be the recollection of an illusory "schöne Welt."

For the finale Schubert again strikes up the tarantella, which now becomes more riotous and relentless than that of "Death and the Maiden." As there, the structure, albeit vast, is entirely logical: a sonata-rondo with displaced reprise of the primary material, as shown in Table 2.2. Yet as in the first movement of this G Major Quartet, the nature and treatment of material in the finale is at odds with its formal outline. In this case, the perpetual rhythmic drive, endless two-bar phrases, dizzying modal shifts, lurching modulations (frequently by half step, as the table shows), and wild dynamic changes yield forth an intoxicating, restless delirium that obscures formal boundaries; the first movement's moderately paced wanderings have given way to an infinite Dionysian dance, whose purportedly curative powers seem irrelevant. Most striking in this respect are those passages labeled "a, exp.[anded]" in the table (mm. 374, 406, and 650ff.): here the defiantly relentless rise of the melody over the chromatically descending *lamento* bass is hair-raising in its harmonic ambiguity. Moreover, the gesture intensifies in each subsequent appearance by spiraling through seemingly endless circles of thirds, the most suspenseful of which is saved for last (m. 650). Less bizarre, yet of similar abandon, are the impossible triplet arpeggiations that drive the first violin toward cadence in the *d* sections, then swamp the entire quartet in wildly pitching third juxtapositions (mm. 125 and 495ff.). At the opposite extreme lies the "new" melody (*f*) of the development, which emerges in stable C♯ minor (i.e., removed from the tonic by the diabolical interval of a tritone): this hushed, entreating lied fragment is like a muffled plea for release from the frenzied uproar, and seems to recall, in distorted rhythms, the plaintive lyricism of the cello solos in preceding movements of the quartet.[153]

"Has Death and the Maiden, now permeated by the experiences of the D Minor Quartet, been composed a second time—only more extremely, and without direct motivic connection?" This is the question posed by Peter Gülke at the end of his essay on the D Minor Quartet. The answer, in certain senses, is yes. But the monumental strangeness of the G Major has left it something of a work apart. Although Schubert apparently managed to have it read in 1827 and probably included one movement of it on his now-famous private concert of March 1828, to our knowledge it was not performed in its entirety until 1850, and remained unpublished until 1851. Even twenty years later, a Berlin critic would complain of its extreme length, excessive use of tremolo, modulatory and formal ambiguities, modal shifts—in short, just those features that make the work so extraordinary.[154]

Works for Violin and Piano, 1826–27

The Rondeau brilliant in B minor, D. 895 (1826). Nine years had elapsed since Schubert had composed a duo for two of the instruments he himself played. That he returned to the violin-and-piano combination in 1826 is apparently due to the arrival in Vienna that year of the Bohemian violin virtuoso Josef Slawjk. Slawjk participated in the 1827 reading of the G Major Quartet mentioned above, and he gave the first performances of both the *Rondeau brilliant* (D. 895, dated October 1826) and the C Major Fantasy (D. 934, completed in December 1827). Both new duos incorporate notable elements of *style hongrois*, which suggests that Slawjk was conversant with that musical dialect. His keyboard partner for both works was Karl Maria von Bocklet, whose playing Schubert much admired and to whom he had dedicated the D Major Sonata, Op. 53 (D. 850), another work marked by Gypsy idiom.[155] Unlike Schubert's earlier sonatas, these new violin-and-piano pieces are big works for top-flight performers; their

(Exposition)

m.	1	16	25	44	60	73	92	147	209	231
	A						**B**			
	a	b^1	b^2	a	c (codetta)	trans.	d	d′	e	~d
tonal plan	g/G	B♭	b, g	g/G→b♭	G	~	D; ~	b; ~	b→D	D
	I						**V**	**(iii)**		**V**

(Development)

m.	256	267	298	307	323	339	355	374	390	406
	A'	**C**								
	a	b^1	b^2	b^2	f (new—from b^2)	f + $b^{2\prime}$	b^2	a, exp.	c	a, exp.
tonal plan	c, a	A♭–a–e–b	B	c→V/c#	c#	c#	f#~~	d/D~~!	D	c#~~!
	I									→**V/G**

(Reprise)

m.	430	441	462	517	579	601	627	642	650	680
	A, truncated	trans.	**B**				**A''**			**Coda**
	c		d	d′	e	~d	a	b	a, exp.	c, exp.
tonal plan	G	~	G; ~	e; ~	e→G	G	g/G	B♭	b♭~~!!	G
	I		**I**	**(vi)**		**I**			→**V/G**	**I**

unusual titles and formats apparently indicate Schubert's desire to provide the proliferating sect of virtuosi with music both challenging and more substantial than their usual flamboyant fare. In that regard, the success of the *Rondeau brilliant* is evident from an anonymous review that appeared in 1828, the year after its publication:

> The grandiose talent of the renowned song and romance composer [i.e., Schubert] is many-sided and tries itself in every branch, as do all those who possess the spirit of true and upward-striving art. The work under notice shows a bold master of harmony, who gives his picture a strong, vigorous fundamental tone and within that knows how to unite his shapes and groups in such a way that they all go to the making of a beautiful whole. A fiery imagination animates this piece and draws the player to the depths and heights of harmony, borne now by a mighty hurricane, now by gentle waves.
>
> Although the whole is brilliant, it is not indebted for its existence to mere figurations, such as grin at us in thousandfold contortions from many a composition and fatigue the soul. The inventive spirit has here often beaten its wings mightily enough and lifted us up with it. Both the pianoforte and the fiddle require a practised artist, who must be prepared for passages which have not by any means attained to their right of citizenship by endless use, but betoken a succession of new and inspired ideas. The player will feel attracted in an interesting way by a beautiful harmonic interchange.[156]

This is perceptive yet circumspect criticism: the piece sounds weird, even today. In certain respects it seems like a pendant to the finale of the G Major Quartet—restless rhythmic energy and unexpected harmonic turns overrun the bounds of a somewhat sprawling hybrid rondo structure. But greater contrasts of pulse and melodic style in its various components, plus the recurring interaction of its slow introduction, lend the rondo an impromptu, patchwork quality befitting the Gypsy flavor apparent in much of the music. In the quartet's finale the relentless leitmotif from the opening bars was split-second minor-major juxtaposition; here it is the half-diminished seventh chord. First heard at the end of the introduction, this eerie sound and its milder derivative, the "added sixth chord," punctuate the rondo theme in both its minor and major manifestations respectively (see Example 2.13). Like a nagging obsession, this two-sided sonority seems never to resolve decisively, but crops up anew, even in unlikely contexts, right into the final return of the rondo before the coda—promissory notes unfulfilled, so to say.[157] As the pivot from ambivalent introduction to pungent rondo, the chord sums up the unsettled vacillation between declamatory severity, sensual delight, and wandering lassitude of the Andante's Gypsy-like improvisatory style, which is shot through with deceptions, double plays, and diminished sevenths. The work's maniacally brilliant coda finally pushes ambivalence aside, although even here harmonic flashes of indecision are apparent (mm. 677 and 689ff.).

EXAMPLE 2.13.   Schubert, *Rondeau brilliant* in B Minor for Violin and Piano, D. 895 (1826), (a) mm. 47–54; (b) mm. 65–68.

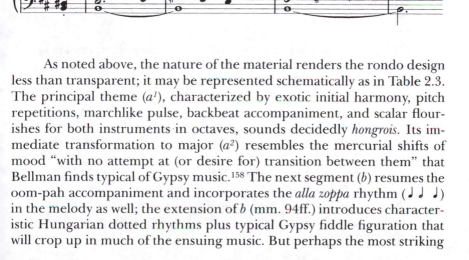

As noted above, the nature of the material renders the rondo design less than transparent; it may be represented schematically as in Table 2.3. The principal theme (*a¹*), characterized by exotic initial harmony, pitch repetitions, marchlike pulse, backbeat accompaniment, and scalar flourishes for both instruments in octaves, sounds decidedly *hongrois*. Its immediate transformation to major (*a²*) resembles the mercurial shifts of mood "with no attempt at (or desire for) transition between them" that Bellman finds typical of Gypsy music.[158] The next segment (*b*) resumes the oom-pah accompaniment and incorporates the *alla zoppa* rhythm (♩ ♩ ♩) in the melody as well; the extension of *b* (mm. 94ff.) introduces characteristic Hungarian dotted rhythms plus typical Gypsy fiddle figuration that will crop up in much of the ensuing music. But perhaps the most striking passage in *style hongrois* is that labeled *e'* (mm. 437ff.), in which the added-sixth chord, dotted rhythms, Gypsy fiddling, and wholly unpredictable harmonic twists yield music of truly exotic, even bizarre, character.

The C Major Fantasy, D. 934 (1827). Composed more than a year later, the C Major Fantasy is a more stable, substantial work, yet nevertheless intriguingly original in design. As in Schubert's earlier "Wanderer" Fantasy, D. 760 (1822), four principal sections are joined without pause, but no longer in the sequence and spirit of a four-movement sonata, as Einstein notes.[159] Rather, they form a *cordon bleu* layering that highlights both the distinctiveness and blending of all four ingredients. To this end the two quick movements (second and forth) eschew the closure of sonata or rondo in favor of modified strophic designs that promote transition and recall. In addition, all major sections of the piece are linked by head motives based on prominent thirds, ascending and descending, both major and minor (see Example 2.14). And the tonal scheme of the whole—C–a–A♭–C—is based on thirds as well.[160]

EXAMPLE 2.14.   Schubert, Fantasy in C for Violin and Piano, D. 934 (1827): motivic connections among the principal sections.

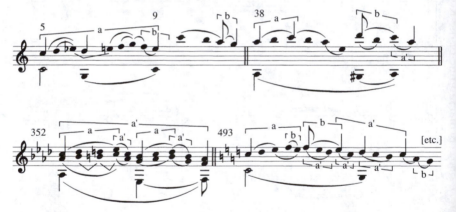

The richly colorful introduction, *andante molto,* features keyboard tremolos in imitation of the Hungarian cimbalom, the malleted string instrument central to Gypsy bands in both soloistic and accompanimental capacities. As Franz Liszt observes,

> The *zymbala* shares with the first violin the right to develop certain passages and to prolong certain variations indefinitely according to the good pleasure of the moment. He is necessarily one of those who conduct the musical poem; having either created it at leisure, or being about to improvise it at the moment; and he imposes upon others the duty of surrounding him, sustaining him, even guessing him in order to sing the same funeral hymn or give himself up to the same mad freak of joy.[161]

TABLE 4.3. *Rondeau brillant* in B Minor, D. 895, Formal Outline of the Rondo

m.	51	65	83	89	103	110	124	164	178	192	224	244	262
	A a¹	a²	b	b, ext.	(~a)	**B** c	c, ext.	c	c	c	d (new; ~b)		(c)
tonal plan	⌀7 → **b** **i**	B	B		⌀7 → b	D **III** *circle of thirds	D∼→f#	F#; → D **(V)** *	Bb *	D **III** *	D	F#→D	D

*circle of thirds

m.	269	281	296	314	320	334	345	402	413	437	467	489
	(A) recall of Intro.	**A** a¹	a²	b	b ext.	b	**C (developmental . . .)** e (new; cf. intro.)	e (recall of intro.)	e, developed	e' (Gypsy)	e	e
tonal plan	⌀7 →	B **i**	B	B	⌀7 → b	B	G; (B) G **VI**	g∼	F(+6); ↝ C; Eb	Eb → G	e	e

m.	527	549	575	586	601	621	627	653	667
	e, dev. (cf. m. 413)	e' (Gypsy)	a²	**A** a¹	a²	b	b ext.	(~a)	**Coda** b
tonal plan	g	C(+6); ↝ G →	⌀7 [!]	b → D **i**	D **(III)**	B	B → D∼	⌀7 → b	**B** **I**

Broadly speaking, that characterizes the quixotic interaction of parts in this two-strophe introduction, which concludes on the dominant of A with Gypsy-style flourishes for each instrument.

The Allegretto that follows (mapped in Table 2.4) is based on a rather stiff, square marching tune *all'ongarese,* replete with syncopations, snapped grace notes, and, as it inflects the relative major (mm. 53ff.), spondees. Its second statement (mm. 64ff.) manifests, as Einstein puts it, "a charming tendency towards 'canon.'"[162] This moves directly into a complementary major section laden with Gypsy figurations for both instruments, and the ensuing modulations lead to a dominant pedal (mm. 131ff.) prolonged by lengthy, quasi-improvisatory scale flourishes in contrary motion, spiced with unpredictable chromatic neighbors and passing tones. The second strophe (mm. 182ff.) initially proceeds like the first, except that the change to major is also a shift to the mediant. There follows a new contrapuntal treatment of the head motive, beginning in tonic minor and sequencing sharpward by fifths all the way to G♯/A♭ minor (m. 297), with changes of instrumentation for the rushing sixteenths at each tonal juncture. Five measures later these swirling scalar lines are fused with *alla zoppa* accompaniment in the piano to launch a fifty-bar dominant preparation of A♭: this ushers in the slow-movement variation set.

As in previous chamber works, the theme is derived from one of Schubert's enchanting songs, "Sei mir gegrüßt"; what grows out of it, however, is less akin to the splendid quartet variations he penned in 1824 than to the travesty of "Trockne Blumen" written in the same year. While some listeners find the Fantasy's set less annoying than the earlier one for flute and piano, critical opinion has been less than favorable: Einstein regards this Andantino as the "brilliant weakness" of the Fantasy as a whole, and Westrup likens it to "watching performing seals at a circus."[163] Typically, the diminutions become progressively busier in each variation, and they place heavy demands upon both performers. The instruments share the lead in alternation (violin/piano/violin), and each new variation absorbs something from the rhythmic patterns of the previous one. Noteworthy amid all this *broderie* is Schubert's skillfully maintained allusion to the regular offbeat accompaniment pattern so characteristic of the theme's first appearance. After three elaborations the song returns in simpler guise (mm. 458ff.), and through slight extension of a characteristic phrase (m.

TABLE 2.4. Fantasy in C Major, D. 934, Formal Outline of First Allegretto

m.	38	83	131	182	219	263
	A			**A**		
	a	b	b′	a	b	a′ (~developmental)
tonal plan	a	A ⟶V—		a	C	a–e–b–f♯–c♯–a♭– V/A♭
	i	**I**		**i**	**III**	**i** ⟶**V/A♭**

464), the dominant of C is at hand, embellished seemingly impromptu by both soloists (mm. 465–79).

Now the cimbalom flutter resumes, and the reentry of the fiddle underscores how closely the variation tune resembles the quietly fervid melody of the Fantasy's introduction; moreover, in measures 484ff. we realize that the keyboard had already foreshadowed one of the notable figurations of the third variation (mm. 434ff.; cf. also mm. 9 ff.). But the course of the introduction is already being curtailed, which signals transition rather than reprise. As before, A minor arrives beneath the violin's high e³ (mm. 487–88; cf. mm. 28–29). But now that line continues in a slow chromatic rise as the harmonic course becomes intensely ambiguous: a modified "omnibus" progression (mm. 489–91) is followed a pair of descending $\frac{4}{2}$s—and suddenly C major emerges, Allegro vivace.

The ebullient finale is closely related to the second movement, both in its vigorous main theme (a joyful major-mode transformation of the stocky Hungarian tune heard earlier) and in its overall design, outlined in Table 2.5 (cf. Tables 2.4 and 2.5). Once again, there are two open-ended strophes, the second of which moves away by third relation (m. 579), then modulates farther, precipitating an A minor articulation of the head motive (m. 611) that ultimately yields to a dominant preparation. At the end of the second movement, dominant preparation led smoothly to the A♭ variation theme; here in the finale, however, A♭ is a deception, and the recurrence of the song is an unexpected bonus that quickly becomes the lyrical culmination of the entire Fantasy.[164] The coda provides a short, high-spirited tag with delightful flecks of harmonic color.

Despite its many charms, the Fantasy was not immediately successful. Following the premiere (20 January 1828), one Viennese critic claimed Slawjk's playing was conspicuously lacking in solidity, while another noted that the Fantasy "occupied too much of the time a Viennese is prepared to devote to pleasures of the mind. The hall emptied gradually, and the writer confesses that he too is unable to say anything about the conclusion of this piece of music."[165] An unfavorable notice also appeared in the Leipzig *Allgemeine musikalische Zeitung*, which dissuaded the publisher H. A. Probst from accepting the work. It did not appear in print until 1850 and is today performed and recorded only sporadically.

Consolidation: The Piano Trios and the Quintet

It is curious that, save for the youthful Sonate of 1812, Schubert did not turn to the piano trio until the last years of his life. Nor have we any clue as to why he did so then, unless perhaps the duos written for Slawjk and Bocklet sparked his interest in the fuller form of string and keyboard music. He must long since have known Beethoven's efforts in the genre.

TABLE 2.5. Fantasy in C Major, D. 934, Formal Outline of Concluding Allegretto

m.	493	508	525	533	555	563	579	587	611	639	665
	A				**A**					**song quotation**	**Coda**
	a¹a¹	a²a²	b	b, ext. (~a)	a¹	a²a²	b	b, ext. (~a)	a¹′a²′		
tonal plan	C	Vped	C	C → a–e–b	C	Vped ↝	A	A → f♯–c♯–g♯	a → V/C	A♭; →V/C	C
	I				**I**		**VI**	**♭VI**	**vi—V**	**♭VI**	**I**

(A passage in the slow movement of his own B♭ Trio would certainly suggest he knew the "Archduke," and he probably heard that piece performed in March 1826.)[166] But whether he found the Beethoven trios pleasing, uninteresting, or intimidating remains unknown. To judge from Schubert's chamber music of 1824, however, he was by then fully prepared to address the piano trio on his own terms, as indeed he did within the next three years.

Yet there remain questions about the chronology of the two trios, particularly as regards the dating of the B♭, about which little is certain. Opinions vary from that of John Reed, who places the B♭ Trio in 1825, to the view held by Arnold Feil and Robert Winter that it may have been written in early 1828—that is, after the E♭ Trio.[167] Eva Badura-Skoda's review of the documentary evidence may be summarized as follows: Schubert's autograph manuscripts of the E♭ Trio indicate he had written three movements of that work by November 1827; we know as well that in the course of arrangements with the publisher Probst the following year, Schubert insisted that it bear the opus number 100. For the B♭ Trio, no autograph or specific date has come down to us. However, in addition to the trios as we know them, there survives a slow movement in E♭, posthumously published as the Nocturne (later "Notturno"), Op. 148 (D. 897): this has long been assumed to be a rejected slow movement for the B♭ Trio, and it is written on a paper type that Schubert used only between October 1827 and April 1828. In 1829, the year after Schubert's death, the catalogue of the Viennese publisher Leidesdorf lists the B♭ as "Opus 99. Premier grand Trio," although the piece was not actually published until 1836 (and then as "Premier Grand Trio . . . Oeuvre 99"), after Leidesdorf's business had been absorbed by Diabelli. It thus appears plausible that Schubert himself designated the B♭ Trio his First, Op. 99. The E♭ was presented in Schubert's concert of March 1828 as "New Trio for piano-forte, violin, and violoncello, performed by Herrn Karl Maria von Bocklet, Böhm [violin] and Linke [cello]." But a "New Trio" by Schubert had also been introduced by Schuppanzig, Bocklet, and Schuppanzigh's cellist Linke at a public subscription concert of the Schuppanzigh Quartet in late December 1827. As Badura-Skoda points out, it was a matter of honor in Vienna for composers who arranged their own concerts (as Schubert did in March 1828) to present one or two works that were genuinely new to the public. We know that Schuppanzigh and colleagues also played a trio at a Schubertiade held in late January 1828. Therefore it is possible, but not certain, that the B♭ Trio had been performed in December 1827, and perhaps also January 1828.[168]

In any case, unlike the two quartets of 1824, the two piano trios form a balanced pair of opposites, as Robert Schumann was among the first to note when the B♭ Trio was published in 1836:

> A glance at Schubert's trio, and all miserable human commotion vanishes, and the world shines in new splendour. About ten years ago a

Schubert trio in E flat went across ordinary musical life of the day like an angry thunderstorm. It was his hundredth opus. Shortly after, in November 1828, he died. This recently published trio seems to be an older work. To be sure, its style does not refer to any earlier period, and it may well have been written a short time before the famous one in E flat major. Intrinsically, however, they bear little resemblance to each other. The first movement, which in the other is inspired by deep indignation as well as boundless longing, is graceful and virginal in the one before us. The adagio, there a sigh tending to swell anxiety, is here a happy dream, a rising and falling of genuine feeling. The scherzos somewhat resemble each other, but I give preference to that in the earlier published [E♭] trio. I cannot decide as to the last movements. In a word, the Trio in E flat major is more spirited, masculine, and dramatic; this one is move passive, lyric, and feminine. Let the work, which he bequeathed to us, be a precious legacy! Time, though producing much that is beautiful, will not soon produce another Schubert![169]

Despite gender metaphors unpopular today, Schumann's review highlights many of the contrasts in character between the two trios. Yet both are more stable, poised, and less experimental than the other chamber works of 1826–27, the most imposing of which—the G Major Quartet and C Major Fantasy—Schumann could not then have known.

The B♭ Major Piano Trio, D. 898, and the "Notturno" Movement, D. 897

In key, tempo, and triadic main theme, the opening movement of the B♭ Major Piano Trio seems to recall Beethoven's "Archduke," Op. 97. But in other respects the two works differ: whereas Beethoven seems bent on dispersing the powerful dynamism of sonata form characteristic of his earlier "heroic style," Schubert is concerned with the successful linking of two lyrical, liedlike thematic groups, a compositional challenge that dates back to his "Unfinished" and culminates in the String Quintet, his last chamber work. In both the "Unfinished" Symphony and the A Minor Quartet (D. 804), the predictable minor-to-major change of mode in the modulatory scheme provides necessary contrast between the song themes; in the B♭ Major Trio, broadening the first theme into asymmetrical phrase lengths and expanding the transitional materials serves that purpose rather differently. The traditional twofold presentation of the main theme (mm. 1 and 26ff.) here sandwiches a mildly developmental extension of its triplet motive (mm. 12ff.) that sets up a false modulation to the submediant (V/G, m. 18ff.). In its second statement the melody moves timidly to the dominant (m. 37), followed by more triplet expansion, this time yielding expectations of the mediant (V/D, m. 49ff.). Schubert then deploys his characteristic device of sustaining a single tone and slipping an unexpected third beneath it (mm. 57–59), thereby giving full rein to the restrained rapture of the second lied. Following its double statement, the tail of this melody is also extended and developed (mm. 77ff.), and in such a manner that the exposition closes with the serenity of its second theme in question, inflected by a rather grim-sounding chromatic neighbor (f–g♭, mm. 100–101ff.)—an excellent bit of stage-setting for the development.

That such rhetorical *dubitatio* should precipitate modal transformation of the main theme at the double bar—tonic minor, no less—sounds implausible, and is quickly rejected.[170] Instead, the theme's head motive is contrapuntally combined with dotted arpeggiation (derived from mm. 37ff.) and put into blocklike sequences, largely but not unequivocally major in orientation, leading to three bars of chromatic contrary motion that bring on the dominant of F (mm. 132–34 and ff.; cf. also m. 90): this is the first high point of the development. By means of the "third-under" modulation that originally introduced it, the second theme reappears (in A♭) together with the oft-heard triplets from the end of the principal idea: treated as invertible counterpoint, this charming phrase passes through a circle of thirds (A♭–E–C), becoming *pianissimo* in the process. Now follows a long rise in both pitch and dynamics as the first bar of the second theme ascends sequentially in two-bar units. A dominant pedal has arrived by measure 161; however, the tension only increases, peaking in the high g♭'s for all three instruments: the same menacing shadow that darkened the second theme at the close of the exposition has now decidedly shifted the music's modal orientation, and B♭ minor seems to be the inevitable next step.

Yet the crisis does not ensue: the pedal remains, but the upper lines descend, becoming quieter. Major and minor alternate in conflict for ten bars (beginning in m. 173) as the g♭ chromatic neighbor pulls at the dominant pedal without dislodging it. From this standoff emerges a charming false reprise, softer than *pp*, in, of all keys, G♭ (m. 187)—as though the foregoing conflict could be resolved through unexpected magical synthesis. In the exposition, the second presentation of the main theme had modulated "timidly" by fifth: so, too, here (with mild intensification), as if to back away from G♭ through the circle of fifths (D♭, m. 198). But D♭ is closely related to B♭ minor (mm. 206–8), and only when g♭¹ yields linearly to g♮¹ (208–209) is the return to tonic major permitted; the third thematic reprise is the genuine one. This is the most remarkably sophisticated process of development and reprise encountered to date in Schubert's chamber music, and arguably, in the whole corpus of it.

Equally remarkable is the ensuing Andante un poco mosso, a movement of exceptional warmth and richness of nuance. Based on liedlike material almost throughout, it is cast in the large ternary format (ABA') favored by the Romantics that, as Winter notes, Schubert adopts for the majority of his later slow movements.[171] The initial A section is bipartite: its second half, a wistful variation of the first, is repeated, recalling strophic procedure in lieder. Throughout the opening twenty-two bars, returning-note triplets undulate in the right hand of the piano part as bass motion is kept to a minimum; over this placid accompaniment the cello unfolds a melody that, serene yet delicately touched with longing, is among the most memorable in all of Schubert. Part of its reassuring calm is due to repetitive symmetry—five two-bar groupings in the pattern *aba'b'c;* only the *c* phrase, with its chromatically descending bass, hints vaguely of agitated spots in the first movement (an allusion to be heard subsequently).

Almost as enchanting as the melody itself is the countermelody given to the cello when the violin takes over the second presentation of the theme (mm. 13ff.). Just before the double bar the music modulates to the dominant; now the triplets quietly vanish as the piano assumes the principal singing role, abandoning the middle register to the strings, which weave still richer countermelodies. The basic pattern of the ten-bar theme is maintained, but a hushed shift of mode recalls the chill associated with B♭ minor in the first movement. Major mode and lulling triplets return with the dominant pedal at measure 33, only to be questioned four bars later by a dip to G♭ (another troubled area of the first movement): chromaticism now intensifies the *b'* and *c* segments of the theme, and the bass descends in the familiar *lamento* manner. This upsurge is delicately quelled, seemingly at the last moment, and the serenity of E♭ returns temporarily (m. 41) in a phrase echoing both the opening theme and its accompaniment in slightly displaced rhythms.

The undercurrent of passion in this music breaks forth in C minor at the beginning of the B section, and again the role of anguished singer falls to the piano. Now the melodic emphasis of raised seventh and lowered sixth degrees, along with the syncopated accompaniment, suggests Gypsy influence. But most striking is the dissolution of this episode well before its fury seems spent—first toward G♭, then to the home key of E♭, and finally settling into C major for what turns out to be a sunny, full-scale variation of it (mm. 71ff.). Thus the B section is bipartite as well. When the variation has drawn to a close, Schubert invokes yet again the "third-under" modulation of the first movement, here with ravishing effect as the violin executes a long *messa di voce*. Like the recapitulation in the first movement, the reprise of the A section comes about gradually, in this case through third modulations that will arrive in E♭ only for its second half (the varied version of the theme, m. 104). In the reprise, the violin leads: the harmonic frisson of E major (mm. 88ff.) as it sings the *b'* and *c* phrases of the theme is most delightful, and when the cello reenters, the violin takes the countermelody beneath it, yielding a warm sonority reminiscent of the development in Beethoven's "Archduke" (mm. 107ff.). This extraordinary music takes its leave only reluctantly, and then in another apparent bow to Beethoven—a sixfold sounding of the "Lebewohl" horn call motive from his Sonata in E♭, Op. 81a (g¹/e♭¹–f¹/b♭–e♭¹/g, mm. 127–31).

If there is a just criticism to be made of the B♭ Trio as a whole, it is that the work is somewhat "top heavy," owing to the richness and complexity of both the first and second movements. If the so-called Notturno in E♭ of 1827–28 was indeed the trio's slow movement at some point, the work as a whole may thereby have been better balanced. Yet while Schubert's preference for the current Andante seems justified, the very different Notturno is unique: whoever named it must have recognized that this is love music. Indeed, it is perhaps the most erotic movement in all of Schubert's chamber music, and ought not to be dismissed as a failure rejected by the composer. The piece is a simple ABA′B′A″ rondo, sonorously sensuous throughout, based on two related, endlessly recurring one-bar motives in parallel motion: the cumulative effect of so much luscious ostinato can be intoxicating, even slightly numbing. Cello and violin almost never emerge as individual voices, but rather remain intertwined in parallel motion, together trading the leading and accompanying roles with the piano.

The opening indication in the piano part, *pp appassionato,* summarizes the character of the A section—a static yet highly charged atmosphere in which the minor variants of the recurrent caressing motive seem to take on magnified significance akin to the semiarticulate utterances of lovers. The latent passion becomes triumphantly overt in the B section, where mounting excitement is projected through contraction of the basic dactylic rhythmic ratios (¢ ♩. ♩ → 𝄵 ♩ ♩) and through "expressive" tonality that ascends from E♭ to E, and then to F at the climax (mm. 66ff.).[172] The outcome of this culmination, however, is immediate dynamic collapse followed by wistful chromaticized harmonic wandering over a slowly descending bass (mm. 72–82); E♭ returns, but with little sense of fulfillment. The second B section (mm. 101ff.) is notably shorter and less ecstatic, and its high point arrives in the less elevated region of the tonic (mm. 118ff.). In the final return of the principal material the music nearly evaporates, *ppp,* in bars uncannily tinged by the minor subdominant (mm. 138–40; cf. mm. 22ff.). A brief rally of energy brings a recall of the previous modulations to E and F before the piece fades into serene somnolence.

Einstein has observed that the main theme of the finale in Op. 99 is derived from Schubert's 1815 song "Skolie," the text of which runs: "Let us, in the bright May morning, take delight in the brief life of the flower, before its fragrance disappears."[173] That indeed seems to be the mood of both remaining movements in the B♭ Trio. The scherzo is cheerful throughout, clouded only momentarily by the contrary-motion chromaticism that signaled unease in the previous movements (mm. 35–41), while the trio has the open warmth of a simple ländler. The last movement, however, is an unusual approach to the seemingly endless finale that Schubert had preferred for his chamber works since 1824. Both pulse and tempo are more moderate than the tarantella movements of the D Minor and G Major Quartets or the Gypsy finale of the Octet; in place of speed, Schubert here invokes formal ambiguity to create the illusion of a spring day without end.

The movement is labeled "Rondo" in the first edition (presumably based on the lost autograph), and its thematic components are indeed blocklike and symmetrical in the manner of a rondo. But as Thomas Denny has shown, the piece is best grasped as a sonata form in which the functions of development and recapitulation are elided.[174] The exposition has arrived solidly in the dominant by measure 152, and there is strong closing material in measures 176–230. Following a simple transition, the development proper gets underway in Db (bVI/V) at measure 250 with an episode derived from the transitional material of the exposition (mm. 52ff.). A mere thirty-two bars later, however (m. 281), the complete first theme appears in Eb. Clearly it is too early for a subdominant recapitulation, and more developmental material in fact follows; then the main idea returns in Bb (m. 345), followed by yet another developmental digression. Only with the tonic recurrence of the transitional material (m. 385) does the music resume the exposition's course of events and rationalize it to the tonic key. Thus development and reprise overlap to an extraordinary and perhaps unique extent, as Denny notes.[175]

The endless nature of the movement is highlighted at the onset of the coda, which seems to launch the development yet again in a modulation of a third to the previously problematic tonal center of Gb (m. 583); this is set right by semitone shift to the dominant thirteen measures later, which resolves into a dozen bars of tonic-ostinato and diminuendo. A madcap chaser brings the piece to its final tapering close and terminating cadence. Yet, as is often the case in Schubert, the music seems to resound into the silence that frames it.

The Eb Major Piano Trio, Op. 100, D. 929 (1827)

Schumann was certainly right in characterizing the Eb Major Piano Trio, Op. 100, as more spirited and dramatic than the Bb. It is also longer, more complex, and in its way more unified: drawing on the precedent of Beethoven's Fifth Symphony, Schubert laces the work with cyclic connections that culminate in the finale, which recalls both the first and, more hauntingly, the second movement. The overall effect is a striking extension of the ambivalence manifest in so many of the chamber works from 1824 on. Schumann found "deep indignation as well as boundless longing" in the first movement of Op. 100—and such there is, within a framework of ostensible joyousness. This is music that sets forth an exceptional number of disjunct ideas in seemingly random array; yet as Example 2.15 shows, all are related through three motivic kernels: the neighbor note (marked " ♪ " and "n"), the third-unfolding (𝒩), and the arpeggiation ("arp.," slurred). In addition, the neighbor-note motive is also deployed linearly in the unexpected harmonic shifts, usually by third, that pepper the movement.[176]

The first of these, to Gb (m. 24), disrupts what had been a seemingly ordinary consequent phrase beginning at measure 16. Yet this jolt is so powerful that the tonic is never firmly reestablished until the recapitulation, more than three hundred bars hence. The same Gb neighbor to F is

EXAMPLE 2.15.   Schubert, Piano Trio in E♭, D. 929 (1827), mvt. 1: motivic kernels.

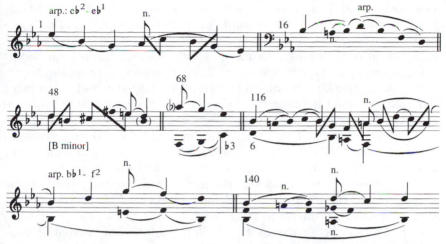

enharmonically reinterpreted in measures 44–47, which precipitates the shocking drop to B minor (enharmonically C♭, the lowered sixth scale degree) and the onset of the repeated-eighth motive—both of which will play a crucial role in the trio as a whole. Beneath the hushed clatter that ensues looms a melody, yet a somewhat insipid one; it wanders, vacillating from minor to major, and ultimately brings on the dominant of the main key (mm. 84ff.). But only after thirty bars of indecisive rehash does this third key area yield a new tune (mm. 116ff.), one so airy that the music is all but dispersed from the wisp of a single f¹, *ppp*, held onto by the cello (mm. 138–39). What follows is the movement's single moment of uncomplicated lyricism, yet it, too, is piqued by chromatic neighbor inflection. As a fairly stock closing gesture (mm. 156ff.) seems about to wind things up, an utterly unexpected flash of nearly celestial brightness brings a sharp pang of Schumann's "boundless longing" (again by means of neighbor notes and third relation: m. 161). But the dominant returns, and the exposition closes with additional expanded neighbor activity.

In contrast to the unpredictable variety of the exposition, the would-be development proceeds with the formulaic regularity of a parabolic curve moving into infinity. Three long episodes based solely on the simple lyrical idea of the exposition's close (mm. 140ff.) move through a circle of thirds followed by a half step. The first runs as follows: B/b (m. 195) → D (m. 212) → F (m. 220) → (f♯) (m. 239) → V/f♯ (243); the second and third begin at measure 247 and 299 respectively. This trancelike pattern is broken to arrest the limitless motion on B♭, the dominant, near the end of the third passage (m. 337), and there follows a seemingly interminable interchange between dominant and ♭6̂ (C♭); texture and dynamics dwindle. Then, with no motivation (other than the prolonged dominant) to do so, the reprise launches itself, *forte,* as though the foregoing music were perfectly normal. Very likely Schubert is responding to the sort of minimal development, even "anti-development," occasionally encountered in Beethoven from the time of the "Archduke" onward; the latter piece certainly comes to mind as an example of unmotivated reprise. But Schubert's procedure in this trio is so blatantly simplistic, especially by comparison to the developments of "Death and the Maiden" or the B♭ Trio, that one can only suppose he chose to project precisely the sort of undirected, repetitive, infinite wandering we find here. Still, it is a piece that does not want to cease: the coda marches resolutely up (and down) to C♭, the disputatious lowered sixth degree active in so much of the movement. And no sooner does a final-sounding tonic cadence countermand this move (mm. 581–83) than the second subject recurs with tonic minor leading to ♭VI once more—as though the music might cycle through its course indefinitely. Restoration of the tonic is made to call a halt; yet the final gesture is the rhythm of the second subject (♩ ♫♫♩), which echoes in the ear well after the music has ceased.

Since 1874, when Gustav Nottebohm published the first attempt at a thematic catalogue of Schubert's music, literature on the composer has hinted that the second movement of Op. 100 was related to a Swedish song, "Se solen sjunker" (The sun is going down), which Schubert is said to have learned from a singer named Berg. This song has since been located (see Example 2.16), and there now seems no doubt that Schubert appropriated several striking gestures from it.[177] The text runs thus:

> See the sun is going down behind the peak of the high mountain,
> Before night's gloomy shadows you flee, O beautiful hope.
> Farewell, farewell, ah, the friend forgot about
> His true dear bride, his true dear bride, his true dear bride.
> La, la, la, la.

The gist of the poem is clear: time is running out, hope has fled, the opportunity for love has been lost. And as the brackets in Example 2.16 show, the musical motives Schubert adopted—the twofold octave drop on "Farewell, farewell," and the sweeping upward tenth followed by a dejected descending seventh for "bride, his true dear bride"—are closely allied to the poetic theme of loss and separation. The Swedish song's accompaniment moves in treading eighth notes (also prominent in the second subject of the trio's first movement); Schubert subtly modifies them to echo the rhythm of his own song "Gute Nacht" from *Winterreise* (written earlier in 1827), in which the lovelorn protagonist begins his cold, dark journey away from humanity into isolation, irrationality, and suicide. Noteworthy, too, is the Swedish song's bittersweet turn toward the mediant major with the line "Before night's gloomy shadows you flee, O beautiful hope," which is reflected in the B section of Schubert's Andante (mm. 41ff.); here the prominent thirds from the word "bride" are linked and developed, but the prevalent rhythm— ♪♩. ♪♩. ♪ (first across bar lines, later squarely within the bars at mm. 58ff.)—clearly comes from the octave-drop "farewell" motive (cf. mm. 34–36) and thus tinges the music with irony.

The form of this slow movement could hardly be simpler: ABA′B′A″ in which the last section funcitons as a coda. But the second statements of both segments (A′, B′) swell in length and intensity, nearly to the point of hysteria. In measures 103ff. the first phrase of A (perhaps related to the line "See the sun go down"?) is set to tremolo accompaniment and begins to sequence up by fifth, arriving in F♯ minor—the "diabolical interval" from C minor—at measure 114. The rage and horror of what follows surpasses even the wild outbursts in the Andante of the G Major Quartet; then F♯ is displaced by simple motivic neighbor-note motion (m. 122), the

EXAMPLE 2.16.   Swedish song "Se solen sjunker" (The sun is going down), either composed or notated from folk sources by Isaak Albert Berg; reproduced through courtesy of *Österreichische Musikzeitschrift*.

EXAMPLE 2.16.   *(continued)*

anguish subsides, and section B′ arrives in the bittersweet calm of C major. This material also mushrooms (mm. 158ff.), but into overblown heroic bravado that, upon close listening, ironically manifests several gestures echoing the A expansion (cf. mm. 167–69 and 119–23). This noisy episode ends in a standoff; as in the first movement, there is no synthesis or resolution, and it would seem as though the alternation of sections might continue indefinitely.

The seventeen-bar coda, however, is as delicate and subtle as the preceding music is bloated. The a♮ grace note of the piano (m. 199)—heard for the first and last time—deflates C major at a stroke. And during the single moment of the piece in which the relentlessly treading pulse is truly held in check (mm. 208–10), the piano quotes the last lamenting wind flourish from the funeral march of the *Eroica* Symphony (mm. 236–39). Appropriately, the movement's final gesture is the "farewell" motive from "Se solen sjunker."

Slightly tongue-in-cheek is the chipper scherzo, with its learned canons at the unison or octave (even during the rustic ländler passages of its second half); Schubert's precedent here is probably Haydn.[178] The trio assumes the confident bar-by-bar triadic stride of the first movement's opening, only to be interrupted by the questioning rhythm of that movement's second subject and parting gesture (♩ ♫♫, mm. 39ff.). Then the two conflicting notions are combined (mm. 51ff.), and all seems fine for the time being.

On the whole, scherzo and trio set the stage well for the opening of the finale, a bright ⁶⁄₈ theme in light marching style bordering upon triviality[179] that is set forth in three sections (mm. 1–32, 33–49, with a move to VI major, and 50–72). Then a simple scalewise drop brings on C minor, the tonality of the slow movement (mm. 73ff.), as well as recollection of its ostinato tread in the bass (¢), while repeated eighths in the melody strum a contour recalling the second subject of the first movement—all of which hints that sweetness and light may not prevail. In its third statement this B material reaches the dominant, and a sweeping new idea resumes the ⁶⁄₈ meter, accompanied by rolling sixteenths seemingly bound for closure (mm. 121ff.).[180] A variant beginning at measure 137 introduces notable syncopations in the accompaniment, and the music grows brash in manner, recalling the overplayed C major heroism in the Andante con moto. The long-awaited cadence in B♭ is abruptly shunted by the impact of a stunning diminished seventh (m. 163)—the first of several brusque disruptions in the movement's course. Now the B idea is back, first in C minor, then major. It gives way to a triumphant-sounding variant upon the movement's initial idea (mm. 193ff.), but even this fades to a disquieting *pianissimo* (mm. 225–30). What follows is further treatment of the first idea, up a chilling semitone in B minor (mm. 236ff.)—which is, enharmonically, the problematic lowered sixth degree of the first movement. And this, after lamenting wails on its Neapolitan (mm. 265ff.), leads to the quiet climax of the entire trio: the recall of the second-movement theme, accompanied by the aforementioned piano syncopations (mm. 279ff.), as though the farewell song had been lingering just beneath the surface of consciousness throughout the entire finale. This stroke of cyclic unity culminates the expressive disjunctiveness of a movement that will never resolve, but rather alternates between, its affective polarities. It is another version of the ambivalent finale Schubert has adopted in all his chamber works since 1824.

The movement's structure serves this ambivalence well, and in its initial casting did so even more. Schubert's autograph contains a repeat sign in the middle of measure 230 that is not found in the first edition: this repeat indicates he considered the B minor episodes just discussed to be part

TABLE 2.6. Piano Trio in E♭, D. 929, Finale, Outline of the Development

	Development									Recap.
m.	230	237	279	319	337	362	377	388	415	
	trans.	a¹	C	b¹	b¹'	b¹	b¹	b¹'	trans.	A
			(2d. mvt. [!])							
tonal plan	B♭ → b	b	b	d	d; °7 →	b; °7 →	F	e♭ → b	b → B♭	E♭
	V		(♭vi)		*				* V	I

of a development section, from which he subsequently cut a hundred-odd bars.[181] In the shorter version we know today, which Schubert himself authorized for publication, the development proceeds from the recall of the second movement in B minor to B variants, as summarized in Table 2.6.

The points marked "*" in the table are where the cuts occurred. The first, following what is now measure 357, took away an additional fifty bars of b¹ material that modulated through a long circle of minor thirds (d–f–A♭/a♭) before the disruption of the diminished seventh that occurs at measure 358. The second deletion was principally another statement of the second-movement theme (C) in B minor for cello, intermingled with b¹ in repeated eighths for the piano. The overall effect of these passages, aside from about two minutes' greater length, is a greater sense of aimless, agitated wandering in the development, yet also a clearer perception that it was indeed a development section, rather than a developmental rondo episode. The distinction is crucial, as follows: When the recapitulation has run its course (m. 660), the music proceeds directly with what had been the transition into the development at measures 230ff. (cf. Table 2.6), and E♭ gives way to E minor (once again raising the possibility of indefinite replay). A modification of the a¹ segment that had opened the development then restores the tonic pitch level, but the mode remains minor (mm. 693ff.), and the second-theme recall recurs again (mm. 697ff.). If that event has been heard only once before, as in the authorized cut version, the movement's form may be perceived as a curtailed binary: I—V → ♭vi~~V || I—I → i–I, in which the thematically repetitive modulatory episodes of measures 319ff. have been dropped. Thus the cuts (including the deleted repeat) tighten the local course of events, but also heighten the ambivalence of what has transpired in broader perspective.

In any event, the trio's major-tonic close seems conventional rather than convincing, and the work's palpable contradictions remain unresolved. This Schubert finale is among those often criticized for excessive length;[182] yet given the nature of its material and the cuts the composer already made, it is difficult to imagine what else could be deleted without substantially diminishing the overall effect.

Schubert chose the E♭ Trio as the principal instrumental work for his private concert in March 1828, which was virtually ignored by the press: Paganini had arrived in Vienna and, as one correspondent put it, "the minor stars paled before the radiance of this comet in the musical heavens."[183] The Leipzig publisher Probst finally issued Op. 100 in October 1828, but it is uncertain whether Schubert lived long enough to see a copy. After his death, however, it was among the first of his works to become widely known.[184]

The C Major String Quintet, D. 956 (1828)

Little is certain about the origins of Schubert's last chamber work, the C Major Quintet (D. 956), except that he offered it to Probst on 2 October 1828 while anxiously awaiting the appearance of the E♭ Piano Trio.[185] Numerous quintets with two cellos by Boccherini and George Onslow had appeared in print, but it seems more likely that Schubert was inspired by a combination of long-standing admiration for Mozart's viola quintets plus his own delight in the deep-voiced, homophonic, warmly Romantic sonorities of the *Singverein* (or *Männerchor*) idiom (two tenor and two bass parts), for which he wrote several pieces in later years, and which had become a symbol of genial sociability in his 1827 song cycle, *Winterreise*.

The first movement of the C Major Quintet is Schubert's most successful, and indeed, ingenious, synthesis of two liedlike thematic groups into large-scale sonata form. Its famous opening—a long *messa di voce* on the closed-position tonic suddenly and sensuously recolored by neighbor tones into a diminished seventh—takes on rhythmic definition and broader direction only gradually, and it seems almost to vanish into the high-range dominant of the tenth bar. The consequent phrase immediately introduces the *Männerchor* texture in its usual register, with the melodic line in the tenor range of the first cello. Halting gestures continue: this is the manner of a slow introduction, not a first thematic group. Only during the precadential crescendo of measures 26–32 do we realize that latent within this material is an opposite and rather stormy character, which bursts forth *ff* at measure 33. This leads to a portentous dominant pedal (mm. 49ff.) agitated by ascending chromatic triplets that culminate in diminished-seventh neighbors (fourth beat of mm. 52 and 56): these neighbor notes echo the movement's alluring initial harmonies, and they also embellish the loud cadence that concludes this passage (mm. 57–58).

Out of that cadence emerges a single g¹ for both cellos, and within seconds the previous tension melts in three descending semitones: as in the B♭ Trio, the new song theme arrives through a delightful "third-under" modulation, yielding in this case ♭III (E♭). Yet owing to the introductory nature of the opening group, this warm, rich duet for cellos is no "secondary theme," but rather becomes the affective center point of the entire first movement.[186] It moves back to the orbit of C (mm. 73ff.), which, although no longer strongly tonic, serves as a starting point for the violins to repeat the ravishing third modulation as they take over the theme (mm. 79ff.). As the music emerges from this repetition, the dominant of C is maintained (mm. 100ff.), and first violin and viola spin forth sixteen bars of beautiful cantilena in canon over pedal points, swerving gracefully to the third-related dominant of E minor (mm. 106ff.), then back to G. The rather extended approach to the closing material is rich in neighbor-chord coloring and delicate development of previous lyrical gestures. Yet the closing idea itself ("C^1," m. 138), a brief march theme hinting at minor mode and *style hongrois,* is a quietly brusque contrast to what precedes it; only in retrospect do we realize that its dotted rhythms stem from the movement's halting introduction. Yet as the march yields to and blends with a reassuring recall of the second theme ("C^2," m. 146), it seems in and of itself of little consequence.

But like Brahms later in the century, Schubert here seizes upon the seemingly inconsequential as the major source of the development, which is based entirely upon the two closing elements just noted. (Here, then, was a viable solution to the problem of developing lyrical themes that seem inherently inimical to working out.) Following brief allusion in A major to both closing components (mm. 157ff.), the first of two large sequential episodes begins in F♯ minor at measure 167: now element C^1 is treated canonically by second cello and viola plus second violin, as first cello and violin snap stingingly unyielding C♯'s in alternation. Reversing the trend of the triplet buildup from the movement's introduction (mm. 175ff.; cf. mm. 49ff.), the music softens into D♭ (enharmonic major of c♯, mm. 181ff.), and C^1 becomes legato. The warm tenor-range parallelism between viola and first cello reveals (again à la Brahms) a striking latent thematic connection: originally presented in martial guise, C^1 is actually derived from the movement's singing second subject.[187] The texture is extraordinarily rich here, and even the wide-ranging syncopated arpeggiations of the second violin remain memorable well into the movement's reprise.

Out of the march's lyrical transformation soars a long arch for first violin, which is gently renewed at its cadence point (m. 197). Here a change of mode makes C♯ minor a pivot chord, and the music moves by third relation toward E. The second developmental episode begins in E minor (m. 203) and pursues a parallel path, ending up in D (m. 239). Then follows, apparently, yet a third developmental episode comprising a canon at the third for second violin and cello, and imitative triplets in first violin and viola.[188] But after a dozen bars of sequencing, the dominant is at hand; this retransition and the ensuing delicate reprise are, like those of the G Major Quartet, among the most exceptional such passages in all of Schubert. Equally striking is the movement's coda: the exposition had, as it were, marched quietly into the distance humming the second theme; that could hardly serve as the conclusion of such a movement. Accordingly, Schubert appends a brief summary of its broad affective contrasts—emerging raw energy from the introduction, versus the sweet lyricism of the second subject. The latter finally prevails; fully freed from the martial demands of the closing section and development, its rhythm dissolves into slow-moving harmonies of Brahmsian warmth. The last arpeggiation of the first violin recalls the neighbor-note gesture of the introduction, and the movement finally rests after a *messa di voce* echoing its first sound.

Directly out of this peaceful close emerges the exquisitely drawn-out slow motion of the Adagio. But E major—a third relation to C foreshadowed yet never realized in the first movement—marks the entry into a different world. A long, nostalgic song unfolds in close three-part *Singverein* harmony, with simple bass underpinning and delicate decoration from the first violin. It sounds familiar; the first eight melodic pitches (counting the rearticulated f#¹ in measure 2) are an augmentation of the last phrase from the variation theme of "Death and the Maiden," and the slow 3:1 pulse, parallel motion, plus certain details of harmony recall the Notturno movement for piano trio. But perhaps no other passage of Schubert's chamber music so fully reveals his subtlety and control in matters of harmonic color and voice leading. Effortlessly the music floats from the initial E to the unexpected, intensified realm of F# major, reaching its poignant climax on the minor subdominant of that center (m. 11), then returning slowly back to tonic, with delicate surprises that make each note vibrantly alive. The theme begins anew at measure 15; this time it pursues a simpler harmonic course and cadences (m. 24) in time for a five-bar tonic epilogue, without, however, disturbing the fourteen-bar symmetry between its two strophes.

Like the Andante un poco mosso of the B♭ Trio, this slow movement is a broad ternary structure with a middle section influenced by Gypsy idiom.[189] But entirely unexpected is the outburst of raw anguish that launches the B section, beginning with the semitone lurch up to F minor. Exotic Hungarian syncopated rhythms and triplet tremolos rage relentlessly in the accompaniment, and a song of bitter lament wails in octaves throughout the next thirty bars as the five-part texture is deployed for maximum sonic effect. A long sequential ascent in measures 35–38 brings on C minor (minor tonic of the quintet as a whole), and that remains the principal tonal center for the remainder of this wild episode. Inflections of its Neapolitan add to the pathetic tone (mm. 40, 44, 54ff.), as do loud melodic crying gestures (mm. 42, 46–47, 50–52). Then, fury spent, the melodic line slowly descends through two octaves in a lengthy diminuendo (mm. 53ff.), during which the dominant of C is reasserted.

Suddenly all is hushed and fragmented, without pulse or harmonic goal. For no discernible reason the subdominant of E emerges from these shards (m. 62), and the original tonic and tempo are resumed in an agonizingly slow cadence. Once again the long *Singverein* song unfolds in two strophes, which follow the same course as before. But now quasi-improvised embellishments in fiddle and bass enhance the theme with delicate recollection of the exotic *style hongrois* that swamped the heart of the movement. Its final bars explicitly recall the stormy F minor outburst, only to let it go through augmented-sixth reinterpretation of its dominant. The music comes to rest on a swelled, sustained tonic reminiscent of the gestures that open and close the first movement.

In the event, however, this peaceful conclusion does not dispel the raucous Gypsy style and energy that emerged during the course of the Adagio; *style hongrois* is prevalent in both the scherzo and finale to come. Characteristic elements in the scherzo are the low drones and gritty dissonances in the main idea, the unexpected progressions and sudden leaps into unforetold key areas, tremolos and repeated notes, syncopations, and occasional virtuosic flights for the fiddle, all of which give the movement more dash and pungency than the scherzos of either the piano trios or string quartets. The first half, which lasts only about thirty seconds, makes rapid forays from C into D minor (mm. 12–16) and A♭ (mm. 29–37); then follows unpredictable ascending parallelism that falls onto the dominant seventh of A♭, immediately reinterpreted as an augmented sixth leading toward the structural dominant of C.

The leap into E♭ that slams open the second half is another shock (notwithstanding its analogous relation to the C–A♭ move of the first half). This launches a circle of major thirds (G–E♭–B [m. 83]–G [m. 107]) that leads to return of the tonic—which is hardly surprising in itself. Unforgettable, however, is the approach to G through the roar of unison cellos developing the neighbor-note idea from the opening bars; when the G[7] has been heard twice, the neighbor motive is expanded into the harmonic interrelations of both melody and bass, such that the dominant is prolonged and cast in doubt simultaneously (mm. 112–30). The brief coda is a final reprise of the opening tune-plus-drones expanded into a grating yet persuasive cadence over an unrelenting tonic pedal (mm. 198ff.).

The trio is, unusually, in duple meter; an obvious precedent for that feature alone is Beethoven's Ninth (or the "Pastoral"). But as Jonathan Bellman notes, here, too, the style is markedly Gypsy.[190] As the melancholy, quasi-improvised opening line weaves its way downward in heavily dotted rhythms, the most likely tonal center seems to be A♭, or possibly F minor. But when the ensemble finally catches and cradles the improvisers (as in Liszt's description of the cimbalom player cited in n. 114), it pulls the harmonic center unexpectedly to D♭, with drone parallel fifths in the second cello; the ensuing minor iv–I cadence sounds even more exotic (mm. 9–10). Equally striking is the chain of modal interplay and functional relations in measures 31–38. Ultimately this passage is understood as D♭/c♯ → vi–IV–V in E; B/b → vi–IV–V in D—but the manner in which this hushed, slow-moving sequence unfolds is disorienting. Indeed, it recalls a related moment of confusion in the slow movement—the collapse at the end of its B section (mm. 58ff.). There, tonic focus returned as if by lucky chance. But here follows one of the most luminous moments in the entire quintet, which hinges upon a remarkable expressive detail: in measure 39 there is no seventh requiring resolution, yet in the context of warm low-range string tone growing fuller, the voices of the simple A major sonority melt apart as though it had actually been an augmented sixth. And only here, at long last, does the strange Gypsy tonic of D♭ sound naturalized and fulfilling.

The influence of *style hongrois* in the Quintet culminates in the finale. Here the main idea begins with a defiant pickup and sforzando downbeat, off-tonic and evidently minor in mode; in addition, it is peppered with grace-note snaps on weak beats and accompanied by drones in *alla zoppa* dance rhythms.[191] More exotic are the unexpected, nonfunctional leap into E♭ minor before the tonic has been fully articulated, and the semitone slide (mm. 17–19) into C at last, which is driven home heavy-handedly for nearly thirty bars. The second theme of the sonata-rondo (mm. 46ff.) simply "backs into" the dominant, with delightful Viennese *Schwung* in its third and fourth bars. Soon the triplet rhythms of its accompaniment are taken over as the basis of Gypsy-style ornamentation in the first fiddle, and this filigree plus fragments of the tune are spun out over a dominant pedal for a leisurely twenty-bar interlude. A second version of this group (mm. 79ff.) leads to transitional material (m. 107), which broadens into further transience (mm. 118ff.). Expectations of closure in G diminish as the cellos introduce a wistful new idea in parallel motion (mm. 127ff.); but this is short-lived, and the dominant (G) is restored, albeit *ppp*, at measure 141. Meanwhile a sinuous seven-note accompaniment motive has taken over the upper voices and is now heard alternately in the upper and lower choirs of the ensemble (mm. 141ff.). Although a mere arpeggiation, it has nevertheless an uncanny and foreboding quality. At measure 153 the disposition of voices changes, neighbor-note activity increases, and a long chromatic ascent begins in the viola, all of which is shortly followed by a lengthy crescendo: while the dominant-prolongation function of the passage is never seriously in doubt, its increasingly tortuous convolutions suggest a mounting horror that imbues the ensuing return of the rondo, now *fortissimo*, with ominous overtones (m. 169).

The developmental C section deploys Schubert's favorite device of parallel sequential episodes (mm. 214–32, 233–51). They begin sternly and *fortissimo* with stretto treatment of the rondo's motto in minor, and end up insouciantly a semitone lower, homophonic, *pianissimo*, and major, with its tail motive. Yet more serendipitous is the passage immediately following the second of these episodes, which wanders onto the dominant (albeit $\frac{4}{3}$ [m. 256]), overshoots it, and then, as though with a shrug, backs up and resumes the second theme (m. 268). There is delicate irony in all of this, and one comes away with the impression that development per se is scarcely germane to this musical world. As expected, the ominous buildup at the close of the B group returns, but now it is lengthened and intensified. And as in so many previous finales, the music finishes by simply dancing away from the conflict, *più allegro* through a wide range of sequencing, then *più presto* in motivic fragments, finally ceasing in a neighbor-note flourish that once again echoes the initial gesture of the entire quintet.

Although Franz Grillparzer probably did not know the C Major Quintet, that work justifies down to the present day his famous epitaph of Schubert: "The art of music here entombed a rich possession, but even far fairer hopes."[192] The Quintet continues to yield new delights even after years of familiarity, much as do the chamber works of Mozart's last decade and the late quartets of Beethoven. Entirely on his own terms and in his own voice, Schubert has here achieved a synthesis of expressivity and logic, form and drama, fineness of detail and overall command, that places him firmly in the company of the musical ancestors he revered most deeply—"Mozart, immortal Mozart," who brought "such comforting perceptions of a brighter and better life," and Beethoven, whose "eccentricity . . . joins and confuses the tragic with the comic, the agreeable with the repulsive, heroism with howlings and the holiest with harlequinades"[193] in a manner that both troubled and challenged Schubert. If there is a criticism to be made of the String Quintet, it is the same as for the B♭ Piano Trio: the sublimity of the first two movements is neither recaptured nor transcended in the following two. However one reads the disruption of the quietly ecstatic slow movement by the raw passion of the Gypsy horde, and however moving the fiddler's gloss on the return of the intimate E major song, paradise is not regained. So much seems apparent as well from the orgiastic dancing, the marching and light singing, or the unsettled juxtaposition of contrasts in his chamber music finales from 1824 on. And the inherent autobiographical influence upon such works, Cone's "cold wind" of terminal, sexually transmitted disease, now seems difficult to discount.

Knowing Beethoven's work well, including the Ninth Symphony, Schubert refused to follow the path of heroic triumphalism. How his "far fairer hopes" might have resolved this artistic dilemma had Schubert lived longer is uncertain; that the issue remained a central one for Austro-Germanic music through the end of the nineteenth century is quite certain. Much of Schubert's best instrumental music, including the C Major Quintet as well as the Octet in F Major, the G Major Quartet, and the "Unfinished" Symphony, remained unpublished until midcentury, and many works already in print lay largely unknown until the 1860s. Thus, through quirk of fate, it was the post-Wagnerians—Bruckner, Brahms, and especially young Gustav Mahler—who became the spiritual heirs of Schubert's chamber music.

Notes

1. See Walter Gray, "Schubert the Instrumental Composer," *Musical Quarterly* 64 (1978): 483–94, esp. 490.
2. Otto Erich Deutsch, ed., *Schubert: Memoirs by His Friends*, trans. Rosamond Ley and John Nowell (London, 1958 [cited hereafter as *Memoirs*]), 34 and 212.
3. Ibid., 58.
4. *Quartettsatz* is nothing more than the German for "quartet movement," but the foreign moniker has remained affixed to the piece in English-speaking countries (it is also called simply "the *Satz*").
5. Doris Finke-Hecklinger and Werner Aderhold have suggested (preface to *Franz Schubert: Neue Ausgabe sämtlicher Werke* [cited hereafter as *NSA*] VI/9, *Tänze*

für mehrere Instrumente, xiii) that because these minuets are scored for regimental military ensemble (*Harmoniemusik*) plus trumpet, rather than the traditional dance group of two violins and bass, they may well have been exercises in instrumentation for winds.

6. Concerning the quartet's chronology, see Ernst Hilmar, "Datierungsprobleme im Werk Schuberts, " *Schubert-Kongreß Wien 1978: Bericht,* ed. Otto Brusatti (Graz, 1979), 54.

7. E.g., Symphonies Nos. 97 and 103.

8. James Webster, "Schubert's Sonata Form and Brahms's First Maturity," *19th Century Music* 2 (1978): 30, 35.

9. The reprise of the slow movement in Op. 18, No. 4, by Beethoven comes to mind here.

10. From the obituary by Schubert's close friend Joseph von Spaun, in *Memoirs,* 18, and Otto Erich Deutsch, ed., *The Schubert Reader: A Life of Franz Schubert in Letters and Documents,* trans. Eric Blom (New York, 1947 [cited hereafter as *Schubert Reader*]), 866.

11. Hilmar, "Datierungsprobleme," 54.

12. J. A. Westrup, *Schubert Chamber Music,* BBC Music Guides (Seattle, 1969), 23.

13. See Martin Chusid, ed., *NSA* VI/3, *Streichquartette* 1:178 and 197 (Example 14), and Ernst Hilmar, *Verzeichnis der Schubert-Handschriften in der Musiksammlung der Wiener Stadt- und Landesbibliothek,* Catalogus Musicus 8 (Kassel, 1978), 89. The canonic passage is in G minor, which explains why D major, approached through an augmented sixth, sounds like a dominant in m. 293.

14. Westrup, *Schubert Chamber Music,* 23; the slow movement of Haydn's Op. 74, No. 3 ("The Rider") seems to be one influence.

15. Cf. the C to A relationship between minuet and trio in Haydn's Op. 74, No. 1.

16. E.g., Haydn, Op. 20, No. 2, first movement; Mozart, "Dissonant" Quartet, K. 465, finale.

17. See Martin Chusid, "Schubert's Overture for String Quartet and Cherubini's Overture to *Faniska,*" *Journal of the American Musicological Society* 15 (1962): 78–84.

18. *Schuberts Studien, NSA* VIII, supplement vol. 2, ed. Alfred Mann, provides an excellent account of Schubert's musical education. Such productivity does not, however, indicate that Schubert was unaffected by his mother's death. On the contrary, parts for the *Salve Regina* are dated precisely one month later (28 June), which suggests that the work may have been a memorial for her. Schubert sets the opening of the text (directed to the Virgin Mary) to a melodic line distinctly recalling Cherubino's "Voi che sapete che cosa è l'amor [You who know what love is]" from Mozart's *The Marriage of Figaro*—perhaps not only to identify his mother with divinity but to seek her guidance and comfort at a time of confusion as well.

19. Alfred Einstein, *Schubert: A Musical Portrait* (New York, 1951), 31.

20. On rhetoric in music and *dubitatio* in particular, see, e.g., Leonard G. Ratner, *Classic Music: Expression, Form, and Style* (New York, 1980), part 2, and esp. 91ff.

21. E.g., the Quartet in D minor, K. 421/417b, or the Piano Concerto in A, K. 488.

22. Einstein, *Schubert,* 31; possible precedents include the slow movements of the Quartets in D Minor, K. 421/417b, and in F Major, K. 590.

23. E.g., the Fifth Symphony and the *Coriolan* Overture (one of Schubert's favorite pieces).

24. Einstein, *Schubert,* 32.

25. The main theme of the movement bears striking resemblances in key, pace, texture, and gesture to Monostatos's aria in the second act of Mozart's *Die Zauberflöte,* "Alles fühlt der Liebe Freude" ("Every creature feels love's rapture . . . yet I am supposed to shun it, because a Moor is ugly"); quite possibly this is an early instance of Schubertian irony.

26. Westrup, *Schubert Chamber Music,* 25.

27. Cf. also Einstein, *Schubert,* 32.

28. Schubert's lifelong friend Josef von Spaun reports that during their student days Schubert confided to him, "Secretly, in my heart of hearts, I still hope to be able to make something out of myself, but who can do anything after Beethoven?" (*Memoirs,* 128). Further on this subject, see Edward T. Cone, "Schubert's Beethoven," *Musical Quarterly* 56 (1970): 779–93; Maynard Solomon, "Schubert and Beethoven," *19th Century Music* 3 (1979): 114–25; Richard Kramer, "*Gradus ad Parnassum:* Beethoven, Schubert, and the Romance of Counterpoint," *19th Century Music* 11 (1987): 107–20; and Walter Dürr, "Wer vermag nach Beethoven noch etwas zu machen? Gedanken über die Beziehungen Schuberts zu Beethoven," *Beethoven Jahrbuch 1973/77,* 47ff., reprinted in *Musik-Konzepte: Sonderband Franz Schubert,* ed. Heinz-Klaus Metzger and Rainer Riehn (Munich, 1979), 10–25.

29. Cf. mm. 25–32 and Beethoven, Op. 18, No. 4, second movement, mm. 28–32. Cf. also, e.g., Beethoven's finales to Op. 18, Nos. 2 and 3.

30. A reconstruction by Reinhard van Hoorickx and Christopher Weait has been recorded by the German Wind Soloists (Marco Polo 8.223356).

31. *Schubert Reader,* 32 (translation modified). The German text is in *NSA* VI/i, *Oktette und Nonett,* ed. Arnold Feil, viii and xiii.

32. See *Schubert Reader,* 34–41.

33. The opening Haydn paraphrase is the beginning of the finale from Symphony No. 104; Einstein finds allusions to Mozart's Quartets K. 575 and 499, Beethoven's Second Symphony, and near the end [m. 489ff.], the Overture to *Die Zauberflöte* (see also Westrup, *Schubert Chamber Music,* 25, ex. 16).

34. Schubert's ambivalence about the dedicatees of his works is evident in two other cases: both Beethoven and the brother of Therese Grob received less than first-rate works from his pen (see also below, 59). It is not out of the question that the "knocking" motive may represent Schubert's resentment of his father's sexual activity with his new wife.

35. The memoirs of Schubert's brother Ferdinand suggest that their father was not a strong cellist; see *Memoirs,* 35.

36. *Schubert Reader,* 41.

37. See Doris Finke-Hecklinger and Werner Aderhold, preface to *NSA* VI/9, *Tänze für mehrere Instrumente,* ix–x.

38. Franz Schubert, *Streichquartettsatz C moll (1814),* completed and ed. Alfred Orel, Philharmonia Partituren, no. 350 (Vienna, 1939); parts published by Adolph Robitschek, Vienna, 1939.

39. See Natalie Bauer-Lechner, *Recollections of Gustav Mahler,* trans. Dika Newlin, ed. Peter Franklin (Cambridge, 1980), 147: "How easily he [Schubert] takes things when it comes to developing his ideas! Six sequences follow one after the other, and then comes still another one in a new key. No elaboration, no artistically finished development of his original idea! Instead, he repeats himself so much that you could cut out half the piece without doing it any harm. . . . Schubert's melody, like Beethoven's and Wagner's, is *eternal.* That's why he should-

n't fall back on the formalism of Haydn and Mozart, which was intrinsic to the structure of their works.
"Now I understand why, as we are told, Schubert still wanted to study counter-point even shortly before his death. He was aware of what he lacked. And I can feel for him in this, as I myself am deficient in this technique."

40. Einstein, *Schubert*, 14; *Schubert Reader*, 64.

41. Cf. the slow movements of the Mozart quartets in Bb (K. 589), F (K. 590), and, to some extent, C (K. 465); precedents can be found in Haydn as well.

42. John Reed, *Schubert*, Master Musicians Series (London, 1987), 53.

43. Gray, "Schubert the Instrumental Composer," 488, 492–93.

44. Maurice J. E. Brown and Eric Sams, *The New Grove Schubert* (New York, 1983), 16.

45. E.g., first movement of the E Major, latter half of the development (cf. also mm. 39ff. of this movement and the finale of Beethoven, Op. 59, No. 1, mm. 73ff.); finale of the E Major, mm. 70–85 and passim (cf. Beethoven, Op. 74, finale, mm. 69ff. [third variation]). The elaborate diminutions in the Andante of the same work also suggest Beethoven's influence. Cf. also Einstein's discussion in *Schubert*, 85–86, 106–7.

46. See below, 72ff. The finale of the G Minor Quartet, D. 173, is apparently Schubert's earliest venture in Hungarian style, which he does not pursue further until 1824 (personal communication from Jonathan Bellman to the authors).

47. Westrup, *Schubert Chamber Music*, 28.

48. According to Leopold von Sonnleithner, Schubert "never danced, but was always ready to sit down at the piano, where for hours he improvised the most beautiful waltzes; those he liked he repeated, in order to remember them and write them out afterwards" (*Memoirs*, 121).

49. See *NSA* VI/9, *Tänze für mehrere Instrumente*, esp. preface, ix–xii.

50. Cf. also Einstein, *Schubert*, 106.

51. See William S. Newman, *The Sonata since Beethoven*, 2d ed. (New York, 1972), chapters 1 and 2, esp. pp. 9–14, 27–29, and 37–45.

52. Cited in ibid., 44.

53. E.g., first movement of the C Major Piano Concerto, K. 467.

54. While the chromatic movement in contrary motion of the outer voices (mm. 83ff.) would seem to be a nineteenth-century procedure, one of the earliest ex-amples of such a progression is found in Mozart's Overture to *Don Giovanni*, mm. 7–11; see also below, n. 124.

55. Cf., for example, the Mozart Sonata in Bb, K. 454, second movement, mm. 89–92.

56. Cf. the first movement of the Piano Sonata, Op. 14, No. 1, which Beethoven also rearranged for string quartet.

57. E.g., the G Minor Symphony, K. 550, and the G Minor String Quintet, K. 516; Schubert's diary for June 13 of this year contains fervent praise of a Mozart quintet he heard the previous night, and according to Deutsch it was probably K. 516 (*Schubert Reader*, 60).

58. Cf. mm. 124–26 and Mozart's G Major Quartet, K. 387, first movement, two measures before the recapitulation (mm. 106ff.).

59. In the transition back to the scherzo, however, the a#[1] (violin) on the down-beat of bar 132 shown in the first edition (and played by some performers) should surely be delayed to the third beat: the previous g#[1] is an accented passing tone that must resolve to a sixth chord (A minor) before the augmented sixth (a#) lead-

ing to the dominant of E can be introduced. The downbeat a♯¹ is almost certainly a printer's error; the work was not published until 1851, and the autograph manuscript has been lost.

60. Westrup, *Schubert Chamber Music*, 47.

61. *Schubert Reader,* 93, 99.

62. Ibid., 121.

63. Albert Stadler, in *Memoirs,* 148, 152–53; cf. also *Schubert Reader,* 159.

64. Donald Francis Tovey, "Franz Schubert," *The Main Stream of Music and Other Essays* (New York, 1949), 118.

65. See *Schubert Reader,* 128–30; Brown, *Schubert: A Critical Biography* (London, 1961), 100; Maynard Solomon, "Franz Schubert and the Peacocks of Benvenuto Cellini," *19th Century Music* 12 (1989): 205.

66. Brown and Sams, *The New Grove Schubert,* 25; *Schubert Reader,* 180ff.

67. *Schubert Reader,* 151.

68. See *Schubert Reader,* 44, 46–47, 110, and 153.

69. Brown and Sams, *The New Grove Schubert,* 27–28; Einstein, *Schubert,* 160.

70. See Webster, "Schubert's Sonata Form," 24ff.

71. Ibid., 26ff. Webster regards Schubert's "three-key expositions" as comprising a first group and a "double second group."

72. Concerning the probable influence of Beethoven's F Minor Quartet, Op. 95, on this movement, see Werner Aderhold, "Das Streichquartett-Fragment c-moll D 703," in *Franz Schubert: Jahre der Krise, 1818-1823,* ed. Werner Aderhold, Walther Dürr, and Walburga Litschauer (Kassel, 1985), 61, 65.

73. Such moves are also characteristic of Schubert's transition and closing in later sonata-form movements, as Webster points out ("Schubert's Sonata Form").

74. The autograph manuscript contains a crossed-out passage of twenty-six bars between mm. 120 and 121 of the movement as we know it. This includes a twice-intoned *fortissimo* outburst of scalar sixteenths in G minor. The first of these eruptions leads to the Neapolitan cadential gesture familiar from mm. 122–24 in the published score; the second brings on a digression to an eight-bar oscillation between C♭ and B♭, which once again gives way to the Neapolitan-prepared cadence in G. Thus, reemphasis of neighbor-note relations is readily apparent in the passage, yet so, too, is the redundancy of the cadence pattern. See *NSA* VI/5, *Streichquartette* 3: x, xxi, 173, 203–4, as well as Aderhold, "Das Streichquartett-Fragment c-moll D 703," 62–65.

75. For further discussion of the topical tradition to which the *Quartettsatz* belongs, see Timothy L. Jackson, "The Tragic Reversed Recapitulation in the German Classical Tradition," *Journal of Music Theory* 40 (1996): 61–111.

76. Printed in *F. Schuberts Werke: Kritische durchgesehene Gesamtausgabe* (Leipzig, 1884–97), V, Revisionsbericht, 78–82; *NSA* VI/5, *Streichquartette* 3:168–70; and Aderhold, "Das Streichquartett-Fragment c-moll D 703," 66–70.

77. Aderhold, "Das Streichquartett-Fragment c-moll D 703," 71.

78. Brian Newbould, *Schubert and the Symphony: A New Perspective* (London, 1992), 156–57.

79. *Schubert Reader,* 279.

80. Ibid., 286–87, 270–340 et passim.

81. Letter from Moritz von Schwind to Franz von Schober, in ibid., 327.

82. Ibid., 336, 339; the quotation "My peace is gone . . . " is from the portion of Goethe's *Faust* Schubert had set to music in "Gretchen am Spinnrade," in which the tragic heroine agonizes over her conflicting feelings about her suitor.

83. Edward T. Cone, "Schubert's Promissory Note: An Exercise in Musical Hermeneutics," *19th Century Music* 5 (1982): 241, reprinted in Walter Frisch, ed., *Schubert: Critical and Analytical Studies* (Lincoln, NE, 1986), 28.

84. Jonathan Bellman, *The "Style Hongrois" in the Music of Western Europe* (Boston, 1993), esp. chapter 7.

85. See Maynard Solomon, "Franz Schubert and the Peacocks of Benvenuto Cellini," 193–206, as well as *19th Century Music* 17 no. 1 (1993), special issue: *Schubert: Music, Sexuality, Culture.*

86. Bellman, *Style Hongrois*, 173.

87. *Schubert Reader,* 313, 339; Brown, *Schubert: A Critical Biography,* 137, 146.

88. Heinrich Kreißle von Hellborn, *The Life of Franz Schubert,* trans. A. D. Coleridge (London, 1869), 2:9.

89. Einstein, *Schubert,* 245.

90. Cf. Bauernfeld's report of Schubert's tavern tirade against self-serving virtuosi in *Memoirs,* 230–33; cf. also *Schubert Reader,* 337–38.

91. *Memoirs,* 115–16, 123.

92. Cf. Brown, *Schubert: A Critical Biography,* 182–84, and Westrup, *Schubert Chamber Music,* 13.

93. Tovey, "Franz Schubert," 118–26, esp. 121; Carl Dahlhaus, "Sonata Form in Schubert: The First Movement of the G-major String Quartet, Op. 161 (D. 887)," trans. Thilo Reinhard, in Frisch, *Schubert: Critical and Analytical Studies,* 1–7, esp. 2.

94. See also Webster, "Schubert's Sonata Form," 24ff., and Tovey, "Franz Schubert," 118–26.

95. Cone, "Schubert's Promissory Note"; the principal focus of Cone's article, the *Moment musical* in A♭, Op. 94, No. 6 (D. 780), was also composed in 1824.

96. Cf. Einstein, *Schubert,* 257, who, however, inaccurately observes that "there is no trace of dualism in Schubert's work either."

97. Cf., e.g., the fifth variation in Brahms's B♭ Major String Sextet, Op. 18 (mm. 113ff.). Schubert adapts bars 122–23 from this variation of the Octet in the second half of the trio (mm. 92–95) in the A Minor String Quartet (D. 804), his next completed chamber work (also March 1824).

98. Westrup, *Schubert Chamber Music,* 16–17.

99. Both chords turn out to be Neapolitans, of C and F respectively.

100. On the Gypsy elements, see Bellman, *Style Hongrois,* 104–5, 164–66; the *tárogató* is an ancient Hungarian double-reed instrument.

101. Westrup, *Schubert Chamber Music,* 18.

102. The A Minor Quartet (D. 804) was published in September 1824 as the first in a projected set of three, designated Op. 29, all of which were at that point to be dedicated to Schuppanzigh (see *NSA* VI/5, *Streichquartette* 3:175). In the event, the D Minor (D. 810) was not published in Schubert's lifetime; nor was the third, the G Major (D. 887), which was not written until June 1826.

103. See Christoph Wolff, "Schubert's 'Der Tod und das Mädchen': Analytical and Explanatory Notes on the Song D. 531 and the Quartet D. 810," in *Schubert Studies: Problems of Style and Chronology,* ed. Eva Badura-Skoda and Peter Branscombe (Cambridge, 1982), 169–71.

104. Einstein, *Schubert,* 252.

105. The theme comes from the entr'acte before act 4 of *Rosamunde;* while no copies of the play are known to survive, a long review of it reveals that in the fourth act Rosamunde appears among her flocks in an idyllic valley, having been previ-

ously released from arrest brought on by false accusation (see *Schubert Reader,* 312, and *NSA* VI/5, *Streichquartette* 3: x–xi).

106. Westrup, *Schubert Chamber Music,* 31–32; Einstein, *Schubert,* 253.

107. Cf. also Westrup, *Schubert Chamber Music,* 33.

108. The motive is strongly associated with the remorse of the father; it first occurs—in A minor—at the beginning of the second stanza, on the (italicized) word "*Zitternd* an der Krücke [Trembling on crutches, who is he, with sombre, sunken gaze . . . (who) totters behind the silently borne coffin?]." It recurs (in C minor) in the same stanza with words describing the father, "*Schwer geneckt* vom eisernen Geschicke [Harshly tormented by an iron fate]," and in the third stanza (F minor) as he imagines the boy calling to him, "*Vater* [Father]."

109. Einstein, *Schubert,* 167–68.

110. In mm. 98–99 viola and cello present a stunning augmentation of the eighth-note ostinato accompaniment figure (cf. second half of m. 1)

111. Theodor W. Adorno discusses the notion of music that reflects immediacy in the medium of memory in his *Mahler: A Musical Physiognomy,* trans. Edmund Jephcott (Chicago, 1992), e.g., 155 et passim.

112. See Westrup, *Schubert Chamber Music,* 34–35.

113. In C♯ minor only the third and sixth scale degrees (E♮, A♮) and, when used, the lowered seventh (B♮) generate sympathetic resonance with the open strings of the quartet; it is therefore a "dull" sounding key, and is used for that expressive effect (e.g., Beethoven, Op. 131).

114. This spot is intentionally tricky in performance, as is characteristic of the style. Liszt would later write about the accompaniment of a Gypsy fiddler thus: "The orchestra is so electrified by the fire, or, it may be, the melancholy, of its chief, that, when the latter has come to the end of his explorations—when, having allowed himself sufficiently long to float in air, he gives sign of being about to fall . . . receiving him into their arms they do not allow him to reach the earth, but sustain him, aid him to rebound" (Franz Liszt, *The Gipsy in Music,* trans. Edwin Evans [London, n. d.], 303). On Gypsy characteristics of this movement as a whole, see Bellman, *Style Hongrois,* esp. 164; Einstein, *Schubert,* 242, rightly points to thematic connections between this finale and the *Divertissement à la hongroise,* D. 818, which Schubert apparently composed later in 1824, following a vacation in Zseliz.

115. Einstein, *Schubert,* 253.

116. Wolff, "Schubert's 'Der Tod und das Mädchen,'" 143–47, 156–59, 160ff. (quote from 169).

117. *Encyclopädie der gesammten musikalischen Wissenschaften, oder Universal-Lexicon der Tonkunst,* comp. Gustav Schilling (Stuttgart, 1838), s.v. "Tarantella" by Gustav Schilling.

118. See esp. Henry E. Sigerist, "The Story of Tarantism," in *Music and Medicine,* ed. Dorothy M. Schullian and Max Schoen (New York, 1948), 96–116; *MGG,* s.v. "Tarantella" by Marius Schneider and Anton Würz; J. F. C. Hecker, *The Epidemics of the Middle Ages,* trans. B. G. Babington (London, 1844), 107–33; and George Mora, "An Historical and Sociopsychiatric Appraisal of Tarantism and Its Importance in the Tradition of Psychotherapy of Mental Disorders," *Bulletin of the History of Medicine* 37 (1963): 417–39. J. G. Walther's influential *Musikalisches Lexikon* (Leipzig, 1732) provides a brief account of the tarantella and refers readers to Athanasius Kircher's *Magnes, sive de arte magnetica* (1643) as well as Giorgio Baglivi's *Dissertatio . . . tarantulae* (1695), two of the more detailed treatises on the subject (both of which are discussed in Sigerist). Kircher's ideas on tarantism also

appeared in his *Musurgia universalis* (Rome, 1650; facs. ed., Hildesheim, 1970), book 9, chapter 5; this work influenced German music theory well into the eighteenth century, especially through the German "Philosophischer Extract und Auszug" from it edited by Andrea Hirsch as *Kircherus Jesuita Germanus Germaniae redonatur: sive Artis Magnae de Consono et Dissono* (Schwäbisch Hall, 1662; facs. ed., Kassel, 1988), book 5, chapters 4–5; cf. also Kircher, *Phonurgia nova* (Kempten, 1673; facs. ed., New York, 1966), book 2, section 2, chapters 4–5. (The authors are indebted to Professor Charles E. Brewer for kind assistance in locating the Kircher essays.) According to Baglivi, *The Practice of Physick . . . together with Several New and Curious Dissertations, Particularly of the Tarantula,* trans. anon., 2d ed. (London, 1723), 337, "The impressions of the venereal distemper stick to the blood for 30 years together and better, without any trouble or injury to the patient's health; but then there is as vigorous a return of the symptoms, as if it were upon the first onset. The poison of the *tarantula* renews itself infallibly every year, especially about the same time when the patient receiv'd it." See also ibid., 331, 335–36, and 343 on other aspects of the disease's seemingly incurable symptoms and the nature of the dancing that sought to relieve them.

119. See *MGG,* s.v. "Tarantella," and Michael Tusa, "In Defense of Weber," in *Nineteenth-Century Piano Music,* ed. R. Larry Todd (New York, 1990), 162–68. Weber's incomplete novel, *Tonkünstlers Leben,* compares the then-current (1819) Rossini craze to tarantism: "for just as the bite of the tarantula makes people dance, it is not long before they sink exhausted to the ground—cured" (Carl Maria von Weber, *Writings on Music,* trans. Martin Cooper, ed. John Warrack [Cambridge, 1981], 338). As noted above, however, the "cure" was more problematic than Weber here suggests. (The authors are indebted to Prof. R. Larry Todd for drawing our attention to this reference.)

120. It should be noted, however, that Schubert's syphilis evidently did not progress to the tertiary stage, which is characterized by tissue destruction and frequently fatal neurological deterioration. The immediate cause of Schubert's death was almost certainly an infection, possibly typhoid fever. See John O'Shea, *Music and Medicine: Medical Profiles of Great Composers* (London, 1990), 109–17; the accuracy of O'Shea's discussion was kindly verified for us by Daniel M. Musher, M.D., Chief of the Infectious Disease Section and Professor of Medicine, Microbiology/Immunology, Department of Veterans Affairs Medical Center, Houston, Texas.

121. Peter Gülke, *Franz Schubert und seine Zeit* (Laaber, 1991), 207; Hans Holländer, "Stil und poetische Idee in Schuberts d-Moll Streichquartett," *Neue Zeitschrift für Musik* 131 (1970): 239–41. As Wolff points out ("Schubert's 'Der Tod und das Mädchen,'" 169, n. 38), "galloping" rhythms feature prominently in every movement of the quartet.

122. Baglivi, *The Practice of Physick,* 344; Sigerist, "The Story of Tarantism," 108.

123. See Wolff, "Schubert's 'Der Tod und das Mädchen,'" 150–52, 160–62.

124. On the "omnibus," see Walter Piston, *Harmony,* 5th ed., rev. Mark DeVoto (New York, 1987) and Robert W. Wason, *Viennese Harmonic Theory from Albrechtsberger to Schenker and Schoenberg* (Ann Arbor, MI, 1985), 15–19; the passage from *Don Giovanni* is the Commendatore's "rispondimi, rispondimi, verrai tu" in the finale of act 2. Other omnibus progressions in Mozart are found in the third movement of the G Minor String Quintet, K. 516, mm. 63–65—a piece that apparently moved Schubert deeply (see *Schubert Reader,* 60)—and in the slow movement of the E♭ Quintet for Piano and Winds, K. 452, mm. 62–66.

125. Wolff, "Schubert's 'Der Tod und das Mädchen,'" 167–69; cf. also the passage at mm. 252ff. and 610ff. in the finale.

126. In the late Middle Ages the interval of the tritone was known as *diabolus in musica* (the devil in music); its use was forbidden because of its dissonance, instability, and difficulty of execution. The demonic associations of the tritone are highlighted in the Wolf's Glen scene of Weber's popular *Der Freischütz* (1821), which Schubert knew and admired (*Memoirs,* 137, and Bellman, *Style Hongrois,* 149ff.); see Robert Bailey, "Visual and Musical Symbolism in German Romantic Opera," in *International Musicological Society: Report of the Twelfth Congress, Berkeley, 1977,* ed. Daniel Heartz and Bonnie Wade (Kassel, 1981), 436–43.

127. The sixteenth pickups to the third beat in mm. 177 and 179 are clusters (pitch class set 4-3).

128. See also Wolff, "Schubert's 'Der Tod und das Mädchen,'" 147–50 et passim.

129. See also Gülke, *Franz Schubert,* 207–209. Performers of this movement may wish to consider adopting Schubert's metronome marking for the song "Der Tod und das Mädchen": ♩ = 54 (alla breve).

130. Schubert's knowledge of bowed strings comes to the fore here: the accented quarter-note bass of the chord followed by a three-string rip is among the most powerful sounds such instruments can make.

131. Gülke, *Franz Schubert,* 208.

132. Performers should carefully consider Schubert's dynamic markings on these pages; while cellists understandably find it attractive to maintain full power in the dramatic gestures of mm. 137–40, Schubert has reduced the level from *fff* to *f*. Similarly, the entire quartet is to drop (unexpectedly) to *mf* at m. 141.

133. See also Brown, *Schubert: A Critical Biography,* 129.

134. See also Wolff, "Schubert's 'Der Tod und das Mädchen,'" 164–66.

135. See *NSA* VI/5, *Streichquartette* 3:179, 190, and *Schubert Reader,* 506–8. Although Deutsch (following Kreißle von Hellborn and Grove) suggests that Schubert "cut part of the first movement and made other alterations," the surviving portion of the autograph shows no sign of such alterations (see Wolff, "Schubert's 'Der Tod und das Mädchen,'" 159, n. 24, and Werner Aderhold, preface to *NSA* VI/5, *Streichquartette* 3: xvii–xviii. The Schuppanzigh quotation is from *Memoirs,* 289 (cf. also 372–73); this report comes from Schubert's friend Franz Lachner, at whose apartment the D Minor Quartet was eventually performed in 1826. According to Deutsch (*Schubert Reader,* 506), Schuppanzigh was not then among the performers; thus his reading of the quartet probably took place after he had performed the Octet and A Minor Quartet (which is dedicated to Schuppanzigh) in the spring of 1824. See also Werner Aderhold, preface to *NSA* VI/5, *Streichquartette* 3: xi–xii, who suggests that declining interest in string quartet performance and publication may have been a factor as well.

136. Maynard Solomon, *Beethoven* (New York, 1977), 270–71.

137. See Karl Geiringer, "Schubert's Arpeggione Sonata and the 'Super Arpeggio,'" *Musical Quarterly* 65 (1979): 513–23 (quotation on 522, from *Cäcilia* 1 [1824]: 168).

138. Specifically, the slow movement of the Mozart C Major Viola Quintet, K. 515, and the slow movement of Beethoven's Second Symphony, Op. 36.

139. See Robert Winter, "Paper Studies and the Future of Schubert Research," *Schubert Studies,* ed. Badura-Skoda and Branscombe, 257–68.

140. See Solomon, "Schubert and the Peacocks," 204–5, and *Schubert Reader,* 528–29 and 538.

141. The first two performances of Beethoven's Ninth Symphony, Op. 125, took place in May 1824; his Quartets in E♭, Op. 127, and A minor, Op. 132, were performed by the Schuppanzigh Quartet in 1825, and that ensemble gave the premiere of the B♭, Op. 130, with the *Grosse Fuge* as finale, on 21 March 1826 (*The New Grove*, s.v. "Beethoven, Ludwig van," 374–75). Deutsch, *Schubert Reader,* 536, suggests that "Schubert seems to have been present at all the concerts of Schuppanzigh's quartet during the preceding months" (i.e., prior to mid-1826).

142. Ernst Behler, *Irony and the Discourse of Modernity* (Seattle, 1990), 83.

143. Dahlhaus, "Sonata Form in Schubert," 1, 2, 4, 8, 9 (Adorno discusses musical epic, novel, and remembrance in his *Mahler: A Musical Physiognomy,* trans. Edmund Jephcott [Chicago, 1992]). Dahlhaus's categorization of the five sections as introduction, antecedent, consequent, elaboration, and transition is, however, perhaps too rigid.

144. Dahlhaus, 10, 2.

145. Gülke, *Franz Schubert und seine Zeit,* 212.

146. Dahlhaus, "Sonata Form in Schubert," 11 and 4; cf. also Einstein, *Schubert,* 255.

147. This idea is adumbrated by Tovey in "Franz Schubert (1797–1828)," in *The Main Stream of Music,* 121.

148. Ibid., 119; Tovey, "Tonality in Schubert," in *The Main Stream of Music,* 142–43.

149. The autograph manuscript reveals that Schubert initially planned this movement in B minor, whereby it began with F♯ in all parts—i.e., the motivic descending semitone from the previous tonic, G. (See *NSA* VI/5, *Streichquartette* 3: xxvi, 193, 207.)

150. The semitone drop is a case of "expressive" tonality—unexpected motion by half or whole step, either up to suggest rising energy and brightness, or down to evoke darker, more depressed affect; Schubert uses the procedure frequently in his later songs, and it becomes a commonplace device in later nineteenth-century music (see Robert Bailey, "The Structure of the *Ring* and Its Evolution," *19th Century Music* 1 [1977]: 51–52).

151. Opening of No. 10, "Uhui"; see note 126 above.

152. See R. Larry Todd, "The Chamber Music of Mendelssohn," pp. 182–83 in this volume; cf. also Westrup, *Schubert Chamber Music,* 45.

153. As Judy Gillett observes in "The Problem of Schubert's G Major String Quartet," *Music Review* 35 (1974): 290–91, the C♯ minor episode is actually derived from the material labeled "*e*" in Table 2.2 (mm. 209–15), which in turn is closely related to mm. 2–4 of the movement's opening. "*Everything,*" she writes, "boils down to the *same* thing. Every time Schubert appears to be saying something new—expressing something different—it turns out to be merely what he was saying before said in a different way" (p. 291).

154. Gülke, *Franz Schubert und seine Zeit,* 212; see also *Schubert Reader,* 613–14, 751–52, as well as Werner Aderhold, preface to *NSA* VI/5, *Streichquartette* 3: xix; the Berlin review is cited there from the *Allgemeine musikalische Zeitung* (new series) 6 (1871): 748.

155. See *Schubert Reader,* 350, 522, 524, 599, 613–14, 715, 743; Bocklet also gave the first performance of a Schubert piano trio (possibly the B♭) in December 1827 (*Schubert Reader,* 698). On Hungarian style in D. 850, see Bellman, *Style Hongrois,* 98–99, 168, 226.

156. *Wiener Zeitschrift für Kunst,* 7 June 1828, cited in *Schubert Reader,* 781.

157. Cf. mm. 52, 65, 73, 103ff., 269ff., 296, 304, 334ff., 437ff., 549ff., 575ff., 587, 601ff.

158. Bellman, *Style Hongrois*, 126–27; cf. also Einstein, *Schubert*, 275.

159. Einstein, *Schubert*, 276.

160. The local and large-scale significance of the minor/major third motive is reflected in the first three bass notes of the introduction: c–A–A♭.

161. Liszt, *The Gipsy in Music*, 313; see Bellman, *Style Hongrois*, 106–9, 169–70.

162. Einstein, *Schubert*, 276.

163. Ibid.; Westrup, *Schubert Chamber Music*, 56.

164. There are some subtle preparations for this moment; among them are the lowered-sixth-degree inflections of the dominant pedal in the a^2 passages (e.g., mm. 518–21) and the shimmering treatment of the head motive in parallel motion with offbeat accompaniment in m. 611ff., which emphasizes its connection to "Sei mir gegrüßt."

165. See *Schubert Reader*, 715–16, 767.

166. The "Archduke" Trio in B♭, Op. 97, was performed on 21 March 1826 at Schuppanzigh's last subscription concert of the season (see *Schubert Reader*, 536).

167. John Reed, *Schubert: The Final Years* (New York, 1972), 61–68, 260–61; Arnold Feil, preface to *NSA* VI/vii: xii; Winter, "Paper Studies," 222, 247–50.

168. See *Schubert Reader*, 751–55, 698, 713–14, 724–25, and Badura-Skoda, "The Chronology of Schubert's Piano Trios," 284–88.

169. Quoted in translation by Badura-Skoda, 279.

170. Cf. the similar situation in the development of the "Arpeggione" Sonata, p. 92 above.

171. Winter, "Paper Studies," 250.

172. Since the 1950s this B section has been compared to an Upper Austrian work song for piledrivers, who joined in unison hammer blows on every second beat of the thirty-four measures (see Badura-Skoda, "The Chronology of Schubert's Piano Trios," 281). If Schubert indeed watched and listened to piledrivers while visiting Gmunden in 1825, his treatment of the work song motive in the "Notturno" would seem to be an obvious and amusing double entendre.

173. Einstein, *Schubert*, 278.

174. Thomas A. Denny, "Articulation, Elision, and Ambiguity in Schubert's Mature Sonata Forms: The Op. 99 Trio Finale in Its Context," *Journal of Musicology* 6 (1988): 340–66.

175. Ibid., 355.

176. Schubert's preliminary draft for the first three movements of the E♭ Trio (published in *NSA* VI/vii: 261ff.) provides evidence of numerous compositional changes, including restructuring of the first movement's tonal scheme, that cannot be addressed here.

177. See Manfred Willfort, "Das Urbild des Andante aus Schuberts Klaviertrio Es-dur, D. 929," *Österreichische Musikzeitschrift* 33 (1978): 277–83, from which Example 2.16 is reproduced through courtesy of the *Österreichische Musikzeitschrift*, Marion Diederichs-Lafite, editor. The English translation of the text printed here was kindly provided by Benta Bob.

178. E.g., the minuet of the D Minor Quartet, Op. 76, No. 2, or perhaps those of Symphonies No. 23, 44, or 47.

179. Cf. Brown, *Schubert: A Critical Biography*, 201.

180. In a letter to his publisher dated 10 May 1828 Schubert writes about the E♭

trio: "Be sure to have it performed for the first time by capable people, and most particularly see to a continual uniformity of tempo at the changes of the time signature in the last movement" (*Schubert Reader,* 774). Thus performers must choose the tempo carefully to accomodate the wide variety of materials in the movement.

181. Both versions of the movement are included in *NSA* VI/vii: 57ff.; see also the letter cited in note 180 above. The longer version has been recorded by the Mozartean Players on Harmonia Mundi [France] HMU 907095.

182. On this issue see Thomas A. Denny, "Too Long? Too Loose? and Too Light?: Critical Thoughts about Schubert's Mature Finales," *Studies in Music* 23 ([Australia] 1989): 25–52.

183. *Schubert Reader,* 757.

184. See Brown, *Schubert: A Critical Biography,* 201–2.

185. See *Schubert Reader,* 810–11, 60, 360–64, 552.

186. Cf. also Reed, *Schubert: The Final Years,* 241–42. According to the musicologist Dennis Stevens, "It was so adored by one English chamber-music player that he had it carved on his tombstone" (liner notes for the Heifetz-Piatigorsky Concerts, RCA Soria Series LD/LDS 6159 [1962]).

187. Such moments recall Schubert's comments in "My Dream," the dream or fantasy he wrote out in early July 1822: "Whenever I attempted to sing of love, it turned to pain. And again, when I tried to sing of pain, it turned to love" (*Schubert Reader,* 227).

188. The canonic portions of this movement, along with several impressive contrapuntal passages in both piano trios, clearly justify Schubert's wish to study counterpoint with Sechter during his last weeks—not merely to overcome deficiency, but to expand upon developing interest and strength. See Alfred Mann, "Schubert's Lesson with Sechter," *19th Century Music* 6 (1982): 159ff.; the arrangements with Sechter date from November 1828.

189. The authors are indebted to Jonathan Bellman for personal communication concerning Gypsy elements in this portion of the movement.

190. Bellman, *Style Hongrois,* 106, 126.

191. Bellman, *Style Hongrois,* 115, 117. In a subsequent appearance (mm. 233ff.) the theme is presented in characteristic Hungarian dotted rhythms.

192. *Memoirs,* 143.

193. From Schubert's diary entries of 1816, in *Schubert Reader,* 60, 64.

Select Bibliography

Badura-Skoda, Eva. "The Chronology of Schubert's Piano Trios." In *Schubert Studies: Problems of Style and Chronology,* edited by Eva Badura-Skoda and Peter Branscombe, 277–95. Cambridge, 1982.

Badura-Skoda, Eva, and Peter Branscombe, eds. *Schubert Studies: Problems of Style and Chronology.* Cambridge, 1982.

Beach, David. "Schubert's Experiments with Sonata Form: Formal-Tonal Design versus Underlying Structure." *Music Theory Spectrum* 15 (1993): 1–18.

Bellman, Jonathan. *The "Style Hongrois" in the Music of Western Europe.* Boston, 1993.

Brown, Maurice J. E. *Schubert: A Critical Biography.* London, 1961.

Brown, Maurice J. E., and Eric Sams. *The New Grove Schubert.* New York, 1983.

Chusid, Martin. "Das 'Orchestermäßige' in Schuberts früher Streicherkammermusik." In *Zur Aufführungspraxis der Werke Franz Schuberts,* edited by Vera Schwarz, 77–86. Munich, 1981.

———. "Schubert's Cyclic Compositions of 1824." *Acta musicologica* 36 (1964): 37–45.

———. "Schubert's Overture for String Quintet and Cherubini's Overture to *Faniska.*" *Journal of the American Musicological Society* 15 (1962): 78–84.

Cone, Edward T. "Schubert's Beethoven." *Musical Quarterly* 56 (1970): 779–93.

———. "Schubert's Promissory Note: An Exercise in Musical Hermeneutics." *19th Century Music* 5 (1982): 233–41. Reprinted in *Schubert: Critical and Analytical Studies,* edited by Walter Frisch, 13–30. Lincoln, NE, 1986.

———. "Schubert's Unfinished Business." *19th Century Music* 7 (1984): 222–32.

Coolidge, Richard A. "Form in the String Quartets of Franz Schubert." *Music Review* 32 (1971): 309–25.

Dahlhaus, Carl. "Formprobleme in Schuberts frühen Streichquartetten." In *Schubert-Kongreß Wien 1978: Bericht,* edited by Otto Brusatti, 191–97. Graz, 1979.

———. "Sonata Form in Schubert: The First Movement of the G-Major String Quartet, Op. 161 (D. 887)." Translated by Thilo Reinhard. In *Schubert: Critical and Analytical Studies,* edited by Walter Frisch, 1–12. Lincoln, NE, 1986.

Denny, Thomas. "Articulation, Elision, and Ambiguity in Schubert's Mature Sonata Forms: The Op. 99 Trio Finale in Its Context." *Journal of Musicology* 6 (1988): 340–66.

———. "Too Long? Too Loose? and Too Light?: Critical Thoughts about Schubert's Mature Finales." *Studies in Music* 23 ([Australia] 1989): 25–52.

Deutsch, Otto Erich. *Franz Schubert: Thematisches Verzeichnis seiner Werke in chronologischer Folge.* Revised and enlarged by Walther Dürr, Arnold Feil, Christa Landon, et al. *NSA* viii/4. Kassel, 1978.

———, ed. *Schubert: Memoirs by His Friends.* Translated by Rosamond Ley and John Nowell. London, 1958.

———, ed. *The Schubert Reader: A Life of Franz Schubert in Letters and Documents.* Translated by Eric Blom. New York, 1951. [Also published in London as *Schubert: A Documentary Biography.*]

Einstein, Alfred. *Schubert: A Musical Portrait.* New York, 1951.

Erickson, Raymond, ed. *Schubert's Vienna.* New Haven, 1997.

Frisch, Walter, ed. *Schubert: Critical and Analytical Studies.* Lincoln, NE, 1986.

Geiringer, Karl. "Schubert's Arpeggione Sonata and the 'Super Arpeggio.'" *Musical Quarterly* 65 (1979): 513–23.

Gibbs, Christopher H., ed. *The Cambridge Companion to Schubert.* Cambridge, 1997.

Gillett, Judy. "The Problem of Schubert's G Major String Quartet (D. 887)." *Music Review* 35 (1974): 281–92.

Gülke, Peter. "In What Respect a Quintet? On the Disposition of Instruments in the String Quintet D 956." In *Schubert Studies: Problems of Style and Chronology,* edited by Eva Badura-Skoda and Peter Branscombe, 173–85. Cambridge, 1982.

———. *Franz Schubert und seine Zeit.* Laaber, 1991.

Hilmar, Ernst. "Datierungsprobleme im Werk Schuberts." In *Schubert-Kongreß Wien 1978: Bericht,* edited by Otto Brusatti, 45–60. Graz, 1979.

———. *Franz Schubert in His Time.* Translated by Reinhard G. Pauly. Portland, OR, 1988.

————. *Verzeichnis der Schubert-Handschriften in der Musiksammlung der Wiener Stadt- und Landesbibliothek.* Catalogus Musicus 8. Kassel, 1978.

Kindermann, William. "Schubert's Tragic Perspective."In *Schubert: Critical and Analytical Studies*, edited by Walter Frisch, 65–83. Lincoln, NE, 1986.

Konold, Wulf. *The String Quartet from Its Beginnings to Franz Schubert.* Translated by Susan Hellauer. New York, 1983.

Kramer, Richard. "*Gradus ad Parnassum:* Beethoven, Schubert, and the Romance of Counterpoint." *19th Century Music* 11 (1987): 107–20.

McClary, Susan. "Constructions of Subjectivity in Schubert's Music." In *Queering the Pitch: The New Gay and Lesbian Musicology*, edited by Philip Brett, Elizabeth Wood, and Gary C. Thomas, 205–33. New York, 1994.

McCreless, Patrick. "A Candidate for the Canon? A New Look at Schubert's Fantasie in C Major for Violin and Piano." *19th Century Music* 20 (1997): 205–30.

Newbound, Brian. *Schubert: The Music and the Man.* London, 1997.

19th Century Music 17, no. 1 (1993). Special issue: *Schubert: Music, Sexuality, Culture.*

Sigerist, Henry E. "The Story of Tarantism." In *Music and Medicine*, edited by Dorothy M. Schullian and Max Schoen, 96–116. New York, 1948.

Solomon, Maynard. "Franz Schubert and the Peacocks of Benvenuto Cellini." *19th Century Music* 12 (1989): 193–206.

————. "Schubert and Beethoven." *19th Century Music* 3 (1979): 114–25.

Thomas, Werner. *Schubert-Studien.* Frankfurt am Main, 1990.

Tovey, Donald Francis. "Franz Schubert." In *The Main Stream of Music and Other Essays*, 103–33. New York, 1949.

————. "Tonality in Schubert." In *The Main Stream of Music and Other Essays*, 134–59. New York, 1949.

Truscott, Harold. "Schubert's D Minor String Quartet." *Music Review* 19 (1958): 27–36.

————. "Schubert's String Quartet in G Major." *Music Review* 20 (1959): 119–45.

Webster, James. "Schubert's Sonata Form and Brahms's First Maturity." *19th Century Music* 2 (1978): 18–35; 3 (1979): 52–71.

Westrup, J. A. "The Chamber Music." In *The Music of Schubert*, edited by Gerald Abraham, 88–110. New York, 1947.

————. *Schubert Chamber Music.* BBC Music Guides. Seattle, 1969.

Whaples, Miriam K. "On Structural Integration in Schubert's Instrumental Works." *Acta musicologica* 40 (1968): 186–95.

Winter, Robert. "Paper Studies and the Future of Schubert Research." In *Schubert Studies: Problems of Style and Chronology*, edited by Eva Badura-Skoda and Peter Branscombe, 209–75. Cambridge, 1982.

Wolff, Christoph. "Schubert's 'Der Tod und das Mädchen': Analytical and Explanatory Notes on the Song D 531 and the Quartet D 810." In *Schubert Studies: Problems of Style and Chronology*, edited by Eva Badura-Skoda and Peter Branscombe, 143–71. Cambridge, 1982.

CHAPTER THREE

The Chamber Music of Spohr and Weber

Clive Brown

The music of Louis Spohr (1784–1859) and Carl Maria von Weber (1786–1826) has many common stylistic features. Both composers had a predilection for lyricism, melodic and harmonic chromaticism, brilliant passagework, and colorful instrumentation. They also shared with other contemporaries a liking for certain melodic gestures and for stock rhythmic patterns such as those of the polacca and bolero. Both were virtuoso performers, Spohr on the violin and Weber on the piano, and each composed much for his own instrument. Yet their chamber music outputs are very different in profile and content.

Weber's chamber works, including all his music that might possibly be listed under that heading, number scarcely a dozen, of which only four are substantial compositions. Spohr's, on the other hand, run to more than a hundred, of which at least half are pieces of major proportions. This difference does not arise simply from Spohr's longevity, for by the time of Weber's death in 1826 Spohr had already composed more than fifty chamber works; nor is the contrast between the two composers' outputs merely the result of greater productivity on Spohr's part, although he was certainly the more prolific of the two. The explanation lies partly in their activities as performers. Weber could display his talents as composer/performer by playing his own piano sonatas and brilliant piano solos, whereas Spohr, requiring accompaniment, could only achieve the same end in ensemble music with a prominent violin part. If Weber's piano sonatas, variations, and numerous other piano pieces are taken into account as equivalent to some of Spohr's ensemble pieces, the imbalance is less evident. However, to characterize Spohr's chamber music, even in his earlier years, as primarily inspired by the need to provide vehicles for his own virtuosity would grossly distort the nature of his involvement in the field, and to link Weber's relative lack of interest in chamber music with an absence of compulsion from practical considerations would be to misunderstand the bent of his genius. Differences in temperament and aptitude undoubtedly played a significant part in shaping the profile of their outputs. Although both composers made significant contributions to German opera, Weber's preoccupation with the theater was more intense, while Spohr, despite his substantial output of stage works, was ambitious to prove himself in all the major fields in which his Classical predecessors had distinguished themselves.

Weber's chamber music was composed over a period of about fifteen years and belongs stylistically to the phase in German music, generally perceived as "early Romantic," in which there seems sometimes to be an unresolved conflict between form and content. A portion of Spohr's chamber music is also part of that phase, but his later works, the last of which are coeval with the earlier chamber music of Brahms, foreshadow, albeit tentatively, many subsequent nineteenth-century developments. Finally, it is notable that Weber did not write more than one major chamber work in any genre and that he avoided the principal forms of the day, the string quartet and the piano trio (with violin and cello). Spohr contributed substantially to most of the mainstream forms as well as producing works for several more unusual instrumental combinations. While Spohr's chamber music, therefore, lends itself to discussion in periods and genres, Weber's must be considered mainly in terms of individual compositions.

Carl Maria von Weber

Major works

Piano Quartet in B♭, Op. 8, J. 76[1]

Clarinet Quintet in B♭, Op. 34, J. 182

Grand Duo Concertant for Clarinet and Piano, Op. 48, J. 204

Trio for Piano, Flute, and Cello, Op. 63, J. 259

Minor works

Six Variations on a Theme from Vogler's *Samori*, for piano with violin and cello ad libitum, Op. 6, J. 43

Nine Variations on a Norwegian Theme, for violin and piano, Op. 22, J. 61

Seven Variations on a Theme from *Silvana*, for clarinet and piano, Op. 33, J. 128

Six sonates progressives for violin and piano, J. 99–104

Melody for clarinet (with piano accompaniment by F. W. Jähns), J. 119

Divertimento assai facile for guitar and piano, Op. 38, J. 207

Weber's chamber music output began modestly in 1804 with his six variations on the aria "Woher mag dies wohl kommen" (J. 43) from his teacher Georg Joseph Vogler's opera *Samori,* of which he was at that time preparing a vocal score. The piece has similarities with Spohr's early potpourris and variations, yet it is nearer to solo piano music than chamber music in that the violin and cello parts, which Weber designated *ad libitum,* merely lend support and color to the principal instrument. Weber did not, however, seek simply to provide a display piece for piano; his concern, like Spohr's, in this type of composition was "with the musical rather than the virtuosic possibilities of the theme."[2] This is less the case with his contemporaneous set of solo piano variations on another of Vogler's themes (J. 40), which more uninhibitedly reflects the eighteen-year-old composer's already formidable command of the keyboard.

Four years and several sets of variations later, Weber made a more serious attempt at a concerted chamber work with the Variations on a Norwegian Theme for violin and piano. Weber and Spohr are curiously linked by this piece: it was performed by them in Gotha in 1812 (when, according to Weber's diary, "Spohr played gloriously"), and it shares tonality (D minor) and dedicatee (the Prague banker Ignaz Kleinwächter) with Spohr's *Quatuor brillant,* Op. 11 (1806–7). Like Spohr's quartet, the variations were enthusiastically acclaimed by the influential critic Friedrich Rochlitz;[3] and both works are more than merely display music. Weber's variations anticipate his impressive Grand Duo Concertant, Op. 48, in their virtuoso treatment of the instruments, and belong unequivocally to the genre of composition, cultivated by both composers, in which two or more instruments are treated as equal partners, vying with one another in brilliance.

Weber's first substantial chamber work, the Piano Quartet in B♭ (J. 76), completed in 1809, also suggests comparison with Spohr's music of this period in its mixture of concerted and *concertante* elements. As in the best of Spohr's early string quartets, attention is focused on the leading instrument (in this case the piano) without relegating the others to a merely accompanying role; the strings play an integral part in the statement or elaboration of important thematic material. A significant feature, typical of much nineteenth-century writing for piano and strings, is the tendency to give rapid passagework to the piano while the strings are allotted more flowing melodic parts. Similar treatment, also found in the music of many of Weber's older pianist contemporaries, such as Jan Ladislav Dussek and Prince Louis Ferdinand of Prussia (whose two piano quartets published in 1806 may have served as Weber's direct inspiration), is to be encountered again and again in the piano chamber music of such minor composers as C. G. Reissiger and even such major ones as Mendelssohn. It is particularly evident in the first movement of Weber's Piano Quartet; in the Adagio ma non troppo (apart from the *più moto* middle section) and the Menuetto the distinction is less apparent, although it recurs to some extent in the finale.

In its melodic and harmonic dress and management of material the quartet is also typical of the burgeoning early-Romantic idiom of the first decade of the nineteenth century, again revealing kinship with Dussek and

Prince Louis Ferdinand. The thematic matter ranges from typical Classical triadic motives to characteristic Romantic self-contained, square-cut, chromatically embellished melodies. The diatonic opening gesture of the piece (Example 3.1a) could have provided Haydn or Beethoven with the material for most of a movement, but although Weber recalls it in the codetta to the exposition, the development, and the coda, its reappearances are primarily restatements rather than explorations of its potential. As in so many of Weber's sonata movements, the emphasis is on a juxtaposition of often heterogeneous themes and figures as opposed to organic development from a few germinal ideas. The sixteen-bar cantabile theme (Example 3.1b), decked out in chromatic glad rags, which appears at measure 56 and returns in the tonic in the recapitulation, belongs to a genus frequently encountered in the music of Weber and his contemporaries. Charming as these themes may be in themselves, they are generally inimical to the Classical sonata principal. Weber seems most assured in the slow movement, where he had greater scope to exercise his well-developed feeling for texture, color, and atmosphere; typically, this was the first movement to be composed (as early as October 1806). The *presto* finale, too, in which impetus and character take precedence over formal subtlety, is confident and effective, and his alert feeling for instrumental texture and color is shown in the way the vivacious ideas are playfully tossed between strings and piano.

EXAMPLE 3.1.(a).   Carl Maria von Weber, Quartet for Piano and Strings in Bb, Op. 8, J. 76 (1809), mvt. 1: (a) mm. 1–4

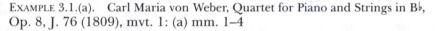

EXAMPLE 3.1.(b)   mm. 54–65.

Whereas the Piano Quartet had occupied Weber over a three-year period, his next chamber compositions, the six *Sonates progressives pour le piano-forté avec violon obligé* (J. 99–104), were composed in less than a month of grueling labor in the autumn of 1810, in fulfillment of a commission from the publisher André, for which he had already been paid. Weber evidently tried to produce the short, pleasant, undemanding sonatinas for amateur consumption that André required. But despite their directness and brevity, and the absence of any really daunting difficulties (especially in the violin part), Weber had clearly aimed too high for the market the publisher had in mind; as he informed his friend Gottfried Weber in a letter of 1 November: "The —— has sent my sonatas back on the splendid grounds that *they're too good,* they must be much more ordinary."[4] Simrock, however, was happy enough to publish them. Although they can scarcely be regarded as significant contributions to the violin sonata repertoire, they contain, within their unambitious remit, music of simple charm that might well be played more frequently by the type of amateur musician for whom they were originally intended. In their eclectic content they reflect a range of styles and genres popular at the time. As well as three "Classical" first movements in compressed sonata form and a couple of short slow movements, there is a typically French "dotted rhythm" rondo, such as Spohr often used (Example 3.2);[5] a "Polish" rondo, a polonaise finale, a bolero ("Carattere espagnuolo"), an "Air russe," a "Romanze," a Siciliano, and a set of variations on "Warum musst' ich dich je erblicken?" from Weber's opera *Silvana*, which he revised and expanded the following year for performance by himself and the clarinetist Heinrich Bärmann in Prague (making the clarinet part more brilliant than the violin part). Curiously, in the clarinet version (J. 128), although Weber added two bars to the second section of the theme, he retained the simple eight-bar structure in the subsequent variations.

EXAMPLE 3.2.   Weber, *Sonate progressive pour le piano-forté avec violon obligé,* No. 1, J. 99 (1810), rondo, opening.

It was also for Bärmann that Weber composed his attractive Clarinet Quintet. He began it during a walking tour in Switzerland in September 1811; the Adagio was completed in March 1812 and, having composed a Menuetto "capriccio," he gave it to Bärmann as a birthday present in April 1813 still lacking its Rondo, which was finished only shortly before the work's first performance in August 1815. Despite its Classical four-movement structure, the Clarinet Quintet owes nothing to Mozart's great Quintet. Like some of Spohr's *quatuors brillants,* it is essentially a display piece, with the strings providing little more than a discreet foil to the virtuosity of the clarinetist; its virtues are those of a concerto rather than chamber music. Only in the scherzo is there more than a hint of genuine chamber music textures and procedures.

In the Grand Duo Concertant, composed during 1815 and 1816, Weber built on the technique developed in his variations, combining the virtuosity of clarinet and piano in the manner Spohr had adopted in his sonatas for violin and harp. This important early nineteenth-century genre of concertante chamber music is related, perhaps, to tendencies apparent in the more extrovert aspects of the late-eighteenth-century French tradition of the *quatuor concertant*. Something similar can be found in Beethoven's early violin sonatas (notably Op. 12, No. 3), written about the time of Rudolf Kreutzer's visit to Vienna, and it culminates in the *Kreutzer* Sonata of 1802–3, though in Beethoven's case it seems less that the nature of the music is generated by his approach to the instruments than that his handling of the instruments arises from his musical intentions. Weber's Grand Duo, as John Warrack succinctly remarks, "bases its entire material and form on the demands of shared piano and clarinet virtuosity."[6] The effectiveness of the work owes much to the theatrical flair with which the composer treats the two instruments as protagonists in a drama, sometimes combining them in brilliant thirds and sixths, sometimes highlighting their contrasting natures.

One other, very different chamber work, the *Divertimento assai facile* (J. 207) for guitar and piano, dates from the end of Weber's three-year period as kapellmeister of the opera in Prague. Although Weber was an excellent guitarist as well as pianist, neither part is particularly taxing, and the piano part is especially straightforward. Its four movements (Andante, Waltz, Variations, Polacca) are quite clearly *pièces d'occasion* with little of the composer's individuality in them, and the modest technical demands are matched by modest musical ones.

After moving to Dresden as Hofkapellmeister of the German Opera, much of Weber's thought and creative energy was focused increasingly on the problems of fostering a national German opera, for which he had attempted to lay the foundations during his Prague years. He began serious work on *Der Freischütz* in 1817, and for the rest of his short life, theater music and court commissions dominated his output. The Trio for Flute, Cello, and Piano (J. 259), completed in 1819 from drafts going back perhaps to 1814, was to be his last piece of chamber music, and it is in many ways his most satisfactory one. There is scarcely a hint of virtuosity for its own sake in this work: each member of the ensemble contributes equally to the unfolding of the musical ideas, and the choice of flute rather than violin allowed Weber to respond to his well-developed feeling for instrumental color. His handling of form is also more assured and imaginative—the recapitulation of the first movement with the second subject (reserving a return to the somber first theme for the coda), the highly unusual structure of the trio-less scherzo, the "Schäfers Klage" (Shepherd's complaint) marked *andante espressivo* (a kind of varied strophic song), the sonata-form finale with its compressed recapitulation—all seem to derive their structure from the richly characterful material, rather than, as in many of Weber's earlier sonata-cycle works, having the material forced into a predetermined form. The treatment of chromaticism, too, is far subtler than in the Piano Quartet; for example, the first appearance of the first movement's second subject with a chromatic inflection nicely eases the transition from the intense mood of the opening to the establishment of the relative major (Example 3.3a), but when the same idea begins the recapitulation, it is firmly in the tonic major (Example 3.3b).[7] In the "Schäfers Klage" the use of the diminished seventh chord, so often a cliché, seems motivated by genuine dramatic need and, in the transition to the final bars, is handled with almost Schubertian delicacy (Example 3.4).

EXAMPLE 3.3.   Weber, Trio for Flute, Cello, and Piano in G Minor, Op. 63, J. 259 (1819), mvt. 1: (a) mm. 49–51; (b) mm. 124–26.

a)

b)

EXAMPLE 3.4.   Weber, Trio for Flute, Cello, and Piano in G Minor, Op. 63, mvt. 2, mm. 54–55.

Weber's growing preoccupation with opera composition seems already to have been exerting its influence strongly in this work. His success in finding effective structures may well be related to the dramatic quality of each of the four movements, which appear almost to have a hidden program. The main theme of the finale forges a direct link with *Der Freischütz*, as Jähns observed, by its resemblance to the piccolo motif in Caspar's drinking song.[8]

Louis Spohr

Major works

Duets for 2 Violins, Opp. 3, 9, 39, 67, 148, 150, 153

Duet for Violin and Viola, Op. 13

String Quartets, Opp. 4, 11, 15, 27, 29, 30, 43, 45, 58, 61, 68, 74, 82, 83, 84, 93, 132, 141, 146

String Quintets, Opp. 33, 69, 91, 106, 129, 144

String Sextet, Op. 140

Double String Quartets, Opp. 65, 77, 87, 136

Sonatas for Violin and Harp, Opp. 16, 113, 114, 115, WoO. 23[9]

Duos for Violin and Piano, Opp. 95, 96, 112

Piano Trios, Opp. 119, 123, 124, 133, 142

Quintet for Piano and Winds, Op. 52 (version for piano and strings as Op. 53)

Quintet for Piano and Strings, Op. 130

Septet for Piano, Winds, and Strings, Op. 147

Octet for Winds and Strings, Op. 32

Nonet for Winds and Strings, Op. 31

Minor works

Fantasias, Potpourris, Rondos, *Salonstücke*, etc., for violin and piano (or harp)

Potpourris and Variations for violin with string accompaniment

Fantasia and Variations on a Theme of Danzi for clarinet and string quartet, Op. 81

By the age of twenty-three, Weber, with several operas to his credit, had just completed his first substantial piece of chamber music and had only begun tentatively to tackle the problems of handling extended sonata structures. At the same age, Spohr had composed several large-scale instrumental works, both orchestral and chamber, and was just beginning to become involved in dramatic composition. From an early stage Spohr, unlike Weber, showed himself at ease with sonata forms. Whereas Weber had grown up in a predominantly theatrical background, Spohr, despite his bourgeois roots, had joined the Brunswick Hofkapelle at the age of fifteen and, through duties in the orchestra as well as the informal performance of chamber music, become familiar with the Classical repertoire. By the age of twenty he was intimately acquainted not only with Haydn's and Mozart's string quartets, but also with Beethoven's violin sonatas Opp. 12, 23, 24, 30, and string quartets Op. 18, which he was one of the earliest North German musicians to champion.

A contrasting influence was the French violin school of Giovanni Battista Viotti and his followers, but this seems to have impinged upon Spohr strongly only after his enthusiasm for the Viennese Classics was already established. The French school had its most powerful effect on his playing and composing after he heard one of its leading representatives, Pierre Rode, performing his A Minor Concerto in Brunswick in 1803. Also significant, especially for the development of Spohr's harmonic idiom, was Luigi Cherubini, whose music, along with that of other French composers, he encountered through his duties in the Brunswick opera orchestra. Spohr's style, like Weber's, but also like Dussek's, Hummel's, and that of many lesser composers of the period, can only be understood as a synthesis of melodic, harmonic, and formal traits derived not only from the language of Viennese Classicism and North German singspiel, but also from a range of other diverse sources.

Spohr's earliest experiments in composition, duets for two violins composed about 1796–97, were primarily subject to German influences, as many of the themes clearly indicate (Example 3.5). His first three published duets, Op. 3 (begun in 1802 but probably revised before publication in 1805), seem also to predate French influence, but clearly reveal the spell exerted on him by early Beethoven, even to the extent of an apparently direct reference to the opening of the F Major Quartet from Beethoven's Op. 18 at the beginning of the first Allegro of Op. 3, No. 2 (Example 3.6). Many of the themes in these duos have a terse, motivic quality reminiscent of Beethoven, while several of the second subjects also have a Beethovenian cast; in addition, Spohr's love of extensively developing short figures, sometimes carried to excess in later works, is already apparent. The equal distribution of material between the two violins also indicates that Spohr already had a genuine feeling for the conversational interplay that is essential to chamber music.

By the time the Op. 3 duos appeared in print Spohr had composed several violin concertos in which the influence of French violin music is evident. It is also apparent in his first essays in quartet writing, made about this time, both in the florid figurations employed at cadence points and in melodic features such as the main theme of the finale of the G Minor Quartet (Example 3.7), similar to the one in Weber's F Major Violin Sonata cited in Example 3.2. By his own account Spohr was already dissatisfied with these early quartets before they appeared in print in 1806, and it is not difficult to appreciate that, comparing them with those of his Classical idols, he should have found them wanting.[10] Apart from the rather undigested mixture of styles, the conversational aspect of the Classical quartet is only intermittently achieved. The two Op. 15 quartets of 1806–8 show greater maturity in this respect, especially the first movement of the D Major Quartet, but Spohr recognized that they still failed to satisfy the most exacting criteria of string quartet writing. None of these quartets displays the assured individuality of the violin concertos Opp. 2, 7, 10, and 17 from the years 1804–7, and he was later forced to accept the justice of Andreas Romberg's observation: "Your quartets will not do yet: they are far behind your orchestral compositions."[11]

EXAMPLE 3.5.   Louis Spohr, Duets for Two Violins (ca. 1796–97): (a) WoO 21, No. 2, mvt. 1, opening; (b) WoO 22, mvt. 3, opening.

EXAMPLE 3.6.   Spohr, Duet for Two Violins, Op. 3, No. 2, mvt. 1, opening.

EXAMPLE 3.7.   Spohr, String Quartet in G Minor, Op. 4, No. 2 (1806), mvt. 4, opening.

Between writing the Op. 4 and Op. 15 quartets, however, Spohr composed the first of his *quatuors brillants* (Op. 11 in D Minor), which he offered to his publisher Kühnel in January 1806 as "of the Rode type."[12] This differed from the other quartets in its three-movement form and in the prominence and virtuosity of the first violin part. The model was evidently Rode's three quartets, Op. 11 (ca. 1803), which are essentially chamber concertos with string trio accompaniment; they had been staple items in Spohr's repertoire, along with pieces by Viotti and quartets of Beethoven and Mozart, on his early concert tours. Friedrich Rochlitz noted Spohr's responsiveness as a performer to the distinctive styles of these compositions in 1804:

> He is altogether a different person when he plays, for example, Beethoven (his darling whom he handles exquisitely) or Mozart (his ideal) or Rode (whose grandiosity he knows so well how to assume, without any scratching and scraping in producing the necessary volume of tone), or when he plays Viotti and *galant* composers: he is a different person because they are different persons.[13]

Yet despite his success in finding the right style for these disparate works and his excellent performance of Classical compositions, a comparison of the Op. 4 and Op. 15 quartets with Op. 11 indicates that at this

stage in his development he was, as a composer, more successful in emu-
lating Rode than in mastering the subtleties of the Classical quartet idiom.
Indeed, in Op. 11 he far surpassed his model; with his highly developed
sense of musical architecture, rich harmonic palette, and rapidly ripening
mastery of compositional techniques, he succeeded, in this and his subsequent *quatuors brillants,* in setting a standard that remained an unattain-
able ideal for others who attempted the genre.

The *quatuor brillant* is certainly closer to a concerto than a string quartet, and it belongs to a class of *brillant* chamber composition, scarcely
performed today, that was cultivated almost exclusively by performer-com-
posers, largely for their own use. These pieces range in style and quality
from the frankly meretricious, in the hands of many scarcely remembered
performers, through competent but uninspired works by a host of medi-
ocre composers such as Rode, Kreutzer, and the Romberg cousins, to compositions of real merit by Spohr, Weber, Hummel, Dussek, and a few others.
The *brillant* music of these composers often transcended its function as a
vehicle for displaying their own virtuosity in a drawing room (or that of
other performers who were incapable of writing their own pieces); although
the accompanying parts may be subordinate, they are, in the best of these
works, sensitively and effectively handled. Spohr showed similar fastidi-
ousness in his more lightweight pieces, the potpourris and variations for
violin with string accompaniment, treating them with as much seriousness
of purpose and attention to detail as his major works.

Spohr was not to return to string quartet composition of either category for several years, but during the period 1805 to 1812, when he was
Konzertmeister to the duke of Saxe-Gotha-Altenburg, he composed other
types of chamber music assiduously. His output at that time included five
sonatas for violin and harp (written for performance with the harp virtuoso Dorette Scheidler, whom he married in 1806), only one of which (Op.
16) was published at the time, two violin duets (Op. 9), a duet for violin
and viola (Op. 13), as well as several of his potpourris and sets of variations with string accompaniment. In the sonatas, which became repertoire
pieces for the concert tours he undertook with Dorette, the *concertante* element predominates, though Spohr gave equal weight to both instruments
and was careful to avoid sacrificing musical substance for the sake of gra-
tuitous effect; but the inevitable emphasis on display and his adoption of
melodic types from the French school (especially dotted themes, as in the
finales of the D/E♭ Major and G/A♭ Major sonatas Opp. 113 and 115)[14]
sometimes seems to sit uncomfortably with his evident reverence for
Classical models. The duets for string instruments, on the other hand, are
masterpieces by any standard; the promise of the Op. 3 duets is fulfilled
in these and the nine later violin duets. Spohr's deep understanding of the
instrument combined with his profound seriousness of purpose enabled
him to achieve an unrivaled richness and variety. The particularly fine
Duo, Op. 13, the only one for violin and viola, is a worthy companion to
the two duets of Mozart, and the whole series triumphantly transcends the
limitations of the medium.

Spohr was deeply interested in the problem of German opera at the beginning of the second decade of the century, and was not idle in this respect. But having resigned his appointment in Gotha to take up a position as leader of the orchestra at Vienna's Theater an der Wien in 1813, he was thrown into the midst of a society in which chamber music was intensively fostered by the music-loving aristocracy and bourgeoisie, and in which the presence of Beethoven and a host of admired performers and composers provided a powerful stimulus. Spohr's long-cherished desire to excel in the composition of chamber music was also given a further fillip by a strange commission from Johann Tost, the dedicatee of Haydn's string quartets Opp. 54, 55, and 64, to compose as much chamber music as he liked, for which Tost would pay on a sliding scale of charges (thirty ducats for a quartet, thirty-five for a quintet, and so on in proportion to the number of instruments involved); the only condition was that Tost should have sole possession of the works and the right to be present at their performances for a period of three years, after which Spohr could dispose of them as he wished. In the years 1812–15, therefore, he produced not only his opera *Faust* and other large-scale works, but also five string quartets (two of them *brillants*), two string quintets, the Octet and Nonet for winds and strings, as well as several slighter chamber pieces.

The first work delivered to Tost under this arrangement, the Quartet in G minor, Op. 27, had already been composed in 1812 and is closer to Op. 11 than Op. 15 in its treatment of the medium. Spohr referred to it in his memoirs as a *Solo-Quartett*,[15] a term that he used interchangeably with *quatuor brillant*, but it was published simply as *Grand quatuor* and seems to occupy a middle ground between the two types, having four movements and more active participation of the three lower instruments than Op. 11. The Quartet, Op. 30, of 1814, referred to by Spohr as a *quatuor brillant*[16] but published simply as *Quartett*, and which became a favorite warhorse for his appearances in Viennese salons, is also in four movements and has a subordinate but not negligible accompaniment. This work is broadly conceived and contains some unusual features; the Menuetto and Trio both appear twice (the movement ending with a short coda to the trio's second appearance), while the finale's alternation of a major-key *moderato* section with a minor-key *vivace* is particularly effective. In both these works Spohr seems to have been aiming to give greater substance to the *quatuor brillant* as a genre of chamber music.

Of the three Op. 29 string quartets, composed between 1813 and 1815, Nos. 1 (1814) and 2 (1815) are quite definitely concerted chamber works; in these he finally found a manner of handling the medium that allowed him unembarrassed expression of his marked stylistic individuality within a genuine quartet texture, albeit one in which brilliance, from all members of the ensemble, played a significant part. The earlier Op. 29, No. 3 (1813), hovers uneasily between the two genres, having more than a hint of the *brillant* style in the trio of the scherzo and in the finale. A similar stylistic distinction exists between the String Quintets, Op. 33, Nos. 1 and 2, although in this case it is the later of the two (in E♭, 1814, published as Op. 33, No. 1) that tends more toward a *brillant* idiom. The G Major Quintet, Op. 33, No. 2, written toward the end of 1813, is a finer composition than its partner, although the E♭ Quintet has many attractive features. The challenge of a new medium often seems particularly to have stimulated Spohr's creative energy. A contemporary reviewer opined that the charming and resourceful *andante* variation movement of the G Major Quintet could "be held as a model for all time, so long at least as the taste for true art does not perish," and maintained that "Haydn, Mozart, and Beethoven themselves have created nothing more magnificent of this kind."[17] Each of its four movements is on the same high level.

The remaining significant chamber works of Spohr's highly productive three years in Vienna, the Nonet and Octet, are written for a mixture of winds and strings. Both compositions, although they are in only four movements, owe something to the serenade tradition that had spawned Beethoven's Septet and was to produce Schubert's Octet. The scoring of the Nonet (violin, viola, cello, bass, flute, oboe, clarinet, bassoon, horn) is unsurprising; that of the Octet (violin, 2 violas, cello, bass, clarinet, 2 horns) more unusual. The combination of horns and violas, together with clarinet, whose lowest register Spohr exploited in a manner scarcely paralleled at that period, gives the Octet a textural richness that makes the sparkling violin part stand out even more strikingly. But it was not only the violin that Spohr treated in a virtuoso manner; his demanding horn parts have given rise to the suggestion that they must have been written for an early valved instrument, although they were certainly intended for the natural horn. Indeed, as in the string chamber music, virtuosity from all members of the ensemble, but not display for its own sake, is a prominent element in the music.

More frankly virtuosic chamber pieces from this period are a Rondo (1813, WoO 33) and a Potpourri for harp and violin (1814, later published as Op. 118). The potpourri was used later in the same year as the basis for the Fantasia and Variations for clarinet and string quartet, Op. 81, the only chamber work among Spohr's virtuoso clarinet compositions (all intended for J. S. Hermstedt).

Spohr's Vienna chamber music displays, as a whole, a considerable advance in compositional technique. It seems likely that his consciousness of the expectations of musicians and connoisseurs in Vienna at that time induced him to pay even greater attention to coherence and compositional subtlety in these works. His fascination with "interesting harmonic progressions" (inspired, according to his pupil Moritz Hauptmann, by Cherubini), his intensification of late-Mozartian chromaticism, his gift for lyrical melody, his contrapuntal expertise (Mendelssohn considered him the best fugue writer of his day),[18] his structural dexterity, his skillful instrumentation, and his flair for effective virtuosity without vapidity allowed him to produce works of real quality. The best of these compositions, technically consummate yet still retaining the freshness of youthful

Spohr, String Quartet in E♭, Op. 29, No. 1, opening (autograph).

inspiration, reach a peak that is sometimes equaled in his later music but never surpassed.

The first movement of Op. 29, No. 1, may be taken as a case study of Spohr's handling of material and of the treatment of harmony and modulation that made his music so fascinating to many contemporary musicians. It begins with a curious two-note motif that is a cryptogram of Spohr's name (E♭ is Es [S] and B♮ is H in German, combined with *po* for *piano* and a quarter rest that looks like an *R*); its harmonic ambivalence seems to generate much of the movement's tonal instability. Even when the tonic key of E♭ has been established at measure 8, the interval of a diminished fourth continues periodically to intrude (Figure 3.1). Measures 8–25 are principally characterized by manipulation of the dotted motive from measure 2 together with versions of the initial motive, expanded to a falling perfect fourth or major or minor sixth as well as the original interval, while the first violin continues its decorative figurations, mostly in triplets. The tonal direction, which until the beginning of measure 20 seems to be toward B♭, is diverted by a rising chromatic bass toward the dominant of D minor (m. 24), where the dotted figure continues insistently in the bass before giving way to an idea derived from the combination of that rhythm with the rising chromatic idea (Example 3.8).

EXAMPLE 3.8.   Spohr, String Quartet in E♭ Major, Op. 29, No. 1 (1814), mvt. 1, mm. 27–30.

A persistent a♮[1] continues uninterruptedly from measures 24 to 36, where it finally resolves itself as the major third of an F[7] chord and the rising chromatic motive settles comfortably in B♭ for what would conventionally be regarded as the second subject (Example 3.9.). Bars 41 to 44 stray, sequentially, as far as the dominant of E minor before returning to a firm, although typically chromatic cadence into B♭. The passage leading toward the codetta of the exposition is characteristic of Spohr's handling of sonata form in movements of this type; a passage of brilliant sixteenths, initiated by the cello, viola and second violin (mm. 49-50) before being handed over to the first violin in measure 54, is combined with constant reference to the movement's basic thematic material. The codetta continues to make use of this thematic material, producing two variants that are to be used after the double bar in the first part of the development (m. 76).

EXAMPLE 3.9.   Spohr, String Quartet in E♭, Op. 29, No. 1, mvt. 1, mm. 35–39.

Although the large-scale tonic–dominant pattern of the exposition is quite conventional, the small-scale harmonic activity is wide-ranging, and chromatic inflection in the melody almost continuous. The most tonally stable section of the exposition—the last twenty-eight bars—seldom seems to be quite firmly in B♭; only eight of these bars are without any notes foreign to the key.

The development, beginning in C minor, combines and recombines the thematic material, passing rapidly through a series of key centers and arriving at C♯ minor after twenty bars, where it immediately shifts enharmonically into a passage of remarkable harmonic daring for the period (Example 3.10). After a five-bar dominant preparation for E major, Spohr slides out of that key two bars before the recapitulation, but not into E♭. The thematic recapitulation does not coincide with the tonal one; the first violin returns to an E♭ key signature while the other instruments remain as before, only changing their key signature when the home tonality reasserts itself (Example 3.11).

The recapitulation keeps fairly close to the structure of the exposition in its restatement of melodic material. Instead of the shift to the dominant of D minor that occurred in measure 24, Spohr bends the end of the previous passage toward E♭ minor and arrives at the dominant of E♭, as might be expected; but then, following the harmonic pattern of the exposition, he slips into C♭ (m. 147) for the "second subject." At measure 160 the brilliant passage recurs in E♭ with the same chromatic inflections as before, although the last seventeen bars of coda, from measure 180, are firmly in the tonic key, providing the only extended passage of unambiguous tonality in the movement.

It is hardly surprising that Beethoven's single recorded comment on Spohr's music should have been that it was "too rich in dissonances, pleasure in his music is marred by his chromatic melody."[19] A more appreciative appraisal of this aspect of his music, one that also indicates the extent to which it was seen as original at that time, was given some ten years later in the journal *Caecilia;* the writer observes that this music could rather be called "chromatic-diatonic than diatonic-chromatic" and continues: "If there were many composers who possessed his deep knowledge of har-

EXAMPLE 3.10.   Spohr, String Quartet in E♭, Op. 29, No. 1, mvt. 1, mm. 97–104.

EXAMPLE 3.11.   Spohr, String Quartet in E♭, Op. 29, No. 1, mvt. 1, mm. 111–18.

mony there would certainly soon be imitators of his style. For although such a manner of writing may well be more suited to the quartet than to the opera, it is not to be denied that it is very attractive."[20] It is difficult for the modern listener, exposed to so much chromaticism in later music, to appreciate the extent to which this aspect of Spohr's style seized the imagination of so many of his younger contemporaries in the second, third, and fourth decades of the nineteenth century, and led to comments such as Sir G. A. Macfarren's, a few years after Spohr's death: "Few if any composers have exercised such influence on their contemporaries as Spohr did, and many living writers may be counted among his imitators."[21]

Another aspect of Spohr's style, conspicuous in the first movement of Op. 29, No. 1, his concern for motivic integration, is equally apparent in his other Vienna chamber works. In the String Quintet, Op. 33, No. 2, a figure introduced in measure 1, or a very close derivative of it, appears in more than 150 of the first movement's 228 bars (Example 3.12). His manipulation of material is resourceful. In the first movement of the Octet, for instance, the opening of the introductory *adagio* (Example 3.13a) provides the material, in reverse order, for the first theme of the ensuing *allegro vivace* (Example 3.13b). The first movement of the Quartet, Op. 29, No. 2, is particularly subtle in its transformations of ideas derived from the initial fourteen-bar theme to provide motivic and melodic material for the whole movement. The process is carried even further in the Nonet, where the first four notes of the piece not only permeate the first movement (Example 3.14), but recur as well in the main theme, codetta, and coda of the Adagio (Example 3.15), and are also jokingly alluded to in the second subject of the high-spirited finale (Example 3.16).

Tovey remarked on Spohr's handling of sonata form: "The masterly scheme (there is only one) of Spohr is (as Schumann remarked) not so easy to imitate as it looks; but it is the prototype of most pseudo-classical work up to the present day; and many teachers believe it to be the only orthodox form."[22] His suggestion of a stereotype form is hardly just; it is true that Spohr stands near the beginning of the period when the mold was beginning to harden, but sonata form was not yet the ready vessel into which a composer's ideas could be poured that it later became. The Vienna works reveal great fertility of invention in Spohr's approach to form. A couple of instances may stand for many. The essentially monothematic F major Adagio of Op. 29, No. 2, unites an exposition containing developmental elements (mm. 23–38) with a combination of development and recapitulation: after a 58-bar exposition in which the dominant has been reached at measure 39, there is a modulation to A♭ major, where, after a statement of the opening theme in that key (mm.

EXAMPLE 3.12.   Spohr, String Quintet in G Major, Op. 33, No. 2 (1813–14), mvt. 1: (a) opening figure; (b) mm. 44–46, derivative of opening.

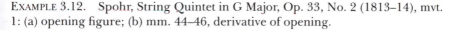

EXAMPLE 3.13.   Spohr, Octet for Winds and Strings in E Major, Op. 32 (1814), mvt. 1: (a) introduction; (b) main theme.

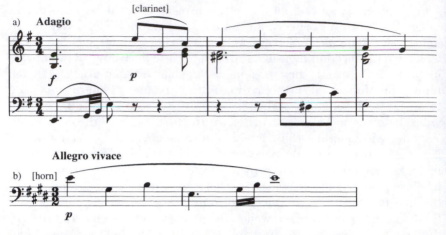

EXAMPLE 3.14.   Spohr, Nonet for Winds and Strings in F Major, Op. 31 (1813), mvt. 1: (a) main theme; (b) m. 28; (c) mm. 125–27.

61–68), a variant of measures 9–22 (mm. 62–78) leads, in measure 79, to the return of the tonic key (and thematic material) that had occurred at measure 39, and the movement proceeds regularly to its close. In the first movement of the Octet, after a fairly regular exposition, there are only ten bars of development before the *adagio* introduction returns, notated in long note values in the *allegro* tempo; this leads directly into a modified bridge passage from the exposition, and the recapitulation begins directly with the second-subject material.

During a period of traveling in Germany, Switzerland, and Italy Spohr composed another *quatuor brillant,* Op. 43, that reverted to the con-

EXAMPLE 3.15.   Spohr, Nonet in F, Op. 31, Adagio: (a) introduction; (b) codetta, mm. 50–52.

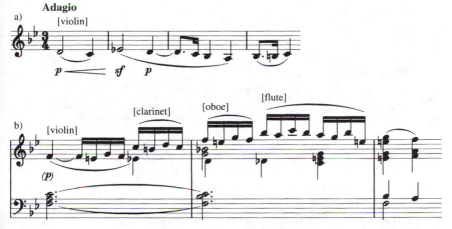

EXAMPLE 3.16.   Spohr, Nonet in F, Op. 31, finale, second subject, mm. 42–49.

ventional three-movement form, and the magnificent Violin Duets, Op. 39, surely among the finest examples of their kind by any composer. Then in 1818 he accepted the post of director of the opera in Frankfurt am Main, where, apart from his duties in the theater (for which he composed his opera *Zemire und Azor*), he took on the organization of public chamber concerts and enriched the repertoire with four further string quartets: the three Op. 45 quartets and the *Quatuor brillant*, Op. 61. Opus 61 is again in the three-movement form typical of the *quatuor brillant* and harks back melodically to the music of the French violin school, as comparison of the opening melody with one by Rode suggests (Example 3.17). The Op. 45 quartets, too, seem to contain rather more of melodic lyricism than the Vienna ones, and there is less intensive motivic work. Chromaticism is still prominent, but Spohr uses it, perhaps, less self-consciously. The sonata-form movements contain fewer formal surprises, though the scherzo/menuetto movements are more extended.

In 1820, having resigned his Frankfurt post the previous year, Spohr also made his first essay in piano chamber music with the Quintet, Op. 52, for Piano and Winds (also for piano and strings as Op. 53), which was intended for performance by his wife, Dorette. Increasing ill health had made harp playing too strenuous for her, but to judge by the extremely taxing piano part of the quintet, her piano playing was unaffected. Chopin

EXAMPLE 3.17.   (a) Spohr, *Quatuor brillant,* Op. 61, mvt. 1, mm. 1–4; (b) Pierre Rode, Violin Concerto no. 8, mvt. 1, opening of first solo.

considered the work "most beautiful" but "intolerably difficult."[23] The quintet is a major work in the repertoire for piano and winds, and each of its four movements is on an equally high plane.

In 1822, through Weber's recommendation, Spohr was offered and accepted the post of Hofkapellmeister in Kassel, where he was to remain for the rest of his life. Although his official duties did not require the composition of chamber music, Spohr held regular musical evenings during the winter months throughout his time in Kassel, and until Dorette Spohr's death in 1834, few years passed without the composition of string quartets, quintets, or double string quartets for performance on these occasions. The three Op. 58 quartets (1822), the first two of which are particularly successful, are similar to the Op. 45 set in many respects, displaying lyricism, brilliance, harmonic ingenuity, and formal innovation within essentially Classical parameters. An example of the latter occurs in Op. 58, No. 2, where *andante* and scherzo are combined in an irregular variation movement, with the scherzo constituting the third of the movement's four variations (Example 3.18). In the same quartet the *all'espagnola* finale continues the tradition of "exotic" movements.

EXAMPLE 3.18.   Spohr, String Quartet, Op. 58, No. 2, mvt. 2: (a) theme; (b) third variation.

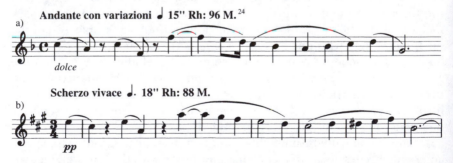

During the period between moving to Kassel and his wife's death, Spohr completed nine more "normal" string quartets (Opp. 74 [1826], 82 [1828–29] and 84 [1831–32]) and two *quatuors brillants* (Opp. 68 [1825] and 83 [1829]). Each of the three sets of quartets contains fine and attractive

music, but few of the individual works are without one or more movements that, although always finely crafted, fall considerably below the best
of which Spohr was capable in terms of inspiration. Tovey's observation of
predictability in Spohr's handling of sonata form is to some extent justified with respect to these and many of his later chamber works. On the
other hand, they contain a number of unusual features: Op. 74, No. 2, has
no scherzo, its middle movements being a Larghetto and an Andante con
variazioni; Op. 82, No. 2 has an Alla polacca instead of a scherzo; the
Andante of Op. 82, No. 3, proceeds for much of the time in alternating
bars of $\frac{4}{8}$ and $\frac{3}{8}$.

The year 1823 saw the composition of Spohr's first double string
quartet, which he described to his friend Speyer as "a wholly new kind of
instrumental work which, so far as I know, I am the first to attempt."
Although Spohr was mistaken in believing that no one had previously
composed for this combination, his Double Quartet in D Minor, Op. 65,
does seem to be without a direct instrumental model. He had apparently
discussed the idea of such a work with Andreas Romberg in 1821, shortly
before Romberg's death, but Spohr's letter to Speyer suggests that the immediate inspiration may rather have come from vocal music: "It is most
like a piece for double chorus, for the two quartets who cooperate here
work against one another in about the same proportion as the two choirs
do."[25] Spohr himself had imaginatively and effectively experimented with
this type of thing in his *a cappella* Mass for five soloists and two five-part
choirs of 1820, and in a number of respects the experience gained in the
composition of the Mass seems to be reflected in the treatment of the
Double Quartet. Although Spohr's conception of the relationship between
the two quartets developed significantly with each of his four double quartets, he never handled the ensemble orchestrally as Mendelssohn did in
his Octet. In Op. 65 the first quartet functions primarily as a concertino,
with the second acting as ripieno. In Op. 77 (1827) and Op. 87 (1832–33)
the subordination of the second quartet is less marked, the two quartets
often being used antiphonally, as in the opening of the scherzo of Op. 77
(although Spohr periodically reverted to giving the second quartet an essentially supporting role). In the much later Op. 136 (1847) the antiphonal relationship of the two quartets is most marked.

Unlike some of the string quartets, the double quartets maintain a
remarkably high level of invention throughout and contain many striking
ideas and textures. The last movement of Op. 77 again shows Spohr's liking for music with a folk flavor; it seems to breathe the spirit of Smetana's
or Dvořák's Bohemia. The fine Third Double Quartet, Op. 87, explores
different emotional territory, its dominant mood being one of restless agitation and passionate urgency. As in the first two double quartets, the challenge of the unusual medium seems to sustain Spohr's imagination at an
impressive level.

The other really outstanding chamber work from Spohr's first
decade in Kassel is the String Quintet in B Minor, Op. 69 (1826). As with

the double quartets, the challenge of a less familiar ensemble seems to have prevented him from falling so readily into the patterns and modes of treatment that recur in many of the string quartets. The Quintet, dramatic and lyrical, impassioned and tender by turns, belongs among Spohr's best chamber works. So, too, on a much more modest scale, do the three Violin Duos, Op. 67 (1824), although they are perhaps less striking than those of Op. 39.

After 1835, which saw only the *Quatuor brillant,* Op. 93, in which, as Schumann remarked, "Forms, modulations and melodic phrases are Spohr's often-heard ones,"[26] the flow of string chamber music dried up almost entirely for a decade. The only exception was the effective though rather routine String Quintet, Op. 106, of 1838. But Spohr's remarriage in 1836 to Marianne Pfeiffer, by all accounts an active and accomplished amateur pianist, inspired him to make an important contribution to the repertoire of chamber music with piano: between 1836 and 1853 he composed his three duos for violin and piano, five piano trios, the Quintet for Piano and Strings, Op. 130, and the Septet for Piano, Winds, and Strings, Op. 147.

The duos, like Weber's Grand Duo Concertant, are pieces in which the emphasis is on brilliance rather than on a Classical sonata dialogue. The style is more polished and intricate than in the violin and harp sonatas, but the impression of two instruments alternately cooperating and vying with one another to produce an effect is the same. The F Major Duo, Op. 96 (1836), entitled *Nachklänge einer Reise in die Sächsische Schweiz* (Reminiscences of a journey in Saxon Switzerland), is notable as Spohr's only programmatic chamber work. (He had made his first excursion into program music four years earlier with the Fourth Symphony, *Die Weihe der Töne* [The consecration of sound] and was to pursue the idea in several more large-scale works.) Spohr described in his memoirs how he tried to capture a different aspect of the journey in each movement of the Duo. The first movement attempted "to describe the love of travel"; the scherzo recalled "the journey itself, by introducing the postillion's horn calls customary in Saxony and the neighboring part of Prussia," while the trio "depicted a daydream such as one so willingly yet unconsciously surrenders to in the carriage"; the Adagio represented "a scene in the Catholic court chapel in Dresden" with organ prelude, intonations of the priest, responses of choristers, and finally, "an aria for castrato, in which the violinist must imitate the tone and style of that kind of singing" (a difficult task for the modern violinist); the rondo finale depicts the journey through Saxon Switzerland itself, with the "grand beauties of nature" and "the merry Bohemian music that one hears echoing from almost every rocky glen."[27] The stimulus of the program resulted in fresher melodic ideas and greater vitality than in the other two duos, the rhythmic irregularity and freedom of phrase structure sometimes reminding one of Schumann. Op. 112 (1837), however, although more intricate in textures and harmony, is also an attractive work.

The first of the piano trios followed in 1841 and, together with the second and third trios (1842), constitutes a major, though still largely unrecognized, contribution to this important nineteenth-century genre. Spohr's treatment of the medium is highly individual, owing little to earlier composers. The title *Trio concertant,* under which all three were published, is absolutely appropriate, for the parts are all demanding and Spohr's tendency to avoid accompaniment textures results in a complex contrapuntal web of sound. This impression is intensified by his characteristically intricate harmonic idiom and by the concentrated use of musical motives. As in some earlier works, this extends to cross-reference between sections and movements. In Op. 123, for instance, the themes of the scherzo and trio are intermingled when the scherzo returns after the trio, and the second subject of the finale is related to the main theme of the scherzo. In Op. 119 the main theme of the Larghetto reappears in the development section of the finale. Another feature that probably arose from Spohr's approaching the composition from the point of view of a violinist rather than a pianist is the frequently unconventional texture. The piano often does not have the real bass of the harmony (very uncommon in earlier trios), and Spohr is thus able to create some fascinating sonorities, as in the opening of the Larghetto of Op. 123, where for the first thirteen bars the cello is consistently more than two octaves below the piano, and for twenty-six bars cello and violin are almost entirely below the piano in pitch. Similar imaginative textures abound, and Spohr makes full use of the extreme registers of all three instruments. Of the two later trios (1846 and 1849), the G Minor, Op. 142, is particularly effective; its style, in common with many of Spohr's later works, is rather broader and less intricate.

The other significant chamber works with piano are the Quintet, Op. 130, and the Septet, Op. 147. The Quintet, composed between the Third and Fourth Piano Trios in 1845, despite its excellent workmanship and some felicitous ideas, seems to lack the freshness of invention apparent in the best of the trios. The Septet, however, with its unusual combination of piano trio plus flute, clarinet, and horn, was written in 1853 at the end of an otherwise rather fallow period, yet it contains some of Spohr's most attractive writing. The combination of tender melancholy and grace, so typical of his style, finds ideal expression in this work, and although the sense of stylistic progress may be more apparent than real, there is an impression that he sought to avoid inessentials and to give the music greater directness (particularly apparent in the finale); his refined feeling for instrumental color even lends appeal to ideas that in other contexts might seem somewhat faded. In relation to the earlier chamber works with keyboard, it is notable that the piano writing is far sparer and the keyboard assumes a much more discreet place in the ensemble than in the Quintet, where it seems often to be pitted against the string quartet.

The 1840s and 1850s also saw the composition of many small pieces for violin and piano, some published in sets as *Duettinen* and *Salonstücke.*

These are typical of the period when salon music was much in demand from publishers, and they display Spohr's qualities and faults in miniature. A few, such as the Barcarole and Scherzo from Op. 135, became popular concert pieces with violinists (for instance, Joseph Joachim), but the majority were neither straightforward enough for amateurs nor technically impressive enough for concert violinists.

Beginning with the String Quintet, Op. 129 (1845), Spohr had returned to the composition of chamber music for strings alone. In the later works for strings, as in the last piano trio and the Septet, there is the emergence of what may be seen, if not as a late style, at least as a late phase, in which there is greater breadth, and detail assumes less importance in relation to the whole. This is particularly apparent in the Double Quartet, Op. 136, the Quartet, Op. 141, and above all the fine Sextet, Op. 140. The last three violin duos (Opp. 148, 150, and 153) are also attractive and stylistically quite distinct from his previous duos, the last of which had been written some thirty years earlier.

The Double Quartet, apart from its exploitation of the two quartets as equal antiphonal bodies, is interesting for a freer treatment of rhythm than is found in many earlier works. Spohr seems to be consciously trying to address the problem of rhythmic stagnation that is common in much early Romantic music. Passages of syncopation (Example 3.19a) and changes of meter (Example 3.19b) are characteristic of the first movement; unusual nebulous rhythm combined with Spohr's most plangent harmony occurs in the Larghetto. Cross rhythm again distinguishes the scherzo (Example 3.20), while in the finale the contrast is between sections in *alla breve* and $\frac{6}{4}$ meter.

The freshness and vigor of the Sextet, Op. 140, composed in March and April 1848, seems to owe much to Spohr's optimistic excitement about the outbreak of revolution against autocratic government in several German states, for he entered it in his catalog of works with the inscription "At the time of the glorious people's revolution for the reawakening of the freedom, unity, and greatness of Germany."[28] The same breadth, expansiveness, and sonority, calling Brahms to mind (see Example 3.21), is apparent here, and the whole work has a consistently high level of inspi-

EXAMPLE 3.19.   Spohr, Double Quartet, Op. 136 (1847), mvt. 1: (a) mm. 55–57; (b) mm. 100–102.

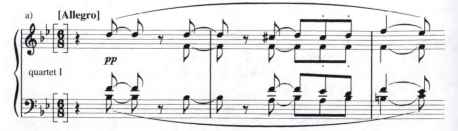

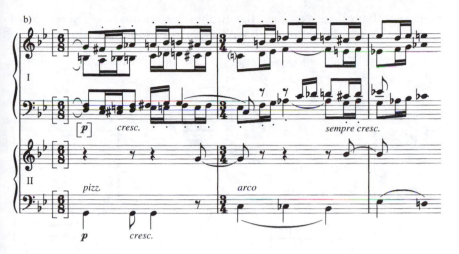

EXAMPLE 3.20.   Spohr, Double Quartet, Op. 136 (1847), scherzo, opening.

ration. An unconventional feature is the combined scherzo and finale. The scherzo is unusual in itself, alternating A minor and A major sections; after a truncated second appearance of the A major section, it is interrupted by the *presto* C major finale, which begins, like the scherzo, with an octave upbeat (Example 3.22). A shortened version of the scherzo reappears at the point where development is expected, and after a regular recapitulation an even more compressed version of the scherzo functions as a coda, only to be dismissed by a final *prestissimo* return of the finale material. Brahms's combination of scherzo and slow movement in his A Major Violin Sonata may, perhaps, have owed something to Spohr's sextet. It seems certain that Brahms's own sextets were inspired by it; not only were there no other obvious models, but Brahms also owned the autograph of Spohr's sextet and is known to have had an affection for Spohr's music.[29]

EXAMPLE 3.21.   Spohr, String Sextet in C Major, Op. 140 (1848), mvt. 1, opening

The C Major String Quartet, Op. 141 (February 1849), although less striking than the sextet, also has a Brahmsian warmth at times, as, for example, in the principal theme of the first movement. Yet as in his other later quartets, Spohr could not resist slipping into the habit of giving the first violin extended sections of passagework in the outer movements and, however much he might integrate these into the work by means of thematic material in the other parts, a degree of predictability about this procedure detracts from the overall impression. Nevertheless, there is considerable freshness in the ideas and their execution. The lilting $\frac{6}{8}$ Larghetto, the polonaise-like scherzo, and the vigorous *presto* finale are well matched with the lyrical first movement.

Although Spohr's creative powers began to wane in the 1850s, he retained his preoccupation with string chamber music almost to the end.

EXAMPLE 3.22. Spohr, String Sextet in C Major, Op. 140 (1848): (a) scherzo, opening; (b) finale, opening.

In 1850 he composed his seventh and last quintet (Op. 144), in 1851 a G Major Quartet (Op. 146), and in 1855 his last published quartet (Op. 152); during 1856–57 he occupied himself with further quartet writing but did not regard the ensuing works as worthy of publication. Although all these works show Spohr's usual careful attention to detail and contain some fine movements, notably the Molto adagio of Op. 146, the sustained inspiration that enlivened the works of 1847–49 is generally missing.

Relatively little of Weber's and Spohr's chamber music has maintained a place in the repertoire. Weber's Grand Duo and Clarinet Quintet are regularly performed by clarinetists (as is Spohr's Fantasia, Op. 81), but Weber's finest chamber work, the Trio, Op. 63, although perfectly accessible to good amateur performers, seems to be less well known than its merit deserves. Wider knowledge of Spohr's chamber music has been hindered partly by its often formidable technical difficulty and partly by the unavailability of many works in modern editions; over the past decades, however, almost all of it has become accessible through recordings, and the best works (particularly the piano trios) have recently begun to find a place in the repertoires of standard ensembles.[30] It is hardly conceivable that Spohr's chamber music should regain the place in the Classical canon that many of his contemporaries considered it to deserve, or that Weber's less substantial contribution to the field should be regarded as more than peripheral to his historical or artistic importance; yet the increasing availability of recordings of their chamber works, together with those of many lesser composers of the period, not only provides us with a substantial body of attractive and often profound music but also gives students, scholars, and listeners an opportunity to appreciate some of the less familiar yet extremely significant currents in European music that played such an important part in forming the experience of Mendelssohn, Schumann, Brahms, Dvořák, and their contemporaries.

Notes

1. J numbers are from Friedrich Wilhelm Jähns, *Carl Maria von Weber in seinen Werken* (Berlin, 1871).
2. John Warrack, *Carl Maria von Weber,* 2d ed. (Cambridge, 1976), 50.
3. *Allgemeine musikalische Zeitung* 11 (1808): 181ff.; 15 (1813): 792.
4. Letter cited in Jähns, *Weber,* 121–22.
5. Particularly characteristic of French opera (e.g., No. 4 from Pierre Gaveaux's *Le petit matelot, ou Le mariage impromptue* of 1796) and French violin music.
6. Warrack, *Weber,* 179.
7. The practice of beginning the recapitulation with the second subject is associated with the Mannheim school, with which Weber's teacher Vogler was connected.
8. Jähns, *Weber,* 281.
9. WoO numbers are as given in Folker Göthel, *Thematisch-bibliographisches Verzeichnis der Werke von Louis Spohr* (Tutzing, 1981).
10. Spohr erroneously gives their publication date as 1807 in his *Lebenserinnerungen,* ed. Folker Göthel (Tutzing, 1968) 1:119.
11. Quoted in ibid. 1:132.
12. ". . . im genre der Rodeschen" ("Briefe L. Spohrs an das Haus Peters in Leipzig." *Leipziger allgemeine musikalische Zeitung,* new series, 2 (1867): 290.
13. *Allgemeine musikalische Zeitung* 7 (1804–5): 202.
14. To avoid broken strings on the harp and to allow each instrument to play in tonalities best suited to it, Spohr (from 1806) scored his violin and harp sonatas with the harp in a key a semitone higher than the violin and had the harp tuned down a semitone. Three of the sonatas were published in 1840 (Opp.113–15) with an alternative for piano and violin.
15. Spohr, *Lebenserinnerungen* 1:164.
16. In the appendix to the holograph calatog of his works, "Verzeichniß

sämtlicher Compositionen von Louis Spohr" (private collection); see Göthel, *Thematisch-bibliographisches Verzeichnis*, 52.

17. *Allgemeine musikalische Zeitung* 22 (1820): 239.

18. Moritz Hauptmann, *Letters of a Leipzig Cantor*, comp. and trans. A. D. Coleridge (London, 1892) 2:138; Robert Schumann, *Erinnerungen an Felix Mendelssohn Bartholdy*, ed. G. Eismann (Zwickau, 1947), 68.

19. *Thayer's Life of Beethoven*, rev. and ed. Elliot Forbes (Princeton, 1967), 957.

20. *Caecilia* 2 (1825): 267.

21. *The Imperial Dictionary of Universal Biography* (London, ca. 1880) 8:104.

22. Sir Donald Francis Tovey, *Musical Articles from the Encyclopaedia Brittanica* (London, 1944), 231.

23. Arthur Headley, trans. and ed., *Selected Correspondence of Fryderyk Chopin* (London, 1962), 55.

24. In works from about 1816 Spohr often employed Gottfried Weber's method of determing tempo by means of a pendulum of variable length. 15″ Rh indicates a pendulum length of 15 Rhenish inches, which is equivalent to 96 on Mäzel's metronome. At first Spohr used the pendulum system alone; for a short time in the early 1820s he marked the tempo with both methods, but later gave only metronome marks.

25. Letter quoted in Edward Speyer, *Wilhelm Speyer der Liederkomponist* (Munich, 1925), 67. Albrechtsberger had published a set of contrapuntal sonatas for this combination in 1804: *Trois sonates à deux choeurs, savoir deux violons, alto[,] basse du premier, et deux violons, alto[,] basse du deuxième choeur.*

26. *Neue Zeitschrift für Musik* 8 (1838): 181.

27. Louis Spohr, *Selbstbiographie* (Cassel und Göttingen, 1860–61), 2:215.

28. "Zur Zeit der glorischen Volks-Revolution zur Wiedererweckung der Freiheit, Einheit und Größe Deutschlands."

29. Eduard Speyer, *My Life and Friends* (London, 1937), 102–3; see also Clive Brown, *Louis Spohr: A Critical Biography* (Cambridge, 1984), 163, 341.

30. Recordings of the complete string quartets and quintets are well under way at the time of writing.

Selected Bibliography

Brown, Clive. *Louis Spohr: A Critical Biography*. Cambridge, 1984.

———. *Selected Works of Louis Spohr*, vol. 9, *Chamber Music for Strings*, and vol. 10, *Chamber Music with Piano*, with introductions. New York, 1987.

Glenewinkel, Hans. "Louis Spohrs Kammermusik für Streichinstrumente." Diss., Univ. of Munich, 1912.

Jähns, Friedrich Wilhelm. *Carl Maria von Weber in seinen Werken: Chronologisch-thematisches Verzeichniss seiner sämtlichen Compositionen*. Berlin, 1871; repr. 1967.

Viertel, Matthias S. *Die Instrumentalmusik Carl Maria von Webers: Ästhetische Voraussetzungen und structureller Befund*. Frankfurt, 1986.

Warrack, John. *Carl Maria von Weber*. 2nd ed. Cambridge, 1976.

Wulfhorst, Martin. "Louis Spohr's Early Chamber Music (1796–1812): A Contribution to the History of Nineteenth-Century Genres." Ph.D. diss., City University of New York, 1995.

The Chamber Music of Mendelssohn

R. Larry Todd

Mendelssohn's chamber music is usually thought to reflect the tastes of a classically inclined nineteenth-century composer who, during a short, meteoric career, remained content to build on the firm foundations of his predecessors Haydn, Mozart, and Beethoven. In this view, Mendelssohn is the supreme representative of the *Restaurationszeit* in Germany and the early Victorian period in England. He is the staunch upholder of conservative aesthetic values; no radical reformer or innovator, he is the composer of finely polished chamber works that fall easily and unobtrusively into the Classical paradigms (duo sonata, piano trio, string quartet and quintet) established by Mozart and Haydn in the eighteenth century and redefined by Beethoven in the early decades of the nineteenth. Mendelssohn is the conservator of historical models, who reveals no great anxiety of influence but a serene confidence that there are "no new paths to be cleared," that in the best case what the accomplished composer does is to manage musical material "imperceptibly better than his immediate predecessors."[1]

In 1840 Robert Schumann anticipated something of this notion when he reviewed Mendelssohn's D Minor Piano Trio, the "master trio of the present," as he termed it. Schumann deemed Mendelssohn the "Mozart of the nineteenth century, the most discerning musician, who looks most clearly through the contradictions of the present and for the first time reconciles them."[2] Schumann would not have had great difficulty with Mendelssohn's historically rooted reanimation of Classical forms, a process that could still yield original results. Thus, in assembling his memoirs of Mendelssohn in 1847, Schumann praised the Octet for its extraordinary perfection, achieved during the precocious composer's sixteenth year.[3] In 1842, when Schumann himself turned to chamber music in earnest, he embarked upon a similar journey of historical self-discovery. Not surprisingly, Schumann chose to dedicate to Mendelssohn the three Op. 41 string quartets—works that, like his friend's earlier Opp. 12 and 13, attempted a *rapprochement* with Beethoven's late string quartets.

By Mendelssohn's time chamber music was being contemplated more and more as an ideal form of absolute instrumental music. In the enigmatic, mystical string quartets of Beethoven's late period, the Classical notion of the genre as a spirited conversation among equals had been reformulated to bring chamber music closer to a metaphysical realm. For Karl Reinhold von Koestlin, writing after the middle of the century, chamber music was nothing less than a Hegelian "dialogue of the (absolute) spirit with itself."[4] As Friedhelm Krummacher has argued, a crucial issue that confronted young Mendelssohn, who attended Hegel's lectures in Berlin and was steeped in Schleiermacher's metaphysics, was how to render chamber music meaningful. As the highest form of instrumental music, chamber music ran the risk of becoming "overly esoteric" by retreating into an autonomous world of absolute music.[5] Mendelssohn answered this challenge by relying on "clarity and formal structure to intensify the emotional power of music," and on "historical models of musical greatness, whose imaginative emulation helped to preserve normative aesthetic values."[6] The result was a substantial body of chamber music that communicated directly to the audience and readily entered the standard canon after Beethoven. Nevertheless, Mendelssohn's remarkable facility and ease of communication were eventually criticized as a lack of originality and depth, an ultimately self-limiting, formalist experiment. The proponents of the "music of the future" (*Zukunftsmusik*) placed the new Wagnerian music drama and the Lisztian symphonic poem considerably ahead of chamber music in the hierarchy of musical genres, and in the revolutionary musical agenda of the years following 1848, chamber music impressed some as a historically bound genre symbolic of the old musical order.[7]

Mendelssohn viewed instrumental music as a language of sounds infinitely more precise than the language of ambiguous words, an agent through which, as Leon Botstein has suggested, "ideas and feelings could be exactly communicated and recognized in purely musical terms."[8] Chamber music played a central role in Mendelssohn's aesthetic and was his constant companion. One of his earliest datable compositions was a *Recitativo* for piano and strings (April 1820); his final compositions included the highly charged String Quartet in F Minor, Op. 80 (September 1847), and Mendelssohn spent his last few weeks contemplating a new string quartet in D minor.[9] Throughout his career the composer also remained active as a performer of chamber music, principally, of course, as one of the distinguished pianists of his age. During the winter of 1831–32 in Paris he performed Mozart piano concertos in an intimate chamber setting, with the accompaniment of a string quartet led by the French violinist Pierre Baillot.[10] And during the 1840s in Leipzig, Mendelssohn won acclaim for his performances of Mozart and Beethoven in the "musikalische Abendunterhaltungen," a series of chamber music concerts that supplemented the regular orchestral subscription series at the Gewandhaus.[11] Finally, as a skilled string musician Mendelssohn was not reluctant to take up a challenging violin or viola part in performances of his Octet.[12]

Our discussion will examine Mendelssohn's chamber music in four chronological groups: (1) an early student period of the 1820s that culminated in (2) the Octet, the First String Quintet, Op. 18, and the two String Quartets, Op. 12 and 13; (3) a middle period of the 1830s, centered around Mendelssohn's early years in Leipzig, that produced the Op. 44 string quartets and ended with the First Piano Trio, Op. 49; and (4) a late period of the 1840s, during which Mendelssohn created four major chamber works—the Second Cello Sonata, Op. 58, the Second Piano Trio, Op. 66, the Second String Quintet, Op. 87, and the final String Quartet, Op. 80.

The Student Period

Under Carl Friedrich Zelter, director of the Berlin Singakademie, Mendelssohn began his training in theory and composition at age ten. By February 1824 the fifteen-year-old had completed an impressive number of compositions, including chamber works, and in a symbolic ceremony Zelter certified him a mature musician in the brotherhood of Bach, Mozart, and Haydn.[13] Drawing on the theoretical writings of the Bach pupil J. P. Kirnberger, Zelter guided the prodigy through figured bass, chorale, invertible counterpoint, canon, and fugue, and assigned three- and four-part fugues for violin and piano and for string quartet.[14] These exercises exude a severely academic quality and record the efforts of a boy striving to assimilate the rigorous complexities of Bachian counterpoint. Zelter granted his pupil some latitude in free composition, and in an early workbook we find Mendelssohn's first attempts at sonata form and theme and variations, including several examples for violin and piano, from the year 1820.

We have it on the authority of Joseph Wilhelm von Wasielewski, Robert Schumann's early biographer, that Zelter encouraged Mendelssohn to model his early efforts after the proven examples of eighteenth-century masters, including Mozart and Haydn.[15] Thus a three-part Fugue in D Major is prefaced by an introduction with scalar flourishes that strikingly revive Bach's Partita in D Major, BWV 828 (Example 4.1a and b). A theme and variations in C major for violin and piano, comprising a squarely symmetrical theme and several variations in progressively faster rhythmic values that culminate in a studious fugue, is strikingly indebted to Classical procedures. Indeed, only a thin disguise separates Mendelssohn's theme from its probable model in a Haydn piano sonata (Example 4.1c and d).

More ambitious efforts are evident in the Trio in C Minor (piano, violin, and viola) and Violin Sonata in F Major (1820), the Piano Quartet in D Minor (ca. 1821), and the String Quartet in E♭ Major (1823).[16] For the

EXAMPLE 4.1.   (a) Felix Mendelssohn, Prelude and Fugue for Violin and Piano (1820), opening; (b) J. S. Bach, Partita in D major, BWV 828, mvt. 1, opening. (c) Mendelssohn, Theme and Variations in C Major for Violin and Piano; (d) Franz Joseph Haydn, Piano Sonata in C, Hob. XVI:48, finale.

a)

b)
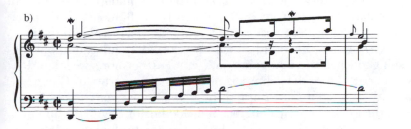

c)

d)

most part these works show the conservative influence of eighteenth-century binary sonata form: typically Mendelssohn adheres to a mono-thematic approach and writes short, uncomplicated development sections. The C Minor Trio begins with a stock eighteenth-century motive centered around a dissonant diminished seventh, and it employs a basso ostinato figure in its Adagio; on the other hand, the trio also includes a stylistically prescient scherzo in G minor, marked *sempre staccato e pianissimo,* that curiously anticipates the scherzo of the Octet. The Violin Sonata in F Major reveals prominent Haydnesque influences. The beginning of the Andante may be indebted to the head motive of the canonic minuet of Haydn's Symphony No. 44 (*Trauer*); from this motive emerges a theme-and-variations movement alternating between F minor and F major, patterned after the double strophic form so frequently employed by Haydn. And in the finale of the Violin Sonata Mendelssohn turns unabashedly to the finale of Haydn's Symphony No. 102 for inspiration.

With the Piano Quartet in D Minor and String Quartet in E♭ Major we reach Mendelssohn's first substantial chamber works. The undated Piano Quartet is preserved in an autograph volume containing works from 1822, but it may well date from 1821.[17] When Julius Benedict, Carl Maria von Weber's young protégé, visited Berlin in May 1821 to attend the premiere of *Der Freischütz,* he found an eleven-year-old Mendelssohn putting the finishing touches on a new piano quartet.[18] Furthermore, we know that in November 1821 Mendelssohn performed a piano quartet for Goethe in Weimar;[19] the undated (and unpublished) D Minor Quartet could well have been the work heard by Benedict and Goethe, for Mendelssohn's first published piano quartet, Op. 1 in C Minor, was not finished until 1822. In three movements, the D Minor Quartet betrays the influence of Mozart's two Piano Quartets, K. 478 and 493, and is Mendelssohn's first sizable chamber work to explore thematic contrast in a sonata-form movement.

The composer's First String Quartet, in E♭ Major, is in four movements, according to classical procedures. Thematic contrast is again employed, and Mendelssohn displays considerable skill in extracting from the ensemble a variety of textures. The finale, a double fugue on two compact, stiffly academic subjects, reflects Zelter's influence, but also draws upon the Classical tradition of fugal finales exemplified by Haydn's String Quartets, Op. 20, and Mozart's String Quartet, K. 387. Mendelssohn presents the two subjects in expositions on the tonic and dominant tonalities, then contraposes the subjects before reintroducing them in augmentation. The application of specialized fugal techniques betrays the impressionable youth's deepening immersion in the music of Bach, as well as his interest in investing the string quartet with the rigor of Bachian counterpoint.

Between 1823 and 1825 Mendelssohn began to publish his music. Significantly, he chose to venture into print with four chamber works, including the three Piano Quartets in C Minor, F Minor, and B Minor, Opp. 1–3, and the Violin Sonata in F Minor, Op. 4.[20] Evident here are not only conservative stylistic features but also indications—initially tentative, then increasingly bolder—of Mendelssohn's exploration of newer modes of expression.

Of the three piano quartets, Op. 1 in C Minor (1822) is heavily indebted to Mozart—a feature not lost on an early reviewer of the work, who in 1824 singled out three Mozartean features: the strict form of the individual movements, division of themes into antecedent and consequent phrases, and remarkable simplicity of the ideas.²¹ Signs of modeling are indeed undeniable: the opening theme of the slow movement suggests the Andante of Mozart's G Minor Piano Quartet, and in the outer movements Mendelssohn draws heavily on the Piano Sonata in C Minor, K. 457. On the other hand, the third movement, a lightly scored scherzo in duple meter, contains the ingredients of Mendelssohn's later scherzos, which, in such works as the Octet and the *Midsummer Night's Dream* Overture, became a hallmark of his mature style.

The Piano Quartet in F Minor, Op. 2 (1823), marks a considerable advance in Mendelssohn's stylistic development. Although dedicated to Zelter, the work clearly shows contemporary styles and may represent Mendelssohn's first serious engagement with Beethoven's music. A good deal of the piano figuration, now featuring widely spaced chords and arpeggiations, scale figures in parallel sixths, and *martellato* passages, reflects the influence of virtuosi such as Weber and Hummel. And the application of sonata form is considerably more adventuresome, with marked Beethovenian emphasis on bridge and closing materials. In the first movement, the development section impresses as a unified whole. Mendelssohn begins with a deceptive cadence on the submediant, D♭ major, and introduces a rising chromatic figure—F–G♭–G♮–A♭—that chromatically retraces the opening motive of the movement—A♭–G–F–E♮. The idea of a motivic chromatic ascent is subsequently reinforced through a sequential series of modulations (b♭–b♮–C–D♭) before a protracted dominant prolongation prepares the reprise.

Toward the conclusion of the movement Mendelssohn revisits the deceptive cadence on D♭, but now moves to the third below, B♭ minor, in order to launch an extended coda. The weighty coda, which culminates in a strettolike *più allegro,* also indicates Beethoven's influence, as Mendelssohn here experiments more freely and forcefully with the structural proportions of ternary sonata form.

The engagement with Beethoven's music is very much evident in Mendelssohn's final Piano Quartet, Op. 3 in B Minor, by far the most sophisticated, expansive, and successful of the early chamber works. This quartet is characterized by a new, daring experimentation with form—especially in the first, third, and fourth movements—and by a concern for thematic relationships between the movements. Thus the opening Allegro is built upon a chromatic turn figure (B–C♯–B–A♯–B) that becomes thoroughly embedded in the thematicism of the entire quartet, as, for example, in the bridge of the first movement's exposition (where it is harmonized by a colorful augmented-sixth sonority), and the opening motive of the scherzo (Example 4.2). The thematic contents of the exposition are conspicuously richer than those of the earlier quartets, and as in Op. 2, Mendelssohn gives added emphasis to the bridge and closing sections. The development begins by abruptly shifting tempo to *più allegro* and intro-

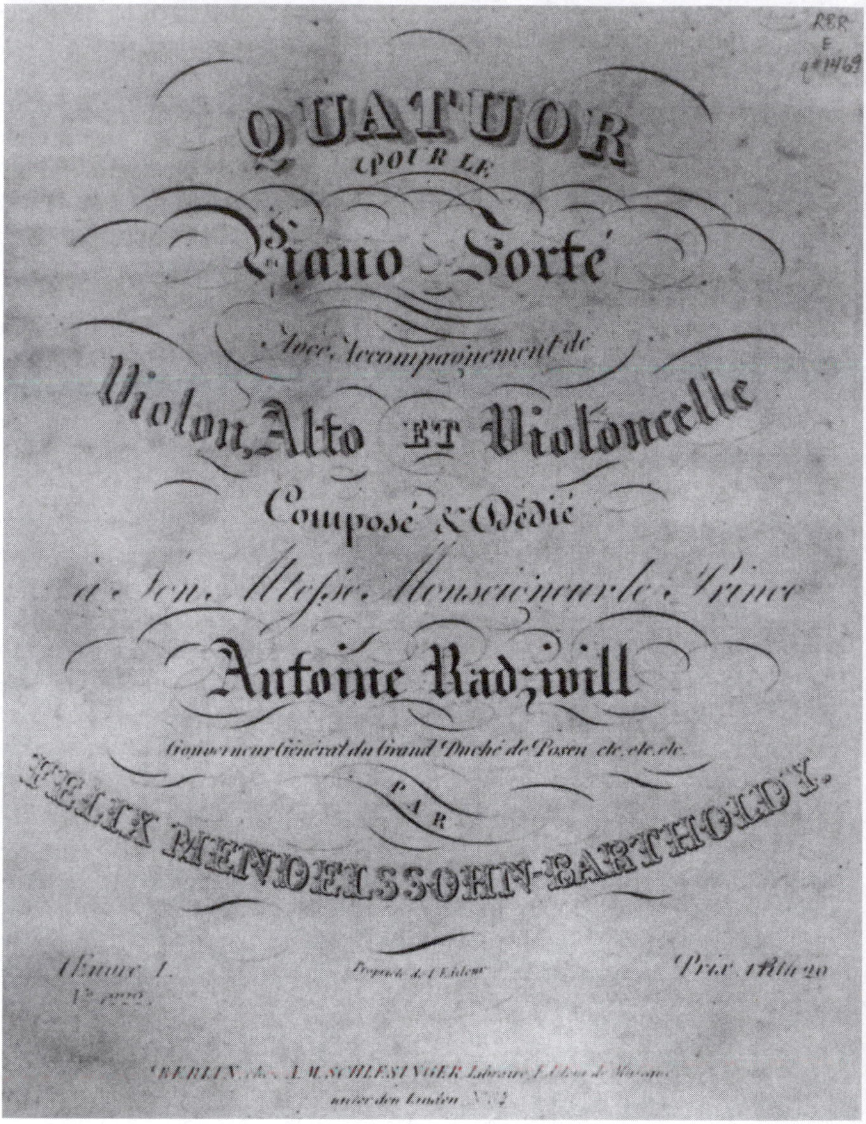

FIGURE 4.1.   Title page of the piano part for Mendelssohn's Piano Quartet in C Minor, Op. 1, first edition, Berlin, Schlesinger, 1822. Special Collections Library, Duke University.

FIGURE 4.2.   First page of the piano part for Mendelssohn's Piano Quartet in C Minor, Op. 1, first edition, Berlin, Schlesinger, 1822. Special Collections Library, Duke University.

ducing a fresh motivic idea that is subsequently developed along with the turn figure. At the end of the movement the *più allegro* returns to form a sizable coda. The thematic fullness of the movement, the addition of a full-length coda to a ternary sonata-form design, and the introduction of new material in the development are all features that Mendelssohn would have studied in the first movement of Beethoven's *Eroica* Symphony.

The expanded design of the scherzo (ABAB′) probably betrays Beethoven's influence as well, although here Mendelssohn succeeded in penning a highly original, fleet-footed movement that approaches the level of the scherzo of the Octet and the *Midsummer Night's Dream* Overture. The imposing finale, spanning nearly five hundred measures, offers a complex amalgam of sonata and rondo form, in which the developmentlike C section returns to form a culminating coda.

The B Minor Piano Quartet occupies a special position in Mendelssohn's oeuvre as his first published work to evince clear signs of his mature style. In 1825 he performed it in Paris for the hypercritical Cherubini, who astonished French musical circles by the positive verdict, "Ce garçon est riche; il fera bien"; and in May of that year Mendelssohn dedicated the quartet to Goethe, with whom he had earlier debated vigorously the significance of Beethoven's music. Some measure of the quartet's success is indicated by its popularity in Paris, where Mendelssohn's music was usually viewed as too complex and Germanic; the piano quartet was still in press during the 1830s, and Mendelssohn may have performed it in 1832 at a gathering of the Saint-Simonian utopian sect.[22]

Very much in the shadow of Op. 3 are three duo sonatas—for violin in F minor (Op. 4; 1823, published in 1825), viola in C minor (1824), and clarinet in E♭ major (1824)—and the Piano Sextet in D Major (Op. 110, 1824).[23] The Violin Sonata commences with a violin recitative reminiscent of the first movement of Beethoven's "Tempest" Sonata, Op. 31, No. 2; possibly drawn from the same work is the descending two-note sigh motive that follows in the *allegro* theme for the piano (this motive, in the affective key of F minor, also conjures up Carl Maria von Weber's *Konzertstück*, a perennial favorite of Mendelssohn's). Similar in mood and style is the Viola Sonata, which concludes with an impressive theme and variations. Mendelssohn closely observes the contours and structure of his classically

EXAMPLE 4.2.(a).   Mendelssohn, Piano Quartet No. 3 in B Minor, Op. 3: mvt. 1.

EXAMPLE 4.2.(b).   Mendelssohn, Piano Quartet No. 3 in B Minor, Op. 3: mvt. 1.

designed theme in the first seven variations, but in the eighth writes a free, florid *adagio* in C major featuring the piano. A brief recitative then leads to a turbulent return to C minor in an *allegro* coda. Though Mendelssohn chose not to publish the Viola Sonata, he did reuse its minuet, the opening material of which became the basis for the Menuetto of the nearly contemporaneous Symphony No. 1, Op. 11 (1824).[24]

EXAMPLE 4.2.(c).   Mendelssohn, Piano Quartet No. 3 in B Minor, Op. 3: mvt. 3.

During the 1820s Mendelssohn had ample opportunities to hear the many German and foreign virtuosi who appeared in Berlin; the Clarinet Sonata and Piano Sextet mirror vividly the shifting fashions of Berlin concert life. The Clarinet Sonata is strongly indebted to Carl Maria von Weber, who explored the technical potential of the instrument in a variety of compositions—including two concertos, several chamber works, and the celebrated E♭ major clarinet solo in the Overture to *Der Freischütz*—in which he explored the dark chalumeau register and set a new standard of writing for the instrument. The peculiar scoring of the Sextet (violin, two violas, cello, contrabass, and piano) may owe its inspiration to Johann Nepomuk Hummel's Piano Septet in D Minor, Op. 74 (ca. 1816; flute, oboe, horn, viola, cello, contrabass, and piano).[25] A good deal of Mendelssohn's piano figuration, featuring translucent scale runs and arpeggiations in the high treble register, is Hummelesque, and the peculiar Menuetto (*agitato*, in ⁶⁄₈ meter) brings to mind something of Hummel's "Menuetto o Scherzo." On the other hand, Mendelssohn's revival of the minuet in the finale, where it serves as a spirited coda to the entire work, is a dramatic gesture that invokes Beethoven's Fifth Symphony and its recall of the third movement just before the reprise in the finale.

"New and Strange Music": Works of First Maturity

Buoyed by Cherubini's positive comments and Goethe's acceptance of the dedication of the Op. 3 Piano Quartet, Mendelssohn returned from Paris to Berlin in June 1825. Within a few months, on 15 October, he completed his first masterpiece, the extraordinary Octet. Although Mendelssohn's correspondence does not divulge the inspiration for this work, we may discern at least four distinct musical stimuli. First, there was the series of string *sinfonie* that Mendelssohn had composed between 1821 and 1824 for performance at the family residence in Berlin. The first few *sinfonie* were scored for four-part string ensemble. Then, by dividing the cellos and double bass or by adding a second viola part, Mendelssohn achieved a five-part texture; a second expansion, to six and eight parts, followed in the Sinfonia No. 9 of 1823. To some degree the opulent textures of the Octet represent the culmination of these *sinfonie* and their systematic augmentation of the string texture; indeed, on the title page of the first edition of the Octet (1832), Mendelssohn emphasized its symphonic character with a special instruction: "This Octet must be played by all the instruments in the style of a symphonic orchestra. *Pianos* and *fortes* must be exactly observed and more strongly emphasized than is usual in works of this type."[26]

A second factor was probably the chamber music of Louis Spohr, who had composed in 1823 the first of his four double string quartets (Op. 65, in D Minor). Mendelssohn had met Spohr in Cassel in 1822 and again in Berlin in 1824. In his memoirs Spohr was careful to distinguish his double quartets, "in which the two quartets frequently concert and answer each other in the manner of double choirs,"[27] from Mendelssohn's effort: "An octet for string instruments by Mendelssohn belongs namely to a completely different genre, in which the two quartets do not concert and alternate in double choral (*doppelchörig*) style, but in which all eight instruments collaborate."[28] Actually, Mendelssohn's Octet contains some passages in which the ensemble does split into two antiphonal quartets (e.g., the first movement, mm. 21ff.). On the other hand, Mendelssohn considerably exceeds Spohr's achievement by exploring a broad spectrum of textures, ranging from minimalist unison passages (first movement, 211ff., and conclusion of the scherzo) to lush, eight-part counterpoint (opening of the finale). The sheer variety of textures and instrumental combinations sets the Octet quite apart from Spohr's double quartets; indeed, Mendelssohn's love of complexity is everywhere evident in the Octet, which attains a degree of intricacy rarely encountered in nineteenth-century chamber music.

Mendelssohn's fascination with intricate contrapuntal combinations was a third stimulus that led to the creation of the Octet. In particular, the composer could not resist exploring fugal procedures in the finale, and here his deep knowledge of the finale of Mozart's "Jupiter" Symphony, with its *ne plus ultra* synthesis of combinative contrapuntal techniques and sonata form, exercised its influence as well. Three years before, in the last movement of the Sinfonia No. 8 (1822), Mendelssohn had produced an overt imitation of the "Jupiter" finale, complete with a strettolike combination of four subjects in quadruple counterpoint.[29] The finale of the Octet, which displays pronounced fugatos at the opening and in the developmentlike middle section—all incorporated into an amalgam of sonata-form and rondo principles—reveals a compositional attitude that traces its roots to the "Jupiter" Symphony.[30]

The expansion of the string ensemble to eight parts was paralleled by a considerable enlargement of the work's proportions and formal design. In fact, Mendelssohn's autograph score of the Octet, now preserved in the Library of Congress, transmits a text conspicuously longer than the published version.[31] Mendelssohn's grand conception is evident in the autograph of the first movement, which, notated in rhythmic values twice as long as those of the final version, yielded an Allegro of over six hundred measures. The urge to expand the length and compass of the work again betrays Beethoven's influence, observed earlier in the expansive size of the Piano Quartet, Op. 3. And Beethoven's shadow looms large, too, in the Octet's finale, where Mendelssohn unexpectedly recalls the scherzo in a playful reinterpretation of the Fifth Symphony.

The Octet exudes a newfound confidence in innovative formal designs, represented by Mendelssohn's imaginative applications of sonata form in the first three movements, and by the remarkable fugal sonata-rondo scheme of the finale. The exposition of the first movement serves as a case in point (see the reduction in Example 4.3a). It divides into five sections. Of these, the first and second present a double statement of the soaring first theme, which rises nearly three octaves from the tremolo opening on the tonic; the third and fourth, a double statement of the compact second theme on the dominant; and the fifth, the closing section on the dominant. Compellingly new in Mendelssohn's exposition is the enrichment of the traditional tonic-dominant axis by unexpected tonal diversions within the five sections. Thus, between the two statements of the first theme (mm. 1, 37ff.) (Example 4.3b), Mendelssohn turns suddenly to C major (m. 23), the third below the tonic, as if to establish F minor (ii). But the implied progression is thwarted by the reappearance of the tonic and second statement of the first theme. Subsequently, in measure 45, Mendelssohn does turn to F minor, and so fulfills the goal of the earlier C major intrusion. What is more, he now reorients the passage toward D major, the third above the dominant Bb, and also the dominant of G minor (iii). Then, between the two statements of the second theme, he touches on G minor and G major, again realizing the implied dominant role of the previously heard D major, and further enriching the tonal palette.

Of the Octet's four movements, the celebrated G minor scherzo, which Mendelssohn later orchestrated as a substitute third movement for the First Symphony (Op. 11), requires special consideration.[32] According to his sister Fanny, the ethereal conclusion, with its delicate *pianissimo* unison writing, was inspired by an extramusical source, a passage from Goethe's *Faust:*

> He tried to set to music the stanza from the Walpurgis-night Dream in "Faust":—"The flight of the clouds and the veil of mist / Are lighted from above. / A breeze in the leaves, a wind in the reeds, / And all has vanished." . . . To me alone he told this idea: the whole piece is to be played staccato and pianissimo, the tremulandos coming in now and

EXAMPLE 4.3.(a).   Mendelssohn, Octet for Strings, Op. 20, mvt. 1: exposition, harmonic reduction.

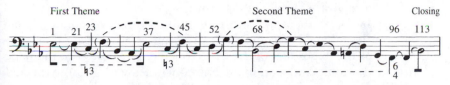

EXAMPLE 4.3.(b).   Mendelssohn, Octet for Strings, Op. 20, mvt. 1: mm. 1–5.

then, the trills passing away with the quickness of lightning; everything new and strange, and at the same time most insinuating and pleasing, one feels so near the world of spirits, carried away in the air, half inclined to snatch up a broomstick and follow the aerial procession. At the end the first violin takes a flight with a feather-like lightness, and— all has vanished.[33]

The passage in question is the closing quatrain of the "Walpurgisnachtstraum, oder Oberons und Titanias goldne Hochzeit" (Walpurgisnight's dream, or the golden wedding of Oberon and Titania), the dreamlike sequence that appears in the first part of *Faust* just after the "Walpurgisnacht" scene. Goethe's "dream" unfolds to the accompaniment of an orchestra, led by a kapellmeister who exhorts his diminutive musicians, "Snout of Fly, Mosquito Nose, / Damnable amateurs! Frog O'Leaves and Crick't O'Grass / You are musicians, sirs!" In Goethe's verse Mendelssohn thus found the literary source for his musical transformation of the fanciful, which he elevated in the Octet to the level of a new aesthetic category and, of course, explored further the following year in another musical dream, the Overture to *A Midsummer Night's Dream.*

Within a year of finishing the Octet Mendelssohn produced his first string quintet, eventually published in 1832 as Op. 18. Completed on 31 May 1826, it originally consisted of four movements: (1) Allegro moderato (A major, 468 mm.), (2) Allegretto (D minor, 313 mm.), (3) Minuetto and Trio (F♯ minor, 230 mm.), and (4) Allegro vivace (A major, 441 mm.). After a private 1831 Parisian performance led by the violinist Pierre Baillot, Mendelssohn was persuaded of the need for a slow movement, and upon learning of the death of his friend, the violinist Eduard Rietz, early in February 1832, quickly composed the deeply felt Intermezzo in F major, which he labeled in his autograph "In memoriam" (*Nachruf*). The new slow movement replaced the minuet, and Mendelssohn incorporated further revisions in the remaining movements—chiefly excisions—before releasing the final version: (l) Allegro con moto (A major, 437 mm.), (2) Intermezzo (F major, 135 mm.), (3) Allegro di molto (D minor, 303 mm.), and (4) Allegro vivace (A major, 354 mm.).

Like the Octet, the A Major String Quintet evinces the new expansiveness in design and the composer's preference for contrapuntal complexity. Thus the exposition of the first movement includes two thematic groups in the tonic and dominant but concludes with an unexpected scherzolike intrusion of the submediant, F♯ minor; in the intermezzo, the exposition is expanded to accommodate three thematic groups, in the tonic, dominant, and dominant minor. Three of the five movements written for the quintet celebrate Mendelssohn's intensifying engagement with learned counterpoint. The delicate filigree of the scherzo is spun from a formal five-part fugal exposition, and a fugato plays a prominent role within the finale, cast in a complex sonata-rondo design. Mendelssohn notated an especially erudite exercise in the trio of the jettisoned minuet: while the minuet employs double counterpoint, the trio is organized as a *canone doppio* (Example 4.4), with the two canons subjected to inversion according to the scheme in Figure 4.1.[34]

EXAMPLE 4.4.   Mendelssohn, String Quintet No. 1 in A Major, Op. 18 (first version), mvt. 2, trio.

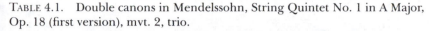

Coda

‖: Canon II at 2nd	‖: Canon I at 2nd	Canon II at 2nd	‖: Canon I at 2nd ‖
‖ Canon I at 6th :‖:	Canon II at 6th ‖	Canon I at 6th :‖	Canon I at 4th ‖

TABLE 4.1.   Double canons in Mendelssohn, String Quintet No. 1 in A Major, Op. 18 (first version), mvt. 2, trio.

The academic tone of the trio may have facilitated Mendelssohn's decision to remove the minuet from the quintet. The similarly studious Fugue in E♭ Major for String Quartet (1827), a double fugue whose opening subject is based on the "Jupiter" motive, was also left unpublished (it appeared posthumously as Op. 81, No. 4).[35] One other minor chamber work from this period, the *Lied ohne Worte*–like "Evening Bell" for Harp and Piano, was composed in 1829 as a private offering for the English musician Thomas Attwood and his daughter. Instead, Mendelssohn chose to release in print three other chamber works in which he found a suitable forum to explore his deepening relationship to the late music of Beethoven. If the *Variations concertantes* for Piano and Cello, Op. 17 (1829), written for his brother, Paul, impress as a conventional although effective display piece, the String Quartets in E♭ and A, Op. 12 and 13, stand as serious contributions to the nineteenth-century quartet canon that in many ways attain the level of inspiration of the Octet.

During the late 1820s Mendelssohn corresponded extensively with the Swedish musician Adolf Lindblad, and their letters reveal the full extent of Mendelssohn's immersion in Beethoven's late string quartets. In this unfathomable repertory Mendelssohn discovered as a guiding principle for his own instrumental music the organic relationship of the parts to the whole, or, in his words, "the relation of all 4 or 3 or 2 or 1 movements of a sonata to each other and their respective parts, so that from the bare beginning throughout the entire existence of such a piece one already knows the mystery that must be in music."[36] In the E♭ Major Quartet, Op. 12, completed in 1829 with a secret dedication to Betty Pistor,[37] Mendelssohn attempted to achieve this structural unity through the use of cyclical techniques: the turbulent finale, most of which is cast in the key of C minor, contains periodic recalls of material from the first movement, and indeed concludes with an extensive quotation that returns us to the opening of the quartet and resecures the tonic key of E♭ major as well.

The urge to interrelate the four movements of the sonata cycle is especially evident in the String Quartet in A Major, written during the summer and fall of 1827. As Mendelssohn explained to Lindblad, this quartet was inspired by the lied "Frage," Op. 9, No. 1: "The song that I append to the quartet is the theme of the same. You will hear its notes resound in the first and last movements, and sense its feeling in all four."[38] Composed as an "impromptu" during a summer party at an estate near Potsdam, "Frage" served as the thematic and expressive basis for the quartet,

FIGURE 4.3.   Mendelssohn, String Quintet No. 1 in A Major, Op. 18. First page of the autograph manuscript. The collection of Robert Owen Lehmann, on deposit at The Pierpont Morgan Library, New York.

prompting Mendelssohn to incorporate explicit quotations from the song in the outer movements and implicit references in the inner movements.

"Frage" begins with the mottolike question, "Ist es wahr?" (Is it true?), rendered musically by a dotted figure (C♯–B–D) that pauses on an inconclusive dominant seventh chord (Example 4.5a). Midway through the song the questions return more emphatically and ultimately are answered by the closing lines of the poem: "What I feel, only she can grasp

EXAMPLE 4.5.(a).   Mendelssohn: "Frage," Op. 9, No. 1.

EXAMPLE 4.5.(b).   String Quartet in A Major, Op. 13, mvt. 1.

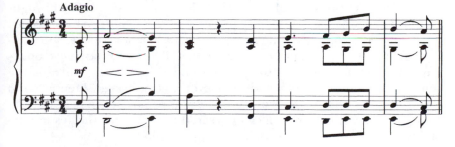

EXAMPLE 4.5.(c).   Quartet in A, mvt. 3.

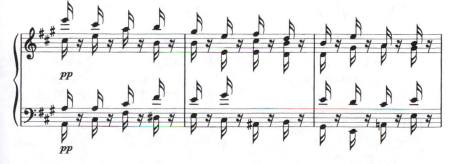

who feels it as well and who remains eternally true to me." Here the song turns unambiguously to A major and concludes with a plagal cadence.

The string quartet begins with a slow introduction that revives the flavor of the closing plagal progression of the lied (Example 4.5b). Within a few bars, the questioning motto of the lied is cited; then, after a pause on the dominant, a brisk transition leads us into the A minor Allegro vivace, a powerfully charged sonata-form movement that recaptures the sound world of the opening movement of Beethoven's String Quartet, Op. 132. In the expressive slow movement we enter the inner, subjective realm of Mendelssohn's inspiration. Literal citations from the lied give way here to more subtle allusions, including, in the opening F major section, a reworking of the dotted figure from the motto. In the central core of the slow movement Mendelssohn presents a complex fugato: its chromatically descending subject, closely related to the fugato in the slow movement of Beethoven's "Serioso" Quartet, Op. 95, impresses as a lament. A tempo change to *poco più animato* and the appearance of the fugato subject in mirror inversion considerably intensify the movement, which, at its climax, is finally interrupted by a free cadenza for the first violin. Concluding with a recitative-like gesture, the solo violin brings us back to the F major opening of the slow movement and the vocal origins of the quartet.

At first glance, the charming Intermezzo in A minor takes us farther from the insistent strains of "Frage," yet here too we may detect an "implicit" allusion. The central portion of the movement, devoted to a transparently scored scherzo in A major, reestablishes the tonality of the lied and subtly outlines its second phrase (Example 4.5c). In the finale the first violin resumes its recitative, and a dramatic passage launches the impassioned Presto reminiscent of the finale of Beethoven's Op. 132. Throughout the finale Mendelssohn recalls materials from the first two movements; by means of the recitative, the first violin, in a Beethovenian gesture, ultimately rejects these in order to return us full circle to the *adagio* opening of the quartet. In the closing bars we hear the final measures of the song, now cited and prolonged for eleven full measures. Mendelssohn thus closes the quartet by reviving the lyrical strains of the lied, thereby bridging the realms of chamber music and the art song and testing the ability of instrumental music to imitate a vocal model.

The Middle Period: the 1830s

In contrast to the later 1820s, when Mendelssohn produced several major chamber works in which he identified his mature style, in the early 1830s the composer turned decisively away from the genre. With the exception of the *Nachruf* written for Op. 18, during these years he composed only two minor chamber pieces, the *Konzertstücke* in F Minor and D Minor, Opp. 113 and 114, for clarinet, basset horn, and piano. Hurriedly dispatched in December 1832 and January 1833, these were designed as lighthearted virtuoso pieces for Heinrich Bärmann and his son Carl. Each is in three connected movements, and each observes a telescoped formal design borrowed from Carl Maria von Weber's *Konzertstück* for piano and orchestra. With their wide registral contrasts, brilliant figuration, and cantabile singing style, Mendelssohn's *Konzertstücke* are heavily indebted to Weber, whose clarinet works had been inspired by the rich, expressive style perfected by Heinrich Bärmann during his extensive concert tours of the 1820s. Mendelssohn celebrated his friendship with the Bärmanns by adding a humorous dedication to the title page of Op. 113: "The Battle of Prague: A Great Duet for Noodles or Cream Pastry, Clarinet, and Basset horn, composed and humbly dedicated to Bärmann sen. and Bärmann jun. by their completely devoted Felix Mendelssohn Bartholdy (All's well that ends well)."[39] Within a few days of completing Op. 113, Mendelssohn orchestrated the piano part, thus contributing further to the growing nineteenth-century clarinet repertoire;[40] curiously, the orchestral version still remains unpublished, and the chamber versions of the two *Konzertstücke* were published only in 1869, some twenty years after Mendelssohn's death.

Not until 1837 did Mendelssohn return to chamber music in a serious way. The intervening years saw his appointment as municipal music director in Düsseldorf, his arrival in Leipzig in 1835 to direct the Gewandhaus orchestra, and his considerable struggle, after his father's death in 1835, to complete the oratorio *Saint Paul*, which was premiered in Düsseldorf in 1836. In March 1837 Mendelssohn married Cécile Jeanrenaud, and during the couple's restful honeymoon that summer he composed the String Quartet in E Minor, Op. 44, No. 2. Two more quartets, in E♭ (Op. 44, No. 3) and D Major (Op. 44, No. 1) followed in February and July 1838, and after considerable revision, the three were published by Breitkopf and Härtel in 1839.

Highly polished and meticulously crafted, Op. 44 reveals a distinctly new, classicizing phase in Mendelssohn's career that celebrates a clarity of expression and structure, a melodious style undisturbed by strong contrast, and a carefully balanced formal design. In comparison to earlier chamber works such as Opp. 12, 13, and the Octet, the Op. 44 quartets have struck many listeners as conservative, if not reactionary, emulations of a Classical chamber-music ideal. It is as though the tranquillity of Mendelssohn's early married years led him to produce serenely graceful music that was somehow less profound than the more adventuresome experiments of his youth.

Signs of a stylistic retrenchment are indeed evident in the first few bars of Op. 44, No. 1, in which the energetic first theme, assigned to the first violin, is delivered in three neatly articulated phrases. This opening, with its rising arpeggiated motive supported by string tremolos, is clearly reminiscent of the opening of the Octet, though the quartet lacks the dynamic power of Mendelssohn's youthful masterpiece. In Op. 44, No. 1, the violin theme is securely placed above the string tremolos and operates within a fairly constrained range, in marked contrast to the Octet, in which the violin melody emerges from the welling string tremolos to chart an ascent of nearly three octaves.

For the second movement of Op. 44, No. 1, Mendelssohn chose to write a minuet (the sole example in his string quartets), as if to acknowledge a new affinity with classical chamber music. The wistful, lightly scored Andante espressivo, on the other hand, takes on a scherzolike quality, and the robust finale, a sonata-rondo movement in $\frac{12}{8}$ meter, impresses as a *perpetuum mobile* whose bravura figuration returns us to Mendelssohn's musical world of the early 1830s.

The second and third quartets of Op. 44 evince similar signs of a classicizing tendency, now fully assimilated into the composer's mature style. The opening theme of the E Minor Quartet offers a pendant to that of the D Major Quartet: here the rising, arpeggiated theme in the first violin achieves a melancholy, elegiac tone that adumbrates the celebrated Violin Concerto in E Minor, Op. 64, which Mendelssohn began to sketch in 1838. In striking contrast is the capricious second movement, a brisk, elfin scherzo in E major. The G major slow movement is a lyrical *Lied ohne Worte* that may well have inspired the slow movement of Robert Schumann's String Quartet Op. 41, No. 1. Mendelssohn assigns the opening theme to the first violin as a solo lied, but then arranges the second theme on the dominant as a duet in parallel thirds in both violins; at the reprise, the opening theme is inverted to the cello. Only in the finale does the composer's inspiration flag noticeably. Here he produced another *perpetuum mobile* finale that, notwithstanding its agitated first theme and lilting second theme, suffers from undue length.

The third quartet of Op. 44 begins with a compact motive that is treated and developed with a Haydnesque intensity and economy of means. The second movement, a brisk scherzo in C minor, must count as the summit of Op. 44. It unfolds as a complex, highly original rondo according to the scheme: ABA C A'BAA' C' A (Coda). The A subject, based on an insistent repeated pitch in the first violin, is accompanied by rapid eighth-note staccato work (Example 4.6a). When the subject returns midway through the movement, Mendelssohn indulges in a favorite device: he introduces a new countersubject, thereby investing the part writing with a new complexity.[41] The *pianissimo* B subject borrows its repeated pitches from A, now broken by rests that momentarily check the unbridled course of the movement (Example 4.6b). The C subject is introduced as a fugato, although—unusual for Mendelssohn—its contrapuntal rigor is soon lost in the delicate tissues of the ensemble (Example 4.6c). When the C subject later reappears, Mendelssohn again adds a fresh countersubject—in this case, the descending chromatic fourth—playfully invoking a traditional fugal figure. This unexpected intrusion prepares the chromatic flavoring of the ensuing slow movement, an expressive Adagio in A♭ major, which opens with a progression from the tonic to minor subdominant, marked by a poignant cross relation between the cello and first violin. But the emotional depth of the slow movement, which contains some of the most impressive writing in all of Op. 44, is regrettably vitiated by the bustling finale, yet another virtuoso *vivace* movement marred by predictable motor rhythms and excessive length.

EXAMPLE 4.6.   Mendelssohn, String Quartet in E♭ Major, Op. 44, No. 3, mvt. 2: (a) opening theme; (b) second theme; (c) third theme (fugato).

Contemporaneous with Op. 44 are two duo sonatas from 1838, the first for violin and piano in F major, the second for cello and piano in B♭ major. The violin sonata, written for Ferdinand David, was drafted by June 1838. By the beginning of 1839, however, Mendelssohn began to have grave doubts, and he described the piece to Karl Klingemann as a "wretched sonata." He then began revising, only to abandon it midway through the first movement. The sonata was to comprise three movements, including an expansive first movement in which the second theme appears in the dominant, C major, and lowered mediant, A♭ major. The slow movement was designed as a *Lied ohne Worte* in A major; the finale, a Weberesque *perpetuum mobile* in rondo form. In 1953 Yehudi Menuhin published the sonata, but for the first movement combined the two manuscript versions without offering a critical editorial apparatus.[42] A full assessment of the work must await a new scholarly edition.

Stylistically similar to the violin sonata is the First Cello Sonata, written for Mendelssohn's brother, Paul; this work did survive the composer's habitual self-criticism to appear in 1839 as Op. 45. For Schumann it seemed to approach ever more closely Mozart's style.[43] The Cello Sonata is especially marked by an avoidance of strong contrast, not only within but also between the movements. Thus, in the second movement (Andante, in ABA ternary form), Mendelssohn endeavors to minimize the contrast between the *scherzando* section in G minor (A) and the singing *Lied ohne Worte* in G major (B) by incorporating the characteristic dotted figure of A into the piano accompaniment of B. What is more, the outer movements are built upon similar opening *piano* themes, each constructed on the third B♭–D embellished by the tritone A–E♭. Whereas in the sonata-form first movement the principal theme moves primarily by disjunct motion, in the rondo finale Mendelssohn smoothes out the tritone by filling it in with stepwise motion, yielding a lyrical theme that resembles more a *Lied ohne Worte* than the refrain of a rondo.

No doubt the summit of Mendelssohn's chamber music efforts during the 1830s was reached in the First Piano Trio in D Minor, Op. 49. Composed in Frankfurt in June and July 1839, the work immediately underwent a thorough revision, and a second, considerably different version was produced in September. The substantial alterations Mendelssohn effected prompted at least one twentieth-century scholar to speak of a fundamental change in style and musical syntax.[44] A particular aspect of the trio that cost the composer considerable effort was the piano part, which he rewrote separately during the winter of 1839 before submitting the manuscript to the publisher, Breitkopf and Härtel, in January 1840.[45] The decision to recast the keyboard part was taken at the urging of Ferdinand Hiller, who saw Mendelssohn frequently during his Frankfurt sojourn:

> I was tremendously impressed by the fire and spirit, the flow, and, in short, the masterly character of the whole thing. But I had one small misgiving. Certain pianoforte passages in it, constructed on broken chords, seemed to me—to speak candidly—somewhat old-fashioned. I had lived many years in Paris, seeing Liszt frequently, and Chopin every day, so that I was thoroughly accustomed to the richness of passages which marked the new pianoforte school. I made some observations to Mendelssohn on this point, suggesting certain alterations, but at first he would not listen to me. "Do you think that that would make the thing any better?" he said. "The piece would be the same, and so it may remain as it is." "But," I answered, "you have often told me . . . that the smallest touch of the brush, which might conduce to the perfection of the whole, must not be despised. An unusual form of arpeggio may not improve the harmony, but neither does it spoil it—and it becomes more interesting to the player." We discussed it and tried it on the piano over and over again, and I enjoyed the small triumph of at last getting Mendelssohn over to my view. With his usual

conscientious earnestness when once he had made up his mind about a thing, he now undertook the lengthy, not to say wearisome, task of rewriting the whole pianoforte part. One day, when I found him working at it, he played me a bit which he had worked out exactly as I had suggested to him on the piano, and called out to me, "That is to remain as a remembrance of you."[46]

One short example illustrates how Mendelssohn redesigned the piano figuration to accommodate Hiller's criticism. In the closing group of the exposition of the first movement (mm. 195–202), he originally assigned thematic material to the treble of the piano in bare octaves, accompanied by routine, nondescript arpeggiations in triplets in the bass. But in the final version, the theme is taken over by the violin, allowing the piano to execute thicker, more adventuresome arpeggiations in the treble and to add syncopated chords in the bass (Example 4.7).

All four movements contain passages of Mendelssohn's most inspired writing. In the first movement, the noble opening theme in the cello is positioned in a dark texture of low syncopated chords in the piano. When the violin takes up the theme a few bars later, the cello's characteristic motive of an ascending fourth (A–D) is expanded to a sixth (A–F), and when the opening thematic complex reaches its climax on a high A, the piano momentarily abandons its syncopated patterns to join the cello and violin in reinforcing the theme. Especially effective is the beginning of the recapitulation, where Mendelssohn sets against the cello theme a violin subject that descends from the high A, previously heard as the melodic goal of the opening measures.

The second movement is a *Lied ohne Worte* in ternary ABA form. In the opening section, melodic phrases for solo piano alternate with duet

EXAMPLE 4.7.(a).   Mendelssohn, Piano Trio No. 1 in D Minor, Op. 49, mvt. 1, mm. 195ff. (piano): first version.

EXAMPLE 4.7.(b).   Mendelssohn, Piano Trio No. 1 in D Minor, Op. 49, mvt. 1, mm. 195ff. (piano): final version.

phrases for the violin and cello. The middle of the Andante is devoted to a contrasting section in the parallel minor, in which the sixteenth-note arpeggiated piano accompaniment of the opening is replaced by triplet chords. In the retransition to the return of A, the sixteenth-note figuration resumes, and Mendelssohn twice reestablishes the dominant, F major, by means of an expressive French augmented-sixth harmony, a distinctive chromatic progression that suggests his knowledge of Schubert's chamber works.

By 1839 Mendelssohn had produced numerous examples of the brisk, elfin scherzo that became associated with his mature style, and the third movement of the Piano Trio offers an especially entertaining specimen. Its playful nature is established in the opening material for piano solo, where Mendelssohn's usual preference for symmetrical phrases yields to an irregular seven-bar phrase that divides into two units of three and four bars. The form of the movement, too, is unpredictable (see Figure 4.2): Mendelssohn produces a rondolike structure with three full statements of the opening refrain, and two statements each for the contrasting B and C sections. In the closing bars an attenuated version of A reappears, and the movement ends by evaporating into *pianissimo* chords, a technique that brings to mind the scherzo of the Octet.

TABLE 4.2.   Mendelssohn, Piano Trio in D Minor, Op. 49, mvt. 3, formal plan.

Like the scherzo, the finale is cast as a rondo, and in fact, observes the same scheme (ABACABCA'), although with a markedly different effect. The questioning opening theme achieves its restless character by destabilizing the tonic: the theme begins on the dominant in first inversion, touches on the tonic in first inversion, and pauses on a half cadence before coming to a ritard on the Neapolitan E♭ major. The songlike C section revives the *Lied ohne Worte* style of the Andante as well as its key, B♭ major. And the final version of A, in D major, suggests a fleeting reference to the scherzo before the trio comes to its triumphant close.

The Final Period: Chamber Works of the 1840s

At first glance, no novel stylistic features mark the chamber works of Mendelssohn's final period, with the obvious exception of the String Quartet in F Minor, Op. 80, the turbulent pages of which record the composer's grief at the death of his sister, Fanny Hensel, in May 1847. Mendelssohn wrote eight chamber works during the 1840s, ranging in scoring from cello and piano (the Second Cello Sonata, Op. 58, and the *Lied ohne Worte*, Op. 109) to the piano trio (Second Piano Trio, Op. 66), string quartet (the Capriccio in E Minor, Op. 81, No. 3, the final String Quartet, Op. 80, and two separate movements of an unfinished quartet, Op. 81, Nos. 1 and 2) and the string quintet (Second String Quintet, Op. 87). But he was able to publish only two, Opp. 58 and 66, which, along with Opp. 80 and 87, represent his final contribution to nineteenth-century chamber music. Much of this music reflects the classicizing tendencies of Mendelssohn's middle period, though the late chamber works now attain a consistently greater depth of expressiveness and denote an increased level of experimentation as he sought to find new solutions to issues of formal organization, treatment of tonality, and handling of the chamber ensembles.

The first of the late works, the Cello Sonata No. 2 in D Major, was sketched as early as 1841, completed late in 1842, and published in 1843. The ebullient first movement duly impressed Robert Schumann, who alluded to its opening theme in the finale of his Piano Trio in D Minor, Op. 63 (Example 4.8a and b). The second-movement scherzo, with its contrasting lyrical section, recalls a similar procedure in the second movement of the First Cello Sonata, though the basic ternary scheme of Op. 45 is here expanded to the five-part ABABA.

EXAMPLE 4.8.(a).   Mendelssohn, Cello Sonata No. 2 in D Major, Op. 58, mvt. 1.

EXAMPLE 4.8.(b).   Robert Schumann, Piano Trio in D Minor, Op. 63, finale.

The heart of the sonata is the remarkable third movement, an expressive Adagio in which a newly composed chorale in G major, performed by the piano with thickly arpeggiated chords (Example 4.8c), is answered by a recitative-like passage for the cello. Mendelssohn's Adagio left its mark on Schumann, who crafted his own G major chorale in the slow movement of the Violin Sonata in D Minor, Op. 121 (1851), dedicated to Ferdinand David, a mutual friend of Schumann's and Mendelssohn's. Schumann's setting, which comprises a series of variations, includes one passage with piano arpeggiations that is strikingly reminiscent of Op. 58 (Example 4.8d). In Mendelssohn's Adagio, after the cello recitative the chorale returns in a higher keyboard register, accompanied by the cello recitative. In the closing bars the piano performs its own version of the recitative, into which Mendelssohn weaves the descending chromatic tetrachord, G–F♯–F♮–E–E♭–D, the traditional symbol of a lament. The movement ends with *pianissimo* rolled chords, elided by means of a diminished seventh sonority to a bright, bravura rondo finale.

A modest companion piece to Op. 58 is the *Lied ohne Worte* in D major, published posthumously in 1868 as Op. 109. This was written for the French cellist Lisa Cristiani, who appeared in concert at the Leipzig Gewandhaus on 18 October 1845;[47] although Mendelssohn's autograph is undated, the *Lied* presumably is from the time of her concert. In ternary form with a contrasting middle section in the parallel minor, Op. 109 offers yet another example of Mendelssohn's attempt to transfer the highly popular piano genre to the domain of chamber music.

EXAMPLE 4.8.(c).   Mendelssohn, Cello Sonata No. 2, mvt. 3.

The Capriccio in E Minor for String Quartet was composed in July and August 1843 and appeared as the third of the four movements for string quartet collected together posthumously in 1850 as Op. 81. The composition consists of two linked sections, a *Lied ohne Worte*–like Andante, featuring the first violin, and a brisk fugue. The subject of the fugue traverses two interlocking tritones that together form a diminished seventh (C–F♯, A–D♯). This feature, and Mendelssohn's indulgence in learned

EXAMPLE 4.8.(d).   Schumann, Violin Sonata in D Minor, Op. 121, mvt. 2.

contrapuntal techniques such as mirror inversion and stretto, relate the Capriccio to several other fugues based on dissonant subjects, among them the Fugue in E Minor for piano, Op. 35, No. 1, the first movement of the Organ Sonata in A Major, Op. 65, No. 3, and the Overture to *Elijah*.[48]

Of the late works, the Second Piano Trio in C Minor, Op. 66, occupies a special position as the last chamber composition Mendelssohn successfully saw through the press. Drafted by the end of April 1845, the trio was reworked and retouched during the summer months, as Mendelssohn began to take up in earnest the composition of *Elijah*. In February 1846 he sent a copy of the trio with a dedication to Louis Spohr;[49] it was published that month by Breitkopf and Härtel in Leipzig and by Ewer and Company in London.

The dark, *pianissimo* opening of the Piano Trio No. 2 stands as one of Mendelssohn's most inspired passages, and the exposition of the first movement as one of his most successful applications of sonata form. The opening period is built up from a compact, arpeggiated motive that is repeated sequentially at three different pitch levels, a technique reminiscent of the *Hebrides* Overture and the first movement of the *Scottish* Symphony. Whereas in those works an essential *Urmotiv* is transposed by ascending thirds, from tonic to mediant and dominant, in the Trio the basic motive moves upward by fourth, from tonic to subdominant and leading tone, a less conventional sequence that invests the opening with a certain aura of mystery and instability. Some twenty bars into the movement, the violin presents the first truly melodic material—as it happens, a short phrase borrowed from the *Lied ohne Worte*, Op. 102, No. 1, composed in 1842 but published posthumously in 1868 (Example 4.9). At this point in the Trio the *Urmotiv* is redeployed as the piano accompaniment, with a rhythmic shift to sixteenth notes. The lyrical second theme, in the mediant, E♭ major, stands in marked contrast to the motivic structure of the opening material. Finally, for the closing section, Mendelssohn modulates to the dominant G minor and contraposes a robust, chordal subject in the piano against the *Urmotiv* in the violin and (in mirror inversion) the cello. The exposition is thus expanded to accommodate three motivic-thematic complexes and three tonal areas, the tonic, mediant, and dominant minor—the keys, as it turns out, of the first three movements of the Trio.

EXAMPLE 4.9.(a).   Mendelssohn: Piano Trio No. 2 in C Minor, Op. 66, mvt. 1.

EXAMPLE 4.9.(b).   Mendelssohn: *Lied ohne Worte*, Op. 102, No. 1.

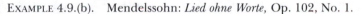

As in Op. 49, the second movement of Op. 66 unfolds as a *Lied ohne Worte* in ternary form, with a contrasting middle section in the parallel minor. But instead of imitating a solo lied or duet, as in so many previous works of this type, Mendelssohn here alludes to the genre of the part song by employing a simple homophonic style. The masterly third movement, a capricious scherzo, follows an unpredictable rondolike course that may be summarized as ABABCACA', with the two B sections in the mediant and submediant and the two statements of C in the parallel major and submediant modulating to tonic minor. The scherzo springs from a characteristic anacrusis of two sixteenth notes followed by a stressed downbeat, a rhythmic idea that recurs in each section of the movement, either in the thematic material or the accompaniment. In typical Mendelssohnian fashion, the scherzo ends by dissolving into a series of soft, detached chords.

Like the scherzo, the finale comprises a complex rondo design based on three ideas: ABACABACB(Coda). The dissonant opening material, which begins with a leap of a minor ninth, may have influenced the scherzo of Brahms's Piano Sonata in F Minor, Op. 2 (Example 4.10a and b). Undoubtedly the most unusual portion of the finale is the central C section, where Mendelssohn introduces a majestic chorale in the piano, with brief reminiscences of A interpolated between the phrases in the strings. Freely composed, the chorale nevertheless begins by quoting nearly intact the first phrase of "Gelobet seist du, Jesu Christ" (Example 4.10c and d). It is, perhaps, no coincidence that the finale of Brahms's Piano Quartet No. 3 in C Minor, Op. 60, also contains a pseudo chorale, though here the chorale appears in the strings, with brief interjections between the phrases from the piano. (As further evidence of Brahms's debt to Mendelssohn, the finale of his Op. 60 begins with a more or less clear allusion to the opening bars of the first movement of Mendelssohn's C Minor Piano Trio.)

The other major chamber work of 1845, the Second String Quintet, Op. 87, was finished in July, during the composer's holiday in Frankfurt. Moscheles found the work energetic, and indeed the first movement, with its brilliant figuration for the first violin, often captures the grandeur and sweep of the Octet. Too, the expansion of the tonal design—as in the first thematic group, structured as a large-scale double period on the tonic with intervening turns toward the mediant and submediant—recalls the experimental character of Mendelssohn's youthful masterpiece.

The inner movements of the quintet were apparently designed to maximize the sense of contrast. The Andante scherzando in G minor, reminiscent of the slow movement of the First Cello Sonata, offers an unassuming scherzo with two alternating sections in a rondolike form. The following Adagio e lento in D minor, on the other hand, is among Mendelssohn's most poignant and serious slow movements. Its dotted rhythms and agitated tremolos attain a high, tragic style, not far removed from the stately slow movement of the *Scottish* Symphony.

By his own admission to Moscheles, Mendelssohn maintained serious doubts about the finale, and here we discover the most probable reason why he chose not to publish the work.[50] As Friedhelm Krummacher has successfully demonstrated in a detailed study of the autograph manuscript, Mendelssohn initially envisioned the finale as a movement in sonata-rondo form, in which A and B served as contrasting thematic com-

EXAMPLE 4.10.(a).   Mendelssohn, Piano Trio No. 2, mvt. 4.

EXAMPLE 4.10.(b).   Johannes Brahms, Piano Sonata in F Minor, Op. 2, scherzo.

EXAMPLE 4.10.(c).   Mendelssohn, Piano Trio No. 2, mvt. 4.

EXAMPLE 4.10.(d).   Chorale, "Gelobet seist du, Jesu Christ."

Ge - lo - bet   seist   du,   Je - su   Christ

plexes, and C as a quasi-development. But he was never satisfied with the thematic material of B and omitted it from the recapitulation. The result was a formally imbalanced movement tending toward a "monothematic *perpetuum mobile* whose thematic material, quite simply, was overtaxed."[51]

A considerably different source situation obtains in the case of Mendelssohn's final major chamber work, the String Quartet in F Minor, Op. 80. Although unpublished until 1850, this composition was left by Mendelssohn, as Krummacher has argued, in an essentially completed form.[52] Most analysts have viewed Op. 80 as representing a bold stylistic departure in the closing months of the composer's life, a musical crisis precipitated by the death of his sister Fanny in May 1847. As we know, the quartet was hurriedly sketched and drafted during Mendelssohn's recuperative Swiss holiday in July and September. Not long after his return to Leipzig, in September, Mendelssohn began to experience the symptoms of his final illness; deeply engaged with the final proofs of *Elijah,* he in all likelihood would have been unable to prepare the quartet for publication before his death on 4 November.

On many counts the quartet stands as the antithesis of the classicizing ideal of Mendelssohn's middle-period chamber music. The smoothly melodious manner of the Op. 44 quartets is here challenged by an intensely dissonant style marked by severe contrast and, at every turn, by the undermining of the listener's expectations. The first movement begins with a burst of agitated tremolos, above which appears in the first violin a short, winding motive stated on the tonic, subdominant, and leading-tone degrees. This highly charged passage is unique in Mendelssohn's oeuvre, although there is a clear enough precedent for its three-tiered sequence in the opening bars of Op. 66. But signs of discontinuity are now everywhere apparent in Op. 80. Thus, the tremolos are abruptly interrupted by an anguished dissonant figure in the high register of the first violin, answered in turn by the lower strings. The modulation to the mediant for the second group is reached through the second inversion of the mediant, a move that works to destabilize the new tonality. What is more, the second group includes some striking chromatic deviations, as when Mendelssohn briefly touches on A major (m. 75, spelled enharmonically as A♭, D♭, and F♭). And finally, the exposition abruptly breaks off on the dominant seventh of the mediant: the anticipated cadence in A♭ major is supplanted by the return of the tremolos, now harmonized with an unpredictable diminished seventh.

The basic motive of the first movement serves as a kind of *Urmotiv* for the entire quartet, the essential glue that holds together the disparate parts of the composition. Thus, in the second-movement scherzo, which begins *in medias res* with biting syncopated figures on the dominant, the rising chromatic bass line that spans the sixth E♮–C is drawn from measure 2 of the first movement. And the soulful Adagio in A♭ major incorporates a portion of the motive in the opening bass line of the cello, which commences by spanning the diminished fourth A♭–E♮, an interval also stated prominently in the opening of the finale.

In the closing weeks of his life Mendelssohn frequently discussed current compositional projects with Ignaz Moscheles. Among them, evidently, was the first movement of a string quartet in D minor, which Moscheles described as "variations, less gloomy, more comforting [than the F Minor Quartet, Op. 80], and harmonically particularly distinguished."[53] No such D minor variations survived in Mendelssohn's *Nachlaß;* rather, Moscheles may have been referring to the Variations in E Major for String Quartet, eventually published as Op. 81, No. 1. Although undated in the autograph, the variations almost surely originated no earlier than the time of the Op. 80 Quartet, and probably represent the very final phase of Mendelssohn's compositional activities.[54] They survive alongside a Scherzo in A Minor, which appeared posthumously as Op. 81, No. 2. Taken together, the two movements probably were conceived as part of a new string quartet, but their exact place in the new work and its tonality remain unclear.

Op. 81, No. 1 is constructed upon a carefully, one might almost say classically, balanced theme that divides into three phrases of eight, eight, and four bars. The rhythmic pulse of the first four variations accelerates from eighth notes to triplets and sixteenths, while the fifth variation, in E minor, shifts from *andante* to *presto* and from $\frac{2}{4}$ to $\frac{6}{8}$. In the closing section Mendelssohn brings back the E major theme, but now breaks it up into short motives, so that the continuity of the original is lost. A similar process obtains in the Scherzo in A Minor, Op. 81, No. 2. At times reminiscent of the puckish scherzo from the incidental music to *A Midsummer Night's Dream,* this last chamber work falls into a rondo structure with two alternating sections. In the final return of A, the opening theme again collapses into motivic units and ultimately disintegrates into a skeletal outline.

Discontinuity and disruption thus mark Mendelssohn's final essays in chamber music, which may have been an "attempt to dissolve the classical cyclical structure by means of a series of miniatures, much as we find in Schumann's smaller chamber works."[55] In sum, these short works from the close of Mendelssohn's life reveal the composer contemplating the Classical tradition that he had inherited and mastered in his chamber music, a tradition that, at the time of his death, he was arguably on the verge of transcending.

Notes

1. Johann Christian Lobe, "Gespräche mit Mendelssohn," *Fliegende Blätter für Musik* 1, no. 5 (1855), trans. Susan Gillespie in *Mendelssohn and His World*, ed. R. L. Todd (Princeton, 1991), 193.

2. *Neue Zeitschrift für Musik* 13 (1840): 198 (19 December; hereinafter cited as *NZfM*): "Er ist der Mozart des 19ten Jahrhunderts, der hellste Musiker, der die Widersprüche der Zeit am klarsten durchschaut und zuerst versöhnt."

3. In the "Erinnerungen an Felix Mendelssohn Bartholdy" recorded by Schumann after Mendelssohn's death in 1847: "Mehr Vollendung in so jungen Jahren kann sich kein Meister der älteren noch der neueren Zeit rühmen." See Robert Schumann, "Aufzeichnungen über Mendelssohn," ed. H.-K. Metzger and Rainer Riehn, in *Felix Mendelssohn Bartholdy* (Musik-Konzepte, vol. 14/15), ed. H.-K. Metzger and R. Riehn (Munich, 1980), 107.

4. Karl Reinhold von Koestlin, "Die Musik," in F. T. Vischer, *Aesthetik, oder Wissenschaft des Schönen* (Stuggart, 1857), 1054–55, cited in Friedhelm Krummacher, "Mendelssohn's Late Chamber Music: Some Autograph Sources Recovered," in *Mendelssohn and Schumann: Essays on Their Music and Its Context*, ed. J. W. Finson and R. L. Todd (Durham, NC, 1984), 72.

5. Ibid., 73.

6. Leon Botstein, "The Aesthetics of Assimilation and Affirmation: Reconstructing the Career of Felix Mendelssohn," in *Mendelssohn and His World*, ed. R. L. Todd (Princeton, NJ, 1991), 33.

7. Thus Franz Brendel placed Mendelssohn in the Mozartian school, which "became the conservator of everything essentially academic in music, the conservator of rule and measure, of the formal element in general," a school "dominated by a certain process of externalization, while the imaginative element and spiritual expressiveness recede" (Franz Brendel, "Robert Schumann mit Rücksicht auf Mendelssohn-Bartholdy und die Entwicklung der modernen Tonkunst überhaupt," *NZfM* 22 (1845): 113; from the trans. by Susan Gillespie in *Mendelssohn and His World*, 342.

8. Botstein, "Aesthetics of Assimilation," 32.

9. According to an account given by Ignaz Moscheles; see Ernst Rychnovsky, "Aus Felix Mendelssohn Bartholdys letzten Lebenstagen," *Die Musik* 8, no. 19 (1908/9): 143.

10. Ferdinand Hiller, *Mendelssohn: Letters and Recollections,* trans. M. E. von Glehn (London, 1874; rpt., 1972), 18.

11. See further my "Mozart according to Mendelssohn: A Contribution to Rezeptionsgeschichte," in *Perspectives on Mozart Performance*, ed. R. L. Todd and Peter Williams (Cambridge, 1991), 185ff.

12. See further F. Krautwurst, "Felix Mendelssohn Bartholdy als Bratschist," in *Gedenkschrift Hermann Beck* (Laaber, 1982), 151ff.

13. Sebastian Hensel, *The Mendelssohn Family (1729–1847)*, trans. C. Klingemann (London, 1882), 1:120–21.

14. Contained principally in the manuscript workbook, Oxford Bodleian Library M. Deneke Mendelssohn C. 43 (figured bass, chorale, invertible counterpoint, and two- and three-part canon and fugue), and in vol. 2 of the Mendelssohn Nachlaß at the Deutsche Staatsbibliothek zu Berlin (twelve four-part fugues labeled "Quartetto"). See further my *Mendelssohn's Musical Education: A Study and Edition of His Exercises in Composition* (Cambridge, 1983), and Gerda Friedrich, "Die Fugenkomposition in Mendelssohns Instrumentalwerk" (diss., Bonn, 1969), 14ff.

15. As reported by the composer Carl Reinecke in "Mendelssohn und Schumann als Lehrer," *NZfM* 78 (1911): 3.

16. The unpublished Piano Trio and Piano Quartet are transcribed in J. A. McDonald, "The Chamber Music of Felix Mendelssohn-Bartholdy" (Ph.D., Northwestern University, 1970); the Violin Sonata is available in an edition by Renate Unger (Leipzig, 1977). The String Quartet appeared posthumously in Leipzig in 1879.

17. Berlin, Deutsche Staatsbibliothek, Mendelssohn Nachlaß Band 3. An edition by Wulf Konaold is available (Leipzig, 1997).

18. Julius Benedict, *Sketch of the Life and Works of the Late Felix Mendelssohn Bartholdy* (London, 1850), 10.

19. J. C. Lobe, "Ein Quartett bei Goethe: Erinnerung aus Weimars großer Zeit," *Die Gartenlaube* no. 1 (1867): 4–8. See also Friedhelm Krummacher, *Mendelssohn der Komponist: Studien zur Kammermusik für Streicher* (Munich, 1978), 82.

20. On Mendelssohn's early dealings with publishers, see Rudolf Elvers, "Acht Briefe an den Verlag Schlesinger in Berlin," in *Das Problem Mendelssohn*, ed. Carl Dahlhaus (Regensburg, 1974), 47–53, and most recently, Peter Ward Jones, "Mendelssohn's Opus 1: Bibliographical Problems of the C minor Piano Quartet," in *Sundry Sorts of Music Books: Essays on the British Library Collections: Essays Presented to O. W. Neighbour on His 70th Birthday*, ed. Chris Banks, Arthur Searle, and Malcolm Turner (London, 1993), 264–73.

21. Anonymous "Recension" of 12 May 1824, *Berliner allgemeine musikalische Zeitung* 1 (1824): 168–69.

22. See further Ralph Locke, "Mendelssohn's Collision with the Saint-Simonians," in *Mendelssohn and Schumann: Essays on Their Music and Its Context*, 114.

23. Published posthumously in 1868, when it was assigned its opus number.

24. See also my "Mendelssohn" in *The Nineteenth-Century Symphony*, ed. D. Kern Holoman (New York, 1997), 83–4.

25. Hummel's influence on Mendelssohn is often overlooked in the literature. During his visit to Goethe in Weimar in 1821, Mendelssohn met Hummel and took some piano lessons with him; Mendelssohn's Piano Concerto in A Minor (1822) is strikingly modeled on Hummel's Piano Concerto in A Minor, Op. 85. See further Wolfgang Dinglinger, "Felix Mendelssohn Bartholdys Klavierkonzert a-moll: Umgang mit einer Modellkomposition," *Mendelssohn Studien* 8 (1993): ł05–30.

26. "Dieses Oktett muß von allen Instrumenten im Style eines symphonischen Orchester gespielt werden. Pianos und Fortes müssen genau eingehalten und schärfer betont werden, als gewöhnlich in Werken dieses Charakters."

27. Louis Spohr, *Lebenserinnerungen*, ed. Folker Göthel (Tutzing, 1968), 2:134.

28. Ibid. For further discussion of Spohr's Op. 65, see Clive Brown, *Louis Spohr: A Critical Biography* (Cambridge, 1984), 164–66, and his essay in this volume.

29. See further my "Mozart according to Mendelssohn," 167ff.

30. The subject of the second fugato (mm. 213ff.), with its alternating fourths and sixths, appears to allude to the fugato in the "Hallelujah" chorus of Handel's *Messiah* ("And He shall reign for ever and ever").

31. A facsimile of the autograph is available (ed. Jon Newsom, Washington, DC, 1976).

32. He performed the arrangement at a Philharmonic concert in London on 25 May 1829.

33. Hensel, *The Mendelssohn Family* 1:131.

34. Throughout the trio the first viola mediates between the two canons by imitating now the one, now the other. For a fuller discussion (and transcription) of the movement see R. L. Todd, "The Instrumental Music of Felix Mendelssohn

Bartholdy: Selected Studies Based on Primary Sources" (Ph.D. diss., Yale University, 1979), 308–22.

35. The motive also figures at the opening of the *Reformation* Symphony, which Mendelssohn composed in 1830.

36. Letter ca. February 1828, in Adolf Fredrik Lindblad, *Bref till Adolf Fredrik Lindblåd fran Mendelssohn . . . och andra* (Stockholm, 1913), 19–20.

37. See Nancy B. Reich, ed., "From the Memoirs of Ernst Rudorff," in *Mendelssohn and His World*, 265–66.

38. Letter of February 1828 in *Bref till Adolf Fredrik Lindblad*, 20.

39. Autograph manuscript, Washington, DC, Library of Congress.

40. Paris, Bibliothèque du Conservatoire Ms. 209; dated "Berlin, d. 6. Jan. 1833."

41. For other examples of this technique, see Claudio Spies, "Samplings," in *Mendelssohn and His World*, 100–120.

42. Regarding Menuhin's edition (New York, 1953), see Friedhelm Krummacher, *Mendelssohn der Komponist*, 110–13.

43. *NZfM* 10 (1839): 138.

44. Donald Mintz, "The Sketches and Drafts of Three of Mendelssohn's Major Works" (Ph.D. diss., Cornell University, 1960), 111, 112.

45. Letter of 21 January 1840, in Felix Mendelssohn Bartholdy, *Briefe an deutsche Verleger*, ed. Rudolf Elvers (Berlin, 1968), 102.

46. Hiller, *Mendelssohn*, 154–55.

47. *Allgemeine musikalische Zeitung* 47 (1845): cols. 748–49.

48. See further my "Me voilà perruqué: Mendelssohn's Six Preludes and Fugues Op. 35 Reconsidered," in *Mendelssohn Studies*, ed. R. L. Todd (Cambridge, 1992), 196–98.

49. Unpublished letter of 14 February 1846 from Mendelssohn to Spohr in the Library of Congress, Washington, DC; letter of 30 December 1845 to Breitkopf & Härtel, in Mendelssohn, *Briefe an deutsche Verleger*, 168.

50. Ignaz Moscheles, *Recent Music and Musicians*, trans. A. D. Coleridge (New York, 1873), 329 (from Moscheles' diary entry for 27 October 1846).

51. Krummacher, "Mendelssohn's Late Chamber Music," 77–80. The autograph score is found in vol. 44 of the Mendelssohn Nachlaß, currently housed in the Biblioteka Jagiellońska in Kraków.

52. Ibid., 80–84.

53. Rychnovsky, "Aus Felix Mendelssohn Bartholdys letzten Lebenstagen," 143.

54. See Krummacher, "Mendelssohn's Late Chamber Music," 81.

55. Ibid.

Selected Bibliography

Cadenbach, Rainer. "Zum gattungsgeschichtlichen Ort von Mendelssohns letztem Streichquartett." In *Felix Mendelssohn Bartholdy Kongreß-Bericht, Berlin 1994*, ed. Christian Martin Schmidt, 209–31. Wiesbaden, 1997.

Gerlach, Reinhard. "Mendelssohn's schöpferische Erinnerung der 'Jugendzeit': Die Beziehungen zwischen dem Violinkonzert, op. 64, und dem Oktett für Streicher, op. 20." *Die Musikforschung* 25 (1972):142–52.

Klein, Hans-Günter. "Korrekturen im Autograph von Mendelssohns Streichquartett Op. 80: Überlegungen zur Kompositionstechnik und zum Kompositionsvorgang." *Mendelssohn-Studien* 5 (1982): 113–22.

Kohlhase, H. "Studien zur Form in den Streichquartetten von Felix Mendelssohn Bartholdy." *Hamburger Jahrbuch zur Musikwissenschaft* 2 (1977): 75–104.

———. "Brahms und Mendelssohn: Strukturelle Parallelen in der Kammermusik für Streicher." In *Brahms und seine Zeit,* ed. Constantin Floros, Hans Joachim Marx, and Peter Petersen, 59–85. Laaber, 1984.

Krummacher, Friedhelm. "Zur Kompositionsart Mendelssohns: Thesen am Beispiel der Streichquartette." In *Das Problem Mendelssohn,* ed. Carl Dahlhaus, 46–74. Regensburg, 1974.

———. *Mendelssohn der Komponist: Studien zur Kammermusik für Streicher.* Munich, 1978.

———. "Mendelssohn's Late Chamber Music: Some Autograph Sources Recovered." In *Mendelssohn and Schumann: Essays on Their Music and Its Context,* ed. Jon W. Finson and R. Larry Todd, 71–84. Durham, NC, 1984.

Lobe, J. C. "Ein Quartett bei Goethe: Erinnerung aus Weimars großer Zeit." *Die Gartenlaube,* no. 1 (1867): 4–8.

McDonald, J. A. "The Chamber Music of Felix Mendelssohn-Bartholdy." Ph.D. diss. Northwestern University, 1970.

Mintz, Donald. "The Sketches and Drafts of Three of Mendelssohn's Major Works." Ph.D. diss. Cornell University, 1960.

Newsom, Jon, ed. *Octet for Strings Opus 20 by Felix Mendelssohn: A Facsimile of the Holograph in the Whittall Foundation Collection.* Washington, DC, 1976.

Todd, R. Larry. "The Instrumental Music of Felix Mendelssohn Bartholdy: Selected Studies Based on Primary Sources." Ph.D. diss. Yale University, 1979.

Todd, R. Larry. *Mendelssohn: A Life in Music.* New York, 2003.

Ward Jones, Peter. "Mendelssohn's Opus 1: Bibliographical Problems of the C Minor Piano Quartet." In *Sundry Sorts of Music Books: Essays on the British Library Collections: Essays Presented to O. W. Neighbour on His 70th Birthday,* ed. Chris Banks, Arthur Searle, and Malcolm Turner, 264–73. London, 1993.

CHAPTER FIVE

"Beautiful and Abstruse Conversations"
The Chamber Music of Robert Schumann

John Daverio

The Revelation of a "New Poetic Life"

Commenting on the fate of many string quartets composed during the nineteenth century, Friedhelm Krummacher writes: "There is scarcely another genre in which the standards set by the Classical masterpieces were so domineering that the victims of later selection included even those works that had sought seriously to engage with the established canon."[1] What Krummacher says of the string quartet resonates with almost the whole of Schumann's chamber music. Of the composer's nearly two dozen chamber works (see Table 5.1), only one, the Piano Quintet, Op. 44, is heard with any frequency, a fact of reception history already grounded in the reactions of listeners during Schumann's lifetime. While some of these compositions are occasionally trotted out in public performances—the string quartets, the piano quartet, the first two piano trios, the first two violin sonatas, the *Phantasiestücke*, Op. 73—a late masterpiece such as the G Minor Piano Trio, Op. 110, is hardly known at all.

Indeed, even though Schumann contributed generously to the repertory, we tend not to think of him as a composer of instrumental chamber music in the same sense as Beethoven, Schubert, or Brahms. But in fact the genre framed his compositional career: among his first (nearly) completed works was a C Minor Piano Quartet; among his last was a set of *Fünf Romanzen* for cello and piano, destroyed by Clara Schumann in the

TABLE 5.1.   Schumann's Chamber Music

Date of Composition	Title	Remarks
November/ December 1828– March 1829	Piano Quartet in C Minor (publ. 1979)	originally designated Op. 5
1828–29 (?)	Piano Quartet in B	sketch for opening of one movement
1828–29 (?)	Piano Quartet in A	sketch for opening of one movement
1829 (?)	Allegro [for melody instrument and piano]	16-measure sketch
April 1838	String Quartet	sketch or draft; lost
June 1838	String Quartet	beginning of sketch; lost
summer 1839 (?)	String Quartet in D	sketch for opening of one movement
summer 1839 (?)	String Quartet in E♭	sketch for opening of one movement
June–July 1842	3 String Quartets, Op. 41, Nos. 1–3 (publ. 1848)	
September– October 1842	Piano Quintet, Op. 44 (publ. 1843)	
October– November 1842	Piano Quartet, Op. 47 (publ. 1845)	
December 1842	*Phantasiestücke* for piano, violin, and cello, Op. 88 (publ. 1850)	
January– February 1843	*Andante und Variationen,* for 2 pianos, 2 cellos, and horn, WoO 10 (publ. 1893)	arranged August 1843 as *Andante und Variationen* for 2 pianos, Op. 46 (publ. 1844)
June/ September 1847	Piano Trio in D Minor, Op. 63 (publ. 1848)	
August– November 1847	Piano Trio in F, Op. 80 (publ. 1849)	
February 1849	*Adagio und Allegro* for piano and horn (cello or violin ad libitum), Op. 70 (publ. 1849)	
February 1849	*Phantasiestücke* for piano and clarinet (violin or cello ad libitum), Op. 73 (publ. 1849)	
April 1849	*Fünf Stücke im Volkston* for cello (violin ad libitum) and piano, Op. 102 (publ. 1851)	
December 1849	*Drei Romanzen* for oboe (violin or clarinet ad libitum) and piano, Op. 94 (publ. 1851)	
March 1851	*Märchenbilder* for viola (violin ad libitum) and piano, Op. 113 (publ. 1852)	
September 1851	Sonata in A Minor for Piano and Violin, Op. 105 (publ. 1852)	
October 1851	Piano Trio in G Minor, Op. 110 (publ. 1852)	
October– November 1851	Sonata in D Minor (*2te Große Sonate*) for violin and piano, Op. 121 (publ. 1853)	

(continued)

TABLE 5.1.   (continued)

Date of Composition	Title	Remarks
December 1852– February 1853	Piano accompaniments to J. S. Bach, Sonatas and Partitas for solo violin (publ. 1853)	
March–April 1853	Piano accompaniments to J. S. Bach, Suites for solo cello (publ. ca. 1870)	
October 1853	*Märchenerzählungen: Vier Stücke* for clarinet (violin ad libitum), viola, and piano, Op. 132 (publ. 1854)	
October 1853	Intermezzo and Finale (movements 2 and 4) to "FAE" Sonata (publ. 1935)	movements 1 and 3 by Albert Dietrich and Johannes Brahms
October 1853	Sonata in A Minor for Violin and Piano, WoO 27 (publ. 1956)	movements 3 and 4 = Intermezzo and Finale from "FAE" Sonata; movements 1 and 2 newly composed
November 1853	*Fünf Romanzen* for piano and cello	lost/destroyed
October 1853/ spring and summer (?) 1855	Piano accompaniments to Paganini, Caprices for solo violin (publ. 1941)	

early 1890s, according to Brahms's testimony, since she felt it didn't meet her husband's usually high level of accomplishment.[2] The chamber music of the intervening years encompasses a broad range of subgenres: works in the larger or "higher" forms, as Schumann called them, often with *concertante* piano parts; compositions for strings, again in the higher forms; character pieces; convivial *Hausmusik* for a variety of combinations; and last, arrangements with piano of works originally conceived for unaccompanied violin and cello. These subgenres hardly constitute rigid categories. The central movements of works in the higher forms, for instance, often partake of the traits associated with the character piece. Similarly, there is a fine line between the poetry of the latter and the easygoing charm of the ostensibly bourgeois *Hausmusik*. Furthermore, Schumann's chamber music was more than receptive to features associated with other genres—the symphony, concerto, and lied among them. This repertory, in other words, may be viewed as a kind of prism through which the composer's achievements in other areas were often reflected.

Not surprisingly, given his background and training, the majority of Schumann's chamber music includes piano. According to several entries in the *Blätter und Blümchen aus der goldenen Aue*, a commonplace book he assembled during his early teenage years in Zwickau, his first exposure to instrumental chamber music involved works for piano and strings such as Mozart's Piano Quartets in G Minor (K. 478) and E♭ (K. 493), and the Piano Quintet (Op. 1) of Prince Louis Ferdinand.[3] While fecklessly pursuing legal studies at the University of Leipzig during the winter of 1828 and 1829, Schumann even tried his hand at composing for this medium. To judge from the surviving manuscript materials, two such projects failed to get very far: all that we have of a pair of piano quartets in A and B are sketches for the opening thematic groups of their respective first movements.[4] Schumann made considerably greater headway with a third project, a Piano Quartet in C Minor drafted nearly complete between late autumn 1828 and March 1829.

The composer's first essay in the higher forms grew out of an atmosphere that approached music as a convivial art. Late in 1828 he formed a piano quartet—comprising Johann Friedrich Täglichsbeck (violin), Christoph Sörgel (viola), Christian Glock (cello), and Schumann himself as pianist—whose reading sessions were often attended by a circle of select listeners, including his piano teacher (and subsequently, his recalcitrant father-in-law), Friedrich Wieck. Schumann's diary entry for 13 March 1829 paints a vivid portrait of a typically lively session given over to hearty music making and good-natured banter:

> Evening: 14th quartet session. Beethoven's ["Archduke"] Trio, Op. 97 (bizarre)—Dussek Quartet in E♭ (Op. 57)—[Schumann's C Minor] Quartet Op. V (went well)—much Bavarian beer—long-winded conversation about the students' and peasants' associations—good cheer—late at night the first movement of Schubert's Trio [Op. 100/D. 929]—very noble music . . . beautiful sleep.[5]

These informal sessions provided Schumann with a laboratory for trying out his latest compositional efforts; no sooner had he finished a movement of the quartet than his friends were on hand for a sympathetic—if not always polished—reading. At its tenth meeting, on 7 February 1829, the group played through portions of the quartet (probably the first movement) no less than three times to "general laudations."[6] A week later, the Minuetto was ready, but the cellist Glock (at the time a student of theology and philosophy) apparently came to grief over its witty rhythmic turns: "bungled quartet—the breakneck cello," Schumann wrote in his diary on 14 February.[7] After the entire composition was treated to a run-through at the group's final meeting on 28 March 1829, we hear nothing of the work until early January of the following year, when Schumann noted: "The quartet will be cobbled into a symphony."[8] But while the autograph is peppered with orchestral designations, the plan for a symphonic realization of the work never materialized.

Schumann's C Minor Piano Quartet, however, is not only a document of convivial music making; perhaps more importantly, it speaks to the young composer's reception of a newly found musical hero. From the start, Schumann associated his quartet with the image of Franz Schubert, word of whose untimely death occasioned the following diary entry for 31 November 1828: "My quartet—Schubert is dead—dismay."[9] Indeed, elements of Schubert's idiom in general, and of his Piano Trio in E♭ Major (D. 929) in particular,[10] abound in Schumann's quartet. In its first, second, and last movements, the glittering passagework in the keyboard part—which, a few exceptions aside, is notated on a single staff—seems especially indebted to the older composer's manner. The work's harmonic language likewise draws liberally on a variety of Schubertian traits: consider the immediate emphasis on the Neapolitan in the opening movement, the rapid-fire modulations by third in the Minuetto, and the thoroughgoing modal mixture of the finale.

At the same time, the C Minor Piano Quartet is hardly a mere imitation of Schubert. On the contrary, it is closely implicated with concerns that Schumann made very much his own. Summarizing his artistic development some twenty years later, he accorded the work a special place in his output: "I remember very well a spot in one of my works . . . about which I said to myself: this is *romantic;* here a spirit different from that of my earlier music opened up for me: a new poetic life seemed to reveal itself (the spot in question was the trio of a scherzo [*sic*] from a piano quartet)."[11]

The new, "Romantic" spirit of the trio from the Minuetto emanates from lilting trochaic and dactylic rhythms, piquant appoggiaturas, and at the beginning of the trio's second half, a simple but evocative scoring in which the melody, assigned to the cello, is accompanied by pizzicati in the upper strings and pulsing chords in the piano (see Example 5.1). This passage in turn plays a key role in the finale, which, as Schumann put it, "gaily muses on the past as if from another world and transports its bas reliefs into this one."[12] Specifically, he recalls the "romantic" trio theme in the quartet's last movement, where it figures in a veritable parade of recurrent ideas from earlier in the piece, including the second theme from the first movement and the opening theme of the Andante. The trio theme, however, serves as the peroration of this process of recall when it appears, transformed into an ebullient C major, in the finale's *più presto* coda. And here, too, we realize in retrospect that the obsessive dactylic rhythm of the finale is none other than a quick-tempo variant of the same pattern from the trio. Hence the "new poetic life" revealed through the charming but initially unassuming trio theme was intimately bound up with a search for coherence on a large temporal scale. It is significant that this search was initiated through the medium of instrumental chamber music.

False Starts and Unbounded Creativity

By the end of the 1830s Schumann was assiduously engaged in the composition of piano music. But the period between 1836 and 1839—during which he completed such enduringly popular works as the *Phantasie* (Op. 17), *Davidsbündlertänze, Kinderszenen,* and *Kreisleriana*—was also crucial in the deepening of his sense for chamber music. Picking up on the thread of his activities in 1828 and 1829, Schumann contemplated writing a piano quintet and a piano trio in August 1836, although neither project got off the ground.[13] At about the same time he began regularly attending (and

EXAMPLE 5.1.   Robert Schumann, Piano Quartet in C Minor, Minuetto (trio), mm. 1–24.

sometimes hosting) the rehearsals of a string quartet lead by Ferdinand David, concertmaster of Leipzig's Gewandhaus orchestra. These sessions continued well into 1838 and provided the impetus for Schumann to write a series of six colorful articles on the contemporary quartet scene for his *Neue Zeitschrift für Musik*.[14] Well known for its renditions of Beethoven's late quartets, David's group likewise offered Schumann firsthand encounters with a repertory that immediately captivated him. As he put it

Example 5.1.   *continued*

in a survey of Leipzig's musical life written in 1838, Beethoven's String Quartets in E♭, Op. 127, and C♯ Minor, Op. 131, were works "for whose greatness no words can be found. They appear to me, next to some of the choruses and original works of J. S. Bach, to represent the extreme limits that human art and imagination have yet reached."[15] Schumann did, however, find enough words to articulate a view of Beethoven's late quartets that departed radically from contemporary opinion. While many of his fellow critics found this music to be bizarre and inscrutable, Schumann was taken by its "soaring flights of fancy," its "folklike strain," and its "romantic humor."[16]

Beethoven's late quartets also spurred Schumann to composition. Inspired in part by the C♯ Minor Quartet, Op. 131, which he heard at a rehearsal of David's group in late February or early March 1838, and feeling that the piano had become "too limited" an outlet for his creativity, Schumann made a first attempt at writing a quartet of his own.[17] According to a letter of 3 April 1838 to Joseph Fischhoff, he may even have completed a draft of the work by that time, though no traces of it survive. Another quartet begun (or at least envisioned) in June apparently came to nothing.[18] Schumann turned again to the quartet medium about a year later, and once again his endeavors were bound up with his reception of Beethoven's late works. Writing on 28 May 1839 to the critic and composer Hermann Hirschbach—who, in the months ahead, would contribute a whole series of articles on the late quartets to Schumann's *Neue Zeitschrift*—he divulged his plan to devote the summer months to the composition of string quartets.[19] By 13 June he was able to report to Clara that he had begun two quartets, both of them "just as good as Haydn's," even if his progress was impeded by a lack of "time and inner peace" (his legal battle for Clara's hand, after all, was about to get into high gear). Within a few weeks he was studying Beethoven's late quartets "right down to the love and hate contained therein," no doubt as a catalyst for his own compositional efforts. Unfortunately, Schumann's plans failed to materialize; all he had to show for the pair of quartets intended to be "just as good as Haydn's" were eight- and ten-bar drafts for the openings of movements in D and E♭, respectively.[20]

Thereafter we hear nothing of string quartets for about three years.[21] In the meantime, other matters claimed Schumann's attention: a messy lawsuit that dragged on for over a year—in the course of which he devoted himself with a vengeance to lieder writing, a more lucrative enterprise than the composition of quartets—a period of settling into married life, and finally, a nearly year-long engagement with symphonic composition.[22] But in 1842, Schumann's so-called chamber music year, the false starts of several years earlier were displaced by unbounded creativity. After a period of compositional inactivity in the first half of 1842, the "continual quartet thoughts" that Schumann noted in his *Haushaltbücher* (household account books) on 14 February rapidly bore fruit in the summer months.[23] After sketching an A Minor Quartet (Op. 41, No. 1) in early June, he immediately sketched a second quartet in F before elaborating both in turn. These two quartets were then joined by a third, in A major, sketched and elaborated between 8 and 22 July.[24] After a brief hiatus came the Piano Quintet in E♭, Op. 44 (23 September–12 October), and then the Piano Quartet, Op. 47, also in E♭ (25 October–26 November). By three days after Christmas, he had completed the *Phantasiestücke* for piano trio, Op, 88, and early in the next year rounded out this remarkable spate of creativity with the *Andante und Variationen* in B♭ (WoO 10), unusually scored for two pianos, two cellos, and horn.[25]

Just as Schumann's output as a whole discloses a systematic conquest of the various musical genres—piano music, lieder, symphonic music, oratorio, dramatic and sacred music—so, too, do the creative products of 1842 and early 1843 represent an orderly exploration of the subgenres of instrumental chamber music. The delicately etched chamber style of the string quartets gives way to the broader strokes of the piano quintet and piano quartet. In addition, Schumann drew on his experience as a composer of character pieces for piano in the *Phantasiestücke* and *Andante und Variationen*, works that likewise foreshadow the bourgeois flavor of the *Hausmusik* written in the late 1840s. Hence the larger system of Schumann's creativity enfolds smaller systems within it.

The present survey of the chamber music year begins where Schumann did—with the string quartet. According to one writer, this genre represented a "stimulating novelty" for the composer, but not an "essential thread."[26] In all likelihood, Schumann would not have agreed. As he put it to Raimund Härtel in a letter of 3 December 1847: "My quartets . . . have taken on a special meaning for me through the death of Mendelssohn, to whom they are dedicated. I still view them as the best works of my earlier period, and Mendelssohn often expressed a similar opinion to me."[27] Schumann's critical writings on the quartet may offer us access to the "special meaning" he had in mind.

Two aspects of Schumann's aesthetic are of particular importance. In the first place, composers of quartets should remain within certain strictly delimited boundaries; specifically, they should be careful to avoid "symphonic furor."[28] In Schumann's view, "everyone has something to say" in a "proper string quartet": it is a "by turns beautiful and even abstrusely woven conversation among four people."[29] Hence the "proper" quartet style embodies an esoteric quality whose compositional correlatives include the self-sufficiency of the individual voices and the contrapuntal integrity of the whole.

Second, Schumann believed that the prospective quartet composer must possess a deep understanding of the genre's history, which embraced the quartets of Haydn, Mozart, Beethoven, and Schumann's great contemporary, Mendelssohn, as well. (Although he gave high marks to the "Death and the Maiden" Quartet, D. 810, Schumann's historical scheme largely bypassed Schubert).[30] But while an awareness of tradition was crucial for the composition of string quartets, Schumann maintained with equal conviction that slavish imitation of older models was to be avoided.[31] Both aspects of Schumann's ideal—the creation of contrapuntally integrated works in which every member of the ensemble makes a substantial contribution, and an imaginative approach to the historical legacy—were aptly realized in the three quartets of his Op. 41.

The results of Schumann's self-imposed course of contrapuntal study in March and April 1842 are obvious in all three quartets he would soon complete. Indeed, the first movement of Op. 41, No. 1, begins with a slow introduction in which nearly every measure features the same plaintive sixteenth-note motive, first treated in fugato, and then as a countermelody to a rhythmically differentiated idea. In the following *allegro,* the transition to the second group likewise proceeds with a fugato on the principal motive of the first group; the ensuing duet texture later serves as the basis for the densely imitative central section of the development. The whole of the second variation in the second movement (*assai agitato*) of Op. 41, No. 3, is in turn conceived as a fugato on a persistently driving figure. Thus the three principal functions associated with the sonata style—presentation, development, and varied repetition—are enriched through the medium of counterpoint.

In his review of the first of Hirschbach's *Lebensbilder in einem Zyklus von Quartetten,* Schumann acknowledged that while young composers were anxious to take Beethoven as their model, "heavily laden trees are also to be found in the fruit gardens of Haydn and Mozart."[32] Schumann's own quartets attest to an intimate familiarity with these gardens. While Clara toured in Copenhagen in March and April 1842, Schumann pored over the scores of Haydn's and Mozart's string quartets, and after Clara's return, the couple read through many of these scores at the piano.[33]

In a sense, there is a built-in affinity between Haydn's and Schumann's approaches to the sonata form. The concentration upon a single motive in the first movement of Op. 41, No. 1, for instance, readily bears comparison with the same feature in any number of Haydn's quartet movements. Furthermore, Haydn's teleological sonata forms (which frequently withhold a solid confirmation of the dominant until the very last moments of the exposition) find a ready counterpart in the delayed articulation of the dominant that characterizes the expositions of the first and last movements of Schumann's Op. 41, No. 2.

Schumann's debt to Mozartean forms is perhaps less obvious but no less noteworthy. In several of Mozart's sonata-style movements (examples from the string quartets include the finales of K. 428 in E♭ and K. 575 in D), development and recapitulation are so closely interwoven or conflated that it is difficult to say where one section leaves off and the other begins.[34] Schumann opts for just this kind of design in the opening movement of Op. 41, No. 3, thereby achieving a kind of concision that the textbook sonata form does not so easily allow. At the same time, the flexible structure of the movement belies the charge of schematicism that has been leveled more than once at Schumann's quartets.[35]

"I love *Mozart* dearly," Schumann wrote in a diary entry of November 1842, "but Beethoven I worship like a god who remains forever apart, who will never become one with us."[36] To be sure, the most powerful model for Schumann's approach to the string medium was furnished by Beethoven, whose late works he was now in a position not to imitate but rather to emulate. Echoes of late Beethoven certainly abound in Schumann's own quartets. But of greater moment than the obvious allusions (the head motive of the hymnic slow movement of Op. 41, No. 1, as many writers have pointed out, recalls the corresponding gesture in the slow movement of Beethoven's Ninth Symphony) are the more oblique references to Beethoven's later works. The slow movement of Schumann's Op. 41, No. 2, for instance, adopts the tone, if not the thematic substance, of the slow movement of Beethoven's Op. 127, with which it shares the same form (variations), tonality (A♭), and meter ($\frac{12}{8}$). The imitative slow introduction of the first movement of Op. 41, No. 1, conflates the detached character (and A minor tonality) of the opening *assai sostenuto* of Beethoven's Op. 132 with the fugal texture of the first movement of Op. 131. The unusual tonal argument of Schumann's movement—its introductory *andante espressivo*, in A minor, prefaces a full-fledged sonata allegro in F—may likewise be viewed in terms of a Beethovenian example: F major is the unexpected counterpole to the tonic, A minor, in the first-movement exposition of Beethoven's Op. 132. The first of Schumann's quartets also invokes late Beethoven in its handling of intermovement connections. The F major of the first movement recurs as the key of the slow movement (Adagio) and again as an important tonal plateau in the finale's development; the scherzo's main theme serves as the basis for the shape of a significant countermelody in the Adagio; the bass line for the beginning of a choralelike passage in the coda of the finale (mm. 264–67) recalls the descending fourths of the main theme of the Adagio. Thus Schumann's attempt to make of his quartet an integrated but varied whole bears comparison to Beethoven's similar intent in his C♯ Minor Quartet, Op. 131.

Still, Schumann's quartets amount to more than the sum of the influences that went into their making. Unique to Schumann is the continuation of the quest for "new forms" that distinguished so many of his keyboard works of the 1830s. The strophic variation design of the slow movements of Op. 41, Nos. 1 and 3, to take an example, is practically without precedent in the earlier quartet literature. The finale of Op. 41, No. 3, unfolds as a mosaiclike succession of miniature character portraits (after the manner of the *Novelletten*, Op. 21), but is given shape by an overarching "parallel" design (the music of mm. 112–84 recalls that of mm. 1–72, for the most part a minor third higher)—an idiosyncratic sonata form variant that, as Linda Roesner has shown, plays a significant role in Schumann's earlier piano sonatas and *Phantasie*.[37]

We may also gauge the individuality of Schumann's quartet style by recognizing its *distance* from the style of his contemporaries' works in general, and of Mendelssohn's in particular. As any practiced quartet player will confirm, Mendelssohn's quartets are eminently more "readable" that Schumann's. Mendelssohn's figurations lie well under the hand, and his rich textures are geared to resonate well without undue effort on the part of the executants. With the possible exception of the F Minor Quartet, Op. 80, his quartets were conceived for the delectation of talented amateurs. Not so Schumann's. Even the most seasoned professionals will be challenged by the rhythmic displacements and skittish arpeggios of the C minor scherzo from Op. 41, No. 2. Yet paradoxically, Schumann may well have been truer to the conversational but agonistic ideals of the quartet style.

We should keep in mind that both Schumann and Mendelssohn reached maturity as composers during a period in which chamber music had come to occupy an intermediary position between private and public entertainment. One of the earliest performances of Schumann's A Minor Quartet occurred on 8 January 1843, as part of a *Musikalische Morgenunter-haltung* (literally, "musical morning entertainment, or conversation") at the Leipzig Gewandhaus.[38] The private character of the occasion was emphasized by its exclusivity: only those especially invited could attend. But at the same time, the audience for chamber music—which, strictly speaking, should be limited to the players themselves[39]—was growing ever larger: the violinist Henri Vieuxtemps's Quartet-matinées, a regular feature of musical life in Saint Petersburg during the later 1840s, generally drew audiences of between 100 and 150 listeners.[40]

This split between private and public dimensions manifests itself in the orchestral textures that encroach more and more on the nineteenth-century string quartet. One thinks of the pulsating tremolos and restless syncopations that support the soloistic flights of the first violin in the openings of Mendelssohn's D Major and E Minor Quartets (Op. 44, Nos. 1 and 2) respectively. Yet it is precisely this kind of "symphonic furor" that Schumann generally eschews in his string quartets. The general impression derived from listening to and playing these pieces is of a discourse—"by turns beautiful and abstrusely woven"—among equals. There is no better evidence for the esoteric quality of the motivic web in his quartets than Schumann's insistence that players study them from the full score.[41] Schumann's quartets, in short, may number among the last representatives of the true chamber idiom wherein players and listeners are one.

In a review of contemporary piano trios, including Mendelssohn's Trio in D minor, Op. 47, Schumann articulated an ideal for the composition of chamber music involving piano and strings that is concordant in part with his aesthetic of the string quartet. Here, too, the appropriate style results when "no instrument dominates, and each has something to say."[42] But even though this repertory shares its social and performative space with the quartet, it evinces a markedly divergent social character. Schumann hinted at this difference in praising Mendelssohn's Trio for the equilibrium it achieved between musical substance and a virtuosic piano part.[43] This balance goes hand in hand with a dialectic of private and public characters.

A similar interplay informs the works for piano and strings of Schumann's chamber music year, and it is particularly evident in the Piano Quintet and Piano Quartet. The unusual position of nineteenth-century chamber music—suspended midway between private and public spheres—leaves its imprint on Schumann's quintet in the form of a tension between symphonic and more properly chamberlike elements. Their mediation is evident in the work's distinctive tone color, which will be best appreciated in neither the bourgeois drawing room nor the grand concert hall, but rather in a space proportioned somewhere between the two. Tovey was among the earliest critics to recognize the aptness of the Quintet's scoring: "every note tells, and the instruments are vividly characterized in spite of the preponderance of the pianoforte throughout."[44] Indeed, the doublings for which this work (like Schumann's orchestral compositions) has been frequently criticized often create an almost impressionistic effect, as in the first episode (C major) of the slow movement, where the triplet quarter notes in the piano (against rippling eighths in the second violin and viola) delicately color the sustained melody in the first violin and cello.

The finely wrought web of contrapuntal lines that characterizes the string quartets gives way, in the Piano Quintet, to a more extroverted, "public" counterpoint, most obviously at the peroration of the last movement. After an emphatic arrival on the dominant, the opening theme of the first movement, in augmented note values, is combined with the finale's main theme (see Example 5.2) in a brilliantly effective double-fugue exposition. Thus with the Piano Quintet Schumann returned to a question he had confronted in several of the symphonic works of 1841: how is it possible to shape the finale of a multimovement work so that it is not only complete in itself but also provides closure for the entire composition? The finale of the piano quintet solves the problem by unfolding first as a "parallel" form (the material of mm. 1–85 is elaborated, a half step higher and then a major third lower, in mm. 136–220),[45] but evolves later into something quite different: an "apotheosis" form culminating in a climactic restatement of the first movement's opening motto in augmentation.[46] This design prefigures the trajectory of the finale of the Second Symphony, Op. 61, which culminates in the recall of the opening idea of the first movement, a solemn but genial chorale. Hence the public character of the piano quintet derives less from Schumann's occasionally scrubby writing for the strings than from his serious engagement with a structural problem more readily associated with the most public of musical genres, the symphony.

In many ways, the piano quartet appears to be a creative double to the quintet: both works are cast in E♭; both bring together the piano and a complement of strings; both make prominent use of thematic recall; both display the extroverted, exuberant side of the composer's art. But in spite of their similarities, they are hardly twins. If, in the Piano Quintet, the mediation of private and public character tips toward the latter, the reverse is true of the Piano Quartet. The presence of one less violin in the later work makes for a more intimate sound world whose most obvious emblem is the sumptuous cello solo at the beginning of the Andante cantabile. Furthermore, the distinctive character of the Piano Quartet derives from a neo-Classical tone largely absent in the Quintet. The hymnlike quality of the first movement's slow introduction (*sostenuto assai*), no less than the figurational, abstract quality of much of the ensuing *allegro ma non troppo*, bears comparison to the tone struck by Beethoven in his "Harp" Quartet,

EXAMPLE 5.2.   Schumann, Piano Quintet in E♭, Op. 44, finale, mm. 316–30.

Op. 74, and "Archduke" Trio, Op. 97. Schumann's decision to head off the last movement with a spirited fugato places his piano quartet in line with a tradition extending back through Beethoven (the finale of the C Major String Quartet, Op. 59, No. 3) to Mozart (the finale of the G Major String Quartet, K. 387). In short, the Piano Quartet is closer than its companion piece to the intimate world of the string quartet.

Intimacy is also the rule in the last two products of the chamber music year: the *Phantasiestücke*, Op. 88, for piano trio and the *Andante und Variationen*. In a letter of 19 June 1843 to the Dutch composer and conductor Johannes Verhulst, Schumann set the *Phantasiestücke* apart from his own earlier works for piano and strings by calling attention to its "much more delicate . . . nature." [47] An important signifier for the work's delicacy is Schumann's employment of German movement titles, tempo markings, and character designations as opposed to their internationally recognized Italian equivalents. This small but telling feature complements a turn from the sonata-style forms of the Piano Quintet and Quartet toward the more sectional designs of the character piece. The second movement ("Humoreske"), for example, is cast as a medley of quasi-independent miniatures, all of them in binary form. First comes a march in F, then another march (which brings the opening idea of the first movement in dotted rhythms) in A minor. A third march (F major) gives way to a fourth (D minor), which draws its characteristic rhythm from the preceding miniature. Restatements of the third march (in B♭) and the first round off a piece that seems to emanate from the world of the *Novelletten* and *Faschingsschwank aus Wien*.

The *Andante und Variationen* partake of the same world. Schumann spelled out the link between his "Quintet Variations" and the compositions of the previous decade in a letter of 7 September 1843 to Breitkopf and Härtel, where he compared them to "a somewhat delicate plant," and requested that the print be "fitted out similarly" to the *Kinderszenen*.[48] The theme of the set recalls the main idea of the second piece from *Kreisleriana* (also in B♭), just as the alternation of boisterous "Florestan" variations and more subdued "Eusebius" variations echoes the similar patterning in the *Davidsbündlertänze*. But, as Eduard Hanslick said of the oratorio *Das Paradies und die Peri*, "Master Florestan is getting a bit older."[49] And indeed, Schumann's rhapsodic temper is held in check in the *Andante und Variationen* by a nearly symmetrical disposition of the "Eusebius" pieces, three of which are strategically placed at the opening, midpoint, and close of the cycle. Its somewhat sentimental theme aside, the "Quintet Variations" make few concessions to popular taste. According to the author of a brief review for the *Allgemeine musikalische Zeitung*, the *Andante und Variationen* attempted to "say much with little ado" (in contrast to virtuoso music, which "says little with much ado"), and hence would demand repeated hearings to create the proper effect.[50] Thus, while innovation and tradition come together in Schumann's string quartets, and while the Piano Quintet and Piano Quartet mediate the demands of symphonism and the chamber medium, the *Andante und Variationen* (and to a lesser extent, the *Phantasiestücke*) provide a foretaste of the dialectic between high art and Biedermeier sensibility that will inform the *Hausmusik* of the later 1840s.

Composing in a "Completely New Manner"

In a rare instance of self-analysis, Schumann confided the following description of his compositional development to his diary sometime after 1846:

> I used to write practically all of my shorter pieces in the heat of inspiration; many compositions [were completed] with unbelievable swiftness; for instance, my First Symphony in B♭ Major [was written] in four days, as was a *Liederkreis* of twenty pieces [*Dichterliebe*]; the *Peri* too was composed in a relatively short time. Only from the year 1845 on, when I began to invent and work out everything in my head, did a completely new manner of composing begin to develop.[51]

Prior to 1845, the year during which Schumann completed a rich array of contrapuntal works for keyboard, the last two movements of the Piano Concerto, and the sketches for the Second Symphony, the composer had depended on his improvisational skills for creative inspiration. In contrast, the "completely new manner of composing" of 1845 and beyond gives primacy of place to the act of reflection. The change in compositional process was accompanied by a subtle but palpable stylistic shift whose principal features include a more refined approach to the art of transition and an increasingly concentrated mode of utterance. Put another way, Schumann's "new manner" demonstrates a profound change in the conception of the musical idea. Specifically, the linear development of melodic lines begins to recede in favor of a rich web of simultaneously developed motivic combinations. Chamber music is a natural medium for a process of this sort. Thus it is hardly surprising that among the most impressive documents of the "new manner" are the Piano Trios in D Minor and F Major (Opp. 63 and 80, respectively), conceived as a pair between June and November 1847.[52]

Both works make telling use of the *ars combinatoria* but without the least touch of pedantry or archaism. Consider the darkly hued opening movement of the D Minor Trio (*Mit Energie und Leidenschaft*). Writing in 1848, the critic Alfred Dörffel was certainly correct in asserting that its most noteworthy aspect resided in neither its rich harmonies nor expansive form, but rather in its novel thematic combinations.[53] More precisely, each of the main formal divisions in the exposition is articulated by a contrapuntal duo. The opening theme, for instance, is arguably an outgrowth of the gestural complex presented in the first measure: a cadential figure in the violin (*a* in Example 5.3) and a turning figure in the bass (*b*). The second measure then subjects the initial complex, slightly varied, to voice exchange, so that what we at first perceive as linear entities (the two-measure motives in violin and bass) emerge as by-products of a vertically conceived unit. The new dotted motive heading off the transition is in turn drawn into a series of imitative parries between piano and strings. The hints of imitation in the first four bars of the second group give way to a full-fledged canon between melody and bass in the varied response to the phrase, a strategy geared to lend even greater urgency to the upward-striving chromaticism, appoggiaturas, and syncopations of the lyrical second theme. And finally, the closing group combines a variant of this lyrical theme with the movement's opening idea. (Performers who fail to take the first ending and repeat will miss the point of the exposition: the presen-

EXAMPLE 5.3.   Schumann, Piano Trio in D Minor, Op. 63, mvt. 1, mm. 1–2.

tation, withdrawal, and gradual restitution of a motivic combination.) Hence the musical idea in this movement is no longer conceived as a leisurely unfolding lyrical entity but rather as a terse combinative unit.

The same kind of concision contributes to the textural richness of the trio's subsequent movements. The nervously dotted main theme of the second movement is smoothed out, in the middle section, as a gracefully rising figure that soon combines with a freely inverted variant.[54] The third movement offers one of the most remarkable mixtures of constructive rigor and unbridled fantasy in Schumann's output, a blend issuing from the employment of contrapuntal artifice on the one hand (the violin's opening arioso, transferred into the bass register, functions as a counter-melodic foil to the subsequent phrase in the cello) and variation techniques (in the piano's highly altered delivery of the arioso near the end of the movement) on the other. The initial paragraphs of the finale strike a considerably lighter tone. The dronelike accompaniments to the opening and transitional themes lend them a pastoral flavor, while the second theme, elided seamlessly with the previous transition, is one of those bittersweet conceits that bear Schumann's unmistakable stamp. Yet neither the sunny first theme nor the wistful second hints at the contrapuntal machinations of the development section, where the transitional theme acts as a kind of cantus firmus and portions of the first theme, in original and inverted forms, are treated in fugato. Hence the *ars combinatoria* affects the whole spectrum of the trio's materials: a compact motive (first movement), a lyric scale fragment (second movement), an arioso (slow movement), and a full-blown melody (finale).

As Schumann put it, the D Minor Trio belonged to a "time of gloomy moods."[55] But with its F major counterpart he seems to have banished melancholy once and for all. The later F Major Piano Trio, again according to Schumann, "is of a completely different character from [the Trio] in D—it makes a friendlier and breezier effect. I'm particularly pleased with the beginning of the Adagio and the Allegretto."[56] Undoubtedly, the two trios diverge widely in character, the second providing the satyr play to the tragedy of the first. But their antithetical characters aside, these works have much in common. It is probably not a coincidence that Schumann called attention to just those movements from the F Major Trio in which the *ars combinatoria*, developed to such a high level in the earlier composition, comes to the fore: the opening five bars of the slow movement feature a canon at the fifth between the cello and the piano left hand, while the principal section of the Allegretto, a siciliano marked *In mäßiger Bewegung*, unfolds as a canon in which all instruments take part. Although the finale eschews strict canons or fugatos, its pervasive play on the combinative possibilities of a limited number of motivic cells makes for a kaleidoscopic alternation of contrapuntal textures.

In addition, both works include moments of what may be called "sublime removal"—the obverse of the impassioned "breakthroughs" in more public works like the symphonies. In the D Minor Trio, such a passage occurs early in the first movement's development section, where *pianississimo* triplets in the upper reaches of the piano color an ethereal chorale, its numinous effect enhanced by the *sul ponticello* in the strings and a modulation from F to A♭.[57] A comparable passage occupies a corresponding spot in the first movement of the F Major Trio and consists of an extended quotation of the second song from the Eichendorff *Liederkreis*, Op. 39, "Dein Bildnis wunderselig." Relatives of the dreamy asides in Schumann's early keyboard music, these passages introduce voices as if from a distant domain, incursions into the "real" time of the piece from afar. In spite of its sophisticated motivic techniques and contrapuntal gamesmanship, Schumann's "new manner of composing" was not without its poetic side.

Toward a Poetic *Hausmusik*

In much of the music of what Schumann called his "most fruitful year" (1849)[58] the accent rests on its convivial function; this is especially true of the choral part songs, ensemble lieder, and *Liederspiele*. However, a tendency toward systematic exploration lies at the heart of the keyboard, solo vocal, and even instrumental chamber music of the same period. No doubt Schumann and his contemporaries would have subsumed this repertory under the heading of *Hausmusik*, a term that gained general currency in the years immediately following the publication, between 1837 and 1839, of a multipartite article in the *Neue Zeitschrift* by C. F. Becker entitled "Zur Geschichte der Hausmusik in früheren Jahrhunderten." Although Becker's largely historical account equated *Hausmusik* with the entire range of instrumental and vocal genres intended for performance in the home as opposed to the concert hall, the contemporary press was quick to employ the term to designate a category distinct from concert music (symphonies, concertos), church music, and dramatic music on the one hand, and *Unterhaltungsmusik* ("entertainment music") and music for *Gesangvereine* on the other.[59] As a repertory cultivated in the privacy of the bourgeois home and intended as a means of heightening the cultural awareness of its practitioners, *Hausmusik* amounts to a quintessentially Biedermeier phenomenon. Indeed, it reinforced a central image of the period between the Congress of Vienna (1815) and the mid-nineteenth-century revolutions: withdrawal from the outer tumult into that most hallowed of spaces, the domestic interior. Schumann's *Hausmusik* of 1849 is directly implicated with that image. But if the chief characteristic of the Biedermeier sensibility in music is an artless naïveté, then Schumann brings to it a strong measure of reflectivity.

To be sure, an interplay of simplicity and artfulness is the distinguishing mark of the *Hausmusik* for various solo instruments and piano that occupied Schumann intermittently throughout his most fruitful year: the *Phantasiestücke* for clarinet, Op. 73; the *Adagio und Allegro* for horn, Op.

70; the *Fünf Stücke im Volkston* for cello, Op. 102; and the *Drei Romanzen* for oboe, Op. 94. Together these compositions—along with the *Märchenbilder* for viola and piano, Op. 113 (1851), and the *Märchenerzählungen* for clarinet, viola, and piano, Op. 132 (1853)—constitute a systematic exploration of the coloristic possibilities of the few-voiced instrumental chamber idiom, thus situating Schumann in the center of a tradition bounded by J. S. Bach on one end and Paul Hindemith on the other. Indeed, Schumann's allowances for ad libitum substitutions—in the *Phantasiestücke*, for instance, violin or cello in place of clarinet—make these pieces into a kind of nineteenth-century *Gebrauchsmusik* and extend their appeal to a wider public.

Except for the *Adagio und Allegro*, all of the instrumental chamber works of 1849 were conceived as cycles of miniatures, each unified by a central tonic (interestingly enough, all three cycles are cast in A minor/ major) and an overall affective profile. The close relationship among the three pieces that make up the *Phantasiestücke*, for instance, is further underscored by the *attacca* indications linking each of the movements and, more importantly, by a web of thematic connections. The counterline to the opening idea of No. 1 is echoed in the overlapping third chains of the

EXAMPLE 5.4.(a).   Schumann, *Phantasiestücke*, Op. 73; No. 1, mm. 1–3.

EXAMPLE 5.4.(b).   Schumann, *Phantasiestücke*, Op. 73; No.3, mm. 9–16.

principal melody of No. 2. Number 3 recalls material from both of the preceding pieces: the allusion, in its opening section, to the main idea of No. 1 is so deftly woven into the melodic fabric that one is apt to miss it on first hearing (see Example 5.4); the coda then recalls the opening of No. 2 (at first *piano, dolce*), which, as we have seen, is traceable to the very beginning of the cycle. Yet the various reminiscences do not overtly call attention to themselves; Schumann's technique of attenuated recall rather makes for a delicate tracery of fleeting allusions and half-remembered ideas. One mid-nineteenth-century critic who was particularly struck by the intimate unity of these pieces came to essentially the same conclusion in describing the cycle as the refraction of a single mood (*Stimmung*) into diverse psychological moments, all of them beautifully captured in sound.[60]

In a sense, the *Adagio und Allegro* defies a cardinal rule of *Hausmusik:* accessibility to amateurs. Only the consummate professional will want to tackle this work, the first substantial solo piece to exploit the full capabilities of the valve horn. The suspension of the *Adagio und Allegro* between the salon and the concert stage is implicit in its form. The Adagio begins with an expressive idea (see Example 5.5) whose immediate recourse to half-step motion stamps the composition as the property of the valve horn. The ensuing Allegro falls into a rondo form (ABACAB′A), both of its episodes drawing on the opening four-note gesture of the Adagio. As it turned out, the linking of an introductory or slow movement with a complementary quick movement would figure in two of the large-scale concerted works from later in the year: the *Concertstück*, Op. 86, for four horns and orchestra, and the *Introduction und Allegro*, Op. 92, for piano and orchestra. The employment of this technique on a more modest scale in the *Adagio und Allegro* is only fitting for a piece that contemporary publishers would have advertised as *Hausmusik.*

EXAMPLE 5.5.   Schumann, *Adagio und Allegro*, Op. 70, mm. 1–4.

Common to all the chamber music of 1849 is an extraordinary melodic flexibility characterized by the fluid passing of brief ideas from one instrument to the other; the result is a sumptuous composite texture shared by solo instrument and piano alike. Yet the apparent simplicity of the ideas themselves is often in subtle conflict with the unusual manner in which they are constructed. This dialectic between naïve lyricism and esoteric syntax is especially prominent in the *Fünf Stücke im Volkston*, where four-bar phrases are frequently enlivened by irregular inner divisions, or conversely, where irregular phrase lengths are regularized through repetition. In the first piece of the cycle, the *Humor* of the overall expressive indication is apparent in the metrically irregular groupings—$1\frac{1}{2} + 1\frac{1}{2} + 1$—within the four-bar phrases of the main idea, an outwardly jaunty, folkish tune (see Example 5.6). The second piece, a lullaby, falls into a simple ABA + Coda form, its sections contrasting both tonally (F major versus F minor) and melodically. Yet the contrasting parts are bound together by an identical—and quite unusual—phrase structure, wherein seven-bar units are first divided into a 3 + 4, then a 4 + 3 pattern. Thus the technique of variation, usually a function of melodic or harmonic manipulation, is here applied to an irregular hypermeter. The opening six-bar idea of the third piece falls into two phrases of $2\frac{1}{2}$ and $3\frac{1}{2}$ bars respectively; its speechlike quality is enhanced by the discrepancy between the broad melody in the cello and the punctuating chordal asides in the piano. And while the fourth piece maintains a generally straightforward metric profile, the rondo theme of the fifth features a skittish interplay of 5, 6, 2, and 4-bar units. In each case, the metric irregularities serve as a means of imparting to the music the character of a spoken utterance. And in this, the *Fünf Stücke im Volkston*—along with the other sets of miniatures for cham-

EXAMPLE 5.6.   Schumann, *Fünf Stücke im Volkston*, Op. 102, No. 1, mm. 1–8.

ber ensemble—partake of a feature shared by all of Schumann's instrumental *Hausmusik*. The entire repertory projects an ineffable "once upon a time" quality, a sense that a narrative is under way, even though no determinate content is being narrated. For Schumann, even the cultivation of *Hausmusik* proved to be a poetic activity.

The Late Chamber Music

During his years as municipal music director in Düsseldorf, Schumann was extremely productive. Between the fall of 1850, when he took up residence in the capital of the Rhine Province, and the fall of 1853, when owing to disputes with the town authorities and deteriorating health he was forced to relinquish his post, Schumann completed upwards of fifty works, touching on every musical genre save opera. At the same time, his compositional habits soon fell into a discernible routine: larger works intended for public performance with his orchestra, chorus, or both alternated with pieces for smaller forces. Personal, professional, and commercial factors intersected in this pattern, for while Schumann could count on handsome profits from his lieder and short piano pieces, his more imposing efforts would both enhance his position as music director and fulfill the compositional imperative, already set in motion in the mid-1830s, to cultivate the higher forms.

He turned again to instrumental chamber music in the spring and autumn of 1851, with the *Märchenbilder*, Op. 113, for viola and piano, the A Minor Violin Sonata, Op. 105, the Piano Trio in G Minor, Op. 110, and the D Minor Violin Sonata, Op. 121, conceived respectively as vehicles for Schumann's concertmaster and first biographer, Wilhelm Joseph von Wasielewski, for the violinist Ferdinand David, and for Düsseldorf's resident piano trio. Thus these works fall within the alternating pattern established the year before. Schumann's founding of a *Quartettkränzchen* (a "little quartet club" whose members read through and discussed chamber music) in November 1851 may be viewed as a further complement to his creative work. After devoting almost the whole of 1852 to vocal music, Schumann wrote piano accompaniments for J. S. Bach's works for solo violin and cello between December of that year and February of the next. In fact, the "Bachiana" project (as Schumann called it)[61] set off a new cycle of compositional activity in 1853, this one centered on instrumental music, and here, too, the chamber idiom figures prominently.[62]

This last burst of chamber activity—during which he completed the *Märchenerzählungen*, Op. 132, for clarinet, viola, and piano, compositions for violin and piano, and the no longer extant *Fünf Romanzen* for piano and cello—coincides with Schumann's first meeting with the youthful composer and pianist whom he would hail as a "young eagle" and a "true apostle whose revelations will not be unriddled by the Pharisees for centuries to come": Johannes Brahms.[63] While Brahms cannot be credited with motivating the final upsurge in Schumann's creativity—he had already been composing steadily for months before his protégé arrived in October 1853—there can be no doubt that the "young eagle" played a significant role in rekindling the older man's "Davidsbündler" spirit—the crusading impulse that led Schumann, in the mid-1830s, to forge a new, poetic keyboard idiom and to battle musical Philistinism in the pages of his *Neue Zeitschrift für Musik*. (A little over a week after Brahms's arrival, Schumann assumed the role of critic for the first time in nearly a decade with "Neue Bahnen" [New paths], the celebrated essay in which Brahms was proclaimed a musical messiah).[62]

The young violinist and composer Joseph Joachim likewise occupied an important place in the reconstituted *Davidsbund* of Schumann's last years. On 14 October 1853, about two weeks after Brahms came to Düsseldorf, Joachim, too, paid a surprise visit. The following day Schumann hatched the idea of composing, along with Brahms and Albert Dietrich (another young colleague), a sonata for violin and piano based on the first letters of Joachim's personal motto: "Frei aber einsam" (Free but lonely). In about a week his contributions to the "FAE" Sonata—an Intermezzo and Finale—were complete; then between 29 and 31 October he added two more movements to these to form a Third Sonata for Violin and Piano in A Minor. Schumann's plan to provide Paganini's Caprices for solo violin with piano accompaniments—a project he worked at sporadically in 1854 and 1855 while confined at the asylum for the mentally ill at Endenich—was inspired by Joachim as well.

But in order to appreciate the richness of Schumann's late chamber music, we should consider more closely its relationship to his later music as a whole. Since this repertory recapitulates, in microcosm, the achievements of an entire creative life, it is not surprising that it embraces such a broad diversity of styles. It will be useful to consider Schumann's late music as the product of a varied array of compositional personae, each associated with a style and a family of genres. While all of these characters figure at earlier points in his career, they come together like a well-rehearsed ensemble only in his last years—and often turn up in unexpected places. Hence Schumann approached not only the verses of Nikolaus Lenau and Elisabeth Kulmann but even the time-honored texts of the Mass (Op. 147) and Requiem (Op. 148), in the manner of a lyric poet. As municipal music director, he composed in a public style that is particularly evident in his symphonic works. Schumann the storyteller wrote oratorios and arguably invented two genres: the choral-orchestral ballade and the ballad for "declamation" (i.e., speaker) and piano. His character as a collector shows through—naturally enough—in his arrangements and collections. As a pedagogue, he wrote contrapuntal works and *Hausmusik* for both children and adults. And finally, Schumann the *Davidsbündler* displayed an esoteric style that shows through, for instance, in his late piano music. Just as a single persona may manifest itself in a variety of genres, so, conversely, may a single genre be linked with a number of personae.

Instrumental chamber music proves to be very mobile in this regard. As we will see, it is especially bound up with the personae of the music director, the storyteller, the collector, and the *Davidsbündler*.

In focusing on each of these personae in turn, I do not mean to imply that they are absolutely fixed or impermeable. On the contrary, just as the younger Schumann brought together Florestan and Eusebius in the same composition, so do many of the late chamber works conflate a number of personae and styles. In the *Märchenbilder*, to take what may at first seem an unlikely example, the storyteller provides the title ("Fairy-tale pictures," or better yet: "Images from the land of make-believe"); the public style dominates in the marchlike portions of the middle movements; and the lyric poet has the first and last words—in the wistful opening movement, and the evocative lullaby that concludes the cycle. Still, my consideration in turn of the personae most clearly associated with Schumann's late chamber music will have the advantage of allowing us to detect relationships that might otherwise have gone unnoticed.

As already noted, the persona of the music director will, of course, adopt a public style. The principal features of this style—seriousness of tone, expansive dimensions, and thematic integration over large temporal spans—all figure in the D Minor Violin Sonata (published, not insignificantly, as a "Second Grand Sonata"). The Sonata not only shares its tonality with a number of the orchestral compositions of Schumann's later years (the revision of the D Minor Symphony of 1841 as the Fourth Symphony, Op. 121; the *Introduction und Allegro* for piano and orchestra, Op. 134; the *Faust* Overture; and the Violin Concerto), but aspires to the breadth and depth of the composer's symphonic works.[65] The first movement of the D Minor Sonata (like the corresponding movement in the Third Violin Sonata) begins with a slow introduction whose solemn chordal opening provides the basis for the principal theme of the main body of the movement (*Lebhaft*)—a transformative relationship that also characterizes the first movements of the First and Second Symphonies, both concert pieces for piano and orchestra (Opp. 92 and 134), and the *Faust* Overture. Likewise, the technique of intermovement recurrence, which lends an epic quality to the Third and Fourth Symphonies, the Cello Concerto, and the Violin Concerto, does much the same for the D Minor Sonata. The dreamy course of its third movement, a set of variations on a serenadelike theme, is interrupted by emphatic, then disembodied allusions to the preceding scherzo (*Sehr lebhaft*). And last, the motion from an austere D minor to a triumphant D major in the finale replicates the tonal and affective trajectory of the Fourth Symphony, the *Faust* Overture, and the Violin Concerto.

Storytellers are free to ply their trades in both public and private spaces. This persona regales us with tales (*Erzählungen*) from far-off lands and thereby transports us into realms far removed in space and time from our own. This is precisely what Schumann does in the *Märchenerzählungen*, particularly in the cycle's third movement (*Ruhiges Tempo, mit zartem Aus-*

druck), where the composer's storyteller persona initially calls up great distances by way of a deftly contrived musical texture, consisting of a bass pedal, murmuring sixteenths supporting a descending arabesque in the right hand of the piano, and, hovering over it all, a gracefully nuanced melody in the clarinet interwoven with the viola's counterline (see Example 5.7). Removal into a distant world is also a function of the harmonic and syntactic ambiguities in this passage. Our sense of harmonic progression is blurred by the stasis of the tonic pedal, while the suspended quality of the music is the product of a phrase structure of which it is difficult to tell whether the first measure is a structural downbeat or an upbeat to the clarinet melody beginning in measure 2. Even the form of the movement is ambiguous, removed: it can be heard as a series of rhapsodic varia-

EXAMPLE 5.7.   Schumann, *Märchenerzählungen,* Op. 132, mvt. 3, mm. 1–5.

tions on the opening four-measure idea, or as a rondo in which that idea functions as a refrain.

While the storyteller gathers tales as a means of preserving communal memory, the collector gathers objects in order to save them from perishing. Although Schumann was an avid collector practically throughout his life, this persona takes on particular significance during his later years. Consider first its literary manifestations: in April 1852 Schumann began to select passages on music from the works of Shakespeare, Jean Paul, and other classics of world literature for an anthology to be entitled *Dichtergarten;* a similar project dates from about the same time, his assemblage of his own writings on music for publication in a collected edition. This passion for collecting had a musical side as well. In the "Bachiana" project begun late in 1852 Schumann displayed the same will to preservation that motivated the *Dichtergarten*. On one hand, the addition of piano accompaniments to Bach's sonatas and partitas for solo violin and suites for solo cello may strike us as a travesty, a typically nineteenth-century lapse in taste. But on the other hand, Schumann's additions were intended as a means of preserving Bach's compositions within the context of a concert life that might otherwise have ignored them. Once a group of objects has been assembled into a collection, it is imbued with an aura, an indefinable quality compounded of nearness and distance that fills the beholder with awe. This too has a musical counterpart in the "Bachiana." We should recall that Schumann did not alter a note in Bach's texts: all he added were keyboard harmonizations. That is, he provided Bach's works for solo strings with an aura in the form of accompaniments that are generally discreet and often transparent—as transparent as the glass case through which we might view a collection of rare coins or stamps.[66]

As we have seen, Schumann's *Davidsbündler* persona was no doubt stimulated by his contact with Brahms and Joachim in the autumn of 1853. Still, it was already in evidence well before; in fact, compositions redolent of the esoteric manner of Schumann's younger days are spread throughout his last years. The finale of the G Minor Piano Trio, for example, unfolds as an idiosyncratic sonata form: its exposition is articulated by three self-contained thematic groups, of which the first is a miniature rondo, while the recapitulation is limited to varied restatements of the first group and fragments of the third. The design, in other words, bears comparison with the sectional, mosaiclike construction typical of the longer character pieces from earlier keyboard cycles such as the *Novelletten* or *Kreisleriana*. Likewise, the A Minor Violin Sonata, Op. 105, is easily unmasked as a cycle of three character pieces "composed" by the prime movers of the original *Davidsbund:* Florestan and Eusebius. Whereas the former prevails in the respectively passionate and demonic first and third movements, the middle movement represents a joint effort of both characters and thus recalls similarly collaborative enterprises in the *Davidsbündlertänze*. And finally, in the Intermezzo and Finale of the "FAE" Sonata (which reappear as the last two movements of the Third Violin Sonata),

Schumann translates a verbal motto into a musical cipher that serves as the foundation for a seemingly endless series of motivic shapes—a practice recalling his generation of thematic material from the "Lettres dansantes" (ASCH) in *Carnaval*.

In all of these instances Schumann evokes the *Davidsbündler* style of the 1830s without simply repeating it. On the contrary, the earlier manner is refracted through the medium of an eminently "late" sensibility; witness the finely differentiated textural palette of the G Minor Piano Trio, the intense motivic economy of the A Minor Violin Sonata, Op. 105, and the subtle mixture of contrapuntal and developmental strategies in the "FAE" Sonata. Nonetheless, it is tempting to think that an often-quoted aphorism of the Viennese critic Karl Kraus—"Ursprung ist Ziel"—has particular resonance for the sometimes recondite (and too often maligned) music of Schumann's later years. Here, too, the "origin," the *Davidsbündler* style of his early maturity, was also a "goal" of sorts. Devotees of the composer's "beautiful but abstrusely woven conversations" (an epithet extending well past the string quartets) may take some pleasure in realizing that Kraus's aphorism is well exemplified by Schumann's late chamber music.

Notes

1. Friedhelm Krummacher, "Reception and Analysis: On the Brahms Quartets, Op. 51, Nos. 1 and 2," *19th Century Music* 18 (1994): 26.

2. See Richard Heuberger, *Erinnerungen an Johannes Brahms: Tagebuchnotizen aus den Jahren 1875 bis 1897,* ed. Kurt Hofmann (Tutzing, 1971), 60.

3. See the entries in the *Blätter und Blümchen* for 11 and 27 November 1823, in Hans Kohlhase, *Die Kammermusik R. Schumanns: Stilistische Untersuchungen,* Hamburger Beiträge zur Musikwissenschaft 19 (Hamburg, 1979) 1:9.

4. For transcriptions of the sketches, see Kohlhase, *Kammermusik* 3:12–15. The main theme of the B Major Quartet movement, which exists in two versions, was later used as the principal idea of the finale of the F Major Piano Concerto that occupied Schumann between 1830 and 1831. A sixteen-measure sketch of an Allegro for melody instrument and piano may also date from the same period as the piano quartets; see ibid. 1:7, 3:11.

5. Schumann, *Tagebücher* (hereinafter cited as *TB*) vol. 1, ed. Georg Eismann (Leipzig, 1971), 180.

6. Ibid., 172.

7. Ibid., 174.

8. Entry for 7 January 1830, in *TB* 1:214.

9. Ibid., 151. Cf. also Flechsig's comment on Schumann's reaction to Schubert's death, in Georg Eismann, *Robert Schumann: Ein Quellenwerk über sein Leben und Schaffen* (Leipzig, 1956) 1:44. Whether or not the quartet represented a sublimation of Schumann's grief over Schubert's death, however, as Peter Ostwald has suggested ("Leiden und Trauern im Leben und Werk Robert Schumanns," in *Schumanns Werke: Text und Interpretation—16 Studien,* ed. Akio Mayeda and Klaus Wolfgang Niemöller [Mainz, 1987], 124–25), is difficult to say.

10. See *TB* 1:152. Returning from a musical gathering at Wieck's on 4 Decem-

ber 1828, Schumann spent an "excited night with Schubert's immortal trio ringing in my ears."

11. *TB* 2:402.

12. Entry for 21 March 1829, in *TB* 1:182.

13. Ibid., 23–24.

14. *Neue Zeitschrift für Musik* (hereinafter cited as *NZfM*) 8 (1838): 181–82, 193–95; and *NZfM* 9 (1838): 41–42, 51–52, 79–80.

15. *NZfM* 8 (1838): 116.

16. See the review for the 1 March 1840 issue of Brockhaus's *Allgemeine Zeitung*, in Schumann, *Gesammelte Schriften über Musik und Musiker*, 5th ed. by Martin Kreisig (Leipzig, 1914) (hereinafter cited as *GS*) 1:420; *NZfM* 15 (1841): 142; *NZfM* 16 (1842): 143. For a detailed account of Schumann's initial reception of Beethoven's late quartets, see Bodo Bischoff, *Monument für Beethoven: Die Entwicklung der Beethoven-Rezeption Robert Schumanns* (Cologne-Rheinkassel, 1994), 189–93, 306–12.

17. See Schumann's letter to Clara of 19 March 1838, in Clara and Robert Schumann, *Briefwechsel: Kritische Gesamtausgabe*, ed. Eva Weissweiler (Frankfurt, 1984) (hereinafter cited as *BrKG*) 1:127. His first encounter with Beethoven's Op. 131 came already on 11 November 1837; see *TB* 2:45.

18. The first reference to quartet composition comes in Schumann's letter to Clara of 11 February 1838, where he mentions his plan to write three such works; see *BrKG* 1:100. The April 1838 letter to Fischoff appears in Schumann, *Briefe: Neue Folge*, 2nd ed. by Gustav Jansen (Leipzig, 1904), 118. On Schumann's abortive attempt at a quartet in the summer of 1838, see his letter to Clara of 13 April (*BrKG* 1:140), and his diary entries for 15–24 June (*TB* 2:58).

19. Wolfgang Boetticher, *Robert Schumann in seinen Schriften und Briefen* (Berlin, 1942), 250.

20. See *BrKG* 2:570–71 and the letter of 30 June 1839 to Hirschbach, in Schumann, *Briefe: Neue Folge*, 158. Schumann's quartet drafts, now in the Deutsche Staatsbibliothek, Berlin, are transcribed in Kohlhase, *Kammermusik* 3:17–18, and Nicholas Marston, "Schumann's Monument to Beethoven," *19th Century Music* 14 (1991): 250–51.

21. According to Marston's provocative hypothesis ("Schumann's Monument," 252–64), Schumann's song cycle *Dichterliebe* (completed June 1840) represents a sublimation of techniques first encountered through his study of Beethoven's Op. 131.

22. On the possibility that Schumann's suspension of his quartet plans in 1839 was motivated by commercial as well as artistic reasons, see Barbara Turchin, "Schumann's Conversion to Vocal Music: A Reconsideration," *Musical Quarterly* 67 (1981): 398.

23. *TB* 3:207.

24. Ibid., 216–20.

25. Ibid., 225–33, 236–37. Owing to the ensemble difficulties posed by the original scoring of the *Andante und Variationen*, Schumann rearranged the work in August 1843, at Mendelssohn's suggestion, for two pianos. The second version was published as Op. 46 in 1844. Apart from the obvious scoring differences, the two versions diverge on a number of other points: the two-piano setting lacks a transition between variations 5 and 6 and features a more compact coda than its earlier counterpart.

26. A. E. F. Dickinson, "The Chamber Music," in *Schumann: A Symposium*, ed. Gerald Abraham (London, 1952), 140.

27. Schumann, *Briefe: Neue Folge*, 450.

28. "Streichquartette" (1842), *GS* 2:75.

29. "Erster Quartettmorgen" (1838), *GS* 1:335; see also "Streichquartette," *GS* 2:75.

30. "Preisquartett von Julius Schapler" (1842), *GS* 2:380.

31. "Streichquartette," *GS* 2:75–76.

32. "Streichquartette," *GS* 2:75.

33. *TB* 2:220, 229, 3:210, 213.

34. For a more detailed account of the form and its rationale, see my "From 'Concertante Rondo' to 'Lyric Sonata': A Commentary on Brahms's Reception of Mozart," in *Brahms Studies*, vol. 1, ed. David Brodbeck (Lincoln, NE, 1994), 115–19.

35. For a spirited defense of Schumann's sonata forms that proceeds from an analysis of the first movement of Op. 41, No. 3, see Joel Lester, "Robert Schumann and Sonata Forms," *19th Century Music* 18 (1995): 190–95.

36. *TB* 2:253.

37. Linda Correll Roesner, "Schumann's 'Parallel' Forms," *19th Century Music* 14 (1991): 265–78. For an alternate account of the finale of Op. 41, No. 3, see Anthony Newcomb, "Schumann and Late Eighteenth-Century Narrative Strategies," *19th Century Music* 11 (1987): 170–74, and Kohlhase, *Kammermusik* 1:158–61, 2:69–74. Both writers view the movement as a kind of rondo form; but while the finale does feature a recurrent (although altered) refrain, the rondo interpretation does not address the larger symmetries of the "parallel" form.

38. See Schumann's brief description of the event in *TB* 2:255.

39. As Schumann put it ("Zweite Quartettmorgen" [1838], *GS* 1:336), the four members of a string quartet, unlike the members of a symphony orchestra, "constitute their own public." The same idea serves as the foundation for Adorno's analysis of the changing social function of chamber music in the nineteenth and twentieth centuries; see his *Introduction to the Sociology of Music*, trans. E. B. Ashton (New York, 1976), 85–86.

40. See *Allgemeine musikalische Zeitung* 50 (1848): col. 23.

41. See his letter of 14 December 1847 to Raimund Härtel: "The published parts of such works [Op. 41, Nos. 1–3] seem to me like a man split into four segments: one can't know how to grasp or seize hold of him. . . . There are seldom four musicians who, without a score, would know how to understand the difficult [motivic/contrapuntal] combinations of musical works like these even after several play-throughs. What is the result? The players set the pieces aside after a cursory reading. With a score in hand they could more easily do justice to the composer. Therefore, I'm certain that a published score would help the sale of the parts." Schumann had his way. On 9 October of the following year he wrote to Härtel, thanking him for publication of the scores for the Op. 41 quartets. See Schumann, *Briefe: Neue Folge*, 452, 456.

42. "Trios für Pianoforte mit Begleitung" (1840), *GS* 1:497.

43. *GS* 1:501.

44. Donald Francis Tovey, *Essays in Musical Analysis: Chamber Music* (London, 1944), 151.

45. Hans Kohlhase's (*Kammermusik* 1:162–66) and Arnfried Edler's (*Robert Schumann und seine Zeit* [Laaber, 1982], 171) classification of the movement as an unusual sonata-rondo form ignores the larger parallelisms that make for a more tightly integrated structure. Schumann's sketches for the movement (which correspond closely to the final version up to m. 137, but then present a series of empty

bars with only occasional motivic entries until the equivalent of m. 212 in the final version) likewise support the notion of a "parallel" form. See Jack Westrup, "The Sketch for Schumann's Piano Quintet op. 44," in *Convivium musicorum: Festschrift Wolfgang Boetticher* (Berlin, 1974), 371.

46. Our perception of this passage as a gesture of return precisely reverses the course of Schumann's compositional process; as Kohlhase points out (*Kammermusik* 1:51), the first movement of the quintet was probably sketched after the other movements of the work. For a detailed account of the intermovement thematic relationships in the quintet, see Dieter Conrad, "Zu Schumanns Klavierquintett," in *Musik-Konzepte Sonderband: Robert Schumann*, vol. 2, ed Heinz-Klaus Metzger and Rainer Riehn (Munich, 1982), 343–56. The Bachian quality of the reprise in the finale is addressed in Susan Wollenberg, "Schumann's Piano Quintet in E flat: The Bach Legacy," *Music Review* 52 (1991): 299–305.

47. Schumann, *Briefe: Neue Folge*, 229.

48. Ibid., 436.

49. From his *Davidsbündlerbrief;* quoted in Gerd Nauhaus, "Schumanns *Das Paradies und die Peri:* Quellen zur Entstehungs-, Aufführungs- und Rezeptionsgeschichte," in *Schumanns Werke: Text und Interpretation—16 Studien*, ed. Akio Mayeda and Klaus Wolfgang Niemöller (Mainz, 1987), 145.

50. *Allgemeine musikalische Zeitung* 46 (1844): cols. 303–4.

51. *TB* 2:402. Cf. Schumann's advice to Carl van Bruyck in a letter of 10 May 1852: "Accustom yourself . . . to conceiving music freely from your imagination, without the aid of the piano; only in this way are its inner wellsprings revealed, thus appearing in ever greater clarity and purity" (*Briefe: Neue Folge*, 356).

52. Schumann's trios may have been composed in part as a response to Clara's G Minor Piano Trio (Op. 17), finished the year before. Her most ambitious composition (though she wrote it off as "effeminate and sentimental"), the G Minor Trio was frequently paired with her husband's D Minor Trio in nineteenth-century performances.

53. *NZfM* 29 (1848): 115.

54. Kohlhase's study of the preliminary material for the D Minor Trio has brought to light sketches and an almost complete draft of a second episode that, if retained, would have imparted an overall ABACA shape to the movement. The ultimately rejected C section, like its earlier counterpart (B), features a contrapuntally dense texture with violin, cello, and piano in close imitation practically throughout. See Kohlhase, *Kammermusik* 3:43–47, for transcriptions of Schumann's sketch and draft.

55. Letter to Louis Ehlert of 26 November 1849, in Schumann, *Briefe: Neue Folge*, 319. In early 1847 he was still recovering from the aftereffects of a severe depressive episode that began in the second half of 1844 and prompted his and Clara's relocation in Dresden in December of that year.

56. Letter to C. Reinecke of 1 May 1849, in Schumann, *Briefe: Neue Folge*, 303.

57. Alluding to a famous verse from the closing scene of Goethe's *Faust*, part 2, Dörffel heard this passage as an emanation "from higher spheres." See *NZfM* 29 (1848): 114.

58. See Schumann's letter of 10 April 1849 to Ferdinand Hiller in Schumann, *Briefe: Neue Folge*, 302.

59. Schumann also recognized the usefulness of such distinctions. As he put it in the *Musikalische Haus- und Lebensregeln:* "In judging compositions you must distinguish between those belonging to the realm of art [*Kunstfach*] and those in-

tended merely for dilettantish entertainment [*Unterhaltung*]. Stand up for the former, and don't be annoyed by the latter" (*GS* 2:169).

60. See E. Bernsdorf's brief review of the *Phantasiestücke* in *NZfM* 32 (1850): 59.

61. *TB* 3:614.

62. For a thorough account of Schumann's works of 1853, and a thoughtful defense of the composer's late style in general, see Michael Struck, *Die umstrittenen späten Instrumentalwerke Schumanns*, Hamburger Beiträge zur Musikwissenschaft 29 (Hamburg, 1984).

63. See the letter to Joachim of 8 October 1853, in Schumann, *Briefe: Neue Folge*, 379.

64. *NZfM* 39 (1853): 185–86.

65. On Schumann's association of the key of D minor with "Hallen" (architectural spaces that unite the temples, or "open halls" of Greek antiquity with the cathedrals, or "closed halls" of the Middle Ages), see Reinhard Kapp, *Studien zum Spätwerk Robert Schumanns* (Tutzing, 1984), 152–54. Markus Waldura (*Monomotivik, Sequenz und Sonatenform im Werk Robert Schumanns* [Saarbrücken, 1990], 322–24) draws a comparison between the first movement of the D Minor Sonata and the finale of the Cello Concerto, both of which, he points out, are characterized by "polymotivic" expositions unified through the elaboration of a persistent accompanimental figure.

66. As Joel Lester has observed ("Reading and Misreading: Schumann's Accompaniments to Bach's Sonatas and Partitas for Solo Violin," *Current Musicology* 56 [1995]: 24–53), even though Schumann left Bach's texts untouched, his accompaniments have a powerful effect on how we perceive the melody, harmony, rhythm, phrase structure, and even the form of the violin part. Thus, in Lester's view, Schumann's accompaniments function as virtual analyses of Bach's music.

Bibliography

Adorno, Theodor W. *Introduction to the Sociology of Music* (*Einleitung in die Musiksoziologie*, Frankfurt 1962), trans. E. B. Ashton. New York, 1976.

Bischoff, Bodo. *Monument für Beethoven: Die Entwicklung der Beethoven-Rezeption Robert Schumanns*. Cologne-Rheinkassel, 1994.

Boetticher, Wolfgang. *Robert Schumann in seinen Schriften und Briefen*. Berlin, 1942.

Conrad, Dieter. "Zu Schumanns Klavierquintett." In *Musik-Konzepte Sonderband: Robert Schumann*, vol. 2, ed. Heinz-Klaus Metzger and Rainer Riehn, 343–56. Munich, 1982.

Daverio, John. "From 'Concertante Rondo' to 'Lyric Sonata': A Commentary on Brahms's Reception of Mozart." In *Brahms Studies*, vol. 1, ed. David Brodbeck, 111–38. (Lincoln, NE, 1994).

———. *Crossing Paths: Schubert, Schumann, and Brahms*. Oxford, 2002.

———. *Robert Schumann: Herald of a "New Poetic Age."* Oxford, 1997.

Dickinson, A. E. F. "The Chamber Music." In *Schumann: A Symposium*, ed. Gerald Abraham, 138–75. London, 1952.

Edler, Arnfried. *Robert Schumann und seine Zeit*. Laaber, 1982.

Eismann, Georg. *Robert Schumann: Ein Quellenwerk über sein Leben und Schaffen*, 2 vols. Leipzig, 1956.

Heuberger, Richard. *Erinnerungen an Johannes Brahms: Tagebuchnotizen aus den Jahren 1875 bis 1897*, ed. Kurt Hofmann. Tutzing, 1971.

Kapp, Reinhard. *Studien zum Spätwerk Robert Schumanns.* Tutzing, 1984.

Kohlhase, Hans. *Die Kammermusik R. Schumanns: Stilistische Untersuchungen.* Hamburger Beiträge zur Musikwissenschaft 19. Hamburg, 1979.

Krummacher, Friedhelm. "Reception and Analysis: On the Brahms Quartets, Op. 51, Nos. 1 and 2." *19th Century Music* 18 (1994): 24–25.

Lester, Joel. "Reading and Misreading: Schumann's Accompaniments to Bach's Sonatas and Partitas for Solo Violin." *Current Musicology* 56 (1994): 24–53.

———. "Robert Schumann and Sonata Forms." *19th Century Music* 18 (1995): 189–210.

Marston, Nicholas. "Schumann's Monument to Beethoven." *19th Century Music* 14 (1991): 247–64.

Nauhaus, Gerd. "Schumanns *Das Paradies und die Peri:* Quellen zur Entstehungs-, Aufführungs- und Rezeptionsgeschichte." In *Schumanns Werke: Text und Interpretation—16 Studien,* ed. Akio Mayeda and Klaus Wolfgang Niemöller, 133–48. Mainz, 1987.

Newcomb, Anthony. "Schumann and Late Eighteenth-Century Narrative Strategies." *19th Century Music* 11 (1987): 164–74.

Ostwald, Peter. "Leiden und Trauern im Leben und Werk Robert Schumanns," in *Schumanns Werke: Text und Interpretation: 16 Studien,* ed. Akio Mayeda and Klaus Wolfgang Niemöller, 121–31. Mainz, 1987.

Roesner, Linda Correll. "Schumann's 'Parallel' Forms." *19th Century Music* 14 (1991): 265–78.

Schumann, Robert. *Briefe: Neue Folge.* 2d ed. Edited by Gustav Jansen. Leipzig, 1904.

———. *Gesammelte Schriften über Musik und Musiker.* 5th ed. 2 vols. Edited by Martin Kreisig. Leipzig, 1914.

———. *Tagebücher.* Vol. 1. *1827–1838.* Edited by Georg Eismann. Leipzig, 1971. Vol. 2. *1836–1854.* Edited by Gerd Nauhaus. Leipzig, 1987. Vol. 3. *Haushaltbücher,* Pts. 1 (1837–47) and 2 (1847–56). Edited by Gerd Nauhaus. Leipzig, 1982.

Schumann, Clara, and Robert Schumann. *Briefwechsel: Kritische Gesamtausgabe.* 2 vols. edited by Eva Weissweiler. Frankfurt, 1984.

Struck, Michael. *Die umstrittenen späten Instrumentalwerke Schumanns.* Hamburger Beiträge zur Musikwissenschaft 29. Hamburg, 1984.

Tovey, Donald Francis. *Essays in Musical Analysis: Chamber Music.* London, 1944.

Turchin, Barbara. "Schumann's Conversion to Vocal Music: A Reconsideration." *Musical Quarterly* 67 (1981): 392–404.

Waldura, Markus. *Monomotivik, Sequenz und Sonatenform im Werk Robert Schumanns.* Saarbrücken, 1990.

Westrup, Jack. "The Sketch for Schumann's Piano Quintet op. 44." In *Convivium Musicorum: Festschrift Wolfgang Boetticher,* 367–71. Berlin, 1974.

Wollenberg, Susan. "Schumann's Piano Quintet in E flat: The Bach Legacy." *Music Review* 52 (1991): 299–305.

CHAPTER SIX

Discourse and Allusion

The Chamber Music of Brahms

Margaret Notley

Brahms came of age as an artist in the 1850s. During those same years the performance of chamber music started to regain some of its former significance in Vienna. Between the death of Ignaz Schuppanzigh (1776–1830), whose string quartet had premiered the music of Beethoven and Schubert, and the formation of the Hellmesberger Quartet toward the end of the 1840s, no string quartet had performed publicly on a regular basis in Vienna. By the time Brahms entered the city in 1862, its musical life had begun to develop along lines more congenial to his tastes. Viennese audiences had started to appreciate the late string quartets of Beethoven and to discover the beauties of Schubert's chamber music, just as he himself had during the previous decade: the Hellmesberger Quartet had programmed late Beethoven since its first series of concerts in 1849–50, and already in its second season played two as yet unpublished masterpieces by Schubert, the C Major String Quintet (17 November 1850) and the G Major String Quartet (8 December 1850).[1] To introduce himself to the Viennese music world, Brahms collaborated with members of the Hellmesberger Quartet in his own G Minor Piano Quartet, Op. 25, and, two weeks later, the A Major Piano Quartet, Op. 26, and he continued to take part in public performances of his chamber music throughout his career.

   To Brahms's contemporaries, his true strength as a composer lay in chamber style, directed at the connoisseur and therefore couched in subtleties: chamber music was considered the vehicle for the most rarefied realizations of music as sounding discourse, a concept long invoked to explain and justify the instrumental genres in general. Early on, he mastered

FIGURE 6.1.   Josef Hellmesberger (1828–93), first violinist of the Hellmesberger Quartet, which began to give annual series of performances in Vienna during the 1849–50 season.

the counterpoint, phrase rhythms, and thematic-motivic work that, to acculturated listeners, make a tonal composition sound coherent, but the uses to which he put this command naturally changed during the course of his life. After the youthful B Major Piano Trio, Op. 8, Brahms's chamber music falls into three groups: those works completed, respectively, in 1860–65, 1873–75, and 1879–94. Broadly speaking, these years indicate stylistic periods in this domain of his work. To evoke the quality of his changing style, I use different kinds of metaphors for each period; the by no means remarkable idea that compositions draw on a variety of codes (of technique, form, genre, style, and other traditions) serves as a loose frame of reference, the relevance of which will become clearer in the discussion of the late chamber music. But let us first consider his struggles as a young man to attain full command of his craft.

Early Striving and Mastery

In January 1854 Brahms finished the first full-length chamber piece that he judged fit for publication, the Piano Trio in B Major, Op. 8, and then did not bring another chamber work to a satisfactory conclusion for more than six years. After this hiatus he completed no fewer than seven chamber compositions, most of them on the largest possible scale, between the summer of 1860 and May 1865. As Tovey points out, Schubert's influence predominates in these works of his "first maturity,"[2] audible above all in the expansive melodiousness. Although the B Major Trio itself alludes to Schubert's "Am Meer" (as well as to Beethoven's *An die ferne Geliebte* by way of Schumann's C Major Fantasy),[3] we do not know if Brahms had encountered Schubert's instrumental music before October 1853, a month he spent in the household of Robert and Clara Schumann, longtime admirers of the composer; nor do we know when he began work on the B Major Trio. Its lyric sprawl does, however, suggest the incompletely assimilated impact of what Schumann called Schubert's "heavenly lengths."

Brahms later criticized the B Major Trio in the most meaningful way. When his publisher and friend Fritz Simrock bought the rights to his first ten published compositions in 1888, he gave the composer the opportunity to revise them as he wished. Brahms settled on Op. 8, rewriting virtually everything except the scherzo—he changed only its coda—and the opening themes of the other three movements. The two versions have fascinated scholars, the more so because he destroyed most of his sketches, drafts, and other documentation of his composing habits and history. The first version is a rare example of near juvenilia, and the second offers an unusual chance to view him, in a sense, at work.[4]

Elements of his later style appear in the first movement of the early piano trio, albeit in somewhat immature form. His fondness for drawing together diverse topics and styles is evident in the shape of the second group: an instrumental recitative (mm. 84–98, 104–18) followed by what sounds like a Bachian fugue subject (mm. 98–103, 118–24), both in G♯ minor, and concluding with an E major theme in musette style (mm. 126–47). All of which is replaced by a fugato (mm. 354–96) in the recapitulation—perhaps in emulation of the fugues and fugatos in late Beethoven. As in later compositions, Brahms tries to make the exposition cohere through motivic means, primarily by presenting augmented, diminished, and otherwise altered versions of a descending scalar motive at important points in the form (e.g., mm. 51–52, 62–63, 84, 158–61). Despite these connnections, however, much of the movement sounds excessively episodic—a loose assemblage of styles with a number of awkwardly placed cadences (to name just two, the cadences in the transition at mm. 63 and 68).

The chamber compositions that Brahms finished after the six-year interruption show a much more clearly directed melodiousness. There is no firm evidence for when he began these works, but he entered the dates of their conclusion in a notebook:[5]

B♭ String Sextet, Op. 18	summer 1860
G Minor Piano Quartet, Op. 25	fall 1861
A Major Piano Quartet, Op. 26	fall 1861
F Minor Piano Quintet, Op. 34	August 1862, revised 1864
G Major String Sextet, Op. 36	mvts. 1, 2, 3, Sept. 1864; mvt. 4, May 1865
E Minor Cello Sonata, Op. 38	mvts. 1, 2, 3, 1862; mvt. 4, June 1865
E♭ Horn Trio, Op. 40	May 1865

This music encompasses at least as much stylistic variety as the B Major Piano Trio, but no single movement of it makes so disparate an impression as the Trio's Allegro con moto; and unlike the early Trio, the chamber works that follow both move and cohere. The opening Allegro ma non troppo of the first of them, the B♭ Major String Sextet, Op. 18, prepares each new section without breaking the flow. Even a harmonic surprise like that at the beginning of the second group is absorbed seamlessly into the form. After the transition has settled on a dominant pedal in the key of F major, a highly colored A major triad enters and is then rationalized as V/ii, as the theme, a hybrid period, goes toward a cadence in F (mm. 61–68).[6] When the same Schubertian chord reappears in an extended repetition of the ländler-like melody, it seems more possible that the triad might become a secondary tonic, but it again proves to fit within F major (mm. 69–85).

Brahms based the Andante, in D minor, on the Baroque *folia* theme.[7] Although he changed the meter from triple to duple time and somewhat altered both the harmony and the usual treble line, the derivation of his theme from the archaic source remains audible; moreover, his own set of variations, five in all, begins as a pastiche of Baroque divisions, with each of the first three variations subdividing the beat into progressively more parts. The first version of the B Major Piano Trio had similarly invoked Baroque topics in the musettelike closing theme and, especially, the unfortunate Bachian fugato of its first movement. Brahms integrated references to the extraneous style much more successfully in the Sextet by making the collision of discourses the point of the movement: the set of variations is formed around the very opposition between latter-day subjectivity and the monumental, impersonal quality of both the Baroque theme and the technique of divisions. Elements that sound somewhat unnatural in Baroque style intrude into the second and third variations. The climax comes at the end of the third variation: tension is released, and identifiably Baroque features disappear altogether in the *maggiore* fourth and fifth variations. When the theme returns after the final variation, this moment juxtaposes minor with major, Baroque with nineteenth-century discourses; the coda synthesizes the two styles. That Brahms then concludes the Sextet with scherzo and rondo movements that would not have been out of place in early Beethoven gives some indication of the range of styles that he mastered during the 1850s.

The command of his craft in the B♭ Sextet and, even more, the turn toward the Classical in its final two movements ally this work with the Serenades in D, Op. 11, and A, Op. 16, from the late 1850s; as Brahms's biographer Max Kalbeck noted, "the Op. 18 Sextet is scarcely thinkable without both serenades as antecedents."[8] On the other hand, traces of compositional struggles in the G Minor Piano Quartet, Op. 25, suggest that Brahms may have drafted it before the serenades and sextet. Joseph Joachim, the great violinist and close friend of Brahms's, told Kalbeck that he had heard the first movements of both the G Minor and A Major Piano Quartets, along with the C♯ minor version of what later became the C Minor Piano Quartet, Op. 60, as early as the mid-1850s.[9] We know for certain that the C♯ minor version of the third quartet dates from then, and another, ambiguous comment by Joachim may lend support to an early genesis for the first. Brahms had sent the autograph of the G minor work to Joachim, who responded on 15 October 1861: "Generally speaking, it

FIGURE 6.2.   Brahms and Josef Joachim in Klagenfurt, 1867.

seems to me that we see the cement more in this [first] movement . . . than in your other compositions, and I've wondered if you haven't wanted to stretch some in part earlier material to fit your present greatness."[10]

We can only speculate, gathering support from revisions in the autograph sources and scattered, sometimes cryptic passages in the letters, about the difficulties Brahms appears to have encountered in completing the two piano quartets. But we have concrete evidence of his difficulties with his next two chamber pieces—what would become the F Minor Piano Quintet, Op. 34, and the original first three movements of the E Minor Cello Sonata, Op. 38. This sonata, the first duo that Brahms saw fit to publish, originally included an Adagio.[11] In the words of Kalbeck, Brahms set the slow movement aside "because the sonata seemed too crammed full with music."[12] The E Minor Sonata thus appeared, lopsided, as two Allegros—the first very broad, the other short—with only an Allegretto quasi Menuetto, also small-scale, between them. Instrumentation rather than balance caused the problems in the case of the F minor work. Before arriving at the final ensemble, he set it, in a version he destroyed, as a string quintet with two cellos on the model of Schubert's C Major Quintet, and then as a sonata for two pianos, which survives as Op. 34b.

If, after mastering the art of coherent phrase rhythms, Brahms still struggled with such matters as scoring, he already had an individual sound and aesthetic stance. He set great store by musical workmanship but did not in general consider conciseness a virtue. He dwelt on picturesque harmonies and figuration; themes expanded into complex groupings. The second movement of the A Major Piano Quartet may provide the most extreme example of his tastes as a young man. This Poco adagio opens as a glorious melody set heterophonically (Example 6.1). The lush, Romantic atmosphere is intensified by a succession of arpeggiated diminished seventh chords and an ominous-sounding figure in the bass, especially striking when it appears against a triplet variant of itself (mm. 36–41). And these elements appear in only the first part of a huge ternary shape.[13] The opening melody certainly bears repeated listening, and return it does, three more times, for each of the outer parts is itself in several sections. An *appassionato* theme in B minor given to the piano is followed by serene, pure counterpoint for the strings and a much looser and more animated continuation with the piano; taken together (mm. 42–85), these passages make up the center of the form. The Brahms of this period clearly preferred to make his points through richly varied materials and vivid rhetoric.

Mode Change and Fugato in the Early Music

In the early chamber music Brahms, surely inspired by Schubert, found original ways to expand the communicative power of a most basic resource in tonal music, the affective difference between major and minor.

EXAMPLE 6.1.   Johannes Brahms, Piano Quartet in A Major, Op. 26, mvt. 2, mm. 1–4.

Mode change, for example, played an essential role in the rethought sonata forms of the two piano quartets with which Brahms introduced himself to the Viennese public. Although the first of these, the G Minor Piano Quartet, proved successful with audiences, features of the opening Allegro had made it controversial among his friends. Joachim believed that the first group had an excess of full cadences and, together with Clara Schumann, considered the D major of the second group to last proportionally too long.[14] Brahms may have been working with older, somewhat intractable material, as Joachim had hinted. The first group plus transition do appear to have at least one full cadence too many (mm. 27 or 35), and the second group seems positively glutted with instrumentally varied repetitions of minor- and major-mode versions of the same theme (mm. 50–78, 79–101), another D major theme (mm. 101–30) that comes in over a drone bass, and a closing section in the same key (mm. 131–60). Still, each thematic group includes a strain in the opposing mode—B♭ major (mm. 11–20) within G minor and D minor (mm. 50–78) before D major—and the divisibility of both the first and second groups had its uses: it allowed modal contrasts on a grand scale.

   After the extended stretch of D major in the exposition, the development begins and stays in the minor mode, sounding even as though it ends in D minor (with a Picardy third) rather than on a retransition dominant. This, of course, undermines the usual effect of built-up tension followed by release at the beginning of the recapitulation. Why in the world would Brahms want to do that? The answer would seem to be: to highlight the issue of mode. With a jolt, the second strain of the opening group, now in G major, initiates the recapitulation; the real retransition seems to take place thereafter with the dramatized move (mm. 247–65) to the G minor of the third strain. The second group also reappears in an abridged and recomposed form. It opens in E♭ major—there is no minor-mode statement this time—but drives inexorably to the entrance of the drone melody in G minor. All of the unusual formal gestures heighten the pathos of a turn to the minor mode.

The first movement of the A Major Piano Quartet, with its sound-world of calm beauty, was apparently conceived as a kind of companion piece to the G Minor Quartet.[15] Brahms also built it around a broad juxtaposition of major and minor, in this instance reserving the minor mode almost exclusively for the development. That section presents its own distorted, reweighted rendition of the exposition, centering upon a C minor transformation of the opening theme and two variations thereof, followed by telescoped material from the transition and second group, a cadence in the tonic minor, and a statement of the exposition's closing theme. This final part of the development moves back and forth between A minor and A major. By cadencing prematurely, Brahms again deemphasizes the question of tonal resolution in favor of that of mode.

After his experience with the hapless fugato in the B Major Piano Trio, Brahms managed to turn contrapuntal episodes into another effective rhetorical device. What gives fugatos their power? For one thing, they draw attention to themselves. While fugatos are usually open-ended, they are always demarcated from what went before; furthermore, they can create harmonically "flat" textures, as Joseph Kerman notes.[16] The abstractness of these basic traits allows fugatos to assume a variety of roles within particular compositions. In one traditional use, the last movement of the E Minor Cello Sonata brings together fugal and sonata procedures.[17] Brahms seems to have derived its "first theme" from Contrapunctus 13 of Bach's *The Art of Fugue*, setting it in his three-voice finale as alternating *dux* and *comes* versions; the first group is thus a fugato. The first theme/subject begins with an accented tonic, and the fugato itself becomes a massive tonic block, trailing off eventually into incomplete statements of the subject that lead into a modulation. Somewhat like a fugal episode, the second group transforms motives from one of the countersubjects, but these gradually become less prominent. An arch shape (of the kind that, for instance, employed on various levels, later became Bartók's signature)—or perhaps better, an inverted arch, since the fugal pillars are the high points—emerges in the movement as a whole: first group–second group–development–second group–first group plus coda. Despite the architectural analogy, the form is neither precisely symmetrical nor static. Only the latter part of the second group reappears, and the recapitulation of what does come back takes place over a dominant pedal (briefly tonicized); the first theme/fugal subject likewise enters in its *comes* version (mm. 132–35). All of this makes for a huge climax of tonic harmony at the end; the fugatos are the main topic in this finale.

The characteristic entrance of a single voice in a fugal texture signifies a beginning, but not necessarily the beginning of a movement, as in the E Minor Cello Sonata. In the scherzo of the F Minor Piano Quintet, Brahms uses a fugato as the developmental center of a reinterpreted binary form. He bases the scherzo proper on three thematic strands (mm. 1–13, 14–22, 23–37), the second of which becomes the most important, each entrance of it distinguished by increasing insistence. The fugato, one of whose subjects derives from this same thematic material, comes in after the second appearance (mm. 57–67; see Figure 6.3). As the fugal texture begins to unravel—the subjects do not complete themselves, and the fragments become models for sequences—the deadpan academicism of the contrapuntal episode is engulfed by the next, even more barbaric crescendo. The fugato thus serves as a foil.

Contrapuntal episodes do not appear only in such rhythmically driven contexts as these two movements provide. Brahms composed a passage of austerely beautiful counterpoint for the E♭ minor slow movement of the Horn Trio, Op. 40 (Example 6.2). For this Adagio mesto he devised a fascinating form that (as we shall see) he would return to in several later slow movements: there are three sections, but since the first is tonally open, this is not strictly speaking a ternary form. After a half cadence, the unaccompanied horn presents a bleak subject in B♭ Phrygian. The answer, in the violin, outlines an E♭ minor triad, locally the subdominant, and is followed by another statement of the subject by the piano. The end of this fugato, a single exposition, leads to a brief development of the subject, which moves through several remotely related triads and then returns to the dominant of E♭ minor. For this work, which he completed in May 1865, Brahms specified the Waldhorn, the valveless version of the instrument. Generally more veiled in sound, the natural horn does not possess the uniformity of the valve instrument; the player must constantly adjust the volume to reduce unwanted unevennness.[18] Perhaps because Brahms had played the horn as a youth, Kalbeck believed that he wrote the trio in remembrance of his mother, who had died only three months before.[19] Although he composed the second and fourth movements in the lively hunting-horn style, the first and especially the third, with its somber fugato, could certainly be construed as elegiac. Some of the impact of this episode derives from the solitary entrance of the subject. As a complex of moving parts that go nowhere—it prolongs the B♭ minor triad, at first in a restricted range, but does not really escape the single harmony, even when the registral space expands, until the very end—the fugato itself seems almost a miniature sound image of suspended time.

Brahms integrated masterly passages of both imitative counterpoint and mode change into each movement of the G Major String Sextet, Op.

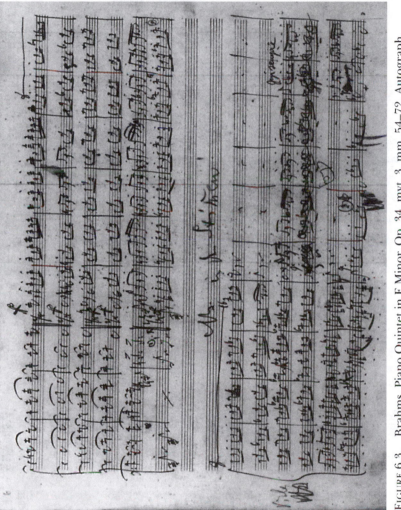

FIGURE 6.3.   Brahms, Piano Quintet in F Minor, Op. 34, mvt. 3, mm. 54–72. Autograph, Library of Congress.

EXAMPLE 6.2.   Brahms, Horn Trio in E♭, Op. 40, mvt. 3, mm. 17–26.

36—which, together with the F Minor Piano Quintet, is perhaps the greatest of the chamber works from this period. In the first and second movements he capitalized again, within a general context of understatement, upon the potential harmonic inertia of contrapuntal episodes. Like that of the F Minor Piano Quintet, this first movement emphasizes the semitone between the dominant and lowered submediant scale degrees, a voice-leading move that seems to have held particular interest for Brahms (as for many other nineteenth-century composers) throughout his life.[20] Rhythmic refinements—for example, the initial six-bar melodic phrase and, later, hemiolas (e.g., mm. 33–40)—give it an asymmetrical swing; with the blending of an E♭ triad into G major and the slowly trilling semitones in the first viola, the opening has a dreamy, unfocused sound. The beginning of the development, which Tovey considered "one of the most brilliant contrapuntal *tours de force* extant,"[21] combines fragments of the first theme (in D minor) canonically with their inversions. After a cadence (m. 229), the entrances come in more closely and then dissolve into a sequence, the entire passage climaxing in an A major triad (m. 249). When the opening theme comes in shortly thereafter in the cellos, the meaning of the oscillating semitones (A–G♯) is reversed: the first has become the decorative note, and the prolonged harmony is a C♯ minor triad. The major-to-minor shift initiates another harmonic plateau with the hypnotic breadth of most of the gestures in this movement.

Brahms called the second movement a scherzo, but it seems to fit better into the category of intermezzo—an introspective substitute for the scherzo that he made his own. Although the trio is a vigorous, hemiola-filled dance in G major and triple time, the scherzo itself (in G minor, $\frac{2}{4}$) stands out for its impassiveness, especially in the second group, a fugato marked *tranquillo*. Unlike the Adagio mesto of the Horn Trio, the subject enters in the dominant minor (D minor, m. 17). The mask of affective neutrality begins to slip after the double bar, as sequences ascend by half step and progressively fragment in a continuous crescendo to an accented G major triad (in m. 50). To haunting effect, the reprise opens in G major (m. 57), only to fall away and begin again in G minor (m. 69).

Imitative, if not fugal, counterpoint pervades most of the variations in the slow movement, becoming especially prominent in the third and fourth. Brahms had sent a fragment of the theme in 1855 to Clara Schumann.[22] From this shadowy, chromatic melody in E minor he composed five variations. The climax comes with the wonderful fifth variation, the only *maggiore*, in which the harmonies implied by the counterpoint in the theme are finally permitted to luxuriate: for the first time, a variation opens on a clear, long tonic in root position, and a later progression between the flat submediant and the Neapolitan has doubled in length from its previous appearances (see m. 10, then mm. 75–76).

Like the other movements, the finale begins indistinctly, in this case on the supertonic (an A minor triad), landing on the tonic with an open fifth above, in measure 6, to introduce the dancelike main theme. Loosely fugal versions of the opening serve as frames at several points in the form—for instance, at the beginning of the development section, where the A minor triad is tonicized. A minor-mode elaboration of the dance theme reaches the tonic before the recapitulation of the main theme, in yet another deliberate undercutting of harmonic tension-and-release in favor of the rhetoric of mode change (Example 6.3).

EXAMPLE 6.3.   Brahms, String Sextet in G Major, Op. 36, mvt. 4, mm. 76 –81.

EXAMPLE 6.3.   *continued*

Music as Logic: The String Quartets and Third Piano Quartet

After finishing the Horn Trio, Brahms would not concentrate on chamber music with similar intensity for some two decades, turning his attention instead to the large choral and orchestral genres. In the mid-1870s he nevertheless managed to complete four chamber pieces in rapid succession:

C Minor String Quartet, Op. 51, No.1	summer 1873; begun earlier
A Minor String Quartet, Op. 51, No. 2	summer 1873; begun earlier
C Minor Piano Quartet, Op. 60	summer 1875; mvts. 1, 2 much earlier; 3, 4 winter 1873–74
B♭ String Quartet, Op. 67	summer 1875

In the first of these, the C Minor String Quartet, terse, undiluted intensity replaces the broad melodiousness of the string sextets and chamber music with piano. The opening group and transition, for example, last only 32 measures, in comparison to 134 in the analogous portion of the G Major String Sextet. While Brahms never returned to the manner of his earlier years, the immediate cause of the stylistic disjunction would seem to have been the change of focus to the string quartet.

Scattered throughout his letters and other sources from the 1860s (and before) are a number of references to string quartets in progress, and in particular, to one in C minor; apparently, however, Brahms had trouble bringing it to a conclusion that pleased him.[23] To judge from the C Minor Quartet that emerged in the end, he seems to have believed that the string quartet ideally demanded the continuous, close working out of musical ideas we associate especially with Beethoven, and that the Schubertian expansiveness of his earlier chamber music would not do. As the highest of the chamber genres, the string quartet appears to have required the purest logic in Brahms's estimation. Not only should its motivic-thematic and harmonic development resemble "discourse, in which every detail forms a consequence to what has been presented previously and a premise for what follows"—Carl Dahlhaus's description of the musical logic long seen as validating all of the instrumental genres[24]—it should also accomplish this with a stringent economy, a minimum of digression.

Already in measure 2 the opening idea of the C Minor Quartet begins to fragment. The second of the two initial motives repeats, briefly expressing an A♭ triad, which resolves onto the dominant in measure 7.[25] A short interlude (mm. 11–22) prolongs the dominant more lyrically, but the ensuing repetition of the first theme leads into a laconic modulation. (The first movement of Beethoven's F Minor String Quartet, Op. 95, a locus classicus of terseness, incorporates similar gestures in an even more extreme experiment in compression.) Fast, nervous elaboration becomes the norm. Toward the end of the development, the opening idea breaks off into its head motive (m. 118). Augmented and again momentarily touching on an A♭ triad, the head motive accelerates into the recapitulation of the first theme, now with a mobile bass line so that it seems to move even more quickly than before. In this composition, every second and every note count.

The Poco adagio of the C Minor Quartet, more songful than the Allegro, as befits a slow movement and especially one entitled "Romanze," still shows some of the same motivic rigor. Like that of the Adagio mesto in the Horn Trio, the form falls into three sections (plus a coda), the first of which does not close completely. Just as an essay writer makes a link between the end of one paragraph and the beginning of the next, Brahms reharmonizes a cadential figure, and, in doing so, both changes its affective value (now it is a minor-mode tonic) and gives it a new formal function, making it the opening gesture (m. 27) of the section that follows (Example 6.4). This attention to motivic connections gives the slow movement of the C Minor Quartet—and that of the A Minor Quartet, admired by Schoenberg in a famous essay—a deliberate sound.[26]

In the finale the fiery restlessness of the first movement returns. Motivic development at times takes precedence over formal conventions, so that incomplete or contradictory signals blur the form. It is by no means clear, for example, where the exposition might be considered to end; the "closing" group transforms the head motive and then elaborates it, not actually coming to a close, but rather leading to further development (mm. 70ff.).

Composed along comparable stylistic lines, the A Minor Quartet is not in general as extreme as the C Minor: less nervous, more lyrical. Certainly, the relationships between sections in the third movement—one of

EXAMPLE 6.4.   Brahms, String Quartet in C Minor, Op. 51, No. 1, mvt. 2, mm. 25–28.

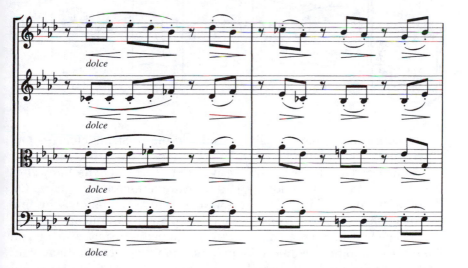

the most original intermezzos Brahms ever wrote and a precursor of an-other, more widely known movement in the Second Symphony—sound less studied than in the Romanze of the C Minor Quartet. He called the movement a "Quasi Minuetto": no real minuet would have contained three-measure phrases. As in the Romanze, the first section in this ghost of a minuet comes only to a half close, ushering in a duple-meter, A major *allegretto vivace* that contrasts sharply with it. When this, too, pauses on a half cadence, a reminiscence of the opening tempo, meter, and mode sug-gests that maybe the two sections are not so different, after all (Example 6.5). The end of the *allegretto vivace* had recalled a motive from the begin-ning of the *quasi minuetto,* and the *tempo di minuetto* interlude superimposes figures from both sections, maintaining the dominant pedal but reinterpreting it for the time being as the bass of a C♯ minor ⁶₃ (the 5–6 move again). Remembering the minuet in this way—at a distance—gives resonance to the archaic status of the genre. Such allusive use of form will reappear in a number of the later chamber works.

EXAMPLE 6.5.(a).   Brahms, String Quartet in A Minor, Op. 51, No. 2, mvt. 3: mm. 1–6.

a)

Commentators have usually considered the B♭ String Quartet, Op. 67, composed in the summer of 1875, to be more relaxed than the earlier pair of quartets (analogous in this respect to the Second Symphony after the First), as if Brahms no longer had to prove himself in the genre. On the other hand, this third quartet shows a new kind of ambition as his first overtly cyclical work, for motives from the opening movement return in the finale.[27] Still, textures are more transparent in this first movement, and it often seems to proceed more by juxtaposition than development; contrasting ways of subdividing the beat and measure become almost as important as the tonal plan. Brahms has again chosen to conceal a formal juncture: where does the second group begin? It takes shape gradually: the change to F major, ²₄, after a cadence in F minor, ⁶₈, sounds like a beginning, but immediately closes again in F minor; only upon repetition does the F major fragment become a full-fledged theme. Strangely enough, the cadential flourish itself (mm. 50–57) seems, after the fact, to mark the beginning of the second group. In a turn of events logical within this movement, the development section places the different subdivisions of the beat and measure next to each other, and the coda culminates by stacking them.

The Andante of the B♭ Quartet, a ternary form, sounds more spontaneous than either slow movement in Op. 51, but we can be sure that the larger course of the movement will be affected by the A major triad formed in passing in the two-measure introduction. In his autograph Brahms changed the scope of the consequences.[28] After the middle section closed on a half cadence in D minor—thus, an A major triad—the opening had originally come back in F major, the tonic. In his revision (that is, in the movement as published), he lengthened a cadenzalike passage leading up to the half close and then allowed the A major triad to become tonicized and expand well into the return of the first theme (decorated and divided between the voices, m. 57). Brahms had separated thematic and harmonic return in isolated early works such as the third movement of the G Minor Piano Quartet, Op. 25, and the first movement of the Horn Trio, Op. 40. But in the string quartets an exploration of such noncoincidence (see, as

EXAMPLE 6.5.(b).   Brahms, String Quartet in A Minor, Op. 51, No. 2, mvt. 3: mm. 71–80.

EXAMPLE 6.5.(b).   *continued*

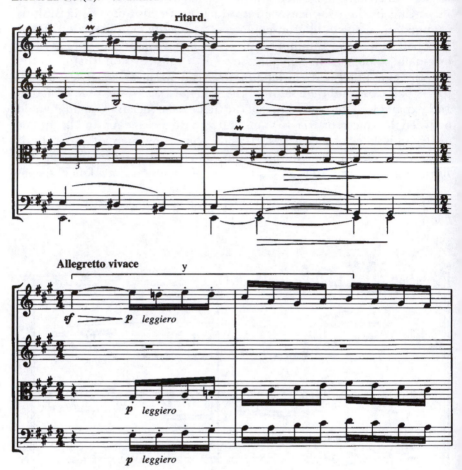

well, the second movement of Op. 51, No. 2) had become part of an increasing obsession with the implications of, and motivations for, obscuring
normative joints in the form.

A decade after the publication of Op. 67, Brahms, as honorary president
of the Wiener Tonkünstlerverein, publicly championed the string quartet
as a neglected genre. The organization decided to sponsor a contest in
which a prize would be awarded to the best new quartet. Brahms initially
suggested that the contest be extended to chamber music of any kind, but
his colleagues convinced him that, since so few string quartets were being
written at the time, the genre deserved special support. Brahms then
served actively on the jury that evaluated all the entries.[29] It is true that he
himself never composed another string quartet after Op. 67. For that reason, a number of commentators have assumed that he did not feel com-
fortable with the genre, that perhaps the legacy of Beethoven weighed too

heavily.[30] On the other hand, he did not publish more than three works in any of the chamber genres. (During the summer before the Tonkünstlerverein contest, that of 1886, he had composed his second and at least part of his third violin sonata, his third and final piano trio—if we do not count the revision of Op. 8—and his second and final cello sonata.)

After completing the first two string quartets, Brahms had resumed work on what had been the C♯ Minor Piano Quartet, writing the third and fourth movements in the winter of 1873–74, according to his notebook inventory, and bringing the piano quartet as a whole to its finished form in 1875, during the same summer in which he composed the B♭ String Quartet. Tovey states that Joachim remembered the C♯ minor version of the first movement as "very diffuse"[31] (a description that would also have fit the original version of the B Major Trio, from approximately the same period). In his customary manner, Brahms destroyed the autograph of the C♯ minor work, but his extant correspondence with Joachim, to whom he sent an early draft, does make it clear that he retained the basic thematic materials of the first movement, and that the declamatory shape of the opening also derives from the earlier version. How did he contrive to reconcile the breadth of his earlier style with the succinctness that he had come to value?

The first movement, as published in C minor, certainly does not seem "diffuse," despite features that could have caused it to sprawl or stagnate. Brahms incorporated a sizable melodic-harmonic model and sequence (the model in mm. 142–53, the sequence in mm. 164–75) into his elaboration of the first group in the development, and he composed the second group (mm. 70–109) as an almost self-enclosed theme and set of four variations, each eight measures long. Despite the odds against the second group, it does not become partitioned into a series of five episodes, largely because the theme and each variation come only to a half close, but also because Brahms rhythmically decentered the third and fourth variations (mm. 86–109): the melody does not enter until the second measure in these variations.

In the recapitulation Brahms came up with a more extravagant strategy to counteract the formal problems posed by the sequence and second group; this is, as far as we know, the first movement since the G Minor Piano Quartet in which he radically recomposed the opening group. To begin with, the dominant pedal of the retransition (mm. 176–97) does not resolve decisively. The first group and especially the transition, fierce in the exposition, become introverted in the recapitulation, and the theme of the second group appears in G major: still no resolution. The variations enter, altered: *pianissimo* and moving ethereally high, now over a dominant pedal in G. Tonal resolution, as well as a return to the minor-mode storminess of the exposition's first half, is postponed until the coda. No longer privileging modal opposition over harmonic tension and release, but rather making the two work together, Brahms came up with a first movement that surpasses those of the two earlier piano quartets in shapliness and momentum; also allowing substantial lyric episodes into the C Minor Piano Quartet, he made the tonal foundation taut. After the extremes of the C Minor String Quartet, he had learned to synthesize Beethovenian rigor with Schubertian melodiousness: the ideal of music as logical discourse had unmistakably acquired a less severe aspect for Brahms.

Borrowing, Allusion, and Recomposition in the Later Chamber Music

With the completion of the C Minor Piano Quartet and three string quartets that finally satisfied him, Brahms brought long-standing projects to a close. At the same time, the reworking of what had been the C♯ Minor Piano Quartet initiated a spate of chamber music recomposition. Thirteen chamber pieces issued from his later years:

G Major Violin Sonata, Op. 78	1879; begun in 1878; mvt. 3 based on two earlier lieder
C Major Piano Trio, Op. 87	1882; begun in 1880
F Major String Quintet, Op. 88	1882; mvt. 2 based on earlier work
F Major Cello Sonata, Op. 99	1886; mvt. 2 based on earlier work?
A Major Violin Sonata, Op. 100	1886; begun in 1883
C Minor Piano Trio, Op. 101	1886
D Minor Violin Sonata, Op. 108	1888; begun in 1886
B Major Piano Trio, Op. 8	1889; based on earlier work
G Major String Quintet, Op. 111	1890
A Minor Clarinet Trio, Op. 114	1891
B Minor Clarinet Quintet, Op. 115	1891
F Minor Clarinet Sonata, Op. 120, No. 1	1894
E♭ Clarinet Sonata, Op. 120, No. 2	1894

What does this list tell us? It shows that Brahms completed most of the works, ten of them, between 1882 and 1891; viewed with respect to instrumentation, the four works with clarinet inspired by the playing of Richard Mühlfeld form a separate group at the end. It also indicates that he built several movements around earlier works.[32]

Although the list does not show this, Brahms stole an idea for another: the middle movement of the A Major Violin Sonata, Op. 100, from a violin sonata by Edvard Grieg. The chamber music aesthetic, after all, traditionally stressed the quality of the elaboration over the inherent beauty of the themes or their originality; as a corollary, composers could make ideas their own by what they did with them. The A Major Sonata is one of only five three-movement chamber works by Brahms. Its second movement alternates sections of an *andante* and a scherzo within a single movement, linking them through proportional tempos, and this formal premise: the two genres represented are in different keys (F major and D minor respectively) as they would be in a traditional four-movement work; the key of either could prevail as the key of the movement as a whole. At least this movement of the sonata was begun during the summer of 1883, which Brahms spent in Wiesbaden near the home of his friend Rudolf von Beckerath, an accomplished amateur violinist. They collaborated repeatedly in playing sonatas from the Classical repertory, as well as works by such nineteenth-century composers as Grieg and Friedrich Kiel.[33]

In a letter to Brahms, his friend Heinrich von Herzogenberg obliquely drew attention to the provenance of the *scherzando* sections of the A Major Violin Sonata: "At first, I didn't really like it that this lovely F major countenance brought along a groom, a cheerfully melancholy Norwegian."[34] Using the stolen idea in exactly the same genre, Brahms did not even try to hide his thievery; the resemblances are in any case straightforward enough (Example 6.6). The Allegretto tranquillo of Grieg's G Major Violin Sonata, Op. 13, and the *vivace* portions of Brahms's Op. 100 share triple meter, minor mode, and an emphasis on progressions between chords with roots a third apart. The contour of Brahms's melody—the opening leap of a fourth, the emphasis on the fifth scale degree, and so on—also obviously derives from Grieg's, and both themes repeatedly use the uninflected seventh degree, which gives each a folkloristic modal sound.

EXAMPLE 6.6.(a).   Edvard Grieg, Violin Sonata in G Major, Op. 13, mvt. 2, mm. 1–8.

a)

EXAMPLE 6.6.(b).   Brahms, Violin Sonata in A Major, Op. 100, mvt. 2, mm. 16–19.

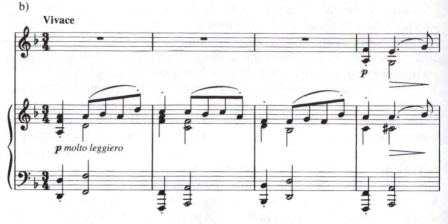

Brahms lifted not only a thematic idea but also the seed of a formal idea from Grieg. After the first movement of Grieg's sonata has ended (in G major, of course), the following movement opens in E minor, but the stability of the minor key is immediately called into question: the second chord is a G major triad, and the second phrase proceeds to tonicize G major (m. 8) before the leading tone of E minor has appeared. Although Grieg did not pursue the possibilities of this situation any further, Brahms explored it thoroughly in his own violin sonata (and a number of later works), for he based his composite on the permeability between a minor key and its relative major, especially in the absence of a leading tone, as suggested in Grieg's Allegretto tranquillo.

Like Grieg, Brahms immediately introduces the mediant, here an F major triad, in the second measure of the *vivace* and again at the end of the first phrase. No process of modulation has led away from the F major of the *andante;* a bare 5–6 voice-leading move prepares the D minor of the *vivace* (Example 6.7). Thus, the most delicate adjustment can cause F major to be subsumed by the key of D minor. On the other hand, D minor can also be integrated back into F major, as ultimately happens in this movement: the coda reconciles the rivaling genres and keys as an F major *scherzando*.

Brahms borrowed from himself for the mournful refrain of the last movement in the G Major Violin Sonata, Op. 78, taking motives intended to suggest rainfall—and tears—from the lieder "Regenlied" and "Nachklang," Op. 59, Nos. 3 and 4, and devising continuations suitable for an instrumental finale.[35] The significance of this self-quotation does not lie only in the solution to the formal problems posed by transferring thematic material to another genre. Another of Brahms's three-movement chamber works, the G Major Violin Sonata expresses in its opening Vivace ma non troppo and especially its concluding Allegro molto moderato the introspective ambivalence he more typically reserved for an intermezzo

EXAMPLE 6.7.   Brahms, Violin Sonata in A, mvt. 2, mm. 11–15.

movement. While the motives that he borrowed from the lieder might not mean much in utter isolation, they do not in fact come into the new composition value-free; as did the audiences of Brahms's time, we know their source and the texts with which he associated them.[36]

   The G Major Violin Sonata also quotes itself: the second episode of the rondo finale weaves in, in the original key, measures 1 and 7 from the middle movement, an austere E♭ major Adagio. Referring to another movement in this way—something that he did as well in the B♭ String Quartet and the B Minor Clarinet Quintet—does not just promote unity in a multimovement composition. Quotation, like reworking an idea from a known source, as we know, reverberates: we hear the original and the new contexts—and the differences between them—almost all at once. Motivic material that had provided a rather stiff opening for the Adagio becomes, as the first substantial major-mode moment in the finale, the agent for change, and it is itself transformed in the process. Breaking free from the formality of its previous appearance, the recalled melodic incipit, followed by motives from the refrain, surges in a quietly ecstatic series of climaxes. In the coda, the same quotation from the Adagio, now in G major, leads into the sunny, transfiguring chord progressions of the close.

For the middle movement of the F Major String Quintet, Op. 88—
the only other composite resembling that in the A Major Violin Sonata—
Brahms revived a sarabande and gavotte from a group of neo-Baroque
dances that he had written in the 1850s. In this case he obviously did not
intend for us to know the sources of the movement: he had destroyed his
own copies of the early dances, and copies that he had given to friends
resurfaced only in the twentieth century.[37] But the preexisting dances do
seem to have been the germ of the quintet, for the compound movement
that emerged from their recomposition and joining is the soul and center
to which he made the outer movements defer.[38]

If Brahms deemphasized the outer movements of the quintet in
favor of the middle, these have their own, for the most part more easygoing, attractions. The first movement of the F Major String Quintet begins with a drone fifth in the cello and second viola; although this specific
pastoral sign, an allusion to rustic bagpipes, quickly disappears, the atmosphere of an idyll is maintained. Themes unfold in a leisurely and lyrical
manner, and Brahms has chosen secondary keys (D major and A major)
that by convention stand in a "bright" relationship to F major.[39]

While Brahms did not mean for us to know that he had based the
core movement on his early sarabande and gavotte, he also did not obscure its Baroque characteristics. Keeping the telltale accented second
beat of the sarabande, the three *grave* portions eventually use all of the
original dance; the two interludes based on the gavotte are respectively in
the manner of a quick pastorale and a distorted—rhythmically inexact,
overly speedy—gavotte. Even more to the point than the allusions to
Baroque genres, the alternating sections with their contrasting tempos
represent the quintet's slow movement and scherzo, the former by tradition much weightier and more deeply felt than the latter.

When Brahms reworked the two dances, both originally in A, he left
the quicker sections derived from the gavotte in A major and transposed
those based on the sarabande to C♯ (minor and major). As in the middle
movement of the A Major Violin Sonata, the dramatic shape of this composite hinges in part on the question of which key will be allowed to end
and thus become "the key of" the movement as a whole. The eventual triumph of A major raises the possibility of arbitrariness—an extraordinary
situation in Brahms's work—since most of the harmonic and formal signals point to C♯ (minor or major) as the overall tonal center of the work.
On at least one level, what seems to matter above all is that the key of the
scherzandi should prevail.

For here the alternation of the two movement types, with the gestures at the boundaries between them, creates a much more intense plot
than in the A Major Violin Sonata. The high spirits of the first quick section seem already to mock the solemnity of the opening *grave*. This *allegretto vivace* retains most of the formal features characteristic of scherzos
and other dance-based movements (such as the original gavotte), preserving even the first repeat sign of the traditional rounded binary form.

The form does not, however, complete itself; falling into fragments toward an inconclusive end, the *allegretto vivace* yields to the returning *grave*. The second *grave* and succeeding *presto* intensify the affective qualities of the first *grave* and *scherzando*, C♯ in the process becoming associated with the tragedy and seeming inexorability of the slow-movement sections, and A major with the good cheer of the scherzo sections. This time A major does not give way, but spills over into the final return of the *grave* (m. 164), which then proceeds to modulate back to C♯.[40] During the course of the movement, Brahms has strengthened the sense of a drama being played out through three codas (mm. 26–31, 110–16, 196–208) that seem to reflect on the action. And in the third of these it seems that he audibly exerts his will; in the end, he (or his musical persona) *chooses* A major, with all of the implications that the key has acquired in the movement: this unusual gesture—quiet yet underscored—is the defining moment in the quintet (Example 6.8).

How does a composer end a multimovement piece after such a richly plotted center? In this instance, with another Baroque reference and much hilarity: Kalbeck wrote that "the spiritually shadowed Mater Dolorosa of his adagio, which bears the scherzo in her womb, must give birth to world-vanquishing humor as Savior" in the finale.[41] The last movement begins with what sounds like a rambling, rhythmically unfocused fugal subject, which enters four times: thus, a fugal exposition, the beginning of a Baroque genre that connoted learnedness and elevation even in Brahms's time—a period when genre and style had supposedly lost all meaning. When the finale does become rhythmically grounded, it also becomes resolutely unfugal, at first both boisterous and homophonic. After this initial juxtaposition of homophonic and fugal textures, Brahms certainly does admit a number of passages in a higher style, including a lovely lyrical second theme in A major and much complex imitative counterpoint. The complete disappearance of fugal signals and the ultimate victory of the exuberantly homophonic theme nevertheless effect a reversal of the expectations originally aroused, and this makes the movement as a whole sound humorous.[42] But it is high comedy.

Brahms's chamber compositions had, from the beginning, been intertextually rich. The first version of the B Major Trio, Op. 8, had quoted music of Schubert, Beethoven, and Schumann. Using a different kind of reference, Brahms had placed two styles in opposition to shape the set of variations in the B♭ String Sextet, Op. 18. Additional kinds of allusion have come up: to other movements within the same work, to traits associated with particular genres, to gestures that we recognize as incomplete or extraordinary—there are many codes and contexts upon which the music draws. Logic and rhetoric do not by themselves seem adequate to convey the eclectic allusiveness and the quality of expression in the later chamber music; the field of metaphors has shifted accordingly to include drama and plot.

EXAMPLE 6.8.   Brahms, String Quintet in F Major, Op. 88, mvt. 2, mm. 196–208.

Late Meditations on the Minor Mode

The much-explored concept of "musical logic" grew out of the long-stand-ing custom of considering music as a language; the logic lay in the tech-niques that make tonal music sound coherent to us.[43] When Brahms himself spoke of logic, however, as he was recorded to have done on many occasions later in his life, he emphasized neither the "speech character" of music nor the traditional techniques that he had long since mastered, but rather the composers themselves as reasoning agents, focused and dis‑ criminating, hence "logical." This view of logic as it applied to music mani‑ festly valorized the individual intellect, an ideologically loaded position in the climate of late nineteenth-century Vienna.[44] To his critics, his cere‑ bralness was a fundamental weakness: while hardly a model of judicious‑ ness, Hugo Wolf was voicing a widely held opinion when he dismissed the older composer's work as "brain music" (*Gehirnmusik*).[45]

If his principle of "thinking logically in music" had to do with the dis‑ ciplined elaboration of musical ideas,[46] Brahms clearly also speculated about the elements of his art. And his intellectual preoccupations became expressive material. A number of late chamber compositions suggest, in particular, ongoing reflection on the properties and possibilities of the minor mode. For example, what place might the natural minor, lacking the leading tone, have in the dominant-oriented discourse of sonata form? Theorists have sometimes considered the half step between the fifth and sixth scale degrees to be more or less as characteristic of the minor mode as the half step between the seventh and eighth scale degrees is of the

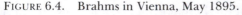

FIGURE 6.4.   Brahms in Vienna, May 1895.

major mode.⁴⁷ According to this dualistic model, the cadence that distinguishes the minor mode would, if only theoretically, be the plagal (iv–i).

In the first movement of the A Minor Clarinet Trio, Op. 114, Brahms opposes two renditions of the minor mode: the initial one "pure," the other not. The dramatic trajectory of this movement encompasses a departure from, and eventual return to, the original, faintly archaic sound world. He centers the opening in A minor without the benefit of the leading tone. Rather than enlisting a G♯, he dwells on F over the tonic pedal as part of an "apparent ii°⁴₂," thereby articulating the tonic through linear neighbor function other than the traditional ♯7̂–8̂.⁴⁸ While the first two phrases (a, mm. 1–13), a period, have a distinctive modal sound, they remain harmonically inert. They are, nevertheless, only the first section in a three-part theme. In this type of theme, the central section (b, mm. 14–17) usually offers harmonic contrast of some sort, often by prolonging the dominant. Here it is harmonically and rhythmically more active than the first section, and it introduces the dominant and leading tone. With its plagal orientation, the abbreviated a′ section (mm. 18–21) then recalls the beginning.

Although the harmonic language in the outer sections of the first theme is not well suited for the dynamism of sonata-form processes—in particular, the almost obligatory move to the dominant at the end of the development section—Brahms nevertheless invokes it at certain points in the movement; the exposition, for example, ends on a plagal half cadence. He thus creates across the span of the movement a network of associations that stand outside the main harmonic thrust, yet make the sound of the composition particular. A related example occurs during the development: motives from the b section of the first theme are set as parallel six-threes in a quasi-fauxbourdon style that recalls the antiquated sound of the opening. This passage effects an expressive reversal: the vigorous motive from the first theme has become dreamy and passive (Example 6.9). As he usually does in these late works, Brahms omits some of the first theme in the recapitulation—here, the initial period (a), which could not effectively follow the retransition dominant—to bring out some new facet in it. The b section enters instead with its former character restored and intensified (m. 126).

The telos of the entire movement is nevertheless its original sound world, and the end of the recapitulation gradually brings back the archaic quality of the opening. The coda begins with an open-fifth chord, which leads into the fauxbourdon transformation of the b motives and then onto sweeping natural minor scales with a Picardy third—all unambiguously in A minor without the presence of its leading tone. In this movement Brahms thus offers two versions of the minor mode: the natural A minor of the opening and coda frames the mixed version necessary for sonata-form discourse.

In the later works Brahms more typically focused on the fluid movement possible between a minor tonic and the keys a diatonic third away. For instance, he built the heart of the F♯ major Adagio affettuoso in the F

EXAMPLE 6.9.   Brahms, Clarinet Trio in A Minor, Op. 114, mvt. 1, mm. 96–100.

Major Cello Sonata, Op. 99, around a struggle between D♭/C♯ major (V/F♯) and the notated key of F minor.[49] This is another slow movement in which the first section of a (modified) ternary form closes on a half cadence— here, a tonicized dominant. The different ways in which he molds this special form and, especially, the kinds of openings that he chooses for the central section highlight his shifting interests at different times in his life. For the middle part of the Adagio mesto in the Horn Trio, Op. 40, he composed a bleakly picturesque fugato; in the Romanze of the C Minor String Quartet, Op. 51, No. 1, he made a tight motivic connection. And the shape of the Adagio affettuoso of the Cello Sonata reflects his growing fascination with the nuances of how firmly a key is established and the effects this can have on conventional formal boundaries.

Gustav Jenner, who began to study with Brahms at the end of the 1880s, recorded relevant comments by the composer on the nature of modulation:

> The tonic key must first of all be fully expressed and its dominion over all the subsidiary keys be maintained through clear relationships, so that, if I may so express myself, the sum of all the keys used in a piece appears as an image of the tonic key in its activity. That, nevertheless, precisely the indefiniteness of a key, even the tonic key, can be an excellent means of expression, lies in the nature of the thing.[50]

Brahms rewrote his B Major Piano Trio, Op. 8, around the time that Jenner began to study with him. In the first movement he kept the opening group—essentially songful and closed, yet also capable of rising to a powerful climax—and recomposed everything else, allowing the breadth and other qualities of the first group to determine the form of the movement. Although the original version was longer, it included a number of small, static gestures. He made the individual gestures of the later version larger and more intense, more in keeping with the sweep of the opening theme. Thus he composed a second group as lyrical as the first, but even more dynamic, and in the key of the relative minor throughout. Toward the end, the second group seems destined to cadence in B major (mm. 101–6) until rerouted at the last moment back to G♯ minor. As the climax of the development section, the opening theme emerges, on the dominant and drastically abbreviated, from G♯ minor (mm. 185–88). Brahms in this way demonstrates the permeability between the two keys as well as the ultimate sovereignty of B major over G♯ minor, asserted at the juncture between development and recapitulation.

G♯ minor is only a secondary key in the B Major Trio. For the middle movement of the A Major Violin Sonata, Op. 100, Brahms had seized on a fleeting hint in Grieg's violin sonata of the possibilities offered by the interpenetrability between a minor tonic and its relative major. What further consequences might this sort of "indefiniteness" have in a sonata-form movement? At the same time that he was completing the A Major Violin Sonata, Brahms composed the first movement of the D Minor Violin Sonata, Op. 108, in which he took up this question.

D minor certainly sounds volatile at the beginning of the sonata, as if it will have no staying power whatsoever: the first two phrases end in an imperfect cadence (m. 4) and a half cadence (m. 8) in F major (Example 6.10). Moreover, during most of the movement the status of D minor as tonic is projected through its dominant, most remarkably by a pedal point throughout the entire development section; even the first group cadences on what sounds like an A minor triad with a Picardy third (m. 24; Example 6.10). Just as F major appears as a facet of D minor in the first group, the dominant of D minor (mm. 56–61) returns in the middle of the F major second group. Brahms seems intent on creating a standoff, a sense that the piece has not really gone anywhere. A pattern of treble A's at important formal joints (mm. 1, 24, 25, 48, 83, 84, 130, 153) until well into the recapitulation also suggests that no real motion has taken place: although held in common by D minor and F major triads, A in the top voice does not indicate full closure in either key.

Two anomalies in this sonata form are well known: (1) the singular, kaleidoscopic development section, as previously mentioned, occurs from beginning to end over a dominant pedal; and (2) the complete first group reappears twice thereafter. Since D minor has almost always been projected through its dominant, the development pedal carries little weight. But with the recapitulation of the second group (mm. 186–217), a tonic triad is finally representing D (now major). Toward the end of this group, definitive motion away from D (mm. 204–8) and back to a chord with the full dramatic force of a structural dominant (m. 214) at last takes place. Logically enough, this dominant leads to the second, "true" recapitulation of the opening group (mm. 218–36), which for the first time closes in D rather than on A: it, too, is in a sense resolved. Resetting the harmonic premises thus led Brahms to a radical, if studied, interpretation of minor-

EXAMPLE 6.10.   Brahms, Violin Sonata in D Minor, Op. 108, mvt. 1, mm. 1–11.

mode sonata form in which the apparent formal divisions do not have their usual meaning.

Brahms focused on modal contrast—and even more, on modal symbiosis—in all four movements of the B Minor Clarinet Quintet, Op. 115. In this regard and in its sheer beauty of sound, the Clarinet Quintet bears comparison with another masterpiece of nearly thirty years before, the G Major String Sextet, Op. 36. In line with the view of tonality that Brahms expressed to Jenner, subsidiary keys tend now more than ever to sound like inflections of the main key rather than strong tonal "others" that will eventually be subjugated. The key scheme of the quintet is organized around B minor and its relative major, D, but at crucial points Brahms undermines the distinction between the two. This eroding of the opposition between major and minor basic to the sign system of expression in tonal music is one of a number of features in the quintet that communicate ambivalence, but also, ultimately, resignation.

Toward the beginning of the first movement, Brahms prominently mixes in D major, the goal of the exposition. The opening only gradually evolves into a theme; for much of its length, this statement seems rhythmically and harmonically ungrounded, as if it would avoid becoming a stable "subject." Each time that the theme reappears thereafter, its fluid design allows it to be in some way truncated or telescoped: for example, when the exposition is repeated, the D major of its close connects directly with the D major moment in the first theme, bypassing the opening measures altogether. A more forceful, fully formed part of the exposition, the transition theme, becomes the center of the development section, where its character undergoes a complete transformation: it is not—or, at least, not only—what it had seemed to be. Brahms's conception of key permits the recapitulation to come almost to a close in G major, which is, nevertheless, only an aspect of the primary key; the last-minute regaining of the tonic in a coda emphasizes the tragic finality of the B minor ending.

The Adagio and the third movement, an intermezzo, continue the pattern of incorporating blunted or equivocal gestures. The latter movement nevertheless ends up sounding more optimistic than the others. In this introspective scherzo substitute, Brahms not only transforms the character of the scherzo, but also plays on the customary three-part form (scherzo-trio-scherzo), again using the interpenetration of B minor and D major. The movement begins as a D major *andantino,* which cadences twice in B minor, only to conclude in D major. A new section, a *presto* "trio" in B minor, turns out to be a sonata form, in which thematic fragments from the D major section reappear (and at the original pitch level). Was the D major *andantino* a slow introduction? Not exactly, since its closing phrases return in the coda of the sonata form, which thus ends in D major with a nod toward the traditional three sections. Yet neither does the movement observe the principles of contrast and containment that help define the genre of scherzo and trio, for it refers to boundaries and distinctions only to blur them.

Brahms composed the fourth movement as a set of variations on a theme of his own devising, with Bachian counterpoint between the cello and first violin. All five variations maintain the form of the theme, which makes D major the goal of its first strain. While each presents the theme in a new guise, the variations otherwise remain discrete entities: the only overall rhetorical plan would seem to derive from the cumulative effect of the theme's recurring form. The final variation changes the meter from duple to triple, turning the theme into a plaintive waltz. Unlike the others, this variation does not close, leading instead into a coda that recalls harmonically reinterpreted shards from the opening of the first movement. Although a series of illusory cadences on major chords delays closure, an unequivocal B minor, as in the first movement, becomes the tragic goal of the finale and thus the quintet as a whole. The differences and the relationships between the modes, already used in powerful and inventive ways in the early chamber music, had become a source of infinite structural and expressive subtlety in late Brahms.

Sonata Form Reimagined

As the list above shows, Brahms completed three chamber works in 1886—the A Major Violin Sonata, the F Major Cello Sonata, Op. 99, and the C Minor Piano Trio, Op. 101—and at least the first movement of the D Minor Violin Sonata, Op. 108. Such remarkable productivity can be attributed in part to his having begun these chamber music projects before then: the Adagio affettuoso of the F Major Cello Sonata may derive from the discarded slow movement of the E Minor Cello Sonata, Op. 38, and he definitely had started work on the middle movement of the A Major Violin Sonata during the summer of 1883. Most likely he had sketched not only that composite movement but also the opening Allegro amabile of the violin sonata three summers earlier at Wiesbaden. In its modest dimensions and reliance on traditional theme types, this first movement certainly resembles the Classical and classicizing repertory that he and von Beckerath had enjoyed together.

Particular themes suggest corresponding forms: Brahms would tell Jenner several years later that a sonata form "must of necessity result from the [thematic] idea."[51] Beyond implying a clear-cut, classicizing form, the opening theme of the A Major Violin Sonata hints at remote harmonies that are finally realized in the coda. And in a brilliant stroke, the otherwise conventionally shaped development—introduction, sequences, retransition—culminates in a nocturnelike thematic transformation, self-enclosed in C♯ minor. The retransition takes place on the wrong dominant, seeming in effect to go to a parallel (non-Classical) universe; the harmonic wrong turn makes this development section semantically rich by both representing and accomplishing a departure from the near routine of before.

Brahms devised a unique plot for the first movement of the A Major Violin Sonata, but a number of the other late development sections (e.g., in the first movement of the Clarinet Quintet) likewise center on thematic transformations. These often help create an aural image of "development" in the sense of growth. Toward the same end, he tends more than ever before to favor blending developmental and recapitulatory processes in accordance with the nature of the opening theme (as we have seen in the second version of the B Major Piano Trio). Beginning with the works from the summer of 1886, these features make each of the sonata forms seem more sharply individualized than before. The first movement of the C Minor Piano Trio, Op. 101, completed during that summer, exemplifies both a *Durchführung* that encompasses *Entwicklung*—the movement is celebrated for its motivic work—and an individual sonata form that results from a thematic idea. The nature of the first theme, which has a disruptive dominant pedal in the middle, almost precludes its recapitulation at the customary point in the form; instead, the development and recapitulation respond together to the thematic configuration in the exposition.

The essential four-note motive appears in the left hand of the piano in measure 1 and in the right hand in measure 2. Within this motive and elsewhere in the movement, the semitone neighbor note will prove to be the most consequential motivic cell (Example 6.11a). In one frequently noted alteration of the four-note motive, Brahms derives a recurring figure in the second group through augmentation (Example 6.11b). Much of the power in this and other transformations lies in the changed harmonic significance of the motive. In its original form, the motive begins with the neighbor note, chromatic and nonchordal; in the derivative, the first note is diatonic and a chordal tone.

Not only does the first theme contain the important motive that Brahms will remold throughout the movement, but the morphology of the theme prefigures important elements in the overall shape of the movement. The opening theme is tonally closed and consists of three segments, each of which has a discrete harmonic function: *a* (mm. 1–4) defines the key by moving from I to V, *b* (mm. 5–11) prolongs the dominant with a pedal, and *c* (mm. 12–20) closes off the theme with a full cadence. (Measures 21–22 extend the cadence.) The segments reappear at points in the form that can make use of their harmonic properties: *a* begins the response (mm. 81–87), *b* becomes part of a massive dominant pedal in the retransition (mm. 135–40) leading to the recapitulation of the second theme, and *c* brings full closure (mm. 200–208) before the coda. The widely separated segments surround and embrace the development of the first theme and the recapitulation of the second.

The reappearance of the opening material in the tonic at the beginning of the development section serves as a foil for the remote modulation to C♯ minor that follows.[52] Jenner quotes remarks by Brahms on this topic:

> An integrated modulation does not in any way rule out the use of the most distant keys. Quite the contrary, these distant keys become so only because another is the governing one. They receive true power of expression in that way; they say something else. They are like colors in a picture that separate from the background color, which both contains and enhances them.[53]

Brahms begins the process of "separation from the background color" by augmenting and freezing the semitone-related upper neighbor note, A♭, after the extended half cadence of measures 85–87. With this upward

EXAMPLE 6.11. Brahms, Piano Trio in C Minor, Op. 101, mvt. 1: (a) mm. 1–4; (b) mm. 38–39.

shift, the piece seems to slip into another world: as in the A Major Violin Sonata, the heart of the development section seems to mean something more than a site for the logical working-out of musical ideas.

Whereas the half-step motivic cell governs the choice of modulations, the development otherwise centers on transformations of the four-note motive. Brahms augments the entire motive (mm. 82–83, 84–85), then the neighbor note alone (m. 87). He contracts the rhythmic values back to the original size (mm. 91–92), changes the position of the motive in the measure (mm. 98 ff.), and both alters the placement of its harmonic and non-harmonic pitches and replaces the final interval (mm. 103–4). What counts above all is the perception of difference and transformation among the versions.

It was suggested above that the compositional strategies of Brahms's later works compel talk of drama and plot; so, too, such dense, constantly evolving, and sometimes unexpected motivic relationships as those in the C Minor Trio call for a new set of metaphors—of growth or even, perhaps, of seemingly *non*rational thought.[54] For by this point, the connections often sound not so much logical as psychological; they seem less a matter of syntax than of association, forming an indistinct analogue to kinds of human experience other than disciplined thinking or the effective use of language. The more continuous variation and transformation of thematic fragments frequently encountered in these later development sections correlates to a preference for free contrapuntal textures over the compartmentalized fugatos of the past (except, of course, for the special use in the finale of the F Major String Quintet, Op. 88).[55]

An illustrative, exceptional development section is that in the opening Allegro vivace of the F Major Cello Sonata, Op. 99, which almost completely avoids conventional motivic work, offering instead pure texture and an improvised manner, until the head motive, a rising fourth, eventually does reappear like the recollection of a distant memory. Brahms manages then to present a full statement of the opening theme, rhythmically flattened and apparently on the tonic, without having it seem as though the tonic has in fact been regained; it, too, sounds like a remembrance.

Another texturally beautiful work, the first movement of the G Major String Quintet, Op. 111, evolves from an incomparably rich beginning. Like that of the C Minor String Quartet, Op. 51, No. 1, this first theme begins to fragment almost immediately, but now with an expansive rather than pressured manner, forming sequences and touching on a variety of harmonies in a semblance from the outset of luxuriant, asymmetrical growth, heightened by the continuous shimmering of tremolos.

The actual development section itself moves between vigorous working out of motives and visionary transformations that become increasingly remote from the original motive forms. During this latter process, a new theme (mm. 84–85, transposed and slightly varied in mm. 87–88) merges motives from the opening with a repeated-note figure, distantly related to the tremolo, it seems. This short theme, too, fragments, and its motives undergo further changes—the succeeding part of the development, indeed, becomes a maze of dreamlike associations and distortions—that culminate with the prolonged leading-tone seventh in measure 99. As if in quotation marks, a version of measure 4 reappears: the recapitulation could in fact have proceeded here, but it would have sounded abrupt. Another leading-tone seventh (m. 102) resolves to a transposition of measure 4, which in turn moves (m. 106) to the dominant sonority of measure 2; measure 107 (= m. 3) finally achieves the full effect of thematic and tonal return. In keeping with the constantly evolving nature of both the first theme and the development section, that theme only gradually takes shape again at the point of recapitulation.

The emphasis on texture and the sound images of growth and non-rational thought do not, of course, mean that Brahms was any less concerned with musical logic in the later chamber compositions—far from it. This is quintessential "logical" music, but the musical elements and procedures Brahms used brought with them traditional connotations that he manipulated into extraordinarily eloquent patterns. We also know, however, from Jenner's account and a variety of other sources, that "logic," as Brahms and certain of his contemporaries interpreted it, had far-reaching implications particular to late nineteenth-century Vienna.[56] And if, as suggested here, the quality of expression had changed in the later chamber music, becoming both more subjective and more evocative, many listeners could not separate the music from their ideologically charged view of Brahms as a coolly intellectual, emotionally constricted person.

The Rosé Quartet, destined also to premiere the early chamber works of Schoenberg, gave the premieres of the G Major String Quintet and the new version of the B Major Piano Trio in 1890, and the first Viennese performance of the Clarinet Quintet with Mühlfeld in November 1892, almost exactly three decades after Brahms's entrance into the city. Since that time, the field of chamber players and the number of public performances had vastly increased. Yet, while this performance was a success, Egon Wellesz noted in his memoirs that during his own Viennese youth around the turn of the century, "the late works of Brahms were perceived in general as austere and brittle," and the Clarinet Quintet, "certainly one of his best works, was performed only on extremely rare occasions because the public found it too hard to understand."[57] Wellesz concluded that he had moved beyond his backward-looking audience. Whether Wellesz's obser-

FIGURE 6.5.   The Rosé Quartet, which began to give annual series of performances in Vienna during the 1882–83 season. From left to right: Arnold Rosé (first violin), August Siebert (second violin), Hugo Steiner (viola), Reinhold Hummer (cello).

vation is accurate or not, we do know that Brahms had at this same time become a model—especially in his chamber music—for a generation of composers coming of age in the city who had begun to use their own version of "musical logic" to express something beyond logic.

Notes

1. The Musiksammlung of the Österreichische Nationalbibliothek has a compilation of the Hellmesberger Quartet's programs from 4 November 1849 to 19 December 1889.

2. See Donald Francis Tovey, "Brahms's Chamber Music," in *The Main Stream of Music and Other Essays* (Oxford, 1949), 220–93, and James Webster, "Schubert's Sonata Form and Brahms's First Maturity (II)," *19th Century Music* 3 (1979):52–71.

3. In the first movement of the Fantasy, Schumann quotes "Nimm sie hin, denn, diese Lieder," the last song of Beethoven's cycle *An die ferne Geliebte;* Brahms worked the same passage into the finale of the B Major Piano Trio. The first interlude in the slow movement alludes to "Am Meer."

4. For discussions of the two versions, see Walter Frisch, *Brahms and the Principle of Developing Variation,* California Studies in Nineteenth-Century Music, vol. 2 (Berkeley and Los Angeles, 1984); Ernst Herttrich, "Johannes Brahms—Klaviertrio H-Dur Opus 8, Frühfassung und Spätfassung: Ein analytischer Vergleich," in *Musik, Edition, Interpretation: Gedenkschrift Günter Henle,* ed. Martin Bente (Munich, 1980), 218–36; and Franz Zaunschirm, *Der frühe und der später Brahms* (Hamburg, 1988). In 1924 the musicologist Ernst Bücken discovered the manuscript of a piano trio in A major, subsequently published in 1938 by Breitkopf & Härtel under Brahms's name, which Bücken dated to approximately the same period as the B Major Piano Trio. He and others have based their attribution of the trio to Brahms purely on stylistic grounds; the manuscript is not in his hand. Since no thorough study of the issues concerning its authenticity has yet appeared in print, I have excluded it from consideration in the text here. For a thoughtful recent discussion of the trio by an author who is convinced that Brahms composed it several years *after* Op. 8, see Malcolm MacDonald, *Brahms* (New York, 1990), 475–76.

5. Brahms's inventory of his works through Op. 79 is transcribed in Alfred Orel, "Ein eigenhändiges Werkverzeichnis von Johannes Brahms: Ein wichtiger Beitrag zur Brahmsforschung," *Die Musik* 29 (1936–37): 529–41.

6. For a discussion of hybrid periods, see William E. Caplin, "Hybrid Themes: Toward a Refinement in the Classification of Classical Theme Types," in *Beethoven Forum 3,* ed. Glenn Stanley (Lincoln, NE, 1994), 151–65.

7. Brahms himself thought highly enough of these variations to arrange them for piano as a birthday present to Clara Schumann.

8. Max Kalbeck, *Johannes Brahms,* rev. ed. (Berlin, 1915–21) 1:415: "Ohne das Antezedens der beiden Serenaden läßt sich das Sextett kaum bedenken."

9. Kalbeck, *Johannes Brahms* 1:445 and 1:232, n. 1: "Übereinstimmend damit bestätigt Joachim daß Brahms den ersten Satz des c-moll Quartetts 1855 komponiert hat; dieser stand aber damals in cis-moll. Von den andern beiden Klavierquartetten sagt derselbe Gewährsmann, sie seien, wenn er sich recht erinnert, zu derselben Zeit begonnen worden. Daß er sie mit Brahms schon in Detmold gespielt habe, wisse er ganz genau. Bargheer erinnert sich des g-moll-

Quartetts und seines Vortragen in Detmold." See also James Webster, "The C-sharp Minor Version of Brahms's Op. 60," *Musical Times* 121 (1980): 89–93.

10. *Johannes Brahms: Briefwechsel* (Berlin, 1912–22) 5:306: "Mir ist's überhaupt als merkte man . . . bei diesem Satz den Kitt mehr wie bei andern Deiner Kompositionen, und es ist bei mir die Frage entstanden, ob Du nicht teilweise früheres Material Deiner jetzigen Größe gemäß habest recken wollen!?"

11. In 1851 Brahms had taken part in a performance of a duo for cello and piano composed by himself but presented under the pseudonym Karl Würth. And Gustav Jenner, who studied with Brahms late in the composer's life, relates that the violin sonata published as his first, Op. 78, was actually his fourth. See Gustav Jenner, *Johannes Brahms als Mensch, Lehrer und Künstler: Studien und Erlebnisse* (Marburg, 1905), 45.

12. Kalbeck, *Johannes Brahms* 2:191: "Brahms, dem die Sonate zu voll mit Musik gestopft schien, das Adagio kassierte." For a discussion of Kalbeck's hypothesis that the Adagio may have been resurrected for the F Major Cello Sonata, Op. 99, see Margaret Notley, "Brahms as Liberal: Genre, Style, and Politics in Late Nineteenth-Century Vienna," *19th Century Music* 17 (1993): 107–23.

13. For varying views of the form of this movement see Elaine Sisman, "Brahms's Slow Movements: Re-inventing the Closed Forms," in *Brahms Studies: Analytical and Historical Perspectives*, ed. George Bozarth (Oxford, 1990), 79–103; Christopher Wintle, "The 'Sceptered Pall': Brahms's Progressive Harmony," in *Brahms 2: Biographical, Documentary and Analytical Studies*, ed. Michael Musgrave (Cambridge, 1987), 197–222; and Christoph Wolff, "Von der Quellenkritik zur musikalischen Analyse: Beobachtungen am Klavierquartett A-Dur op. 26 von Johannes Brahms," in *Brahms-Analysen: Referate der Kieler Tagung 1983*, ed. Friedhelm Krummacher and Wolfram Steinbeck, Kieler Schriften zur Musikwissenschaft 28 (Kassel, 1984), 150–65.

14. *Brahms Briefwechsel* 5:306, and *Clara Schumann—Johannes Brahms: Briefe aus den Jahren 1853–1896 im Auftrage von Marie Schumann*, ed. Berthold Litzmann (Leipzig, 1927) 1:370.

15. This recalls similar pairings by Mozart of major- and minor-mode works in the same genre, e.g., the String Quintets in C Major and G Minor, K. 515 and 516.

16. Joseph Kerman, *The Beethoven Quartets* (New York, 1979), 274.

17. For precendents, see, e.g., the finales of Mozart's G Major String Quartet, K. 387, and Beethoven's C Major String Quartet, Op. 59, No. 2, and D Major Cello Sonata, Op. 102, No. 2.

18. I am grateful to Eva Heater, Carol Padgman Albrecht, and Theodore Albrecht for our conversations about natural horn technique.

19. Kalbeck, *Johannes Brahms* 2:185–86.

20. See Webster, "Schubert's Sonata Form" on the semitonal relationships in the F Minor Piano Quintet.

21. Tovey, "Brahms's Chamber Music," 245.

22. *Schumann-Brahms Briefe* 1:75.

23. See Michael Musgrave and Robert Pascall, "The String Quartets Op. 51 No. 1 in C Minor and No. 2 in A Minor: A Preface," in *Brahms 2: Biographical, Documentary and Analytical Studies*, ed. Michael Musgrave (Cambridge, 1987), 137–44.

24. Carl Dahlhaus, "Musikkritik als Sprachkritik: Musikalische Logik," in *Klassische und romantische Musikästhetik* (Laaber, 1988), 283. Throughout their work, both Dahlhaus and Theodor Adorno have addressed some of the many ramifications of this complex analogy.

25. For discussions of this movement, see Allen Forte, "Motivic Design and Structural Levels in the First Movement of Brahms's String Quartet in C Minor," in *Brahms 2: Biographical, Documentary and Analytical Studies,* ed., Michael Musgrave, (Cambridge, 1987), 165–96; Frisch, *Brahms and the Principle of Continuing Variation,* David Lewin, "Brahms, His Past, and Modes of Music Theory," in *Brahms Studies: Analytical and Historical Perspectives,* ed. George Bozarth (Oxford, 1990), 13–28; and Peter H. Smith, "Liquidation, Augmentation, and Brahms's Recapitulatory Overlaps," *19th-Century Music* 17 (1994): 237–61.

26. Arnold Schoenberg, "Brahms the Progressive," in *Style and Idea: Selected Writings of Arnold Schoenberg,* ed. Leonard Stein, trans. Leo Black (Berkeley, 1975), esp. 429ff.

27. A motive toward the end of the scherzo in the B Major Piano Trio, Op. 8 (violin, mm. 125–29, and piano, mm. 137–41) had anticipated the beginning of its trio, just as a short passage in the slow movement of the Horn Trio, Op. 40 (mm. 63–65) had foreshadowed the opening of the affectively very different finale.

28. For the original version, see Karl Geiringer, *Brahms: His Life and Work,* 3d ed. (New York, 1981), 235. The autograph is now in the Robert Owen Lehman Collection on deposit at the Pierpont Morgan Library in New York.

29. Richard Heuberger, *Erinnerungen an Johannes Brahms: Tagebuchnotizen aus den Jahren 1875 bis 1897,* ed. Kurt Hofmann, 2d ed. (Tutzing, 1976), 140–43. The prize was awarded to Julius Zellner.

30. See, for example, Carl Dahlhaus, "Brahms and the Chamber Music Tradition," in his *Nineteenth-Century Music,* trans. J. Bradford Robinson, California Studies in Nineteenth-Century Music, vol. 5 (Berkeley and Los Angeles, 1989), 78.

31. Tovey, "Brahms's Chamber Music," 254, and James Webster, "The C-sharp Minor Version of Brahms's Op. 60."

32. The inventory mentioned above extends only through Op. 78. The information in this list derives from a variety of sources, including letters, memoirs, and Kalbeck's biography.

33. Kurt Stephenson, *Johannes Brahms und die Familie von Beckerath mit unveröffentlichten Brahmsbriefen und den Bildern und Skizzen von Willy von Beckerath* (Hamburg, 1979), 29–39. Another likely precedent for Brahms's fusion of scherzo and slow movement is Spohr's C Major Sextet, Op. 140 (see above, chap. 3, pp. 165–66).

34. *Brahms: Briefwechsel* 2:147: "Anfangs wollte es mir nicht behagen, daß dieses liebliche F dur-Gesicht schon einen Bräutigam mitbrachte, einen munter-traurigen Norweger."

35. Dillon Parmer, "Brahms, Song Quotation, and Secret Programs," *19th Century Music* 19 (1995): 161–90, esp. pp. 168–69, and MacDonald, *Brahms,* 280–81, give the beginnings of the lieder and the finale.

36. For a persuasive programmatic interpretation of the G Major Violin Sonata, see Parmer, "Brahms, Song Quotation, and Secret Programs."

37. See Robert Pascall, "Unknown Gavottes by Brahms," *Music and Letters* 57 (1976): 404–11. The opening of the scherzo movement of the G Major String Sextet, Op. 36, clearly derives from another gavotte from the same neo-Baroque project, but Brahms's reuse of earlier material was much more thorough in Op. 88.

38. Tovey, "Brahms's Chamber Music," 262, called the middle movement of the A Major Violin Sonata, Op. 100 "a counterpart in pastoral comedy" to the "sublime mystery" of the corresponding movement in the F Major String Quintet.

39. Brahms had used a similar bright chord progression in the coda of the finale of the G Major Violin Sonata, Op. 78.

40. This technique, which Brahms used in a number of slow movements, thus took on particular meaning here. For a discussion of Brahms's approach to the traditional closed forms of slow movements, see Sisman, "Brahms's Slow Movements."

41. Kalbeck, *Johannes Brahms* 3:351: "Die vom Geist beschattete Mater dolorosa seines Adagios, welche das Scherzo in ihrem Mutterschoß trägt, soll den weltüberwindenden Humor als Erlöser begären."

42. For a discussion of this finale, see Victor Ravizza, "Möglichkeiten des Komischen in der Musik: Der letzte Satz des Streichquintetts in F dur, op. 88 von Johannes Brahms," *Archiv für Musikwissenschaft* 31 (1974): 137–50.

43. See, for example, the chapter "Musical Logic and Speech Character" in Carl Dahlhaus, *The Idea of Absolute Music*, trans. Roger Lustig (Chicago, 1989), 103–16.

44. See Margaret Notley, "Brahms as Liberal: Genre, Style, and Politics in Late Nineteenth-Century Vienna," *19th Century Music* 17 (1993): 107–23.

45. From a conversation with Hermann Bahr, quoted in Bahr, "Brahms," in *Essays* (Leipzig, 1912), 41–42.

46. Jenner, *Johannes Brahms als Mensch, Lehrer, und Künstler*, 57. Brahms prescribed composing sonata forms after models so that Jenner would "learn to think logically in music [*musikalisch logisch denken lernen*]."

47. In a provocative book, Daniel Harrison has revived the modal dualism of such theorists as Hugo Riemann, Moritz Hauptmann, Rudolf Louis, and Ludwig Thuille as an analytic tool for understanding the complex chromatic music of the late nineteenth and early twentieth centuries. See Daniel Harrison, *Harmonic Function in Chromatic Music: A Renewed Dualist Theory and an Account of Its Precedents* (Chicago, 1994).

48. "Neighboring or, sometimes, passing motion over a sustained bass can produce an apparent $\frac{4}{2}$" (Edward Aldwell and Carl Schachter, *Harmony and Voice Leading*, 2d ed. [Orlando, FL, 1989], 391).

49. On this analytical point, see Margaret Notley, "Brahms's F-Major Cello Sonata and Its Genesis: A Study in Half-Step Relations," in *Brahms Studies*, vol. 1, ed. David Brodbeck (Lincoln, NE, 1994), 139–60.

50. Jenner, *Johannes Brahms als Mensch, Lehrer, und Küntsler*, 38: "musste stets die Grundtonart zunächst voll zum Ausdruck kommen und ihre Herrschaft über alle Nebentonarten durch klare Verhältnisse gewahrt werden, sodass, wenn ich mich so ausdrücken darf, die Summe aller im Stück angewandten Tonarten als ein Bild der Haupttonart in ihrer Aktivität erschien. Dass nichtsdestoweniger gerade das Unbestimmtlassen einer Tonart, ja der Haupttonart ein vorzügliches Ausdrucksmittel sein kann, liegt in der Natur der Sache."

51. Jenner, *Johannes Brahms als Mensch, Lehrer, und Künstler*, 6: "die Sonatenform mit Notwendigkeit aus dem Gedanken hervorgehen muss."

52. Brahms proceeds similarly in a number of other first movements in which the exposition is not to be repeated: see, for instance, the G Minor Piano Quartet, Op. 25, the *Tragic* Overture, Op. 80, and the Fourth Symphony, Op. 98. Brahms originally did, however, include a repeat sign in the autograph of the C Minor Piano Trio, which he then scribbled over.

53. Jenner, *Johannes Brahms als Mensch, Lehrer, und Küntsler*, 39: "Eine einheitliche Modulation schliesst nun keineswegs die Anwendung auch der entferntesten Tonarten aus. Ganz im Gegenteil werden diese entfernten Tonarten erst

dadurch entfernte, dass eine andere die herrschende ist; sie bekommen dadurch erst wahre Ausdruckskraft; sie sagen etwas anderes; sie sind wie Farben eines Bildes, die sich von der Grundfarbe loslösen, durch die sie gebunden sowohl wie gehoben werden."

54. The first movement of the F Minor Piano Quintet, Op. 34, offers an isolated early example in the chamber music of the same kind of development section.

55. Michael Musgrave, *The Music of Brahms* (London, 1985), 206, also notes the change in Brahms's preferred contrapuntal textures.

56. See Notley, "Brahms as Liberal."

57. Egon Wellesz and Emmy Wellesz, *Egon Wellesz: Leben und Werk*, ed. Franz Endler (Vienna, 1981), 16: "Im allgemeinen empfand man die späten Werke von Brahms als herb und spröde; so wurde zum Beispiel das Klarinettenquintett, das gewiß eines seiner besten Werke ist, zur Zeit meiner Jugend nur äußerst selten aufgeführt, weil das Publikum es zu schwer verständlich fand. Der Geschmack des Wiener Publikums war gewissermaßen der Vergangenheit zugewandt."

Selected Bibliography

Bozarth, George, ed. *Brahms Studies: Analytical and Historical Perspectives.* Oxford, 1990.

Brinkmann, Reinhold. "Anhand von Reprisen." In *Brahms-Analysen: Referate der Kieler Tagung 1983,* ed. Friedhelm Krummacher and Wolfram Steinbeck, 107–28. Kieler Schriften zur Musikwissenschaft, vol. 28. Kassel, 1984.

Brodbeck, David, ed. *Brahms Studies.* Vol. 1. Lincoln, NE, 1994.

———. "Medium and Meaning: New Aspects of the Chamber Music." In *The Cambridge Companion to Brahms,* ed. Michael Musgrave, 98–132. Cambridge, 1999.

Dahlhaus, Carl. "Brahms und die Idee der Kammermusik" (1973). Reprinted in *Brahms-Studien,* vol. 1, edited by Constantin Floros, 45–57. Hamburg, 1974.

———. "Issues in Composition." In idem, *Between Romanticism and Modernism: Four Studies in the Music of the Later Nineteenth Century,* translated by Mary Whittall. California Studies in Nineteenth-Century Music, vol. 1, 40–78. Berkeley and Los Angeles, 1980.

———. "Brahms and the Chamber Music Tradition." In idem, *Nineteenth-Century Music,* translated by J. Bradford Robinson, 252–61. California Studies in Nineteenth-Century Music, vol. 5. Berkeley and Los Angeles, 1989.

Daverio, John. "From 'Concertante Rondo' to 'Lyric Sonata': A Commentary on Brahms's Reception of Mozart." In *Brahms Studies,* vol. 1, ed. David Brodbeck, 111–38. Lincoln, NE, 1994.

Forte, Allen. "Motivic Design and Structural Levels in the First Movement of Brahms's String Quartet in C Minor." In *Brahms 2: Biographical, Documentary and Analytical Studies,* ed. Michael Musgrave, 165–96. Cambridge, 1987.

Frisch, Walter. *Brahms and the Principle of Developing Variation.* California Studies in Nineteenth-Century Music, vol. 2. Berkeley and Los Angeles, 1984.

Fry, J. "Brahms's Conception of the Scherzo in Chamber Music." *Musical Times* 84 (1943): 105–7.

Graybill, Roger C. "Harmonic Circularity in Brahms's F Major Cello Sonata: An Alternative to Schenker's Reading in Free Composition." *Music Theory Spectrum* 10 (1988): 43–55.

Herttrich, Ernst. "Johannes Brahms–Klaviertrio H-Dur Opus 8, Frühfassung und Spätfassung: Ein analytischer Vergleich." In *Musik, Edition, Interpretation: Gedenkschrift Günter Henle,* ed. Martin Bente, 218–36. Munich, 1980.

Kalbeck, Max. *Johannes Brahms*. Rev. ed. 4 vols. Berlin, 1913–22.

Korsyn, Kevin. "Directional Tonality and Intertextuality: Brahms's Quintet op. 88 and Chopin's Ballade op. 38." In *The Second Practice of Nineteenth-Century Tonality*, ed. William Kinderman and Harald Krebs, 45–83. Lincoln, NE, 1996.

Krummacher, Friedhelm and Wolfram Steinbeck, eds. *Brahms-Analysen: Referate der Kieler Tagung 1983*. Kieler Schriften zur Musikwissenschaft, vol. 28. Kassel, 1984.

Lewin, David. "Brahms, His Past, and Modes of Music Theory." In *Brahms Studies: Analytical and Historical Perspectives*, ed. George Bozarth, 13–28. Oxford, 1990.

MacDonald, Malcolm. *Brahms*. New York, 1990.

Mohr, Wilhelm. "Johannes Brahms' formenschöpferische Originalität, dargestellt am ersten Satz seiner Violinsonate, Op. 108, und seiner Rhapsodie, Op. 79, Nr. 2." In *Bericht über den Internationalen musikwissenschaftlichen Kongress Leipzig 1966*, 322–25. Basel, [1970].

Musgrave, Michael. *The Music of Brahms*. London, 1985.

———, ed. *Brahms 2: Biographical, Documentary and Analytical Studies*. Cambridge, 1987.

Musgrave, Michael, and Robert Pascall. "The String Quartets Op. 51 No. 1 in C Minor and No. 2 in A Minor: A Preface." In *Brahms 2: Biographical, Documentary and Analytical Studies*, ed. Michael Musgrave, 137–44. Cambridge, 1987.

Notley, Margaret. "Brahms as Liberal: Genre, Style, and Politics in Late Nineteenth-Century Vienna." *19th Century Music* 17 (1993): 107–23.

———. "Brahms's F-Major Cello Sonata and Its Genesis: A Study in Half-Step Relations." In *Brahms Studies*, vol. 1, ed. David Brodbeck, 139–60. Lincoln, NE, 1994.

———. "Brain-Music by Brahms: Toward an Understanding of Sound and Expression in the Allegro of the Clarinet Trio." *The American Brahms Society Newsletter* 16/2 (Autumn 1998): 1–3.

———. "Late-Nineteenth-Century Chamber Music and the Cult of the Classical Adagio." *19th-Century Music* 23 (1999): 33–61.

Parmer, Dillon. "Brahms, Song Quotation, and Secret Programs." *19th Century Music* 19 (1995): 161–90.

Pascall, Robert. "Ruminations on Brahms's Chamber Music." *Musical Times* 116 (1975): 697–99.

Ravizza, Victor. "Möglichkeiten des Komischen in der Musik: Der letzte Satz des Streichquintetts in F dur, op. 88 von Johannes Brahms." *Archiv für Musikwissenschaft* 31 (1974): 137–50.

Sachs, Hans-Jürgen. "Zur Konzeption des ersten Satzes aus dem Klaviertrio c-Moll op. 101." In *Brahms-Analysen: Referate der Kieler Tagung 1983*, ed. Friedhelm Krummacher and Wolfram Steinbeck, 139–49. Kieler Schriften zur Musikwissenschaft, vol. 28. Kassel, 1984.

Schoenberg, Arnold. "Brahms the Progressive." In *Style and Idea: Selected Writings of Arnold Schoenberg*, ed. Leonard Stein, trans. Leo Black, 398–441. Berkeley and Los Angeles, 1975.

Scott, Ann Besser. "Thematic Transmutation in the Music of Brahms: A Matter of Musical Alchemy." *Journal of Musicology Research* 15 (1995): 177–206.

Sisman, Elaine. "Brahms's Slow Movements: Re-inventing the 'Closed Forms.'" In *Brahms Studies: Analytical and Historical Perspectives*, ed. George Bozarth, 79–103. Oxford, 1990.

Smith, Peter H. "Brahms and the Neapolitan Complex: bII, bIV, and Their Multiple Functions in the First Movement of the F-Minor Clarinet Sonata." In *Brahms Studies*, vol. 2, ed. David Brodbeck, 169–208. Lincoln, NE, 1998.

———. "Brahms and the Shifting Barline: Metric Displacement and Formal Process in the Trios with Wind Instruments." In Brahms Studies, vol. 3, ed. David Brodbeck, 191–229. Lincoln, NE, 2001.

———. "Liquidation, Augmentation, and Brahms's Recapitulatory Overlaps." *19th Century Music* 17 (1994): 237–61.

Tovey, Donald Francis. "Brahms's Chamber Music." In idem, *The Main Stream of Music and Other Essays*, 220–70. Oxford, 1949.

Webster, James. "The C-sharp Minor Version of Brahms's Op. 60." *Musical Times* 121 (1980): 89–93.

———. "Schubert's Sonata Form and Brahms's First Maturity (II)." *19th Century Music* 3 (1979): 52–71.

Whittall, Arnold. "Two of a Kind? Brahms's Op. 51 Finales." In *Brahms 2: Biographical, Documentary and Analytical Studies*, ed. Michael Musgrave, 145–64. Cambridge, 1987.

Wintle, Christopher. "The 'Sceptred Pall': Brahms's Progressive Harmony." In *Brahms 2: Biographical, Documentary and Analytical Studies*, ed. Michael Musgrave, 197–222. Cambridge, 1987.

Wolff, Christoph. "Von der Quellenkritik zur musikalischen Analyse: Beobachtungen am Klavierquartett A-Dur op. 26 von Johannes Brahms." In *Brahms-Analysen: Referate der Kieler Tagung 1983*, ed. Friedhelm Krummacher and Wolfram Steinbeck, 150–65. Kieler Schriften zur Musikwissenschaft, vol. 28. Kassel, 1984.

Zaunschirm, Franz. *Der frühe und der später Brahms*. Hamburg, 1988.

CHAPTER SEVEN

Chamber Music in France from Luigi Cherubini to Claude Debussy

Joël-Marie Fauquet

translated by Stephen E. Hefling
and Patricia Marley

Chamber Music: A Mode of Sociability

It is generally understood today that, contrary to traditional wisdom of long standing, the French Revolution neither interrupted nor impoverished musical activity in France.[1] If one accepts explicit testimony such as that of the violinist Pierre Baillot (1770–1842), during the last decade of the eighteenth century chamber music came to the fore as a privileged mode of sociability, diverse in practice, that brought together amateurs and artists as well as bourgeoisie and aristocrats.[2] Until at least the middle of the nineteenth century the string quartet, the most demanding form of chamber music, was thought of in images of musical conversation in which the discussion leader is the first violinist.[3] Frequently the amateur performer rubbed shoulders with the artist (i.e., the professional, practicing musician). Parisian music publishers made the works of Haydn, Mozart, and Beethoven available to these players, occasionally at precisely the moment when they were also being issued in Germany.

In approximately 1830, however, the practice of chamber music changed, for two reasons: difficulty of execution (most notably in the works of Beethoven), and idealization of the Classical repertory as a normative standard. Amateurs now began to pay for the privilege of hearing works that were beyond their technical means. This latter development is apparent from the quartet and quintet sessions organized by Baillot between 1814 and 1840, for which admission was charged: many of the audience in these subscription concerts were amateurs or music students. Nevertheless, although amateur music making may have diminished, it did not disappear entirely. And whereas the proper venues for opera and symphony in Paris were readily apparent, those appropriate for chamber music were much less clearly identifiable until the showroom-halls of piano manufacturers such as Pleyel, Erard, or Herz became the salons of choice for the performance of sonata, quartet, or quintet. But various constraints—including decrees limiting concerts so as not to interfere with the activities of the emerging light opera theaters (known as *théâtres lyriques*) and the levying of the "poor tax" on gross concert receipts—would come to burden the concert, which had become a fact of social life. The difference between "private" and "public" space regarding the proper place for chamber music gatherings began to erode. If indeed, as noted, amateur performers became less numerous after 1830, many professionals in turn held chamber music sessions in their homes, occasionally attracting an audience just as significant as if they had rented a hall. Moreover, the various private venues delineated distinct aesthetic trends: at the regular performances given by the contrabass player Gouffé between 1836 and 1874, the music of Onslow and Blanc was heard; those of the violinist Eugène Sauzay presented composers of the eighteenth century, including concertos by Mozart; and the chamber music séances of the pianist Wilhelmine Szarvady, which began in 1871, included works of Schumann and Brahms.

However, the performance of chamber music was increasingly subject to the same process of ritualization as was symphonic music: it centered chiefly on the works of Beethoven, who was the object of what Leo Schrade calls "a French religion."[4] The designation of a particular place for chamber music, the approbation of an audience that remained aristocratic, and the seasonal nature of the concerts (each organization that presented quartets gave an average of six performances during the winter months) were all factors favorable to the establishment of new ensembles. A case in point is Delphin Alard's quartet, founded in 1835: it took as its model the concerts of the Paris Conservatoire that had been established in 1828 to give a perfect performance of Beethoven's symphonies, in addition to selected works of chamber music.[5] This evolution in the socioartistic context would bring with it transformations in the technique of instrumental ensembles. Following a relative dearth of string instruments during the 1840s, the great Italian instruments were modernized in Paris, resulting in a bigger and better-balanced quartet sound.[6] The extensive refinement of wind instruments during this period completely redefined their place in chamber music. Throughout the course of the century, whether with or without piano, the winds were destined to take part in engaging scores such as the twenty-four quintets of Antonin Reicha, Opp. 88, 91, 99, and 100 (published between 1817 and 1820), the Quintet, Op.

81, by George Onslow, (1852), the Quintet of Paul Taffanel (1878), or the Octet, Op. 20 (composed in 1890) by Sylvio Lazzari.[7]

The Piano Trio: A Predominant Genre

Before 1850, people for whom the quartet and quintet were the essence of instrumental music regarded the piano as detrimental to "pure" music. Unlike the making of stringed instruments, which remained the work of artisans, piano manufacture benefited from the rise of industrialization. This instrument, adapted to the bourgeois domicile of which it became a symbol, underwent spectacular expansion. From 1830 on, through its capacity both to make its players seem brilliant and to provide diversity in a concert program, the piano established itself as the frequent partner of the strings. A single genre unquestionably dominated the creation of chamber music in France during the greater part of the century: the piano trio (piano, violin, and violoncello), which was frequently chosen to assure representation of instrumental genres in a mixed program, taking its place next to vocal music. The evenings of 1837 in which Franz Liszt, Chrétien Urhan, and Alexandre Batta played the Beethoven trios were an immense success and exercised long-lasting influence on French composers. George Onslow was first through the gate, with ten piano trios (Op. 3, Nos. 1–3 [1808], Op. 14, Nos. 1–3 [1818], Opp. 20, 26, and 27 [1823–34]), the last of which (Op. 83) would be published in 1853. Although the first six trios remain under the direct influence of Haydn and Beethoven, that in D Minor, Op. 20, is more personal in style. It is also one of the most homogeneous: all three instruments are treated equally. After Onslow, the most important composer in this genre is Henri Reber, whose first trio appeared in 1836–37. Reber's remaining six trios (Opp. 12 [1840], 16 [1862], 25 [1864], 30 [1872], 34 [1876], and 37 [1880]), the most remarkable of which is the "trio serenade," Op. 25, established his reputation in Parisian chamber music circles, wherein Achille Dien and Camille Saint-Saëns were among his notable performers. The two trios brought out by Edouard Lalo (1823–92) in 1851 and 1853 draw upon sources more German in style. The first of these (Op. 7) pales in comparison to the later B Minor Trio (no opus number), which is expressively powerful and elaborately polyphonic in texture. The sole work of chamber music Lalo composed after 1870 is his Third Trio, Op. 26 (composed in 1879, published in 1881). Lalo's friend and contemporary Théodore Gouvy (1819–98) devoted a great deal of creative energy to the piano trio during the first half of his career; his five trios (Opp. 8, 18, 19, 22, and 33) were published between 1852 and 1860. During the same period, Félicien David wrote three piano trios (1857) of somewhat pallid hue, which confirm the special interest the trio held for composers during the Second Empire. Indisputably, the most original contribution to the genre is the First Trio, Op. 18, by Camille Saint-Saëns (composed in 1863, published in 1867). Saint-Saëns's Second Trio, Op. 92

(1892), nearly equals this earlier success, whereas the two trios of Alexis de Castillon (Op. 4 [composed in 1865] and Op. 17 [composed in 1872]) represent a setback, despite their formal innovations.

Some of the more notable figures in nineteenth-century French music first broached chamber music by way of the piano trio, including César Franck (1843), Claude Debussy (composed in 1880), and Ernest Chausson (composed in 1881). For pianists such as Sigismond Thalberg (Op. 69), Henry Litolff (Opp. 47, 56, and 100), or Georges Mathias (Opp. 1, 15, 33, 36, 50, and 60), the piano trio was the sole genre of chamber music to which they would contribute. It was also the only form cultivated by Charles-Valentin Alkan (Op. 30), except for the duo sonata. César Franck chose to designate as his *opus primum* the three trios published in 1843. It is noteworthy that each of these works follows a different compositional scheme while employing cyclic elements, and that the piano is the object of remarkably diversified treatment. His Fourth Trio, Op. 2, dedicated to Liszt, is conceived as a single movement, the architecture of which derives from a single theme (Example 7.1). The *concertante* nature of Franck's trios is a characteristic found in other works written during the same period. In this regard, however, his trios scarcely manifest the distinct influence of Hummel evident in other forms of chamber music, such as the Sextets of Henri Bertini (Opp. 79, 85, 90, 114, 124, and 172); the Quintets (Opp. 70 and 76), Sextet (Op. 77*bis*), and Septet (Op. 79) of George Onslow; the chamber music of Frédéric Kalkbrenner (1788–1849); and that of Louise Farrenc (1804–75), who in 1830 had given the second performance of Hummel's *Septuor militaire* in the presence of the composer. Mention of Louise Farrenc, in whose work the piano is omnipresent, brings up the fact that a number of pianists who performed chamber music in Paris were women—among them Thérèse Wartel, Louise Mattmann, Aglae Massart, Ernestine Chabouillé Saint-Phal, and Charlotte Tardieu de Malleville.

EXAMPLE 7.1.   César Franck, Piano Trio No. 4, Op. 2, main theme.

During the July Monarchy the nature of the chamber music concert began to evolve. The human voice was incorporated into the world of chamber music, thanks to the discovery of Schubert lieder and the advent of the *mélodie française,* and also owing to the performance of certain *concertante* works with effectively restricted forces (e.g., the orchestra being reduced to a string quartet or quintet). It was this broadened notion of "ensemble music" that prompted D. F. E. Auber, himself the composer of several quartets, to inaugurate a class in *musique d'ensemble* at the Conservatoire in 1848. The same concept explains the Société Nationale de

Musique. Founded in 1871, it was almost as much an organization of composers seeking to have their works played as it was a society of performing musicians. All of these factors account for the diversity of the groups
that, following the example of Baillot's quartet, were formed beginning
in the 1830s: the quartet of the Tilmont brothers (1833), dedicated to Beethoven and to contemporary compositions; that of Delphin Alard (1835),
which introduced the Mozart quintets and Haydn trios; the Dancla brothers' quartet (1838), focusing on the work of its first violinist, Charles Dancla; the ensemble of Jean-Pierre Maurin and Alexandre Chevillard (1851),
devoted exclusively to the late quartets of Beethoven; that of Jules Armingaud and Edouard Lalo (1856), which explored the music of Schubert
and Mendelssohn; and Charles Lamoureaux's quartet (1860), which
sought to make the classics accessible to everyone through popular concerts.[8] These quartets would remain active through 1870, occasionally
transformed into larger ensembles. During the last third of the nineteenth
century other groups would rise to prominence, such as the Nouvelle Société de Musique de Chambre, founded by Antoine Taudou (1873); Paul
Taffanel's Société de Musique de Chambre pour Instruments à Vent
(1879); the quartet of Armand Parent (1890); that of Lucien Capet (1893);
and the Société Moderne des Instruments à Vent, established by the
flutists Louis Fleury and George Barrère (1895).[9] Meanwhile, in Brussels
in 1889 the violinist Eugène Ysaÿe founded a quartet whose brilliant
championing of new music was considerably influential in France as well
as in Belgium.[10]

An Ideal Genre: The String Quartet

In France the string quartet, from those of Cherubini to the single example by Debussy, is certainly the form that takes on greatest significance.
The entire concept of chamber music gravitates around it, even as that
concept evolves. That quartet writing became progressively rarer after the
eighteenth century is due to a number of causes, among which the one traditionally invoked—the reluctance of composers to approach a form
raised to perfection during the Classic era and enlarged in an imprescrib-
able manner by Beethoven—is not the chief reason. If it were necessary
to characterize the string quartets and quintets written in France between
1800 and 1870, one could say that they result from the will to assimilate
Classical models, in the sense of a reevaluation of writing. It was only after
1870 that, thanks especially to the cyclic procedures applied by Franck and
his pupils, the string quartet was renovated in foundation as well as form,
with Beethoven as the model. Before 1870 the opera house set its mark
upon the French quartet; those of Dancla, the five quartets of Auguste
Morel (1809–80), the works of Pamphile Aimon (1779–1866), and others
as well are cases in point. One detects just as much the influence of the
ballad or popular song in such works.

This interpenetration of vocal and instrumental styles, so important to the art of a Chopin or a Liszt, has been little studied with regard to the string quartet. Is this perhaps a consequence of the moralizing artistic judgment that sets the vocal domain, which is deemed corrupted by Italianism, in opposition to the instrumental domain, the realm of "serious" or "learned" music, just as critics dub it? In reality these domains are not antipodal. Much to the contrary, they are linked by an interactive network of references, above all during the first half of the nineteenth century, when the first violin was still the keystone of the polyphonic structure elaborated by the four voices. Thus Fétis compared the "principal" role of the first violin in the quartet to that played by Mombelli in the sextet of *Cenerentola* or that of Malibran in the first-act finale of *La gazza ladra* by Rossini.[11] This operatic influence on instrumental music and on the string quartet in particular is underscored by the fact that the majority of celebrated quartet players held jobs in the orchestra pit.

One could take the view that schematically, string quartet writing in France indicates two distinct tendencies, especially prior to 1870. The one corresponds to a melodic conception of the quartet (Dancla, Blanc), the other to a clearly more polyphonic conception that goes hand in hand with studied formal refinement (L. Kreutzer, Lalo, Castillon). It is the latter tendency that was favored after 1870.

The considerable work of George Onslow has too long fallen victim to the reductionist notion that it is all up with a Romanticism which is wonderful in ways other than being a fracas of disputatious proclamations. Onslow's production reached its peak during the July Monarchy because it was so much in accord with the bourgeois *juste-milieu*. His quartets and quintets promulgate an aesthetic of conciliation, the acceptance of which was abetted by the widespread playing in France before 1850 of quartets and quintets by Joseph Mayseder, Alexandre Fesca, and especially, Louis Spohr. The quartets, quintets, and octet of Felix Mendelssohn would follow this vein, exercising in their course an important aesthetic influence.

All of these considerations lead up to the question of who composed and who played string quartets and quintets. Having become, with few exceptions, the appanage of professional musicians after 1830, the string quartet was above all considered the touchstone of musical composition. The advisory regulations of the Conservatoire's coveted Prix de Rome provided that each recipient would write a string quartet during his residency at the Villa Medici. Ferdinand Hérold (1812), Ambroise Thomas (1832), Antoine Elwart (1834), Georges Bousquet (1838) and Léon Gastinel (1846) are among those who conscientiously performed this academic duty. In addition, the Société des Compositeurs de Musique, founded in 1862, established an annual composition competition for which the requirement was to write of work of chamber music (the remarkable Piano Quartet, Op. 10, and the Trio, Op. 19, by Léon Boëllmann [1862–97], for example, were prize winners). On many occasions, the stake of the competition was a string quartet. It is also interesting to note that it would be past masters of musical drama, such as Fromental Halévy or Henri Berton, who influenced Charles Dancla and Adolphe Blanc, and that Victor Massé was the mentor of Alexis de Castillon. It is easier to understand that a composer such as Reicha, by the very nature of his instruction, would turn his numerous pupils in the direction of instrumental music. Of these, Scipion Rousselot and Henri Reber are not the best known. Rather, it is the very academic Antoine Elwart, the author of several paltry quartets, who initiated into the profession such different and gifted musicians as Georges Bousquet and Théodore Gouvy—whereas the two most aesthetically progressive musicians of the period, Léon Kreutzer and Edouard Lalo, were to a great extent self-taught.

The nature of a composer's education is, to be sure, hardly a criterion for classification; still, it is important to take into account the quartet composers' diverse modes of apprenticeship when analyzing the repertoire. Two categories may be distinguished. The first consists of string players, chiefly violinists: Charles Dancla (1817–1907), Georges Bousquet (1818–54), Edouard Lalo (1823–92), Adolphe Blanc (1828–85), and the cellist Scipion Rousselot (1804–?). The second category comprises composers who did not play stringed instruments, for whom the piano constituted, to a greater or lesser extent, their compositional medium: Henri Reber (1807–80), Félicien David (1810–76), Léon Kreutzer (1817–68), Theodore Gouvy (1819–98), César Franck (1822–90), Camille Saint-Saëns (1835–1921), Alexis de Castillon (1838–73), Gabriel Fauré (1845–1924), Benjamin Godard (1849–95), Vincent d'Indy (1851–1931), Ernest Chausson (1855–99), Claude Debussy (1862–1918), Louis Vierne (1870–1937), and others. All of these names, which are among the most representative of those who have contributed to the history of the French string quartet, designate in other respects careers of significantly diverse profile.

Luigi Cherubini and George Onslow

The typology of the French string quartet as a musical composition takes into account the stylistic and technical particularities of the ensemble for which the composer's work is intended. The first example one might cite in this regard is the six quartets of Luigi Cherubini (1760–1842), which are the fruit of a rigorous collaboration between the composer and the players whom he had at his disposal—in this case, Baillot and his partners.[12] French publishers entered into association with their German counterparts to copublish works such as string quartets, the diffusion of which would be limited.[13]

It is revealing that Cherubini wrote his first string quartet the same year that Pierre Baillot established his chamber music series in 1814. He was to lead the premieres of Cherubini's first six quartets (the first three of which were dedicated to Baillot), as follows: the First Quartet was heard on 26 December 1814; the Second (composed in 1829) on 27 December

1834; the Third (1834) on 14 February 1835; the Fourth (1834–35), 21 February 1835; the Fifth (1835), 19 March 1836; the Sixth (1835–37) was probably played only in private. This important body of works, to which we must add a string quintet (1837), is inscribed, as it were, in the margin of the German quartet tradition. But the three quartets of Juan Crisostomo Arriaga (1806–26), written in 1824, return to that tradition with a vengeance; the exceptional fullness of their writing makes them direct descendants of Beethoven's Opus 18. Thus, while it is clear that the quartets of Cherubini bear traces of the *concertante* quartet and *quatuor brilliant* in the manner of Viotti, whereby the first violin predominates and stylistic features culled from opera are apparent, it is equally certain that these works are atypical, and in France, at least, their influence would be limited. Yet although Cherubini's quartets are marked by the general characteristics just noted, each one of them has its own character. Cherubini's personality reveals itself in the slightly arid complexity of his polyphonic writing, in the studied elegance of the instrumental coloration, in the motivic work that extends to all four voices, and in the chromaticism of the inner parts. Cherubini adopts frequently subtle cyclic procedures down to his sixth and last quartet: in that work the finale cites the beginning of the three preceding movements, as though the composer were just about to put down his pen, and then cast a look behind himself (Example 7.2).

Baillot and his partners plied their bows as well for the dominating figure in French chamber music during the first half of the nineteenth century, George Onslow (1784–1853), who was performed much more often than Cherubini, particularly in Germany. Onslow had a singular career; fortunately, he did not have to make a living from his art. He spent summers in a château in Auvergne and came to Paris for the winter, the season in which he introduced the new works he had just written. Their dedications faithfully reflect the milieu to whom Onslow addressed himself in order to be played.[14] Onslow's oeuvre consists principally of thirty-six string quartets composed between 1811 and 1846, along with thirty-four string quintets written during the same period. The labor of giving his work greater depth is apparent from the fact that after Op. 47, each quartet was assigned an individual opus number, whereas the preceding ones were published in groups of three. This change in modus operandi took place after an interruption of fifteen years (1817 to 1832), during which Onslow discovered the work of Beethoven, and particularly the late quartets. Onslow was thus to write his own last quartets (Opp. 47–50, 52–56, and 62–69) under the ascendancy of the simultaneous attraction and repulsion that the late works of the German master exercised upon him. Nevertheless, Onslow's first quartets present remarkable strokes of invention (see Example 7.3).

Onslow's quintets were conceived more under the influence of Boccherini's than of Mozart's; the latter became familiar in France only relatively late (they were regularly played by the Société Alard et Franchomme beginning in 1838).[15] Boccherini's works formed the foun-

EXAMPLE 7.2.   Luigi Cherubini, String Quartet No. 6, finale, mm. 92–121.

dation of Baillot's quintet repertoire, and the ensemble he led would also perform some of those by Onslow.[16] However interesting Onslow's evolution may be in the domain of the string quartet, it nevertheless seems less richly diverse than his development in the string quintet, the genre in which Onslow, escaping from the influence of Haydn and Beethoven, showed himself to be more audacious. A notable case in point is Quintet No. 15 in C Minor, Op. 38, called "de la balle" ("of the bullet"), in which

EXAMPLE 7.3.   George Onslow, String Quartet No. 7, Op. 9, No. 1, Minuetto, mm. 1–12.

the minuet, Andante, and finale were inspired by the consequences of a hunting accident suffered by Onslow in 1829. The forces used in the quintets vary. Apart from Opp. 2, 78, and 80, which were originally planned with two violas, the quintets were written for two violins, viola, and two cellos (an additional viola part was provided to replace the first cello); in Opp. 32 through 35, the second cello can be replaced by a double bass.

Almost two-thirds of the string quartets are dedicated to amateurs active in Paris, particularly before 1830, as against only a third of the string quintets. On the other hand, all the principal representatives of the chamber music movement in Paris before 1850 received the dedication of a quartet or a quintet by Onslow—which is indicative of just how frequently the works of Onslow were seen on players' music stands before 1850. Such frequency diminished quickly after the composer's death.

Quartets by Quartet Players

Pierre Baillot, whose example meant so much in the development of chamber music in France, left behind three quartets. He also received the homage of string quartets composed both by his students (e.g., the six quartets, Op. 12 [1821], by Auguste Blondeau) and by admirers such as the cellist Scipion Rousselot, who around 1830 published three quartets, Op. 10, the second of which is undoubtedly the most successful. Nevertheless, it is his Fourth Quartet in B♭ Major, Op. 25, published in 1834, that holds one's attention. It is dedicated to the cellist of the Tilmant Quartet, Alexandre Tilmant.

Trained by Baillot at the Conservatoire where he himself would teach beginning in 1855, Charles Dancla, initially a member of the quartet founded by Alard and Chevillard in 1837, established his own group the same year, in which he was the first violinist alongside his brothers Leopold, violist, and Arnaud, cellist. Amid a great quantity of material for violin, Dancla would also publish fourteen string quartets, most of which he himself performed for the first time. The Quartet No. 1 in F♯ Minor, Op. 5, appeared in 1839; the fourteenth and last, in D Major, Op. 195, in . . . 1900! The dedications of these quartets tell us of his aesthetic parameters. Number 2 in E♭ Major, Op. 7 (1840), is dedicated to Baillot; No. 6, Op. 56 (1855), to Onslow; the Ninth, Op. 101 (1862), is dedicated to Halévy; and the Tenth, Op. 113, to Ambroise Thomas. The Sixth Quartet owes its passing success to an *adagio* entitled "Prayer," the inspiration for which is of autobiographical origin. Léon Kreutzer, whom we will encounter later as a quartet composer, evaluated that work quite well: after having underscored the rigorous Classicism in the first movement of the Sixth Quartet, Kreutzer noted that "it recalls a bit the peculiar style of Onslow, which is to say that one finds more in it of broadly developed inspirations than of minutely sculpted details." Regarding the finale, in which he justifiably draws attention to a certain prolixity, Kreutzer "still finds a trace of the preference that Mr. Dancla so naturally shows for the first violin part, to the occasional detriment of the other three parts."[17]

Not by chance has the name of Felix Mendelssohn already come up: he was himself a Parisian in 1816, 1825, and 1832, and was connected with Baillot, who was the first in Paris to play the Octet, Op. 20, and also gave the premiere of the A minor Quartet, Op. 13. Up through the end of the nineteenth century, Mendelssohn would exert a decided influence on French composers (as, for example, in the scherzo of César Franck's String Quartet). Into this Mendelssohnian orbit came Georges Bousquet, who had won the Prix de Rome in 1838. While in Italy Bousquet had written two quartets that remained unpublished; these are promising essays comparable to his Third Quartet in G Major, Op. 8, which was brought to the boards in both Leipzig and Berlin in June 1841 under the auspices of Mendelssohn himself, to whose memory the work is dedicated. Bousquet's

Third Quartet, although not published until 1852, holds an honorable place beside the three quartets, Op. 44 (1838), of his German colleague. Bousquet was also the author of two string quintets (composed in 1842 and 1852).

The violist of the Armingaud Quartet, which popularized the works of Mendelssohn and Schubert, was Edouard Lalo. In 1856 he began work on his unique String Quartet in E♭ Major, Op. 19 (Op. 45 in its definitive version of 1884); this work unquestionably marks a significant moment in the history of the genre in France. Lalo's score, concise and animated with an intense rhythmic life, includes a slow movement whose density and harmonic daring baffled listeners at its first public hearing in 1859 (see Example 7.4).

EXAMPLE 7.4.   Edouard Lalo, String Quartet in E♭ Major, Op. 45, mvt. 2, mm. 1–18.

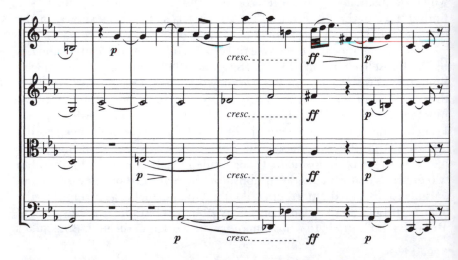

Lalo's course tends toward the unique masterpiece that is already modern in design, in that it raises critical questions of musical language, if not of form. Quite opposite was the aesthetic orientation of the violinist Adolphe Blanc, who seems much more conservative. This composer's instrumental oeuvre is the most important and the most varied after Onslow's, but it has scarcely managed to survive its author. If the substance of this abundant corpus seems rather thin to us today, one must recognize that Blanc's bountiful work exerted a certain attraction until after 1870, an appeal explained by its melodious character. It is, in effect, steeped in stereotypical formulas more or less directly borrowed from the Classical Viennese school, a repertoire the public of the Second Empire had already assimilated. But this type of epigonic, melodic writing had at least the merit of making the string quartet and quintet accessible to players of modest talent. Encouraged by Rossini, Blanc appeared to the public to be the most worthy representative of the Classicism that he perpetuated. The praise accorded Blanc by the Marquis of Queux de Saint-Hilaire, an amateur violinist, in his *Lettre sur la musique de chambre* (Letter concerning chamber music) of 1870 has the flavor of a reactionary manifesto, at precisely the moment when Saint-Saëns and Castillon were getting ready to found the Société Nationale de Musique, which would provide new impetus for instrumental music. To many of his contemporaries, Blanc seemed to be the successor to Onslow. He left four string quartets published between 1856 and 1877 (Opp. 16, 27, 38, and 53), in which the first violin remains the "singer"; three string trios (Opp. 25, 41, and 48); four quintets with string bass (Opp. 21, 22, 36 and 40*bis*); three quintets with two violas (Opp. 15, 19, and 29); and a number of works in which the strings are joined by piano.

String Quartets by Pianists

The figure of Henri Reber brings us in touch with those quartet composers who were not string players and who found in the midst of different artistic foyers a stimulant for their creativity. Coming from a family of Lorraine industrialists, Reber, who was "forgotten by the eighteenth century in the nineteenth,"[18] was known above all during his lifetime for his piano trios. Archaism is one of the most attractive characteristics of this music, which, beyond Viennese models, reflects Couperin, Rameau, and even modal plainchant. Although Reber "dreaded almost with terror the caprices and infidelity of performers,"[19] he found docile interpreters of his wishes in the violinist Eugène Sauzay (1809–1901, son-in-law of Baillot) and his partners. Artists who were sensitive to ancient music, such as the painter Ingres and the composer Alexandre Boëly (1785–1858), frequented the salon of Sauzay. It is perhaps there that Boëly's four string quartets (Opp. 27–30) were first tried out; although published posthumously in 1859, their composition dates from about 1825.[20] These pieces are less striking than Boëly's three trios for violin, viola, and cello (Op. 5, composed in 1808).

Reber's Grand Quartet in B♭ Major, Op. 4, dedicated to François Habeneck, dates from 1832, as does his "Little" Quartet in D♭ Major, Op. 5. These two works present formal and thematic singularities that rupture the academicism which seems to promise a "white" and denuded manner of writing. Opus 4 has no fewer than five movements—three Allegros between which are intercalated an Andante and an Adagio. The Op. 5 quartet, however, has only two movements: an Andante poco adagio and an Allegretto. The Andante is based on the popular song "Vergiß mein nicht" ("Do Not Forget Me"), just as Mendelssohn's A Minor Quartet, Op. 13, takes a part of its thematic material from his Op. 9 lied "Frage" ("Ist es wahr? . . .") ("Question," "Is it true? . . ."). The correspondence between the two works is all the more pertinent because in 1832 Baillot and Sauzay gave the first presentation of the Mendelssohn in Paris, the same year Reber was working on his quartets. Reber's [Third] Quartet in A Major, of grand proportions, seems still more interesting than the two preceding ones. The first version, which dates back to the period of Opp. 4 and 5, was written for string quartet with double bass ad libitum. Several years later Reber reworked the score and suppressed the bass. The movement plan—a very well developed Adagio, an Allegro twice interrupted by an Allegretto, a Larghetto, and an Agitato–Andante sostenuto—is far removed from the Classical scheme. Perhaps this disposition corresponds to philosophical intentions that remain secret; in any case, the tumultuous élan of the last movement interrupts itself to cite in plainchant the theme of the supplication "Parce Domine," which in the Catholic liturgy is sung after the benediction of the Blessed Sacrament.

It was not during the period when Félician David could have found Reber, one of his masters, in the community of the Saint-Simonians,[21] but rather at the end of his life that David wrote four string quartets of Classical bent, and very melodic in their writing. Only the First Quartet in F Minor was published during the composer's lifetime, in 1868. The other three—the Second in A Major, the Third in D Minor, and the Fourth in E Minor, of which only the first Allegro was finished—remained in manuscript for a long time.[22] Despite their somewhat uniform hue, these quartets are of good workmanship, although they reveal no trace of the orientalism that won David his youthful success for the ode-symphony *Le désert* (The desert) of 1844. David's twenty-four string quintets entitled "Les saisons" (The seasons, 1845–46), need only be mentioned for the record.

The personality of Léon Kreutzer stands out in altogether different relief, even though he is forgotten today. Independent and not very sociable, Kreutzer paid dearly for his disdain of success. A virtuoso pianist, he gave free rein to an originality that, sometimes bordering upon strangeness, gradually put him on the margin of the musical mainstream. He possessed a fortune that not only permitted him from time to time to give concerts of his music before a very select audience but also enabled him to publish those of his works that were in essence the least accessible to the public, such as his eight string quartets, which took more than twenty years to compose.[23] The First Quartet in D Major, Op. 15, dedicated to Charles Dancla, was first played in Paris in February 1841 by the quartet of the brothers Franco Mendès, a group Kreutzer himself helped launch; the Second Quartet in F Major is dedicated to Gouffé. The Third, in A Minor, written for Joseph d'Ortigue, stands out for the special ordering of its four parts: the first Andante is a fugato that is interrupted by a Presto before resuming its own course; subsequently this Andante reappears in the final Presto. In the Fourth Quartet in G Major, dedicated to Hector Berlioz, four parts are linked together, in the inner portion of which Kreutzer deploys the resources of variation technique. The Sixth Quartet in C Major approaches the strangeness mentioned above, in that it poses an enigma. On the title page of the manuscript the composer has written in Greek letters the work *sphinx*. In the first and the fourth parts of the quartet, he anticipates later collage procedures by introducing ancient musical pieces: the pavane "Belle qui tiens ma vie" (Thou beauty who holds my life) from Thoinot Arbeau's *Orchésographie* of 1588, and then the 1759 popular song "Dans les gardes françaises" (In the French guards). The Largo integrates into its course a theme of Mendelssohn *al rovesco*—that is to say, "inside-out," and the finale weaves variations on a lullaby that was in everyone's memory. The Sixth Quartet is certainly original. But it is musically less convincing than the Third and Fourth, those rare examples of the French quartet freely conceived in the wake of the late Beethoven quartets, which Kreutzer particularly admired. His eighth and last quartet (1867), in four movements, is the shortest of all (the Largo has only nineteen measures). In this instance the author anticipates aleatoric technique, in that he indicates passages in the scherzo that could be suppressed "in case the piece is judged to be too long"—a precaution that resembles a joke, given the conciseness of the work. The Fifth and Seventh Quartets have not been mentioned, and for good reason: they do not exist as such. But curiously, two different quartets have the number 2, namely, the Op. 15 already mentioned and another quartet in A minor (1864), a beautiful piece ending with a *moto perpetuo vivace*. Finally, the Quartet in G Minor (composed in 1865) has no number whatever. Its plan is most complex: the Adagio, which comes from Kreutzer's Second Symphony in F Minor, reappears in the finale.

Théodore Gouvy, whose background was half French and half German, represents a link between the German musical milieus where his work was favorably received, and the Germanizing milieu of the French capital, where chamber music was held in great honor and was served by such musicians as Lalo, who was one of Gouvy's friends. Of the eleven quartets Gouvy penned (six have remained in manuscript), the first two, grouped under the opus number 16, were published in 1858 by Richault. But the following three—Op. 56, Nos. 1 and 2, and Op. 68—although published much later, exhibit no marked evolution in comparison to Op.

16, save perhaps for a certain prolixity. These works, the fruit of solid craftsmanship, do not do much for the tradition from which they came. The integrity with which the content is joined to the form, plus the moderate expressivity of the thematic material, allied these quartets with the academicism of the Leipzig school inaugurated by Mendelssohn. Preferable, perhaps, is the C Major Quartet, Op. 16, No. 2, in which the Andantino scherzando functions simultaneously as slow movement and scherzo, an arrangement to be encountered again in the Quartet Op. 3, No. 1, of Alexis de Castillon.

The most devoted of amateurs, Castillon took the risk of trying to begin where Beethoven had left off, in two quartets that he thought to publish as his Op. 3. But such an undertaking was beyond the resources of the young musician, who lacked technical mastery. The upshot was that when the two works came to be engraved in 1867, Castillon declined to allow the appearance of the Second Quartet in F Minor, which was even more ambitious than the First. Only the Cavatina from that work had the honor of being published in 1869. My reconstruction of both the overall plan and the entire scherzo of this Second Quartet reveals that Castillon conceived his work under direct inspiration of Beethoven's Quartets in B♭, Op. 130, and C♯ Minor, Op. 131. The contrition of the composer came to bear just as heavily on the First Quartet, which, although primitive in form, had a well-developed finale; at the last moment, however, Castillon replaced it with a rapid fugato of some sixty bars' duration. The composer was much more fortunate in those works that he placed under the direct ascendancy of Robert Schumann: the Piano Quintet, Op. 1 (composed in 1863–64), and above all the Piano Quartet, Op. 7, a piece whose formal scheme follows that of Schumann's Op. 47, but into which Castillon channeled generous personal invention, both in the nature of the thematic material and in the plan of the development.

Attracted all his life to the most demanding of musical forms, Castillon encountered the string quartet in one of the most worldly milieus there was: the Cercle de l'Union Artistique, also called the Cercle des Mirlitons (Circle of the Reed Pipes, or "Kazoos"), where every week the quartet societies enumerated above came to play according to schedule. It was, moreover, to Henri Poencet, who became cellist of the Lamoureux Quartet in 1867, that Castillon dedicated his Quartet, Op. 3.

After 1870

As we have clearly seen, the movement favoring chamber music in France was practically uninterrupted from the eighteenth century on, despite long-standing claims that the "renewal" of the movement did not really begin until after 1870. One wonders all the more why a writer on music as well grounded as Romain Rolland lent credence to this idea.[24] In reality, the feeling that a renewal (although hardly spontaneous, as we have seen) emerged only after 1870 can be explained by the crisis of conscience into which losing the Franco-Prussian War had thrown the French nation. Even while perpetuating the structures of the Ancien Régime, this society was about to give in to a desire for revenge as much as to a willingness for expiation, the latter fed by a counterrevolutionary current that was all the stronger because it was obliged henceforth to combat the ideals of the Third Republic. Since the *théâtre lyrique* had previously been the place for both the consecration of the composer and the triumph of the bourgeoisie, a great effort was made by the bourgeoisie to popularize music with the goal of making the working classes benefit from the moralizing virtues supposedly inherent in the art. After 1870, even if society had not fundamentally changed, intellectual attitudes toward art evolved. Elitist tendencies were affirmed; it was no longer considered necessary that music be a means of edifying the working masses. The moral value of music now consisted, through the elaboration of highly subtilized works, in ransoming the art from the disgrace into which it had supposedly fallen during the preceding period. Aestheticization of the grand forms of instrumental music thus became the stake of an artistic idealism that would be embodied in the person of César Franck. It must be noted, however, that after 1870 the French musicians who gave impetus to this feigned renewal of instrumental music are those who, during the Second Empire, declared as did Edouard Lalo that their "true musical native country" was Germany.[25] And this "French" renewal would essentially rely on formal models and subjects of inspiration that were German: it consecrates Beethoven as the absolute aesthetic touchstone and finds in the work of Richard Wagner a source of expressive and harmonic enrichment.

Three works would come to be esteemed as archetypes: the Piano Quintet (1879), the Violin Sonata (1886), and the String Quartet (1889) of César Franck. But it must be observed that before these works imposed themselves on the spirits of two generations of musicians, certain among them who either did not come under the influence of Franck (e.g., Gabriel Fauré) or who showed themselves hostile to it (Camille Saint-Saëns) had endowed the realm of chamber music with various works, to which we shall return presently.

The Piano Quintet

The history of the piano quintet in France began with the publication of Luigi Boccherini's twelve quintets, Opp. 56 and 57, "dedicated to the French nation," in 1797 and 1799. However, these remarkable compositions are not situated in the same aesthetic line as the sort of piano quintet that would prove attractive to composers through the intermediation of the Schubert "Trout" Quintet and the Schumann Piano Quintet, both of which were played early on in France.[26] Yet there is no trace of either work in the Piano Quintet, Op. 15, of Camille Saint-Saëns, which completely breaks with the quintets in *concertante* style (with double bass) written by Frédéric Kalkbrenner (Op. 30, 1817) or Louise Farrenc (Op. 30, 1842, and Op. 31, 1844–45). Several stylistic traits of Saint-Saëns's score engage one's attention over and above the Mendelssohnian character of the scherzo (third movement). A good example is the slow emergence of the expressive theme in the Allegro assai, ma tranquillo of the finale, which, after a fugato of sixty measures played only by the quartet, is combined with the theme of this fugato.

Undoubtedly the friendship between Saint-Saëns and Castillon influenced Castillon to undertake a piano quintet as his *opus primum* (composed in 1863–64, published in 1865). As we have seen, in working on his string quartets Castillon forced himself to become reengaged with grand Beethovenian form. But in this case he took the Schumann Quintet as a model. His technical clumsiness did not prevent him from finding some ingenious formal solutions: the theme of the Adagio becomes that of the finale, to which it is linked.[27] Moreover, the work as a whole is subject to a supple cyclic scheme. Whatever the merit of these quintets, they would be eclipsed by that of César Franck (composed in 1879), whose student Castillon had been. Little is known about the genesis of the Frank Quintet. The dramatic tension of its sonorous discourse, the monumentality of all three movements—(1) Molto moderato quasi lento–Allegro, (2) Lento con moto sentimento, and (3) Allegro non troppo ma con fuoco—plus the expressive antithesis of the tonalities (F minor–A minor–F major) in this major work of the chamber music repertoire have suggested an autobiographical origin that, however, is by no means proven. At the core of a form that is expansive yet rigorously worked out, the concerted writing for piano holds in check the power of highly chromaticized harmony that is indebted to Liszt. The quintet has been the object of close analysis, notably on the part of Vincent d'Indy.[28] Its cyclic theme is characteristic (see Example 7.5).

EXAMPLE 7.5.   César Franck, Piano Quintet, mvt. 1, cyclic theme.

p tenero ma non passione

The Franck Quintet (dedicated to Saint-Saëns, who gave the premiere on 17 January 1880) was to be of long-lasting influence, whether direct or indirect. Not only such students of the composer as Louis Vierne (Quintet in C Minor, Op. 42, composed in 1918) or Gabriel Pierné (Op. 41, composed in 1916–17), but other musicians as well, including Camille Chevillard (Op. 1, 1882), Charles-Marie Widor (two Quintets, Opp. 7 [composed in 1890] and 68 [1896]), Gabriel Fauré (First Quintet in D minor, Op. 89 [composed 1903–6]; Second Quintet in C Minor, Op. 115), and Florent Schmitt (composed in 1905–8) would give their best efforts to exploit the rapport between piano and string quartet. As for Ernest Chausson (1855–99), he took the original step of adding a principal violin to the quintet formed by piano and strings: the result was the atypical Concerto, Op. 21 (ca. 1889–91), which is neither a sextet nor a modern resurgence of the concerto grosso (as has been claimed).[29] If Chausson's Concerto, built in a cyclic fashion from a single three-note cell, follows directly in the path of the Franck Quintet, it is also steeped in the spirit of French Classical musicians, as evidenced by the Siciliano, the second of the work's four movements. A similar rarity is the Quintet in D Minor, Op. 8, for wind instruments (flute, oboe, clarinet, bassoon) and piano by Albéric Magnard (1894). Although in this work, as in the Chausson Concerto, all four movements are designated by French terms (*Sombre, Tendre, Léger,* and *Joyeux*), these indications are merely fashionable borrowings, as is the rustic accent of the thematic material, which underlines the French character of this music.

The Sonata for Violin and Piano

As in the case of the string quartet, the violin sonatas composed at the beginning of the nineteenth century (Viotti, Boëly, etc.) reveal a quite different aesthetic from those that would be written under the influence of César Franck. French violin sonatas from the first half of the century are neither numerous nor particularly significant; the opposite is true for cello sonatas (Alkan, Op. 48 [composed in 1857], Chopin, Op. 65 [composed in 1845–46], Lalo [no opus number, composed in 1871], Saint-Saëns, Op. 32 [composed in 1872], and Op. 123 [1903–5]). The designation "Grand Duo" attached to the violin sonatas of Alkan (1840) and Lalo (1855) suggests what these works owe to *concertante* style; Alkan's is far more interesting than Lalo's. Not until the Sonata for Violin in C Major, Op. 6 (composed in 1868, published in 1870) of Alexis de Castillon do we encounter an important beacon in the history of the modern French sonata. The prolixity of the work is compensated for by the originality of its tonal plan (as d'Indy emphasizes)[30]—it borrows from modality in the slow movement—and also by original melodic and rhythmic invention. But despite its quality, this work was entirely eclipsed by the First Sonata in A major, Op. 13, of Gabriel Fauré (composed in 1875–76), which reconciles Romanticism and Classicism through masterly equilibrium. The four movements of this sonata possess ideal formal elegance equaled by grand expressive force. Fauré would be just as successful in his Second Sonata in E Minor, Op. 108 (composed in 1916).

During the summer of 1886 César Franck, a musician dedicated to stylistic synthesis, drafted his Sonata for Piano and Violin in A major; he dedicated the work to Eugène Ysaÿe, who played it at the Cercle Artistique in Brussels on 16 December 1886. The intense musicality of the A Major Sonata cannot be reduced merely to the cyclic principle that shapes its four parts—Allegretto ben moderato, Allegro, Recitativo–fantasia / Ben moderato, Allegro poco mosso. The interval of a third, heard in the first measure of the first movement (Example 7.6), constitutes the generative cell of an original structure that serves a broad tonal coherence. The rapport between the violin, treated melodiously as if it were the human voice, and the piano, which constitutes the sonorous foundation of the work, defines in exemplary fashion a model of instrumental dialectic. The numerous analyses to which the work has given rise only confirm the extent to which Franck's use of the cyclic principle, far from being a constraint, actually liberated the composer's musical invention.[31]

EXAMPLE 7.6.   Franck, Violin Sonata in A Major, mvt. 1, mm. 1–4 (violin).

Exceptional works require exceptional interpreters. Owing as much to the artistic merit of the violin sonata as to the passion Ysaÿe would devote to its defense, the genre was to be enriched by scores of vast proportions dedicated to the great violinist. All are governed by the cyclic principle: the Sonata, Op. 24, of Sylvio Lazzari (composed in 1892, published in 1898); the nostalgic work by Guillaume Lekeu (1892); the Sonata, Op. 13, of Albéric Magnard (1902), which is orchestral in conception; the Sonata of Gustave Samazeuilh (1903); that of Louis Vierne (1906); and the First Sonata by Guy Ropartz, in which the generating theme is a Breton popular song (1907). A young violinist, Jacques Thibaud, who was also destined to pursue a career in chamber music with Alfred Cortot and Pablo Casals, received the dedication of the luminous Sonata, Op. 36, by Gabriel Pierné (1900), in which a supple cyclic form blends well with subtle rhythmic variations. Another violinist also devoted to chamber music, Armand Parent, would have dedicated to him the Sonata, Op. 59, of Vincent d'Indy (1903–4) as well as the first of two sonatas by Paul de Wailly (Op. 16, 1904). If the common denominator among these works is recourse to the cyclic principle, they are far from conforming to the same structural model. In addition, their tonal structure is more or less imbued with modality.

Other sonatas would emerge on the shores of the stream created by the Franckian school. One of the most notable of these is the Sonata in D minor, Op. 79 (1879–85), by Camille Saint-Saëns; the second theme of its initial Allegro was to become part of the famous "little phrase" in the Sonata of Vinteuil, a character in Marcel Proust's novel *À la recherche du temps perdu*. If Saint-Saëns regarded this First Sonata as a "concerted sonata," the Second Sonata, Op. 102, had for him the character of a "chamber sonata," subtle in its elaboration, with the first and the last movements constructed on the basis of Greek poetic meters.

The String Quartet

As we have seen, the attitude of composers toward the string quartet varied during the course of the century. Before 1850, the violinist-composers who were assiduous quartet players approached the genre by way of schemas furnished by Haydn and Mozart: the gesture of the composer, so to say, extends that of the interpreter. After 1850, influenced by the revelation of Beethoven's last works (among others), composers considered the string quartet the speculative genre par excellence, which could only be the fruit of long experience. Such experienced musicians as Camille Saint-Saëns and Gabriel Fauré were to be intimidated by the string quartet; whereas it was the "Fountain of Hippocrene" for Saint-Saëns, the string quartet would mark the end of an entire career for Fauré. In this respect it is significant to find Fauré choosing to make his last work a quartet and nourishing it with themes he wrote down during his youth. Otherwise, appropriating the piano enabled these two musicians to tame the form of the quartet (Saint-Saëns, Op. 41, 1875; Fauré, Piano Quartet No. 1 in C Minor, Op. 15 [1876], No. 2 in F Minor, Op. 45 [1886]). The apprehension Saint-Saëns and Fauré felt about venturing into the string quartet may be explained by the powerful influence upon them of a Classical heritage dominated by the emblematic role occupied by this most demanding of genres. It is understandable that Claude Debussy and later Maurice Ravel (1903), feeling much freer with respect to that heritage and being sensitive as well to the influences that had been rejuvenating musical language, chose, on the contrary, to station the string quartet as a founding compositional act in the course of their development.

For Franck, too, the string quartet represents the ultimate level of creative activity. It is customary to designate his String Quartet in D Major (1889–90) as the work that opens the modern period of the genre. However, the master was preceded by a young musician to whom he had given away his advice. Indeed, in 1888 Sylvio Lazzari had his Quartet in A Minor, Op. 17, played before the Société Nationale de Musique; beyond its historical importance, the piece turns out to be a major work as well. Hearing this quartet would have convinced Franck to begin his own. Not only does Lazzari's Quartet have a great richness of thematic elements, but its cyclic construction also seems justified more by expressive intentions than by formal imperatives (which would not always be the case in string quartets subsequently written by other students of Franck's, such as d'Indy). Accordingly, one can note that the end of the development in Lazzari's first movement (Molto agitato) contains an anticipatory citation of the broad and expressive theme of the second movement—a vast Andante, and the heart of the work, which is pervaded by an intense lyricism whose accents are new in France (Example 7.7).

As for the final rondo, separated from the Andante by a scherzo, it incorporates into its course recollections of the preceding movements, but they are transformed by the technique of variation. It remains surprising

EXAMPLE 7.7.   Sylvio Lazzari, String Quartet in A Minor, Op. 17, mvt. 2, mm. 1–14.

that the Quartet, Op. 17, of Lazzari does not occupy the significant place it should in the string quartet repertory, and that it has hitherto evoked only infrequent commentary.

Such, however, is not the case for the String Quartet in D Major of César Franck: as early as its first presentation at the Société Nationale de Musique, on 19 April 1890, the work gave rise to detailed analyses on the part of those who were going to work in this way, namely, d'Indy and Ropartz.[32] It is clear that in composing his own quartet (1889–90) according to principles of rigorous cyclic development—which, however, by no means constrain the expansion of an extremely dense polyphony, in the midst of which each instrument keeps its individuality—Franck inspired those who had forged their artistic ideal upon his teaching to follow the same path.

Of the quartet's four movements—Poco lento–Allegro, Scherzo, Larghetto, and Allegro molto—the first and last are the most original in form. Concerning the introduction of the quartet, which contains its cyclic theme (see Example 7.8), Vincent d'Indy observes that its form, essentially new and original, comprises two components of music, each living its own life and possessing a complete organism; they mutually penetrate each other without getting mixed up, thanks to a perfect disposition of their elements and their divisions.[33] The quartet's finale has drawn all commentators to remark upon the analogies it presents to the finale of Beethoven's Ninth Symphony. But beyond this allusion, Franck's concluding movement adopts the plan of a complex sonata form that effects the recapitulation of the work's constitutive elements.

EXAMPLE 7.8.   Franck, String Quartet in D Major, mvt. 1, mm. 1–3.

Vincent d'Indy, who embarked upon chamber-music composition with a Piano Quartet, Op. 7 (1878–88) and, notably, a very original Trio for Clarinet, Cello, and Piano, Op. 27 (1887), began his First Quartet in D Major, Op. 35, the year that his master, Franck, died. The work was premiered the following February (1891) in Brussels by the Ysaÿe Quartet. The generating motive that constitutes the first measures of the quartet engenders derivative elements from which the structure of the work is freely evolved ([1] *Lent et soutenu–Modérément animé;* [2] *Lent et calme;* [3] *Assez modéré–Assez vite;* [4] *Assez lent et librement déclamé–Vif et joyeusement animé*).

The physiognomy of the French string quartet was to be noticeably rejuvenated by the Quartet in G Minor of Claude Debussy (1862–1918), written in 1892. Once again, the duty of presenting the premiere fell to the Ysaÿe Quartet, which performed the work for the first time at the Société Nationale de Musique on 29 December 1893. That same year, these champions of new music premiered the First Quartet in G Minor of Guy Ropartz. They would in addition receive the dedication of the beautiful First Quartet in E♭, Op. 112 (1899) by Camille Saint-Saëns, the scherzo of which in particular is genuinely original.

In Debussy's Quartet, Op. 10 (his only composition to bear an opus number), the sonorous treatment is entirely novel; if the composer thereby looks toward the future, he remains largely a scion of the Franckian school as regards the work's formal organization. The quartet is subdivided thus: (1) *Animé et très décidé;* (2) *Assez vif et bien rythmé;* (3) *Andantino, doucement expressif;* (4) *Très modéré–Très mouvementé et avec passion.* It is said to be in G minor, but its generative theme, heard as a motto (as in the Franck Quartet), is conceived in the Phrygian mode (Example 7.9). The finale, through its recapitulative structure, confirms the quartet's connections to the Franckian aesthetic.

EXAMPLE 7.9.   Claude Debussy, String Quartet in G Minor, Op. 10, mvt. 1, opening theme.

The very end of the century would be marked by two scores—the Second Quartet, Op. 45, of Vincent d'Indy and the String Quartet, Op. 35, of Ernest Chausson—that demonstrate once again both the sprit of emulation animating the disciples of César Franck and their aspiration to mastery of a form that, for them, practically did not exist except as it was linked to Beethoven.

D'Indy's Second Quartet in E major, Op. 45 (1897), which was first performed by the Parent Quartet in 1898, is much more rigorously subject to cyclic form than his First Quartet. The themes on which the four movements are based are derived from a four-note motive placed as an epigraph at the head of the work. This enigmatic motive has to be read in three different ways: in tenor clef, in alto clef, and in inverted bass clef (see Example 7.10). Many have sought its origin without finding it. But it is actually a motivic archetype well known to students of counterpoint. Moreover, these four notes constitute the head of the subject in J. S. Bach's Fugue in E major, BWV 878, from Book 2 of the *Well-Tempered Clavier,* and they were used even earlier by Josquin Desprez. Mozart, Beethoven, and

Méhul employed this formula as well.[34] That d'Indy chose these four notes as a foundation for his Second Quartet proves how much his headstrong art was rooted in the oldest of traditions. Overall, the Second is more concise than the First and follows a different movement plan as well: (1) *Lentement–Animé;* (2) *Très animé;* (3) *Très lent;* (4) *Lentement–Très vif.*

EXAMPLE 7.10.   Vincent d'Indy, String Quartet No. 2 in E Major, Op. 45, epigraph.

Even as d'Indy was working on the Second Quartet in 1897, Ernest Chausson drafted his Piano Quartet in A Major, Op. 30—a bright and energetic work that contrasts with the somber tension of his Concerto, Op. 21. Op. 30 is permeated by modality and a plenitude of admirable invention that would in turn effect a contrast to the String Quartet in C Minor, Op. 35, which Chausson undertook the next year. "I believe it is neither Franck nor d'Indy, nor Debussy, but I fear that it proceeds somewhat directly from Beethoven," wrote the composer on 12 July 1898 to the work's dedicatee, Mathieu Crickboom. Chausson's perspective was correct, although he died before finishing the quartet. Whereas the Piano Quartet, Op. 30, delineates a new orientation in the composer's aesthetics, the very dense web of the String Quartet does not yield to sonorous seduction. The austere rigor of the two movements of Op. 35 that were finished—(1) *Grave–modéré,* and (2) *Très calme* (the third movement, *Gaiement et pas trop vite,* was finished by Vincent d'Indy)—reveals, notwithstanding the genuine beauty of this music, to what extent the example of Beethoven carried musicians toward a pinnacle of unreasonable expectations that constrained them to a certain asceticism in their musical thought.

It would require the ingenuity of the young Maurice Ravel to dispel the inhibitions that weighed, sometimes heavily, upon the musical creativity of disciples of the Franckian school. To be convinced of this, one need only compare his Quartet in F Major (1902–3) to the vast Quartet in E Minor of Albéric Magnard, which dates from exactly the same time. Whereas Ravel succeeds with quasi-Mozartian ease in reconciling the rigor of Classicism in the two first movements (Allegro moderato; *Assez vif–Très rythmé*) to the rhapsodic freedom of the last two (*Très lent; Vif et agité*), Magnard, haunted by the figure of Beethoven, expands upon the monumentality characteristic of the post-Franckian string quartet. But paradoxically, whereas Ravel deploys the cyclic principle in a very personal and discreet manner, Magnard does not confer a single cyclic theme upon the four movements that constitute his quartet (*Animé, Sérénade, Chant funèbre, Danses*).

One must await the second half of the twentieth century for the French string quartet to take flight anew on the basis of entirely renovated aesthetics.

Notes

1. Jean Mongrédien, *La musique en France des lumières au romantisme, 1789–1830* (Paris, 1986).

2. Brigitte François-Sappey, "Pierre-Marie-François Baillot . . . par lui-meme," *Recherches* 18 (1978): 127–211.

3. Joël-Marie Fauquet, *Les sociétés de musique de chambre à Paris de la Restauration à 1870* (Paris, 1986).

4. Leo Schrade, *Beethoven in France: The Growth of an Idea* (New Haven, CT, 1942), 109.

5. Jeffrey Cooper, *The Rise of Instrumental Music and Concert Series in Paris, 1829–1871* (Ann Arbor, MI, 1983).

6. Joël-Marie Fauquet, "Le quatuor à cordes en France avant 1879: De la partition à la pratique," in *Le quatuor a cordes en France de 1750 à nos jours* (Paris, 1995), 97–117.

7. The dates of works given in parentheses are those of publication, unless otherwise noted.

8. See Fauquet, *Le quatuor à cordes en France,* and Cooper, *Rise of Instrumental Music.*

9. See Serge Gut and Danièle Pistone, *La musique de chambre en France de 1870 à 1918* (Paris, 1978).

10. Michel Stockhem, *Eugène Ysaÿe et la musique de chambre* (Liège, 1990).

11. François-Joseph Fétis, "Soirées des frères Müller," *Revue musicale,* 30 March 1834, 101.

12. Brigitte François-Sappey, "La vie musicale à Paris à travers les mémoires d'Eugène Sauzay," *Revue de musicologie* 40 (1974): 159–210.

13. Opp. 4 and 5 of Reber were published by Richault in Paris as well as by J. André in Offenbach; Op. 8 of Bousquet by Brandus in Paris and by Hoffmeister in Leipzig; and Op. 19 of Lalo by Maho in Paris and by Breitkopf und Härtel in Leipzig.

14. The dedications of Onslow's quartets and quintets are included in the catalogue published in 1852 by the *Revue et gazette musicale de Paris,* 386.

15. Fauquet, *Les sociétés de musique de chambre,* 348ff.

16. Ibid.

17. *Revue et gazette musicale de Paris,* 8 July 1855, 213.

18. Camille Saint-Saëns, *Harmonie et melodie* (Paris, 1885), 283.

19. Ibid.

20. François-Sappey, *Alexandre P. F. Boëlly, 1785–1858* (Paris, 1989), 231ff.

21. Ralph P. Locke, *Music, Musicians, and the Saint-Simonians* (Chicago, 1986), 183–84 et passim.

22. Nos. 2 and 3 were published by Cy in Marseille, in 1993 and 1994 respectively.

23. The first three, redesignated Op. 15, were reissued in score together with the Fourth Quartet by Richault in 1854.

24. "For no one was the legacy [of history] a lighter burden than for French musicians: they had lost all memory of their past; and as regards serious musical education, in France it no longer existed to speak of prior to 1870" (Romain Rolland, "Le renouveau: Esquisse du mouvement musical à Paris depuis 1870," in *Musiciens d'aujourd'hui* [Paris, 1908], 212).

25. Edouard Lalo, letter to Ferdinand Hiller, 27 October 1862, in his *Correspondance,* ed. Joël-Marie Fauquet (Paris, 1989), 77.

26. The Schubert had been played since about 1835 in salons such as that of E. Chabouillé Saint-Phal, and the Schumann since 1858 by the Société Armingaud; it was probably given earlier in salons such as that of W. Szarvady. See J.-M. Fauquet, *Les sociétés de musique de chambre,* 161–65 et passim.

27. See the analysis by Vincent d'Indy in Walter W. Cobbett, *Cyclopedic Survey of Chamber Music* (London, 1929) 1:233.

28. D'Indy, *Cour de composition musicale,* book 2, parts 1 & 2, pp. 381–82 et passim. See also Robert Jardillier, *La musique de chambre de César Franck: Etude et analyse* (Paris, 1929), 87ff.

29. Jean Gallois, *Ernest Chausson* (Paris, 1994), 289ff.

30. In Cobbett, *Cyclopedic Survey,* 1:232ff. See also Joël-Marie Fauquet, "Alexis de Castillon: Sa vie, son oeuvre" (diss., l'Ecole Pratique des Hautes Etudes, 1976), 2:257ff.

31. D'Indy, *Cours de composition,* book 2, part 1, pp. 423ff. The analysis of this work was taken up again by Herbert Schneider, "Analyse der Violinsonate A-Dur von C. Franck," in *Cesar Franck et son temps,* special issue of *Revue belge de musicologie* 45 (1991): 127ff.

32. D'Indy, *Cours de composition,* book 2, part 2, pp. 167–69; Guy Ropartz, "Analyse du quatuor en ré de César Franck," *Revue internationale de musique,* 1 August 1898.

33. D'Indy, *Cours de composition,* book 2, part 2, p. 170.

34. Herbert Schneider, "Das Streichquartett op. 45 von Vincent d'Indy als Exemplum des zyklischen Sonate," in *Studien zur Musikgeschichte: Ein Festschrift für Ludwig Finscher* (Kassel, 1995), 656ff.

Bibliography

Altmann, Wilhelm. *Kammermusik-Katalog.* Leipzig, 1942.
Baillot, Pierre. *L'art du violon.* Paris, 1834. Edited and translated by Louise Goldberg as *The Art of the Violin.* Evanston, IL, 1991.
Bonnerot, Jean. *Camille Saint-Saëns.* Paris, 1922.
Chorley, Henry Fothergill. *Music and Manners in France and Germany.* 2 vols. London, 1844.
Cobbett, Walter Wilson. *Cyclopedic Survey of Chamber Music.* 2 vols. London, 1929.
Cooper, Jeffrey. *The Rise of Instrumental Music and Concert Series in Paris, 1828–1871.* Ann Arbor, MI, 1983.
Della Croce, Vittorio. *Cherubini e i musicisti italiani del suo tempo.* Turin, 1983.
Emmanuel, Maurice. *Histoire de la langue musicale.* 2 vols. Paris, 1911.
Fauquet, Joël-Marie. "Alexis de Catillon: Sa vie, son oeuvre." 2 vols. Diss., l'Ecole Pratique des Hautes Etudes, 1976.
———. "Le quatuor à cordes en France avant 1870: De la partition à la pratique." In *Le quatuor à cordes en France de 1750 à nos jours,* 97ff. Paris, 1995.
———. *Les sociétés de musique de chambre à Paris de la Restauration à 1870.* Paris, 1986.
Francks, Richard Nelson. "George Onslow (1784–1853): A Study of His Life, Family, and Works." Ph.D. diss., University of Texas, 1981.
François-Sappey, Brigitte. *Alexandre P. F. Boëly, 1785–1858.* Paris, 1989.
———. "Pierre-Marie-François de Sales Baillot . . . par lui-meme." *Recherches* 18 (1978): 127–211."
Gallois, Jean. *Chausson.* Paris, 1994.

Gut, Serge, and Danièle Pistone. *La musique de chambre en France de 1870 à 1918.* Musique-musicologie 5. Paris, 1978.

Indy, Vincent d'. *Cours de composition musicale.* 3 vols. Paris, 1903, 1909, 1950.

Jardillier, Robert. *La musique de chambre de César Franck: Etude et analyse.* Paris, 1929.

Lalo, Edouard. *Correspondance.* Edited by J.-M. Fauquet. Paris, 1989.

Lesure, François. *Claude Debussy: Biographie critique.* Paris, 1994.

Locke, Ralph P. *Music, Musicians, and the Saint-Simonians.* Chicago, 1986.

Mahaim, Ivan. *Beethoven: Naissance et renaissance des derniers quatuors de Beethoven.* 2 vols. Paris, 1964.

Mongrédien, Jean. *La musique en France des lumières au romantisme, 1789–1830.* Paris, 1986.

Nectoux, Jean-Michel. *Gabriel Fauré: Les voix du clair-obscur.* Paris, 1990. Translated by R. Nichols as *Gabriel Fauré: A Musical Life.* Cambridge, 1991.

Rolland, Romain. "Le renouveau: Esquisse du mouvement musical à Paris depuis 1870." In *Musiciens d'aujourd'hui.* Paris, 1908.

Schrade, Leo. *Beethoven in France: The Growth of an Idea.* New Haven, CT, 1942.

Stockhem, Michel. *Eugène Ysaÿe et la musique de chambre.* Liège, 1990.

Vidal, Louis-Antoine. *Les instruments à archet: . . . les joueurs d'instruments, leur histoire sur le continent européen, suivi d'un catalogue général de la musique de chambre.* 3 vols. Paris, 1876–78.

CHAPTER EIGHT

The Chamber Music of Smetana and Dvořák

Derek Katz and Michael Beckerman*

The Czech lands, dubbed "the conservatory of Europe" by Charles Burney, have supplied composers and performers to the cultural centers of the continent for centuries. The history of music during the eighteenth and early nineteenth centuries is peppered with such surnames as Benda, Dusík, Stamitz, Koželůh and Reicha, but only in conjunction with the emerging nationalist movement of the mid-nineteenth century did Czech composers consciously orient their efforts towards a distinctively national culture. Czech music from the latter part of the nineteenth century has been most frequently evaluated as part of an independent musical tradition, one in which such nationalistic features as patriotic programs and allusions to folk culture are held to be self-evident virtues. *The Moldau* (*Vltava*), for example, from Smetana's *Má Vlast*, has long been a fixture in music history and appreciation texts; yet that is due less to its purely musical qualities than to its indulgence in local color.

The reception of Czech music, particularly that by two of its leading lights, Bedřich Smetana and Antonín Dvořák, has perhaps been disproportionately shaped by such emphasis on nationalist elements, especially as regards their chamber music. While the cultural agenda of stage works or programmatic orchestral pieces such as Smetana's *Má Vlast* and Dvořák's folk-ballad tone poems may be inescapable, these composers' chamber works are much less obviously nationalistic. Their critical reception has too often been confined to searching for obvious Czech elements, such as dance rhythms. As a result, many compositions in which such fea-

---

*Other contributions were made to this chapter by Erik Entwistle, Diane Paige, Marilee Mouser, Alicia Doyle, and Frank Natale.

tures are not abundant (such as Dvořák's last quartets) have been under-valued, and manifold connections between Czech chamber music and western European works have been neglected. One aim of the present essay is to approach the chamber oeuvre of Smetana and Dvořák as less exotic than it is usually regarded, in the hope that this music will seem no less attractive for being less quaint.

Smetana was by far the less active of the two, and of his few chamber works, only two, the G Minor Piano Trio and the Quartet in E Minor, *Z mého života* (From my life), have any currency in the repertoire. The latter, however, ranks among the great hits in the string quartet literature, and has achieved a certain historical stature as the first well-known piece of programmatic chamber music. Smetana's rarely performed Second Quartet, generally dismissed as a flawed product of the composer's final illness, also merits a wider audience.

Dvořák, on the other hand, was among the most prolific chamber music composers of the nineteenth century: he is the author of more than forty works for various ensembles. Just as his earlier symphonic essays are overshadowed by the immense popularity of the "New World" Symphony, so, too, the most frequently played of his quartets (outside the Czech lands, in any case) is the "American," Op. 96. But the warhorse status of the music Dvořák wrote in the United States has not necessarily led to a broader appreciation of his oeuvre as a whole. The early works in particular have been neglected, and pieces that seem neither American nor Czech have been insufficiently examined.

Smetana's Chamber Music

Bedřich Smetana was strongly influenced by both the musical and cultural politics of his time. A follower of Wagner and Liszt, he was also actively involved in the struggle over national music, in a way that the younger Dvořák was not. By localizing certain ideas embodied in the New German notion of "The Music of the Future," Smetana was determined to create a recognizable Czech style and, particularly, to bring it to both the stage and concert hall. His most notable successes in this regard were his operas (*The Brandenburgers in Bohemia* and *The Bartered Bride*, 1866; *Dalibor*, 1868; and *Libuše*, 1869–72) and his program music (*Má Vlast*, 1874–79). Recent Czech history offers a measure of Smetana's enduring achievement: his opera *Libuše*, which inaugurated the Prague National Theater in 1883, was again chosen for the gala reopening of that theater a century later, and the Prague Spring Festival traditionally begins with a performance of *Má Vlast;* that cycle of tone poems, conducted by expatriate Rafael Kubelik, also opened the first festival following the 1989 Velvet Revolution.

Despite some serious setbacks along the way, Smetana's plan for a Czech national music was undeniably successful, and until the early 1870s he was a highly visible and politically influential figure. But in 1874 Smetana suffered the sudden loss of his hearing; the cause was syphilis.

Ironically, illness forced him to spend more time on composition, and although it eventually drove him to madness and death, the first works he wrote after the onset of declining health are among his best. The autobiographical Quartet in E minor, subtitled *From My Life,* dates from 1876. Smetana's last chamber works include *Z domoviny* (From my homeland) for violin and piano (1880) and the Quartet in D Minor (1883). The Second Quartet, although only eighteen minutes long, is miniature neither in scope nor ideas. Certain technical difficulties and an unusual treatment of dissonance may have been responsible for its poor initial reception, yet none other than Schoenberg realized its importance and regarded it as a progressive composition, years ahead of its time.

Early Works

Smetana's first efforts in chamber music composition date from 1839–40, when he was studying in Prague. Two polkas and a quartet have been lost; only the violin part for a set of waltzes survives, and there are fragments of a Fantasy on Operatic Themes for string quartet.[1] The only complete chamber work extant from the 1840s is the *Fantazie na českou národní píseň* (Fantasy on a Czech folk song), although sketches for both an oboe-and-piano piece and a piano quartet probably stem from this period.

The *Fantazie* dates from 1843, the year Smetana completed his Gymnasium studies in Plzeň. Scored for violin and piano, it is a set of nine variations on the folk song "S'il jsem proso na souvrati" (I was sowing millet), which was the unofficial school song at Německý Brod, Smetana's grammar school.[2] The piece is of greater interest as a historical document than as a composition: its extravagant keyboard writing demonstrates the young Smetana's pianistic prowess as well as his Lisztian sympathies, and a brief fugato before the coda is one of the few moments not devoted chiefly to virtuoso display. There is no evidence of a performance during Smetana's lifetime, and the composer gave this bit of juvenilia to a friend in 1881 with instructions to burn it.[3]

It is noteworthy that the folk-song theme of the *Fantazie* also appears in the third movement of the Piano Trio in G Minor, Op. 15, written in 1855. The trio is not only Smetana's first mature chamber piece but, indeed, his first major work of any kind. The practical impetus for the composition was the arrival in Prague of the violinist Otto von Königslow, who formed a trio together with Smetana and the noted cellist Julius Goltermann.[4] The three musicians premiered Smetana's trio as part of a chamber music evening on 3 December 1855.[5] (Critical response was not enthusiastic; the noticeable influence of Robert Schumann, whose Piano Quintet ended the program, came in for particular censure.) But the more personal impulse behind the trio was Smetana's wish to memorialize his daughter Bedřiska, who had fallen victim to scarlet fever at age three. She was the second of three daughters to die during childhood, and Smetana mourned her all the more since she had shown traces of an exceptional musical gift. As he wrote to a friend, "The loss of my oldest daughter, that so unusually gifted child, caused the chamber composition, that is, the Trio in G minor, to be written in 1855."[6]

Due to this biographical connection, the trio has been regarded as an essentially tragic work, and indeed, it easily supports such a reading, at least superficially. All three movements are in G minor, and the plangent opening theme, chromatically inflected and covering an octave and a half of the violinist's G string, sets a dark tone at the outset (Example 8.1). Yet simply hearing the work as a lugubrious response to personal misfortune neglects large portions of the piece. The second theme of the first movement, in the relative major, is much more tranquil, and the scherzo and finale, although nominally in the minor mode, both contain substantial contrasting major sections and conclude in the major.

EXAMPLE 8.1.   Bedřich Smetana, Piano Trio in G Minor, Op. 15, mvt. 1, mm. 1–8 (violin).

Both the heroic "horn call" figures (Example 8.2) and the opposition of noble and sinister gestures become typical of Smetana's later works, particularly the operas *Dalibor, Libuše,* and *The Devil's Wall;* they occur in the Second String Quartet as well.

EXAMPLE 8.2.   Smetana, Piano Trio, mvt. 1, mm. 176–78 (piano).

These passages of contrasting character are tied together by a number of motivic devices. Within the first movement, both themes outline the interval of a descending fifth; they share a similar tessitura (when the second theme returns in the recapitulation, it outlines exactly the same d^1–g as the first theme); and both use dotted eighth/sixteenth figures. In addition, an accompanimental figure derived from the opening idea is used in conjunction with both themes (Example 8.3).

All three movements of the trio are linked by the motive of the work's first measure, which recurs in the theme of the scherzo (Example 8.4a).

EXAMPLE 8.3.   Smetana, Piano Trio, mvt. 1: (a) m. 3 (violin); (b) m. 18 (violin and cello); (b) m. 55 (violin).

Its descending fifth is then filled in chromatically (Example 8.4b), and in this form the cyclic idea launches the finale (Example 8.4c).

EXAMPLE 8.4.(a)   Smetana, Piano Trio: mvt. 2, mm. 1–8 (cello).

EXAMPLE 8.4.(b)   Smetana, Piano Trio: mvt. 2, mm 233–45 (violin).

EXAMPLE 8.4.(c)   Smetana, Piano Trio: mvt. 3, mm. 1–7 (violin).

FINALE

The pitch C♯, highly prominent in the opening of the first movement, also plays an important structural role in the trio as a whole. The enharmonic ambiguity between C♯ and D♭ is exploited twice—once to reach C major in the development of the first movement, and once again to return to G minor in the scherzo.

The putative influence of Robert Schumann is most strongly apparent in the scherzo, whose G minor unison theme strongly recalls the analogous passage in Schumann's E♭ Piano Quartet, and whose two major *alternativo* sections evoke the naïve confidence of the older composer's *Davidsbund* music. It has also been argued that the critics identified the wrong member of the Schumann household, and that Smetana's first movement is based on Clara Schumann's Trio in G Minor: on this reading, Smetana may have had Clara in mind as a model of the musician his daughter Bedřiska might have become.[7]

Brian Large has proposed that the quotation of "S'il jsem proso na souvrati" in the trio's finale (Example 8.5) may have political significance, since the folk song was associated with the Young Czech nationalist movement.[8] But it is difficult to gauge Smetana's intentions, given that the opening of the last movement was cannibalized from an 1846 piano sonata. From our perspective, this earlier material seems less well integrated into the rest of the trio than the other thematic components. It is also the only section of the piece in which the thematic material is not first given to the strings; perhaps in composing the newer portions of the trio Smetana wished to defer to his distinguished colleagues Königslow and Goltermann.

EXAMPLE 8.5.   Smetana, Piano Trio, mvt. 3, mm. 7–14 (piano).

Late Works

Smetana's late chamber music comprises the short violin-and-piano cycle *Z domoviny* (From my homeland) and two string quartets. The Quartet in E Minor, composed between October and December 1876, is the earlier of two quartets Smetana wrote following his success with the nationalist operas *The Bartered Bride* (1866) and *Dalibor* (1868). As noted above, the E Minor Quartet is evidently a reaction to the onset of deafness; in 1878 he described it as "almost a private composition, and therefore purposely written for four instruments which, as it were, are to talk to each other in a narrow circle of friends of what has so momentously affected me. No more."[9]

Smetana submitted the E Minor Quartet for performance under the auspices of the Prague Chamber Music Association; it was rejected on grounds of its doubtful "orchestral" style and insurmountable technical difficulties.[10] Its first hearing (1877) was private, held in the flat of Josef Srb-Debrnov, the musicographer who was Smetana's closest friend during his last years; the violist on this occasion was none other than Antonín Dvořák. Only a year later was the quartet presented publicly, in Prague on 29 March 1879. The following year Liszt personally requested parts for use by the Weimar Quartet, and was "most warmly appreciative" of their performance of it.[11]

The notoriety of *From My Life* as the first exemplar of overtly programmatic chamber music is not entirely deserved. Smetana does not literally depict a series of events, but rather suggests a general scenario for each of the movements, which he described in a letter to Srb-Debrnov as follows:

> I did not intend to write a quartet according to recipe and according to custom in the usual forms. . . . I had wanted to give a tone picture of my life. First movement: My leaning towards art in my youth, the romantic atmosphere, the inexpressible yearning for something I could neither express nor define, and also the presage, as it were, of my future misfortune. . . . Second movement: *Quasi a polka*, takes me back to the happy times of my youth where, as a composer of dance tunes, I lavished these upon the young world and was myself known everywhere as a passionate dancer. The middle movement is the one, which in the opinion of the gentlemen who play this quartet, cannot possibly be performed. . . . it recalls to me the happiness of my first love for the girl who later became my first wife. Fourth movement: Understanding of the potentialities of the folk music element, joy at the success of this course up to the time it was checked by the catastrophe of the beginning of deafness, the outlook into the sad future, the tiny rays of hope of recovery, but, at the thought of the beginnings of my career, nevertheless sadness.[12]

The first movement, Allegro vivo appassionato in E minor, opens with an impassioned first theme, presented by the viola over murmuring thirds in the violins. The beginning of the theme, with its distinctive eighth-note pickup and descending fifth, reappears in various guises throughout the movement to articulate formal divisions. The second theme, lyrical and expressive in G major, is announced by the viola with a variant of the opening motive. The melody is presented three times at increasingly higher pitch levels, such that the initially sweet lyricism of the line becomes urgent and demanding. This procedure, derived from Wagner, is one of Smetana's favorite compositional gambits, and one that Dvořák cultivates as well—a series of sequences with "surprise" resolutions. The next formal juncture, the development, is also heralded by a variant of the opening motive, this time in the cello. This development is entirely concerned with harmonic manipulations of the first theme, which takes on an increasingly agitated character; as a result, it is dramatically appropriate that the recapitulation begin with the second theme, now in the tonic major. The first theme never returns in its entirety, but the movement's extended coda is based upon fragments of it.

The second movement, Allegro moderato a la Polka, a scherzolike polka in F major, presents two contrasting dance tunes. The first is light-hearted and almost disjointed, punctuated by rests and a cello line that echoes the initial three-note idea. The second theme is introduced by the viola; marked *solo, quasi tromba*, it is to be played entirely on the C string. This tune features another device frequently found in stylized "folkish" music, namely, the direct repetition of a melodic figure a fifth higher. The humorous potential of awkward passages on the lowest strings of the inner voices is fully manifest in the scherzo, and in the trio where swelling chords in the fiddles conjure up the squeeze box of a Pilsner-soaked accordionist.

The third movement, Largo sostenuto, begins with an extended cello solo, whose use of the descending fifth so central to the first movement suggests that it will be a structurally significant element. But this material never returns, and in the event serves only as an introduction to the theme on which the movement is based— an exceptionally beautiful melody supported by a tonic pedal. This Largo is usually described as monothematic, yet the main theme is never literally repeated, and the continuation from the opening sequential pattern is different in each successive statement.

According to Smetana the fourth movement, a Vivace in E major, reflects his pleasure in weaving folk elements into his music. Appropriately, he uses another polka theme to symbolize these thoughts. But near the movement's end, Smetana's playful dance is abruptly interrupted by a C major seventh chord, followed by two measure of silence. Then, over a C pedal, the first violin plays a piercing e^4, imitating the sound Smetana heard ringing in his ears as his hearing deteriorated (Example 8.6). Fragments of the first and last movements follow as the music gradually fades away. The result is a fairly transparent reversal of what unfolds in the finale of Beethoven's Ninth: instead of each earlier movement's attempting to speak in turn, followed by all of them giving way to song, here each thematic recall is in turn dissolved, leading only to silence.

EXAMPLE 8.6.   Smetana, String Quartet No. 1 in E Minor, *From My Life*, mvt. 4, mm. 222–24.

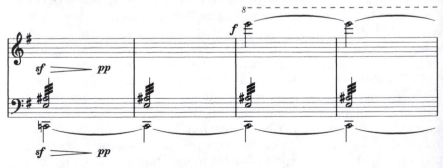

There are no hints of Smetana's misfortune in his next chamber work, *Z domoviny*, two pieces for violin and piano composed in 1880.

FIGURE 8-1.   Page of the score of the quartet *From my Life*, including the passage shown in Example 8.6.

Smetana wrote these duos for Prince Alexander Thurn-Taxis, the son of Count Hugo von Taxis. (Beginning in 1876, when he could no longer afford to live in Prague, Smetana and his married daughter occupied the gamekeeper's lodge on the count's estate at Jabkenice.) The young prince, to judge from the duos, must have been a capable but unexceptional fiddler: the violin part contains all of the melodic material, but is not technically demanding. The few passages in octaves are placed in the lowest positions, and bravura effects for the violin are carefully calculated to avoid frequent left-hand shifts. The melodies are, however, quite charming, and in the days when light music figured more prominently on recitals, Smetana's duos were in the repertoire of many concert violinists (albeit mostly in an abridged arrangement by Hans Sitt); the second duo was particularly popular and was twice recorded by Fritz Kreisler.

The Second String Quartet stems from the final throes of Smetana's illness. It was completed on 12 March 1883, by which time syphilis had robbed Smetana not only of his hearing but, much of the time, of his sanity as well. Prone to hallucinations and only sporadically capable of recognizing his closest friends and immediate family, he nevertheless continued to compose in his lucid moments. Owing to the dire circumstances of the quartet's genesis, critical reception of it, especially outside the Czech lands, has generally been dismissive. The brevity of the work, whose four movements last only eighteen minutes, plus its frequent and abrupt changes of character, suggest that Smetana's intentions were compromised by his infirmities. Yet closer examination reveals much that is beautiful in the piece, and it becomes apparent that its structural and harmonic oddities are anticipated in earlier works.

The form of the first movement has proven problematic, even for the composer himself, who worried that his mental decline and inability to remember musical ideas had rendered it difficult to grasp. Once again Smetana shared his reflections with Srb-Debrnov:

> I have completed the first movement of the quartet, but as regards the style of this movement, I am in something of a quandary; this movement is quite unusual in form and difficult to follow, a kind of conflict dominates it which will, it seems to me, present great difficulties for the players.[13]

The same variant of sonata form found in the First Quartet—i. e., reversed thematic presentation in the recapitulation—can be teased out of this movement as well. However, the primary dramatic contrast is not between the first and second themes, but rather between the opening unison figure and the ensuing F major answer (Example 8.7a and b). As noted in discussing the piano trio, such stark juxtapositions crop up frequently in Smetana's later operas, particularly in *The Devil's Wall*, where the forces of good and evil are represented by major and augmented sonorities respectively. The quartet contains similar abrupt contrasts in all four movements, each of which begins with a harmonically ambiguous unison passage.

EXAMPLE 8.7.   Smetana, String Quartet No. 2 in D Minor, mvt. 1: (a) mm. 1–5; (b) mm. 10–12.

a)

b)

The second movement, like the corresponding movement in the First Quartet, is a polka; this one, however, is a reworking of a sketch for piano from 1848–49. This dates the music to the period of Smetana's first attempts make of the polka the sort of flexible artistic vehicle that Chopin had fashioned from the mazurka. Smetana's unsettling, unpolkalike syncopations, bizarre for an 1848 dance, seem sly and witty in an 1883 chamber work (Example 8.8). This peculiar polka is paired with a warm E major trio.

EXAMPLE 8.8.   Smetana, String Quartet No. 2, mvt. 2, mm. 13–20.

The third movement, Allegro non più moderato, ma agitato e con fuoco, like the first, begins with a chromatic unison passage, this time made even more agitated with tremolos. Then follows a calm fugal exposition, beginning in the cello. The initial ascending sixth C–a and the imitative treatment (Example 8.9) seem to recall the "Heiliger Dankgesang" of Beethoven's Op. 132; perhaps this movement also carries wishes for a return to health.

The fourth movement, Presto, is harmonically nebulous. Part of the elusive *presto* theme (Example 8.10) adopts the sliding parallel harmonies also found in the late operas. Its foil, a heroic F major outburst, establishes that the movement's harmonic contrast is between general instability and F major, rather than between relative major and minor. Indeed, D minor

EXAMPLE 8.9.   Smetana, String Quartet No. 2, mvt. 3, mm. 13–16.

is never really established as tonic, and it comes as something of a surprise that the quartet ends in D major, a tonality that has not played an important role elsewhere in the quartet.

EXAMPLE 8.10.   Smetana, String Quartet No. 2, mvt. 4, mm. 19–22.

Despite its novelties, the Second Quartet is convincing and successful on its own terms. Were the sad details of Smetana's mental decline not known, the work would probably be regarded as a significant harbinger of Smetana's late style, and might well be praised for its progressive qualities rather than dismissed as a flawed effort.

Dvořák's Chamber Music

Whereas Smetana's reputation as a chamber music composer rests almost entirely upon a single work, the E Minor String Quartet, Dvořák is recognized as the composer of numerous favorites in the standard repertoire. The String Quartet in F Major, Op. 96 ("American"), is of course a staple, as are the Piano Quintet in A Major, Op. 81, and the "Dumky" Trio; several other works are frequently performed as well. Dvořák wrote chamber music throughout his career, beginning with the Op. 1 string quintet, and these compositions steadily delineate his artistic development.

Most of the early works (1861–74) remained unpublished during Dvořák's lifetime, and have only recently been revived. Although artistically uneven, they nevertheless reveal the young composer's infatuations, particularly with the music of Wagner. And much of the music is worth revisiting. Dvořák himself did not discard these pieces, but instead recycled portions of some in better-known works, and revised others for performance long after the fact.

Dvořák's middle period (1875–92), has traditionally been viewed as a time of increasing preoccupation with Czech folk materials, and the chamber works from these years often incorporate Czech folk songs and dances. Perhaps more significant during these years, however, is Dvořák's return to Classical forms and proportions following his early struggles with more progressive tendencies.

The late chamber works include the three compositions written during Dvořák's stay in America (1892–95), plus two string quartets completed after his return to Bohemia. Although his enthusiasm for the music of Native and African Americans is apparent in his "American" works, Dvořák denied using folk, Negro, or American Indian melodies in them. The most popular of the three quartets is the "American," Op. 96, composed immediately after Dvořák completed his Symphony *From the New World*.

In his last chamber works, the String Quartets Opp. 105 and 106, Dvořák's return to his homeland seems to be reflected in his resumption of a more "Classical" or Czech style. Connections between the New World Symphony and Op. 106, begun in New York and completed in Bohemia, are evident in the scherzos of each work. And just as apparent in Op. 105 is Dvořák's conscious rejection of the "American" elements characteristic of his recent compositions.

Early Works for Strings, 1861–1874

Early in his compositional career Dvořák, like Smetana, was captivated by the music of Liszt and Wagner. Indeed, Smetana, as both conductor and composer, was partially responsible for introducing Dvořák to the more progressive elements of Romantic music. Dvořák played in the viola section for performances of Liszt's oratorio *The Legend of Saint Elizabeth* as well as the premieres of Smetana's operas *The Brandenburgers in Bohemia* and *Dalibor,* all under the leadership of the older composer. But Dvořák also had more direct contact with the "Music of the Future." As a sixteen-year-old student, he had already played portions of Wagner's *Das Liebesmahl der Apostel* and *Rienzi,* and, more significantly, had played under Wagner himself in an 1863 Prague concert that included the *Faust* Overture, the preludes to *Die Meistersinger* and *Tristan und Isolde,* and the overture to *Tannhäuser.*[14] Dvořák's early chamber works reveal his efforts to reconcile his progressive enthusiasms with the models of the Viennese Classicists that he had come to know as performer and student. A third strand in his development, the influence of Brahms, can be discounted with respect to the early works, since Dvořák probably did not encounter any major work by Brahms before 1876.[15]

The Viola Quintet in A Minor, Op. 1, is Dvořák's earliest surviving chamber work, written in 1861 when the twenty-year-old musician was still fresh from his organ and counterpoint studies at the Prague Organ School. The curriculum there did not include formal instruction in large-scale secular composition, so we may assume that Dvořák drew as much from his experience as a violist as from what he learned at the Organ School. To judge from his A Minor Quintet, he must have been familiar with quartets and quintets by Mozart, Beethoven, and Schubert: the A Minor Quintet strongly evokes specific pieces by Dvořák's predecessors at various points, the most obvious being the first theme of the last movement, which resembles the opening of Mozart's G Minor Piano Quartet.

The strengths of the quintet are its idiomatic string writing and attractive melodies. Thematic material is frequently redistributed when recapitulated, whereby all five players are assigned exposed passages. The best tune of the piece is the theme of the slow movement, which is repeated a number of times, with varied instrumentation and accompaniment figures. Alhough fundamentally conventional, the quintet does not always adhere to Classical models of form. It lacks a scherzo, and the tonal plan is sometimes unusual. Most of these deviations, such as deployment of the tonic during much of the first movement's development, are apparently owing either to inexperience or to misguided ambition; some, however, like the A major return of the main theme in the F major slow movement, are fortuitous. In 1887 the quintet underwent revisions, including removal of the exposition repeats in the outer movements; it was, however, not performed until a concert honoring what would have been Dvořák's eightieth birthday, in 1921.

In 1862, a year after writing the quintet, Dvořák was rejected from military service; like most Czechs, he had no desire to serve in the Habsburg army and was delighted to be deemed unfit. The autograph score of the String Quartet in A, Op. 2, bears a note indicating that he gave vent to his delight in this new work. This is the only one of his first six quartets that Dvořák heard in performance, and as with the Op. 1 quintet, he abridged the work in 1887.

In the A Major Quartet Dvořák seems to be looking toward somewhat more recent music for models. The generally Mozartian textures of the A Minor Quintet have been replaced with frequent tremolo accompaniments and a more extravagant use of both dynamics and the upper reaches of the first violin and cello. The work also manifests a certain degree of unity among its four movements: both the slow introduction and the main section of the first movement begin with the pitches E and F♯, as do the scherzo and the last movement (Example 8.11). In addition, a reminiscence of the first movement's opening occurs just before the close of the finale, a device that Dvořák could have picked up from Mendelssohn's quartets, Opp. 12 and 13.

Wagner's Prague concert took place the year after the composition of the A Major Quartet. During the next decade, Dvořák's aesthetic sympathies are clearly evident in two operas written along explicitly Wagnerian lines: *Alfred* (1870) and *King and Charcoal Burner* (1871). Although neither was immediately produced, Dvořák ingratiated himself with the pro-Smetana faction in Prague by casting his lot with the progressives, and was praised in the influential musical weekly *Hudební listy*.[16] Harmonic and

EXAMPLE 8.11. Antonín Dvořák, String Quartet in A Major, Op. 2: (a) mvt. 1, mm. 1–4; (b) mvt. 1, mm. 39–42; (c) mvt. 3, mm. 1–5; (d) mvt. 4, mm. 1–3 (violin 1).

formal experimentation are also the most striking features of his next three string quartets, in B♭ major, D major, and E minor, which probably date from 1869-70. Little is known about the circumstances of their composition; the autograph scores are no longer extant and were probably destroyed by Dvořák in 1873, when he rejected many of his earlier works. Scores have, however, been reconstructed from parts that had been copied from the autographs.

Dvořák's experimentation is most obvious in the E Minor Quartet. This single-movement work consists of contrasting sections, and ends in B major rather than the expected tonic. Part of its B major *andante religioso* section was reused in a slow movement for the later String Quintet (with bass) in G Major, Op. 77, but was subsequently removed from the quintet and finally published in 1883 as a Nocturne for String Orchestra, Op. 40. The D Major Quartet, in addition to a number of harmonically adventuresome gestures, features a persistent *Rienzi*-esque turn in its melodies, as in Example 8.12.

EXAMPLE 8.12. Dvořák, String Quartet in D Major, mvt. 1, mm. 62–65.

Its third movement quotes a melody that resembles the Polish national anthem, but is in fact, as Hartmut Schick has conclusively demonstrated, the Czech patriotic song "Hej, Slovane" (Hey, Slavs!).[17] Dvořák may have been making a political statement—the song was frequently sung at demonstrations of the Czech national liberation movement and was banned by official censors on more than one occasion.[18] Given that the quartet was not destined for public performance, however, it seems more likely that it was meant as a sort of in-joke whose meaning has been lost, much like the otherwise enigmatic quote of the Wedding March from Mendelssohn's *Midsummer Night's Dream* in the finale of the B♭ Major Quartet.

Dvořák's next two quartets, in F Minor, Op. 9, and in A Minor, Op. 12, represent a transitional stage in his chamber music style. Both date from the end of 1873, after the self-evaluation that resulted in his destroying the previous three quartets; nevertheless, they still have the sprawling length characteristic of the discarded works. The first movement of the F Minor Quartet is a particularly egregious example, weighing in at 630 bars. Like the earlier E Minor Quartet, the A Minor was conceived as a single-movement work. But Dvořák quickly became dissatisfied with this arrangement and began to split it up into four movements. He did not complete this revision (when performed today, the quartet is heard in a reconstruction of the four-movement version), nor did he ever return to the single-movement design in his chamber music. Despite structural similarities to his earlier works, the 1873 quartets are markedly different in character. Gone are the Wagnerisms and monothematic tendencies, replaced by simpler textures and more clearly de-

EXAMPLE 8.13.(a).   Dvořák, String Quartet in A Minor, Op. 16: mvt. 1, mm. 1–6.

EXAMPLE 8.13.(b).   Dvořák, String Quartet in A Minor, Op. 16: mvt. 2, mm. 42–45 (violin 1).

fined themes. While the F Minor Quartet was not intended for publication, Dvořák did salvage its slow movement, which he fashioned into the Romance for Violin and Piano, Op. 11, one of his most successful early compositions.

Dvořák's Seventh Quartet, Op. 16 in A minor, written in 1874 and published the following year, was the first of his quartets to appear in print. With this work the composer finally arrived at a chamber music style that would serve him for the rest of his career. The Classical four-movement pattern is back, and with it more modest proportions: the new first movement is barely half as long as that of the F Minor Quartet, and the main theme of the scherzo is a slender eight bars. Although Otakar Šourek finds the formal excellence of the piece to be achieved at the expense of its invention,[19] there are numerous charming features. The quartet uses many of the melodic devices that mark Dvořák's popular American works, such as the sudden drop of a fifth in the first movement theme and the expressive repeated notes and *portati* in the slow movement (Example 8.13).

The "Nationalist" Period, 1875–1892

The ensuing years of Dvořák's career are traditionally regarded as a period of increasing interest in Czech folk material, which brought him both professional success and international recognition. Šourek, the earliest and most influential of Dvořák's biographers, sums this up as follows:

> He was aided in the final steps of liberating himself from the stupefying music of the German neo-romanticists by the happy example of the works of Bedřich Smetana. As this brilliant and farseeing artist had previously felt, now Dvořák also came to feel that the roots of the new art, while maintaining their contact with world art, must penetrate deeply into the spirit of the artist's own people. Dvořák now began to create a very individual music, giving it also an essentially Czech national tone. . . . It then sufficed merely for him to come in close contact with the rich source of national music, for the corresponding harmonic elements to echo in the artist's soul and thus free his work from the domination of foreign ways of expression which were inducing him toward formalism and complexities in construction.[20]

While it is undeniable that such self-consciously "national" works as the Moravian Duets and the Slavonic Dances played a significant role in establishing Dvořák's international stature, and that from the mid-1870s on Czech dances, including polkas, *dumky*, and *furianty* frequently appear in Dvořák's instrumental works, Šourek's formulation glosses over several points. As noted above, it was in fact Smetana who encouraged Dvořák's early infatuation with Wagner and Liszt, both by exposing Dvořák to their works and through his own example as a composer. In addition, as we have seen, Dvořák had already given up on his efforts to infuse chamber music with a Wagnerian spirit by the early 1870s, well before making any obvious nationalist gestures. Finally, it should be noted that much of the pressure to write "nationalist" music was external: the Berlin publisher Simrock, for example, specifically commissioned Dvořák's Slavonic Dances in an attempt to repeat the success of Brahms's Hungarian Dances, and the Florentine Quartet explicitly requested that the work written for them (Op. 51) should be "Slavonic" in character. That Dvořák's mature compositional voice has a Czech accent has at least as much to do with the robust market for exported exoticism as it does with any personal artistic agenda.

From this point on, Dvořák was no longer writing for private performances by friends, or for his desk drawer; rather, he crafted pieces for specific opportunities. The Quintet in G Major for string quartet plus double bass was written for an 1875 chamber music competition sponsored by the music division of the Umělecká Beseda, a society of Czech artists founded in 1863.[21] Dvořák was awarded a prize by a jury that praised the quintet for its "noble theme, the technical mastery of its polyphonic composition, the mastery of form and . . . the knowledge of the instruments."[22] As noted above, the piece was first performed in a five-movement form that included the *andante religioso* from the E Minor Quartet, but was eventually published with only four movements. Its opus number, 77, reflects the tardy publication date of 1888; Dvořák had wanted the work to appear as Op. 18, which would better indicate its place in the chronological sequence of his works.

Of the virtues praised by the jury, the contrapuntal aspect of the quintet seems relatively insignificant today, but its melodic material and scoring remain striking. The function of the string bass is twofold: at various points it frees the cello to assume a tenor role, while in other passages it doubles the cello to yield an orchestral effect. Melodies in the quintet are never less than catchy, and often reach the sort of noble lyricism that would become a Dvořák hallmark. The second section of the scherzo is frequently cited for its use of a "Moravian modulation," dropping from the tonic E major to the flattened subtonic.

The Umělecká Beseda competition was not Dvořák's sole opportunity to obtain financial reward as a composer: beginning in 1874 the Austrian Imperial Ministry of Education offered an annual stipend for indigent artists. Among the judges for musician applicants were Eduard Hanslick, and later Johannes Brahms. Dvořák received an award, having submitted some fifteen compositions including his Third and Fourth Symphonies, a set of songs, and, probably, the F Minor String Quartet. Dvořák continued to apply for the stipend each year; he was rewarded again in 1876 for his Fifth Symphony and a new string quartet in E major, which was written in the first months of that year.

Like the bass quintet, the E Major Quartet is also known by a misleading opus number, thanks to the publisher Simrock. Originally designated Op. 27, the quartet was not published until 1888, and then as Op. 80 to give it the appearance of a new work. Performance was delayed as well; the first known rendition took place in 1889 in London. Just as Smetana's G Minor Piano Trio is traditionally regarded as a musical response to the loss of his daughter, so, too, are Dvořák's compositions of 1876 linked to the tragic death of his first daughter, Josefa, shortly after she was born in the fall of 1875. Like Smetana, Dvořák wrote a Piano Trio in G Minor immediately after the tragic event, although unlike the older composer, Dvořák left no indication that his trio was intended as a memorial. He then turned to the E Major Quartet and sketches for the Stabat Mater. Critical reception of the E Major Quartet has been colored by the expressions of personal and religious sorrow that surround it, and it is frequently asserted that the insistent use of minor tonalities in an ostensibly major-key work is indicative of the composer's grief.

However, the thematic material of the quartet manifests a variety of characters. The opening theme is initially presented in imitation (Example 8.14a), with passing nods to B minor and F♯ minor, but later reappears (Example 8.14b) in a setting whose harmonic simplicity, pulsing eighth notes, and subsequent interplay between treble and bass strongly recall the Serenade for Strings, also in E, which Dvořák had written less than a year before.

EXAMPLE 8.14.(a).   Dvořák, String Quartet in E Major, Op. 80, mvt. 1: mm. 1–4.

EXAMPLE 8.14.(b).   Dvořák, String Quartet in E Major, Op. 80, mvt. 1: mm. 38–39.

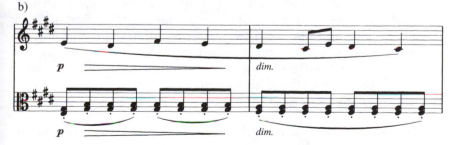

The second theme is foreshadowed in a transitional passage prior to its full statement in both minor and major modes.

The wistful slow movement is similar in mood to many of the pieces that Dvořák later labeled *dumky*, but here the composer seems more concerned with contrapuntal imitation than with any sort of folk effect. Portions of the opening theme are combined with each other and, near the end of the movement, with the second theme (Example 8.15).

EXAMPLE 8.15.   Dvořák, String Quartet in E Major, Op. 80, mvt. 2, mm. 133–39 (violin 1 and cello).

Any lingering impressions of Slavonic melancholy are quickly dispersed by the lilt of the waltz that follows. In the finale, the first theme begins in G♯ minor, and the movement does not arrive in the tonic until thirty-one bars have passed. Dvořák had made a similar experiment in the closing movement of the Fifth Symphony (1875), which also begins with a substantial section in the mediant. A likely precedent is the finale of Beethoven's String Quartet in E Minor, Op. 59, No. 2, in which the first theme also begins in a key a third away from the tonic.

Dvořák's fourth application for the Austrian State Stipend in 1877 was clearly the most consequential. Not only was he awarded a prize, but both Hanslick and Brahms offered to assist in publicizing his music abroad. Brahms recommended Dvořák to his own publisher Simrock, who not only accepted Dvořák's Moravian Duets but commissioned the Slavonic Dances as well, issuing both in 1878. Brahms also urged Simrock to bring out the E Major String Quartet and the 1877 D Minor String Quartet (eventually Op. 34), assuring him that "the best that a musician can have *Dvořák has,* and it is in these compositions."[23] Simrock demurred, pending successful sales of the duets and dances; within the next year, however, he would publish a number of other compositions by Dvořák, who had also entered into successful negotiations with the Berlin firm of Bote & Bock. At this juncture it is interesting to note the similarities to Brahms's career, in which light, popular pieces for amateur consumption (such as the four-hand piano waltzes, Op. 39) played a crucial role; in Dvořák's case, however, it was his strongly national pieces that were most attractive to publishers, rather than the less regionally distinctive string quartets.

Dvořák's D Minor String Quartet was dedicated to Brahms, who declared himself honored by the gesture, but nevertheless scolded the composer for errors in the part writing.[24] Like the E Major Quartet, the D Minor was written during a time of personal tragedy, and also in the shadow of the Stabat Mater: Dvořák's two remaining children had died in the fall of 1877, and shortly thereafter he completed the monumental choral work that had occupied him intermittently for nearly two years. But as in the E Major Quartet, the craftsmanship of the D minor overshadows any autobiographical intent. The first theme of its opening movement initially seems to be little more than an elaboration of a descending fourth (Example 8.16a). The key to the phrase, however, is the sparse cello part, which creates ambiguity between treble and bass functions by nearly doubling the first violin in measures 2–5, and simultaneously emphasizes measures 3 and 4, which foreshadow the head motive of the second theme (Example 8.16b). The connection between the two themes is subsequently highlighted by their contrapuntal combination in the development (Example 8.16c).

EXAMPLE 8.16.(a).   Dvořák, String Quartet in D Minor, Op. 34, mvt. 1: mm. 1–5.

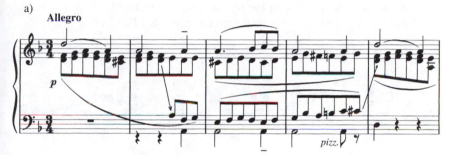

EXAMPLE 8.16.(b).   Dvořák, String Quartet in D Minor, Op. 34, mvt. 1: mm. 63–66 (violin 1).

EXAMPLE 8.16.(c).   Dvořák, String Quartet in D Minor, Op. 34, mvt. 1: mm. 173–78 (violin 1 and cello).

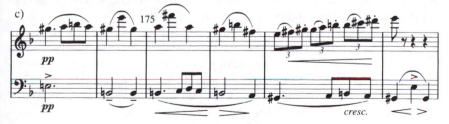

The second movement is a polka: this is Dvořák's first substitution of a Czech dance for the scherzo of a major work. While this is generally assumed to be a further expression of the nationalism inherent in the Slavonic Dances and the Slavonic Rhapsodies, the adoption of a polka may also have been a ploy to make the quartet more attractive to Simrock. Quite possibly it was suggested by the polka in Smetana's *From My Life*, which Dvořák had played a number of times in private performances during April and May of 1877;[25] another likely precedent is the polka in Zdeněk Fibich's String Quartet No. 1 in A Major (1874).

As regards Dvořák's next string quartet, the E♭ Major, Op. 51 (1879), there is no need to speculate about the motivation for its Czech flavor: first violinist Jean Becker of the Florentine Quartet had specifically requested a "Slavonic Quartet" in the spirit of the dances and rhapsodies. Dvořák began writing the work in 1878 but did not finish until 1879, too late for performance during the Swiss tour on which Becker had hoped to program it. Although the Florentine Quartet did not premiere the E♭ Quartet, it is nevertheless dedicated to Becker. Dance rhythms and folk gestures can be found throughout the work; a notable instance is the polka figure accompanying the second theme of the opening movement, which is later used extensively in the development (Example 8.17).

EXAMPLE 8.17.   Dvořák, String Quartet in E♭, Op. 51, mvt. 1, mm. 63–66 (violin 1).

The second movement, labeled *dumka*, begins with an elegiac melody over strummed arpeggios in the cello, perhaps imitating the harp of a legendary Slavonic bard. The pitches of the melody are retained for a contrasting major *vivace*, which incorporates the Czech dance rhythms of the *furiant*. Also dancelike in character is the finale, which apparently does not replicate a specific dance; it is probably closest to the *skočná*, although other types of leaping dances have been suggested.[26]

The last of Dvořák's quartets from this period, the Quartet in C Major, Op. 61 (1881), was also commissioned by the leader of a great quartet—Joseph Hellmesberger (senior), the court kapellmeister, concertmaster, and conservatory director in Vienna who was first violinist of the string quartet that bore his name. Hellmesberger made no stipulation that the new work be "Slavonic," and Dvořák probably suspected that a less obviously ethnic work would stand a better chance in conservative Vienna. Hellmesberger, renowned for both his wit and his authoritarianism, went so far as to announce the date of the quartet's premiere before Dvořák had started to compose it. Despite the pressure he was under to complete the work, Dvořák wrote the first movement twice; the original version, in F major, was completed by Jarmil Burghauser and published in 1951. Burghauser suggested to John Clapham that Dvořák might have discarded the F major movement because of the similarities between its opening bars (Example 8.18a) and the beginning of Agathe's recitative "Wie nahte mir der Schlummer" in the second act of Weber's *Der Freischütz*.[27] In addition, the rhythmic cell of the theme also recalls the opening of Mendelssohn's Op. 12 quartet, and, by association, Beethoven's "Harp" Quartet. Only the rhythmic shape is retained in the new C major movement (Example 8.18b), whose sudden turn to minor in measure 3 must have been inspired by the Schubert cello quintet .

EXAMPLE 8.18.(a)   Dvořák, String Quartet in C Major, Op. 61: discarded F major opening movement, mm. 1–4.

EXAMPLE 8.18.(b)   Dvořák, String Quartet in C Major, Op. 61: replacement opening movement, mm. 1–5.

To hasten the completion of the quartet, Dvořák reused material from other compositions for the main themes of the remaining movements. The second movement is based on a discarded sketch for the Violin Sonata in F Major, Op. 57, and the third and fourth movements draw upon a polonaise for cello and piano.[28] Overall, the C Major Quartet seems concerned with grand gestures, far more so than the E♭ Quartet. The harmonic rhythm is slower than usual for Dvořák, and pedal points are frequent, while double stops and arpeggiated accompaniments add to the sheer volume of sound. Dvořák also takes pains to demonstrate his tonal deftness, as in the second movement's unconventional trip to the dominant of F major, shown in Example 8.19.

The scherzo, based on a motive derived from the second measure of the opening movement, includes a brilliant trio demanding great agility from both violinists. The finale, although beginning with the pitches C and E of a C major triad, swiftly hints at E minor and actually cadences in the

EXAMPLE 8.19.   Dvořák, String Quartet in C Major, Op. 61, mvt. 2, mm. 56–62.

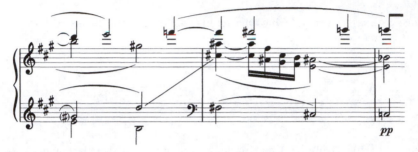

mediant at the end of the first phrase; the tonic does not return until the thirty-third measure. Dvořák thereby continues his experimentation with off-tonic finale openings such as those in the E Major Quartet and the Fifth Symphony.

In the F Minor Piano Trio, Op. 65 (1883), Dvořák achieved the perfect confluence of folk elements plus an international style characterized by a Brahmsian approach to motivic handling and variation techniques. This work, colored by the pallor of melancholy and elegiac melodies, is thought to have been the composer's response to the death of his mother a year earlier. Whatever the impetus, the trio reveals most fully Dvořák's ability to create slow movements rarely matched in substance and affect.

The first movement, in sonata form, introduces the pathos that pervades much of the trio. The tireless scherzo that follows soon gives way to a flowing lyrical section. If the work is indeed a response to the death of the composer's mother, that is most apparent in the elegiac third movement, which, as Šourek observes, carries "the tone of spiritual suffering."[29] The opening melody presented by the cello above the solemn harmonies of the piano represents the paradigmatic Dvořákian lament.

The sonata-rondo finale features a percussive opening octave leap and a *furiant,* the Czech dance characterized by alternation of duple and triple meters. A tranquil secondary theme answers the vigorous opening statement, only to reappear in the recapitulation in a folklike rendition, a gesture that eases the work's melancholy.

The interpolation of Czech song and dance forms was not confined to commissioned exotica such as the E♭ Major Quartet. In particular, the *dumka* (plural: *dumky*), a soulful Ukrainian ballad originally for the recitation of epic tales or heroic deeds, features frequently in Dvořák's works. Through his stylization the *dumka* becomes an episodic instrumental form akin to Liszt's Hungarian Rhapsodies, with sudden and unpredictable changes of mood and tempo, and often elegiac in character. *Dumky* begin to appear in Dvořák's works around the time of the Eb Major Quartet, the Second Slavonic Dance, and the String Sextet in A Major, Op. 48. In all of these instances a *furiant* complements the *dumka,* either as an adjacent movement or as an episode within the *dumka* movement itself.[30] A high point in this trend is the broad slow movement of the Piano Quintet in A Major, Op. 81 (1887), which over-shadows all of Dvořák's previous *dumky.* Apparently it so pleased him that a series of six *dumky* would form the large-scale structure of his later Piano Trio, Op. 90 (1890–91), known of course as the "Dumky" Trio.

The Piano Quintet's extended *dumka* movement sets the tone for the entire work, which is epic in scale and lasts a full forty minutes in performance. Such adventurous scope is particularly indicative of Dvořák's complete confidence in his mastery of extended sonata-allegro and slow movement forms. This stands in marked contrast to the revision of the 1872 Piano Quintet, Op. 5, also in A major, that he carried out shortly before composing Opus 81: the sprawling earlier work was trimmed by some 170 bars to just under half an hour in duration. It was probably Dvořák's ultimate dissatisfaction with Opus 5 that led him to compose a new quintet in the same key.

The opening bars in the first movement of Opus 81 aptly prepare the listener for the ensuing musical journey. A soothing, berceuselike melody for solo cello accompanied by rocking triplets begins comfortably in the tonic; the repetition of the opening phrase, however, turns to the parallel minor. There follows an unexpected A minor cadence coupled with a sudden *subito forte* that abruptly dissolves the peaceful, relaxed opening. The energetic music that follows yields substantial contrast, which Dvořák fully exploits during the course of the movement.

The structure of the second movement is indebted to more than folk models: it bears striking similarity to the second movement of Robert Schumann's Piano Quintet, Op. 44. As David Beveridge observes, Dvořák adopted Schumann's formal design to provide cohesive organization for the characteristic juxtaposition of highly contrasting sections in his *dumka.*[31]

The generously proportioned opening sonata-allegro and the broad arch structure of the second movement (whose form is roughly ABA-CABA) are followed by the unexpected simplicity of a brief ternary *furiant.* The principal section of this movement completely lacks the duple syncopations associated with this dance: rather, these are delayed until the middle of the trio section, where they appear in a ghostly *pianissimo.* Thus, evidently Dvořák did not always regard cross-rhythms as crucial to his conception of *furiant*; an earlier instance is the *furiant* of the String Sextet (1878), which lacks the syncopations entirely. The Piano Quintet concludes with a lively fourth movement, full of engaging contrapuntal inge-

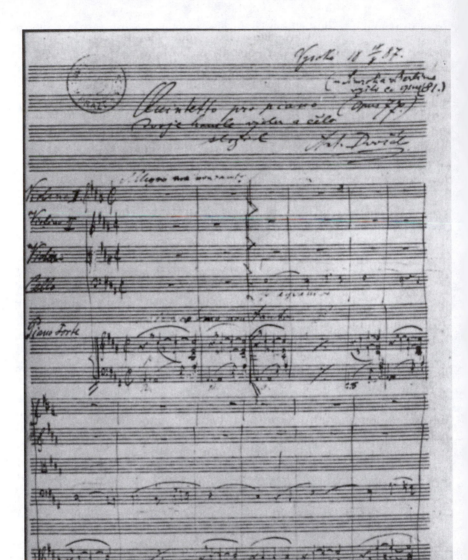

FIGURE 8-2.   First page of the autograph of Dvořák's Piano Quintet in A Major, Op. 81 (1887).

nuity and melodic charm, which, after a brief excursion into the minor mode, returns to the major to end the work in a bustling recapitulation.

As noted above, Dvořák's affinity for the *dumka* culminates in the "Dumky" Trio, Op. 90. Whereas in the quintet he had borrowed a plan from Schumann to mold his *dumka* into a quasi-traditional framework, here he allows each of the six *dumky* to stand fully realized on its own. With the exception of the fifth, which behaves like a scherzo throughout, all six movements manifest the typical alternation of highly contrasted sections. In its presentation of Slavic coloring and use of idiomatic rhythms, the work may best be compared to Dvořák's popular Slavonic Dances.

The Late Works, 1892–1895

During his stay in America between 1892 and 1895, Dvořák wrote three chamber works: the String Quartet, Op. 96, the String Quintet, Op. 97, and the charming Violin Sonatina, Op. 100. Inspired by his visit to the Midwest, all three were composed in the space of seven months, between June and December 1893. These pieces bear the hallmarks of a distinct musical style Dvořák forged during his American sojourn. The personality of the mature composer is as strong as ever, but is now complemented and enhanced by echoes of the indigenous Native and African American musics he encountered during this time. Dvořák's arrival in New York in September 1892 coincided with celebrations of the four hundredth anniversary of Columbus's voyage to the New World. The numerous musical bands Dvořák heard around this time afforded him immediate and plentiful exposure to American popular music.[32] Subsequent encounters with Negro spirituals and the music of different Native American tribes also greatly stimulated his musical imagination. Indeed, such was Dvořák's enthusiasm for Americana that in December 1892 he even attempted his own setting of the text "My Country, 'Tis of Thee," which he hoped would become the future American anthem.[33] That never came to pass, but the melody later found life as the theme for the slow movement of the String Quintet, Opus 97.

Dvořák claimed that he did not actually incorporate any African American, folk, or American Indian melodies into the compositions of his American period; nevertheless, certain scores reveal more than mere echoes of such tunes. It is, however, true that melodies are never quoted in an original form; perhaps Dvořák's substantial alterations somewhat justify his disavowal. In any case, he appropriated the melodies and rhythms that best suited him, and in so doing added "exotic" touches to his already well-formed musical style.[34]

The F Major Quartet, as New York music critic Henry Krehbiel pointed out in 1894, was composed "while Dr. Dvořák's mind was yet warm with the glow created by his work on the [New World] symphony."[35] Thus, it is scarcely surprising to find that the "American" Quartet draws from the same well of musical inspiration as its symphonic predecessor.

The principal themes of both works reveal this plainly: each begins with an ascending arpeggiated figure followed by a repeated compact motive featuring dotted rhythms, as shown in Example 8.20.

EXAMPLE 8.20.(a)   Dvořák: Symphony No. 9, *From the New World*, mvt. 1, main theme.

a)

EXAMPLE 8.20.(b)   Dvořák: String Quartet in F Major, Op. 96, the "American," mvt. 1, main theme.

b)

The quartet was composed in the farming community of Spillville, Iowa, a Bohemian immigrant colony where Dvořák found temporary respite from the overwhelming activity of New York City. The change of scenery and opportunity for relaxation enabled Dvořák to work with ease, and the quartet was finished in only two weeks. The warmth and joy he must have felt during this time are reflected in this new work. Formally uncomplicated and filled with delightful melodies, the "American" has proven the most popular of all the Dvořák quartets. At least two discernible allusions to the environs of Iowa can be found in it. First and most famous is the song of the scarlet tanager, a colorful bird Dvořák encountered during frequent solitary walks in the woods surrounding Spillville. Dvořák's amanuensis Josef Kovařík notated the birdsong in his memoirs, demonstrating its similarity to the melody found in measures 21–24 of the scherzo (Example 8.21).

EXAMPLE 8.21.(a)   The call of the scarlet tanager, notated by Josef Kovařík

a)

EXAMPLE 8.21.(b)   Dvořák, "American" Quartet, mvt. 3, mm. 21–24.

b)

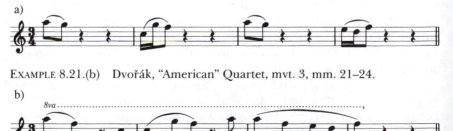

Secondly, the opening of the quartet's slow movement (Lento) contains a melody in the first violin that seems to imitate the vocal style of the Plains Indians. The dronelike, syncopated accompaniment in the inner voices as well as the percussive cello pizzicati provide an unobtrusive, "primitive" accompaniment akin to the drums and rattles used by the Plains Indians to complement their melodies.

The "American" Quartet has since overshadowed its immediate successor, the String Quintet, Opus 97. In this work Dvořák's confidence and assurance are once again manifest to a remarkable degree, but the relaxed atmosphere pervading the recently completed quartet is supplanted here by a more serious intent. Not only does the quintet achieve a greater degree of subtlety and complexity, but the second viola enriches the texture and results in a darker sound color. Unusual key areas such as A♭ minor, an increased harmonic chromaticism, and the apparent use of Native American dance rhythms all contribute to the work's exotic atmosphere.

An unusual formal feature of the quintet is the disposition of metrical patterns in its first two movements: the opening Allegro non tanto is in triple meter, whereas the scherzo, *allegro vivo*, is in common time. The scherzo pits two distinct dances against one another: the first is in Dvořák's "Indian" style, while the colorful fiddling of the second tune is reminiscent of Anglo-American folk dance, or a polka (Example 8.22).

EXAMPLE 8.22.(a)   Dvořák, String Quintet, Op. 97, mvt. 2: mm. 1–6 (viola II).

a)

EXAMPLE 8.22.(b)   Dvořák, String Quintet, Op. 97, mvt. 2: mm. 41–44 (violin I)

b)

In the slow movement, a set of variations, Dvořák's "American anthem" melody is poignantly cast; the first half of the theme appears in the key of A♭ minor, followed by a magical second half in the parallel major. The sentiments suggested here are not those of external pomp and circumstance, but rather of solemn and profound national pride.

Arguably the simplest and most concentrated representation of Dvořák's "American" style is the Sonatina for Violin and Piano. Completed in New York in December 1893, it is dedicated to his children. Two of them, Otakar and Otilie, gave the first performance, which Dvořák described as his "favorite premiere." Assigning the formidable opus number of 100 to this most unpretentious work reflects Dvořák's characteristic modesty and ironic sense of humor.

344 The Chamber Music of Smetana and Dvořák

There is a particularly charming anecdote concerning the composition of the Sonatina. In September 1893 Dvořák visited Minnehaha Falls near Saint Paul, Minnesota, where he was apparently inspired to notate a melody on his shirt cuff; this, we surmise, later appears as the watery G major theme in the middle of the Larghetto movement (Example 8.23).

EXAMPLE 8.23. Dvořák, Sonatina for Violin and Piano, Op. 100, mvt. 2, mm. 44–49.

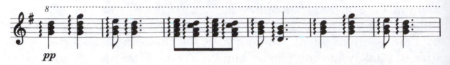

In Dvořák's Sonatina, all of the features prominent in the recently composed quartet and quintet—the pentatonic scale, dotted and syncopated rhythms, and the use of modes (Aeolian in particular)—completely dominate the music. The marked formal and technical simplicity of the piece places these "Americanisms" in high relief, and the overall musical expression is direct and disarming.

These three American-period works form a veritable catalogue of Dvořák's stylistic tendencies at that time, and bear striking resemblance to one another in their musical language. Accordingly, connections can easily be drawn even between the unassuming Violin Sonatina and the formidable "New World" Symphony. For example, a remarkable reminiscence of the symphony's principal theme occurs in the sonatina's finale, transformed to the parallel major (Example 8.24).

EXAMPLE 8.24. Dvořák, Sonatina for Violin and Piano, Op. 100, mvt. 4, mm. 106–13.

Pentatonic melody, a basic building block of the "American" Quartet, is also a crucial thematic component in the quintet and the sonatina. In addition to its associations with folk music, this scale, which lacks semitones, produces an "open" melodic line and harmonic texture that could be said to reflect the vast spaces of the American prairie.

Dvořák's three American chamber works were not his last word in the genre. After he left the New World, two string quartets, Opp. 105 and 106, were completed in Bohemia in 1895. Contented to be at home again among family and friends, Dvořák composed two masterly works filled with his characteristic optimism and *joie de vivre*. The first movement of the Quartet in A♭ major, Op. 105, was begun in New York shortly before his departure, but the entire work was not completed until nine months later. In the meantime, he composed the Quartet in G Major, Op. 106, and these two works crowned his achievements in the field of chamber music. After this Dvořák composed only programmatic works, including operas and symphonic poems.

It is fascinating to compare these two quartets in light of the composer's experience overseas. One could argue that Op. 106, completed first, served as a musical purgative for Dvořák since it is the last work written in his distinctively "American" style. The roots of its scherzo can be clearly traced to the trio section in the scherzo of the "New World" Symphony (Example 8.25). Likewise, the beautiful slow movement recalls its counterpart from the String Quintet, Opus 97, with a similar theme-and-variations structure and a restrained but deeply felt principal melody, whose hymnlike, essentially pentatonic profile is highlighted in the movement's climax.

EXAMPLE 8.25.(a)   Dvořák: "New World" Symphony, mvt. 3, mm. 175–83.

a)

EXAMPLE 8.25.(b).   String Quartet in G Major, Op. 106, mvt. 3, mm. 1–8.

b)

In Opus 105, on the other hand, Dvořák has all but removed his American mask and writes once again in his more familiar "Czech" style; the inclusion of a *furiant* as the scherzo is the most obvious instance of this "return to normalcy." The quartet is also marked by a conspicuous return to a more "Classical" melodic style, readily apparent in the sweetly lyrical slow movement, which commences with a question-and-answer four-bar period. Equally Mozartian is the first movement's opening melody, which recalls the beginning of the Clarinet Trio, K. 498. The finale might be a nod toward Brahms, so similar is its melodic material to the finale of that composer's Violin Concerto.

Both of these final quartets show Dvořák striving to invest Classical molds with greater flexibility and subtlety by means of rhythmically complex textures, liberal use of chromaticism, and cyclic thematic components. His successful blending of these myriad elements resulted in some of the most beautiful pages of music to come from the composer's pen.

Notes

1. The surviving material is reprinted as an appendix in Bedřich Smetana, *Komorní Skladby* (Prague, 1977), which also contains the sketches mentioned below and a reconstruction of the original version of the piano trio.

2. Brian Large, *Smetana* (New York, 1970), 34.

3. Smetana, *Komorní Skladby*, xl.

4. Best remembered as the teacher of David Popper, who arrived at the Prague conservatory around this time at the age of twelve.

5. The program for the concert is reproduced in Large, *Smetana*, 64.

6. Letter to Dr. Ludevít Procházka, 26 September 1877, in Bedřich Smetana, *Letters and Reminiscences*, ed. František Bartoš, trans. Daphne Rusbridge (Prague, 1955), 37.

7. Louise Duchesneau, *The Voice of the Music: A Study of the Role of Inspiration in Musical Composition* (Frankfurt am Main, 1986). (We are grateful to Jeremy Smith for bringing this source to our attention.) Smetana had corresponded with Clara Schumann a few years earlier in an unsuccessful attempt to find a publisher for his *Album Leaves*, Op. 5.

8. Large, *Smetana*, 34.

9. Letter to Joseph Srb-Debrnov, 12 April 1878, in Smetana, *Letters*, 191.

10. Ibid., 189.

11. Ibid., 222–23.

12. Ibid., 190–91.

13. Ibid., 259.

14. John Clapham, *Dvořák* (New York, 1979), 17, 22; the concert program is reproduced in *The New Grove*, s. v. "Dvořák, Antonín," by John Clapham, 5:766.

15. David Beveridge, "Dvořák and Brahms: A Chronicle, an Interpretation," in *Dvořák and His World,* ed. Michael Beckerman (Princeton, NJ, 1993), 58.

16. Clapham, *Dvořák*, 25, n. 10.

17. Hartmut Schick, *Studien zu Dvořáks Streichquartetten* (Laaber, 1990), 68.

18. Miroslav Černý, introduction to Antonín Dvořák, *String Quartet in D Major* (Prague, 1982), viii–ix.

19. Otakar Šourek, *The Chamber Music of Antonín Dvořák,* trans. Roberta Finlayson Samsour (Prague, 1956), 15.

20. Otakar Šourek, *Antonín Dvořák* (Prague, 1952), 12–13.

21. Smetana was the first president of the music division.

22. František Bartoš, introduction to Antonín Dvořák, *String Quintet in G major* (Prague, 1958), x.

23. Brahms to Simrock, 5 April 1878, in Otakar Šourek, *Antonín Dvořák: Letters and Reminiscences,* trans. Roberta Finlayson Samsour (Prague, 1954), 43.

24. Brahms to Dvořák, March 1878, in Šourek, *Letters,* 42–43.

25. Smetana, *Komorní Skladby*, xliii.

26. John Clapham, *Antonín Dvořák: Musician and Craftsman* (New York, 1966), 175.

27. Ibid., 175.

28. Ibid., 175–76.

29. Šourek, *Chamber Music,* 157.

30. For an overview of the composer's use of the *dumka,* see David Beveridge, "Dvořák's Dumka and the Concept of Nationalism," *Journal of Musicological Research* 12 (1993): 303-25.

31. David Beveridge, "Dvořák's Piano Quintet, op. 81: The Schumann Connection," *Chamber Music Quarterly* 6 (Spring 1984): 2.
32. Jarmil Burghauser, "My Country, 'Tis of Thee," in *Dvořák in America,* ed. John C. Tibbetts (Portland, OR, 1993), 203.
33. Ibid., 204.
34. For a discussion of Dvořák's use of Native American musical materials, see John Clapham, "Dvořák and the American Indian," in *Dvořák in America,* ed. John C. Tibbetts (Portland, OR, 1993), 113-22.
35. Henry E. Krehbiel, "Dvořák's American Compositions," *New York Daily Tribune,* 1 January 1894, repr. in Beckerman, ed., *Dvořák and His World,* 168.

Select Bibliography

Bartoš, František, ed. *Bedřich Smetana: Letters and Reminiscences.* Translated by Daphne Rusbridge. Prague, 1955.
Beckerman, Michael, ed. *Dvořák and His World.* Princeton, NJ, 1993.
_____. *New Worlds of Dvořák: Searching in America for the Composer's Inner Life.* New York, 2003.
Beveridge, David,"Dvořák's Dumka and the Concept of Nationalism in Music Historiography." *Journal of Musicological Research* 12 (1993): 303–25.
_____, ed. *Rethinking Dvořák: Views from Five Countries.* Oxford, 1996.
Burghauser, Jarmil. *Antonín Dvořák.* Prague, 1967.
Clapham, John. *Dvořák.* New York, 1979.
_____. *Antonín Dvořák: Musician and Craftsman.* New York, 1966.
_____. *Smetana.* London, 1972.
Döge, Klaus. *Dvořák: Leben, Werke, Dokumente.* Mainz, 1991.
_____, ed. *Dvořák-Studien.* Mainz, 1994.
Katz, Derek. "Smetana's Second String Quartet: Voice of Madness or Triumph of Spirit?" *Musical Quarterly* 81 (1997): 516–536.
Large, Brian. *Smetana.* New York, 1970.
Schick, Hartmut. *Studien zu Dvořáks Streichquartetten.* Laaber, 1990.
_____. "What's American about Dvořák's 'American' Quartet and Quintet." *Czech Music* 18/2 (1993–4): 72–83.
Šourek, Otakar. *Antonín Dvořák.* English translation. Prague, 1952.
_____. *Antonín Dvořák: Letters and Reminiscences.* Translated by Roberta Finlayson Samsour. Prague, 1954.
_____. *The Chamber Music of Antonín Dvořák.* Translated by Roberta Finlayson Samsour. Prague, 1956.
Tibbetts, John C., ed. *Dvořák in America.* Portland, OR, 1993.

CHAPTER NINE

Fin de Siècle Chamber Music and the Critique of Modernism

John Daverio

Preservation and Innovation

In the penultimate chapter of his magisterial history of nineteenth-century music (*Die Musik des 19. Jahrhunderts*), Carl Dahlhaus grapples with the vexing problem of hitting upon the term that best captures the essence of European art music at the turn to the twentieth century. Drawing on the historiography of Hermann Bahr, Dahlhaus ultimately decides in favor of *modernism* as the designation for the musical era bounded by Richard Strauss's *Don Juan* and Gustav Mahler's First Symphony (1889), on the one hand, and the advent of atonality in Arnold Schoenberg's *Drei Klavier- stücke*, Op. 11 (1909), on the other. Characterized structurally by a will to monumentality and affectively by a heightened, feverish intensity, musical modernism emerges most clearly in the tone poem and the post-Wagnerian music drama.[1]

While chamber music figures little (if at all) in this scheme, Dahlhaus goes on to note the curious reversal in which the genre was implicated in the twentieth century's first decade. Turning to a persistent theme in the writings of Theodor Adorno, Dahlhaus argues for the centrality of cham- ber music as the "carrier genre" of the New Music. An enclave of conser- vatism in 1860 or so, chamber music would furnish the medium for the innovations wrought by Schoenberg and his colleagues near the close of the first decade of the twentieth century. Coterminous with the rise in im- portance of the chamber idiom was the plummet in prestige of the tone poem and other programmatically motivated forms. Within about a twenty-year period, in other words, the "carrier genres" of musical mod- ernism came to be viewed as trivial and obsolete.[2]

How and why did this extraordinary reversal take place? For some writers, the flowering of chamber music around 1910 represents a reaction against the gargantuanism cultivated so vigorously in the previous century.[3] According to Dahlhaus's characteristically dialectical reading, chamber music was able to provide, through its pervasive employment of thematic-motivic development, a logical counterforce to the threat of incoherence inherent in a style where dissonance has been emancipated.[4] Psychological reasons might be adduced as well. Carl Schorske writes:

> As his sense of what Hofmannsthal called *das Gleitende*, the slipping away of the world, increased, the bourgeois turned his appropriated aesthetic culture inward to the cultivation of the self, of his personal uniqueness. This tendency inevitably led to preoccupation with one's own psychic life. It provides the link between devotion to art and concern with the psyche.[5]

It may well be that chamber music best reflected this inward turn of *fin de siècle* bourgeois sensibility.

At the same time, the shift of emphasis in the system of musical genres around 1910 may not represent as marked a *volte face* as at first seems to be the case. Writing in 1884, Hugo Wolf observed that many of his contemporaries, whose symphonies and operas "would have driven Job right out of his mind," were "producing their most tolerable music" in the chamber idiom. Indeed, he claimed to be "truly encouraged by the zealous cultivation of chamber music and the public's enthusiastic participation in this category of the musical art."[6] In the course of the next two decades Wolf himself, together with Brahms, Reger, Richard Strauss, Busoni, Zemlinsky, and the young Schoenberg, would make notable contributions to the genre. Working outside of or on the fringes of the Austro-German tradition, figures such as Debussy, Bartók, and Ives likewise played key roles in effecting the shift from "modernism" to "modernity" in their chamber works.

The rise to prominence of chamber music around 1910 may be even better understood as a manifestation of the "progressive" side of a dialectic between preservation and innovation that had informed the genre for at least a century before. Already in the definition of *Kammermusik* in his *Musikalisches Lexikon* of 1802, Heinrich Christoph Koch recognized the split between a conservative social character aimed at the private delectation of music-loving aristocrats and a finely wrought compositional style characterized by motivic interplay and nuance.[7]

With the displacement of the aristocracy by the bourgeoisie as the main consumer class of nineteenth-century musical culture, the production and reception of chamber music came more and more to reflect the profound conservatism of the latter group. Safely ensconced in the bourgeois drawing room, the ideal acoustical space for a genre wherein players and audience are one, chamber music served as a correlate of *Bildung* ("cultured formation"), the acquisition of which was deemed so essential to the nineteenth-century burgher. Courtesy, gentility, and conversational eloquence, all of them qualities of the cultivated middle-class purveyors of high art, would resonate in the practice and even in the production of chamber music.[8]

At the same time, this apparently conservative art form harbored a "progressive" dimension in the potential esotericism of its compositional style. The entry on *Kammermusik* in Gustav Schilling's *Encyclopädie* (1835–37), echoing a theme encountered in earlier accounts, relates that the chamber style was both more "difficult" and more "artful" than the "public" styles associated with opera, symphony, and church music.[9] By 1882, A. Tottmann would locate this artfulness primarily in the propensity toward ever-tighter thematic integration in the masterworks of the chamber repertory since Haydn, thus prefiguring a crucial strand in the Adorno-Dahlhaus interpretation of the link between the chamber style and the New Music.[10]

The dialectic between the notions of chamber music as *Hausmusik* for dilettantes and as an esoteric art for cognoscenti is reflected in two complementary aspects of late nineteenth-century concert life. The gradual effacement of the distinction between "chamber" and "concert" music that eventually led to generically hybrid works such as Schoenberg's First *Kammersymphonie*, Op. 9, and Berg's *Kammerkonzert* had as its precondition the proliferation of professional chamber groups in the late nineteenth century. For the period between 1890 and 1914 in Berlin, Hugo Leichtentritt counted no fewer than seven professional piano trios and twelve string quartets, among the most prominent of the latter being the ensemble led by Joseph Joachim.[11] Vienna served as home base for the Hellmesberger Quartet (founded in 1849) and the famous Rosé Quartet, both of which, if at times reluctantly, contributed to the public's awareness of the modernist chamber repertory. (Although the Rosé Quartet twice rejected Wolf's D Minor String Quartet for performance, first in 1884, then a year later, it did participate in the premiere of Schoenberg's *Verklärte Nacht* [Transfigured night] in 1902.)

Musical life, especially in larger centers such as Vienna, began to change radically as a result of the professionalization of a practice long associated with talented dilettantes. In the early nineteenth century there was often little distinction between performers and listeners in the musical salons of the *haute bourgeoisie*, if only because both groups alternately served in both capacities; by the end of the century, professionals were regularly being hired to entertain a select group of invitees. The Dreililienverlag of Berlin sold fifty-seven copies of the score to Schoenberg's *Verklärte Nacht*, but only nine sets of parts, a sign that most interested individuals were contemplating this music in the privacy of their studies while leaving its performance to those with the requisite technical proficiency.[12] Whereas composers in the late eighteenth and early nineteenth centuries had capitalized on the marketability of ensemble music for a burgeoning class of domestic music makers, they catered less to the sometimes limited capabilities of the bourgeois music lover as the century proceeded. Thus by the early years of the twentieth century a peculiar reversal had set in: professional groups were now assembled to cope with the far greater demands of modernist chamber music. The Waldbauer-Kerpely Quartet, to cite an example, came together for the express purpose of interpreting Bartók's First String Quartet, a work that met with incomprehension and hostility at its first performance in Budapest in March 1910.[13]

If the development of a public and professional chamber music practice suggests something of an oxymoron, then a complementary aspect of *fin de siècle* musical life maintained the privacy regularly associated with the chamber idiom. In the private musical society, again a feature of Viennese culture, *haute bourgeoisie* and professional musicians alike joined forces, often toward the end of forwarding the modernist program. The increased number of these organizations in the first part of the twentieth century makes good sense when considered against the background of late nineteenth-century institutions devoted either to the furtherance of contemporary musical practice, such as the Akademischer Wagner Verein and the Wiener Tonkünstlerverein, or to the cultivation of modernism in the visual arts and architecture, where the Vereinigung bildender Künstler (best known as the "Secession" presided over by Gustav Klimt, Alfred Roller, and Otto Wagner) took primacy of place as a model. Indeed, the stated aim of a specifically musical group such as the Ansorge-Verein— founded in 1903 and largely but not exclusively devoted to performing the works of the pianist and composer Konrad Ansorge—was the propagation of "musico-poetic modernism."[14] The short-lived Vereinigung schaffender Tonkünstler, organized in 1904 by Schoenberg and his mentor, friend, and eventually father-in-law, Alexander Zemlinsky, likewise sought to showcase the most recent developments in the musical world.

But if the Vereinigung schaffender Tonkünstler was intended to serve an educative function for the musical public at large, then Schoenberg's Verein für musikalische Privataufführungen (1918-1921) turned inward to a select group of musicians and listeners with weekly performances for members only. According to Alban Berg's prospectus, the goal of the Verein was an "accurate knowledge of modern music" acquired through "clear, well-prepared performances," "frequent repetitions," and a withdrawal of the performances from "the corrupting influences of publicity."[15] While chamber works had appeared with some frequency on the programs of the Wiener Tonkünstlerverein (Zemlinsky's First String Quartet, Op. 15, was premiered at one of its 1897 concerts) and the Ansorge-Verein (Schoenberg's early lieder figured in the 1904 season), the performance of chamber music took on even greater prominence in Schoenberg's Verein, whose standing ensemble consisted of a handful of pianists and singers and a string quartet. Among the roughly two hundred compositions given during the three-year existence of the organization were dozens of chamber works by the leading exponents of musical modernism: Reger, Busoni, Szymanowski, and Zemlinsky.[16] Thus the dialectic played out in *fin de siècle* chamber music between preservation and innovation emerges here with particular clarity: in Schoenberg's Verein für musikalische Privataufführungen, the chamber idiom takes on the character of a modernist *musica reservata*.

To demonstrate the singular importance of chamber music for *fin de siècle* modernism—to argue, in other words, that the emergence of chamber music as a leading genre of the New Music around 1910 was not as abrupt as the Adorno-Dahlhaus critical tradition suggests—it will be helpful to consider, first of all, the rich and varied responses to the music of Johannes Brahms in the chamber repertory at the turn of the century, and second, this repertory's absorption and reflection of the "carrier genres" of the period, program music and music drama. The receptivity of the chamber idiom both to Brahmsian and Lisztian-Wagnerian influences lends further support to the claim that the essence of the genre lies precisely in a dialectic play of conservatism and progress. At the same time, the forms and aesthetic suppositions of modernism were neither replicated nor unquestioningly embraced in all chamber music of the period. We may in fact discover that the chamber idiom served as the arena in which the critique of modernism was first carried out.

Brahms's Legacy

In a letter of 1893 the twenty-year-old Max Reger spoke eloquently, if tersely, to the depth of Brahms's influence on the younger generation of *fin de siècle* composers by describing him as "the only composer of our time . . . from whom one can learn something."[17] Although Brahms exercised a profound effect on the keyboard and vocal music of the late nineteenth century, nowhere did the instigators of musical modernism put their Brahmsian lessons to such good use as in their instrumental chamber music. To be sure, the nurturing force of earlier masters can also be detected in this repertory; echoes of late Beethoven, in particular, are easily heard in the propulsive dotted rhythms of Wolf's D Minor String Quartet (first movement) and Schoenberg's String Quartet in D Minor, Op. 7, in the chorale variations of Busoni's Second Violin Sonata, Op. 36a, and in the introspective fugato that opens Bartók's First String Quartet. But Brahms, as Reger implied, could speak more directly still to his younger colleagues, if only because he was a living presence.[18]

By his own account, Schoenberg was a "Brahmsian" when he met Alexander Zemlinsky in 1895.[19] Shortly after this meeting he would set to work on his first sustained effort for a chamber ensemble. Completed in 1897, Schoenberg's D Major String Quartet owed much to the advice of his new friend (at Zemlinsky's urging, Schoenberg wrote two new middle movements and substantially revised the first movement) and to the example of Vienna's greatest exponent of the Austro-German musical tradition. As Walter Frisch has shown, the opening movement of this work reveals just how thoroughly the young Schoenberg had absorbed the

Brahmsian technique of developing variation.[20] Likewise, the textural richness of the slow movement, a set of variations, attests to more than a passing acquaintance with the chamber works of the older master. But while the texture of Schoenberg's youthful quartet betrays the influence of Brahms, its melodic idiom (characterized in the first and last movements by a strong emphasis on the sixth degree), jaunty rhythms, and modal fluctuations hearken more to Dvořák's style.[21]

A perhaps more mature appropriation of the Brahmsian manner is evident in the first movement of Zemlinsky's First String Quartet in A, Op. 15 (1896). (Brahms himself was impressed enough with the work to facilitate its publication.) The contrast between lyric, closely spaced upper voices and supporting cello pizzicato at the beginning of the second group, as well as the assignment of the closing theme to the warm middle register of the viola, both recall the older composer's sound world. So, too, does the almost continual play of $\frac{3}{4}$ and $\frac{6}{8}$ meters. Of course, there is nothing particularly Brahmsian about hemiola effects in themselves. What matters most is Zemlinsky's attempt to coordinate these effects with tonal motion and form, much as Brahms was apt to do in the works of his maturity. Hence, the tripartite shape of the movement's opening theme group (mm. 1–13, 14–20, 20–26) is articulated not only by melodic and modal contrast, but also by a shift from triple or compound to implied duple meters and back again. Similarly, the tripartite second group is framed by passages solidly in $\frac{6}{8}$ surrounding a central, metrically divagating section in which $\frac{3}{4}$ and $\frac{6}{8}$ are superimposed.[22]

According to Zemlinsky, Brahms's music supplied the pervasive atmosphere in which he and his colleagues lived and breathed: "It was fascinating, its influence inescapable, its effect intoxicating."[23] Well to the east of the Austrian capital, in Budapest, the young Béla Bartók fell under its "intoxicating" sway. His Piano Quintet, DD 77 (1903–4), like Zemlinsky's A Major String Quartet, abounds in surface imitations of Brahms's style—witness the luxuriant textures in the opening movement, the persistent hemiolas in the scherzo, and the *zigeunerisch* finale. But here, too, there are signs of a more deeply thought emulation of the Brahmsian manner. The rhythmic "modulation" leading to a highly varied repetition of the scherzo recalls the subtle use of metric and melodic variation in the third movement of Brahms's Second Symphony.

One of the warmest tributes to Brahms's fascinating and inescapable influence comes in Reger's Quintet for Clarinet and Strings, Op. 146 (1915). This mellow, elusive, and delicately textured work encapsulates a lifetime preoccupation with the Brahmsian style in the form of an obvious but sensitively handled thematic allusion. Drawing on Brahms's own Clarinet Quintet, Op. 115, Reger introduces a four-note motive—E–D♯–B♯–C♯—at the clarinet's response to the main lyrical idea of the second group (mm. 48–49). But in retrospect, this apparent bow in the direction of Brahms's Quintet (first movement, m. 3: D–C♯–A♯–B) turns out to be more than a mere citation. The "Brahms" motive had in fact insinuated itself into the fabric of the preceding transition, where it figured, in slightly varied form, in the frenetic climax and liquidation of measures 25–39. It surfaces again in the development, first as the basis for a fugato, and next in a climactic passage based on the earlier transition. But its most telling appearance comes at the interface between development and recapitulation. The retransition closes with A–G♯–E♯–F♯ in the first violin, while the reprise, like the exposition, begins with E–F♯–A–G♯ in the clarinet, thus demonstrating, after the fact, that the "Brahms" motive in inverted form lurks behind the movement's suave opening idea. Reger's gestures of homage are at once latent and manifest.[24]

So, too, are those of Arnold Schoenberg, who in moving toward compositional maturity entered into a profound dialogue with the Brahmsian legacy. It is probably safe to say that, in Schoenberg's view, Brahms was responsible for a radical rethinking of what constituted a musical idea. According to Schoenberg's historical outlook, musical practice divides into two great eras: a "contrapuntal" period extending from the "Netherlanders" to Bach, and a "homophonic" period extending from Haydn and Mozart to the end of the nineteenth century. Each era is in turn linked with its own characteristic musical technique, the contrapuntal period with the vertical combination and elaboration of melodically fixed ideas (according to the principle of "unraveling" or *Abwicklung*), the homophonic period with the horizontal unfolding of a melodically mutable idea through development (*Entwicklung*) or "developing variation."[25] What the future demands, according to Schoenberg's utopian historiography, is the simultaneous deployment of both techniques. The horizontal and vertical saturation of musical space for which Schoenberg strove in his twelve-tone works can thus be seen as the response to a historical imperative.

Although he never made the argument outright, it is likely that Schoenberg prized Brahms's music so highly precisely because it prefigured this utopian fusion of horizontal and vertical dimensions, of *Entwicklung* and *Abwicklung*. And indeed, the chamber idiom would provide the medium par excellence within which to effect the shift from a merely developmental to a developmental-contrapuntal notion of the musical idea. The opening measure of the first movement of Brahms's C Minor Piano Trio, Op. 101 (1886), conjoins two rhythmically parallel but melodically distinct motives in the right and left hand of the piano part (see Example 6.11a, p. 277 above). With the *Stimmtausch* in measure 2 it becomes evident that the basis for the musical proceedings is less a single motive than the combination of disparate melodic strands. Moreover, each element of the basic combination as stated in m. 1 is elaborated separately throughout the course of the movement in accordance with the principle of developing variation: motive *a* serves as the point of departure for the continuation of the opening gesture in measures 3–11; the rising triplet from motive *b* informs the expansive melody at the initiation of the second group (mm. 38ff.). But most remarkable are those passages where both motives are elaborated concurrently; in measures 81–85 of the development, for instance, the violin and cello state *b* in augmentation while the piano presents material largely spun out from *a*. A single-minded focus on the contrapuntal density of the movement thus misses the point.[26] What counts, at least from a Schoenbergian perspective, is Brahms's simultaneous reliance on two theoretically opposed procedures.

To be sure, the art of thematic combination was not solely Brahms's property. When Richard Strauss, at the climax of the finale of his Violin Sonata, Op. 18 (1887), brings together the two main themes of the movement's exposition, the result hearkens more to a Berliozian *réunion des thèmes* than to Brahms. Similarly, the model for the impressive passage near the conclusion of Schoenberg's *Verklärte Nacht*, where several of the work's principal motives are interwoven in a luminous D major (mm. 370ff.), is rather to be sought in the "poetic" counterpoint of the orchestral close of Wagner's *Götterdämmerung* than in Brahms's more finely etched art.

The nature of the contrapuntal elaboration in Schoenberg's First String Quartet in D Minor, Op. 7 (1904–5), is of a different order. Here the combinative gesture is no longer held in reserve for moments of apotheosis; it actually serves as the point of departure for the work's unfolding. Much of the opening theme group (mm. 1–96) derives its substance from the working out of a basic motivic combination comprising a rhetorically profiled idea in the first violin (*x* in Example 9.1) and a countermelody (*y*) moving by step in the cello. In accordance with what Dahlhaus calls the principle of multidimensionality,[27] Schoenberg's opening group discloses the structural properties, in miniature, of a complete sonata-form movement. And as it turns out, each station of the form is articulated by a variant of the basic combination or one of its motivic components. The first group (D minor) of the miniature sonata conjoins *x* and *y*, while its second group (Bb minor; from m. 14) introduces simultaneously varied forms of both motives. The development opens in Eb minor with a restatement of the basic combination (from m. 30), now with *y* assigned to the violins and *x* to the cello, and proceeds to evolve a number of derivative contrapuntal units that combine *y* with a propulsive dotted figure (mm. 44ff.) and *x* with the head motive of the second group (m. 54). With the restoration of the D minor tonic and the basic combination at measure 65, the recapitulation begins its inexorable drive toward a climactic conjunction of a transitional motive from measure 8 (fanned out in the three upper voices) and a rhythmically augmented variant of *x* in the cello (mm. 79ff.).

In response to the rhetorical question, "Why is Schoenberg's music so hard to understand?" Alban Berg looked to the motivic and textural density of the String Quartet, Op. 7, for an answer.[28] (If anything, Berg's discussion reminds us that Schoenberg's quartet is even more difficult to understand than I have made it out to be: the two-voice framework of the basic combination, as Berg rightly points out, is often enriched by a third melodic strand, a nervous figure in the viola). But the "boundless opulence" that Berg praised in this work results from more than its densely

EXAMPLE 9.1.   Arnold Schoenberg, String Quartet in D Minor, Op. 7, mvt. 1, opening.

wrought contrapuntal web—which Schoenberg himself did not hesitate to call "remarkable."[29] Owing to its dual reliance on both contrapuntal combinations and developing variation, on *Abwicklung* and *Entwicklung,* the D Minor Quartet presents real challenges to players, listeners, and critics alike. In this, Schoenberg proved to be a more than able pupil of Brahms.

Chamber Music and the "Taking Back" of Program Music

The argument for the essential conservatism of the chamber repertory during the Age of Romanticism rests in large measure on a piece of negative evidence: the repertory's relative indifference to the programmatic genres deemed by critical opinion to be carriers of musical progress. Hermann Hirschbach's association of his *Lebensbilder* for string quartet with passages from Goethe's *Faust,*[30] Joachim Raff's "cyclic tone poem" for violin and piano *Volker,* Op. 203 (1876), Bedřich Smetana's autobiographical string quartet *Z mého života* (From my life; 1876/1880)—all are arguably exceptions adduced to prove the rule. Yet by the end of the nineteenth century and into the first years of the twentieth, the chamber idiom began to evince an ever-greater receptivity to the programmatic impulses of musical modernism.

Schoenberg's *Verklärte Nacht,* Op. 4, for string sextet (1899) provides the locus classicus of this development.[31] As Schoenberg put it, "an almost sudden turn toward a more 'progressive' manner of composing" followed on the completion of his D Major String Quartet in 1897. Intrigued by the orchestral works of Mahler and Strauss, he soon began to write "symphonic poems of one movement" after their model.[32] With *Verklärte Nacht* Schoenberg brilliantly demonstrated the compatibility between the poeticizing aesthetic of musical modernism and the traditionally more abstract demands of the chamber style. As Dahlhaus has suggested, Richard Dehmel's emotionally charged poem (published in 1896 in the collection *Weib und Welt*) furnished Schoenberg with the premise if not the actual content of his music, for the symmetrical structure of the poetic text—three brief stanzas for the narrator framing the woman's confessional monologue and the man's consoling rejoinder—already suggests a common musical form.[33] But even this rondo design is overruled in Schoenberg's sextet by the sheer virtuosity of a crisscrossing network of motivic references. As so often happens in the symphonies of Mahler and the tone poems of Strauss, the poetic starting point for the composition, as well as its outward formal symmetry, is swallowed up by an all-embracing developmental process.

Schoenberg's *Verklärte Nacht* draws on the aesthetic and the compositional techniques of yet another modernist genre: music drama. The brevity of the sextet's rich profusion of melodic ideas, no less than their disposition according to what Schoenberg called the principle of "model and sequence,"[34] lends them the character of leitmotives. Not surprisingly, the tendency toward Wagnerian syntax is most evident in transitional and developmental passages. The opening portion of the first lengthy development section (mm. 135–52; see Example 9.2 for the beginning of this passage), for instance, surely counts as one of the most remarkable spots in the work. Eerie sextuplets, pizzicati, and tremolos in the inner voices (*con sordino*) stand in marked contrast to a "wild" and "passionate" motive (a kind of primal scream) in the first violin, at one extreme of the texture, and ominous asides in the second cello at the other. The logic of the passage derives neither from its tortured harmonies nor its sublimated periodic structure, but rather from the associative magic of the leitmotivic web: each element in the texture points back to earlier motivic landmarks (the sextuplets and pizzicati to m. 34, the primal scream to mm. 41–45, the cello asides to mm. 55–56), which appear here in grotesquely altered forms. In addition, the whole passage coheres as a large-scale model and sequence insofar as measures 135–43 essentially restate the music of measures 144–52 a step higher.

Music-dramatic thinking likewise governs the design of the entire work. The prominence of semitonal motion in its overall tonal organization (d–e♭–D–D♭–D), for instance, recalls the similarly "expressive" harmonic shifts in Wagner's music dramas.[35] And although some writers have argued for the centrality of sonata-form procedures in Schoenberg's sextet, it is probably more sensible to recognize that the remnants of traditional forms have been subsumed (a Hegelian would say *aufgehoben*) under larger musicopoetic processes.[36] Recapitulation, for example, is displaced by apotheosis in the second half of the work, where the languorous, chromatic, minor-mode leitmotives of the first half by and large recur in a transcendent major-mode context. Schoenberg's employment of a transfiguring variation technique at the broadest level (reminiscent of Liszt's practice in

EXAMPLE 9.2.   Schoenberg, *Verklärte Nacht*, Op. 4, mm. 135–40.

EXAMPLE 9.2. *continued*

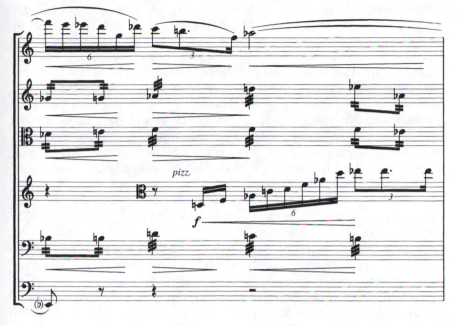

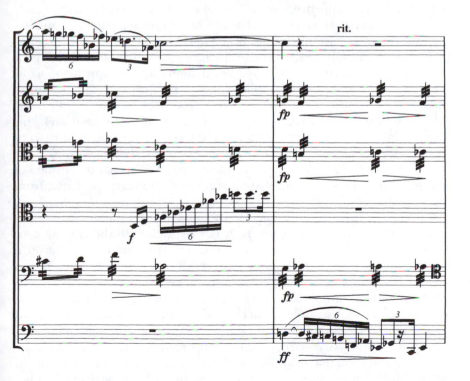

the *Faust* Symphony and Wagner's in *Tristan*) thus serves as a musical cipher for the theme of *Verklärung* (transfiguration) articulated in Dehmel's poem.

With the D Minor String Quartet, Op. 7, Schoenberg claimed to have "abandoned" the programmatic and poetic pretensions of modernism in favor of an abstract employment of sophisticated contrapuntal, harmonic, and motivic techniques.[37] But Christian Martin Schmidt's identification of Schoenberg's "very definite—but private" program for the work in a sketchbook of 1904–5—taken together with the composer's remarks, made late in his life, on the existence of a poetic catalyst for his quartet—suggests that the turn to "absolute" music was less absolute than Schoenberg originally implied.[38] In fashioning his program, Schoenberg eschewed external literary or pictorial stimuli, opting instead for a generalized description of internal psychological states, each of which can be readily linked with a major section of the sprawling quartet: "revolt," "defiance," and "despair" with the opening *Nicht zu rasch;* "feeling new life" with the scherzolike *Kräftig;* the "dream image" of "forsaken ones . . . in mourning" with the equivalent of a slow movement (*Mäßig; langsame Viertel*); and the protagonist's "return home" to feelings of "peace and harmony" with the major-mode coda (*Breit, ruhig*).

At the same time, the relationship of the quartet to its program is considerably more complex than that between musical and poetic texts in *Verklärte Nacht*. Whereas Schoenberg began sketching his D Minor Quartet in March 1904, the program in all likelihood was not drafted until mid-July of the same year, at a point, that is, when a creative impasse impeded further progress with the composition. Hence the "definite" but "private" program, as Mark Benson has recently shown, was little more than a provisional spur to Schoenberg's stymied imagination, a prop to be withdrawn as soon as it had accomplished its task.[39] Just as Thomas Mann's Adrian Leverkühn attempted to "take back" Beethoven's Ninth Symphony, so did Schoenberg, in the Op. 7 quartet, begin to "take back" his own earlier essays in the programmatic genre: the tone poem for string sextet, *Verklärte Nacht*, and its orchestral counterpart, *Pelleas und Melisande*. The D Minor Quartet, in other words, initiates a far-reaching critique of the aesthetic presuppositions that had nurtured musical modernism from the start.

Nor was this critique limited to the immediate confines of the Viennese circle around Schoenberg. Béla Bartók, although thoroughly conversant with the music of the Austro-German tradition, registered a similar protest in his First String Quartet (1907–9), a work premiered in March 1910 on the first of two infamous concerts that came to represent the "double birthday of modern Hungarian music."[40] The first movement opens with a plaintive and sinuous melody in the first violin, imitated two beats later at the lower fourth by the second violin. The first violin's descending sixth, F–A♭, when coupled with the answering C–E, yields a four-note configuration that bears comparison with another four-note pattern whose importance for the confessional side of Bartók's early music is beyond question. Specifically, the pattern D–F♯–A–C♯—a musical symbol for the young Bartók's *inamorata* (the violinist Stefi Geyer) and a source for the pitch material of the First Violin Concerto, the *Two Portraits* for orchestra, and the last two of the Bagatelles, Op. 6, for piano—lurks behind the imitative opening of the String Quartet, the first movement of which Bartók described as his "funeral dirge" in a presumed reference to the demise of his love affair.[41] But to generate the quartet's opening configuration from the "Geyer" motive, we must first transpose the latter to F, then substitute A♭ for A, and finally replace the first and last rising third of the originary motive with descending sixths. In the following movements, the "Geyer" motive recedes even farther into the background. In effect, it disappears: all that remains are allusions to the octatonicism of the melody spun out of the F–A♭ and C–E head motives.[42] The arguably programmatic starting point for the work thus retreats deep within the musical texture, where it figures as a highly mutable, subthematic element. For all intents and purposes, the biographical subject of Bartók's First Quartet is extinguished, and with it one of the chief aesthetic premises of modernist composition.

Fin de Siècle Forms

The principal genres of late nineteenth-century music were driven by a will to monumental forms. But this imperative posed a daunting compositional challenge owing, among other reasons, to the brevity of the musical ideas upon which the larger forms were necessarily based. In response to the challenge, composers adopted new approaches to thematic recurrence, variation technique, and the art of transition, always with an eye toward weaving ever tighter relationships between whole and part, general and particular. And while their endeavors first bore fruit in the symphony and the tone poem, composers were quick to transfer these new means of ensuring monumental breadth to the chamber idiom.

The attempt to impose a higher unity over the discrete movements of a multimovement work through transformational recurrence owes much to the example of Berlioz and Liszt. Claude Debussy's String Quartet in G minor (1893)—written before the composer adopted an intensely skeptical attitude toward the late Romantic aesthetic—draws liberally from this example. The opening idea of the first movement, unfolding first as a pentatonic pattern around G but soon colored by a Phrygian A♭, provides the basis for much of the quartet's thematic material. In the second movement, the same idea undergoes a series of Lisztian transformations, appearing in the guise of an impish viola solo, a suave violin melody, and a rapid-fire pizzicato variant, while in the finale it is deftly interwoven with a series of new ideas prior to its apotheosis at roughly midmovement. The work is thus saved from devolving into a sequence of character pieces through the epic handling of its opening theme.

Bartók adopted a similar principle in his early Piano Quintet, DD (1903–4), where the main idea of the finale, a swaggering and virtuosically developed Gypsy tune, derives from a motive presented near the beginning of the first movement. The resilience of this fundamentally Lisztian technique is demonstrated by its use a full decade later in Ernö Dohnányi's Second Piano Quintet, Op. 26, the last movement of which culminates in a grandiose restatement, *con brio,* of the work's opening idea (combined with the quasi-fugal main subject of the finale) and closes with a varied recall of the first movement's coda, transformed from minor into major.

Not only motives or themes but indeed entire movements may lend themselves to transformation. Such cases, wherein Lisztian-Straussian transformative techniques are raised to a higher power to ensure maximal coherence, warrant description as a kind of affective doubling. We have seen this principle at work in a massive single-movement work such as Schoenberg's *Verklärte Nacht,* the luminous second part of which reconfigures the tortured music of the first. Bartók also brings a similar device to bear on the second and third movements of his First String Quartet. On the surface, each movement projects a radically different character: the middle movement plays on a graceful waltz topos, the finale on a vigorous, peasantlike dance theme. Yet both draw extensively on the same motivic source, a pair of half steps separated by a sixth.[43] Furthermore, both movements are conceived as full-blown, if idiosyncratic, sonata-allegro designs animated by a tonal scheme in which A is symmetrically surrounded by major thirds above and below.[44]

In Alban Berg's String Quartet (1910), however, the principle of affective doubling is cast in a new and troubling light. To be sure, both movements of the work, his first extended essay for string quartet, proceed from the same complex of motives; both allude to the architectural paradigm of sonata form (or sonata-rondo form); and both place increasing emphasis on D as a point of tonal reference.[45] Yet here we sense neither a Schoenbergian *Verklärung* nor a Bartókian resolution in the heady whirl of the dance. On the contrary, many of the knotty, chromatic figures from the first movement are merely transplanted, unaltered, into the largely atonal sound world of the second. Nowhere is Berg's "taking back" of modernism's favored gestures of affirmation more in evidence than in the final moments of the piece, where a D minor chord is unceremoniously swept aside by an atonal cluster. Berg's quartet invokes the nineteenth-century will to monumentality—through its employment of affective doubling—only to deny it.

In some compositions the pursuit of monumental forms goes hand in hand with an effacement of traditionally distinct movement structures; a noisome threat to continuity, the customary caesura between movements was frequently bridged by a transitional link. Ferruccio Busoni's too seldom heard Second Violin Sonata, Op. 36a (1898/1900), originally titled *Sonata quasi fantasia,* after Beethoven,[46] strives for coherence in just this way. All of its major sections—a seemingly rhapsodic, but in fact symmetrically designed introduction, a tarantella, a brief Andante, and a concluding series of chorale variations—proceed logically one from the other, not only in temporal but also in material terms. (Each successive section, that is, recalls at some point the music of its immediate predecessor.) The violin sonata, perhaps the most resistant to change of all the subgenres within the chamber tradition, would thus appear to become an agent of progress in Busoni's hands. Yet his work shows a peculiar Janus face. For one thing, it would be an exaggeration to speak of a network of recurrent themes: many of the recurrences, especially those in the final section of the sonata, are more like citations or fleeting reminiscences; they are incidental, not fundamental to the structure. Furthermore, it is not difficult to discern a clear succession of movements, disposed slow-fast-slow-fast, despite the uninterrupted flow of the composition. Poised between *sonata da chiesa* and tone poem, Busoni's Second Violin Sonata projects an odd blend of conservative and innovative traits.

When a dense web of motivic cross-references is coupled with a highly developed art of transition, the resultant form is of a wholly different order. Traceable to Liszt's B Minor Piano Sonata, and earlier still to Schubert's "Wanderer" *Fantasie*, D. 760, this approach informs the extended symphonic essays of Mahler and Strauss alike. It is not without justification that Dahlhaus describes these most characteristic of *fin de siècle* designs as "multidimensional." Like Rorschach inkblots, they lend themselves to markedly different interpretations depending on our point of view. Specifically, superimposing the structural properties of a unitary design (typically the sonata-allegro) over the entire span of a widely ranging and affectively differentiated work will allow for a single passage to function in a variety of ways. What at first appears in the guise of an opening "movement," for example, may ultimately function as the "exposition" of an overarching sonata form.[47]

Schoenberg's adoption of this method in his D Minor Quartet, Op. 7, imparts a monumental breadth to the chamber idiom. He described his aims with customary succinctness: "In accommodation to the faith of the time, [the] large form [of Op. 7] was to include all the four characters of the sonata type in one single, uninterrupted movement. *Durchführungen* (developments) should not be missing and there should be a certain degree of thematic unity within the contrasting sections."[48]

According to Schoenberg's schematic account, which has served as the basis for all subsequent analyses, the D Minor Quartet falls into four principal parts, each a rough equivalent of one of the traditional movement types: (1) an opening quick section, (2) a scherzo and trio, (3) an Adagio, and (4) a concluding rondo. But interleaved with the four "movements" are developmental and recapitulatory sites, all hearkening back to the material and character of part 1.[49] And as the work proceeds, it becomes clear that the individual "movements" may just as easily be interpreted as the constituents of a mammoth sonata form: the scherzo, which draws on a transitional theme from part 1, functions at the largest level as a development; the rondo, built mainly on the music of parts 1 and 3, serves as a reprise. If the "faith of the time" demanded monumental forms, then Schoenberg readily and brilliantly responded to this historical imperative. Indeed, it is difficult to imagine a more sophisticated mediation of unity and variety, cohesion and contrast, than that achieved in the D Minor Quartet.

With Schoenberg's multidimensional approach to design, our typology of *fin de siècle* forms arrives at a culmination. But at the same time, the appearance of this high point in the chamber idiom—a realm of intimacy and introspection—coincides with a breaking point as regards form. As Dahlhaus has shown, multidimensionality operates on both global and local "orders of magnitude." To cite an example: not only may the sonata form furnish the metastructure for a composition's diverse materials, but its functional components might also be imprinted, in miniature, on the individual sections of the multidimensional work.[50] And the latter, as we have seen, is precisely the case in the "first theme group" (mm. 1–97) of Schoenberg's Op. 7 insofar as a contrapuntal combination and its variants mark off the various stages of a compact but nonetheless recognizable sonata form. Extreme compression thus serves as a corrective to the expansive breadth in which the "time" invested its "faith." Given that Schoenberg's D Minor Quartet finds a place for both monumentality and miniaturism, it is possible to argue that the work embodies a guiding aesthetic claim of musical modernism while simultaneously subjecting this claim to a critique.

Another work conceived at roughly the same time assumes a more radically critical stance vis-à-vis the monumental forms of its day. Brought to light as recently as the early 1960s by Hans Moldenhauer, Anton Webern's String Quartet of 1905 is remarkable both for its foray into atonality and for its anticipation of the cellular technique that would soon become the composer's trademark. Like Schoenberg's D Minor Quartet, this is a multidimensional work, each of its three main divisions doing double duty as movements and as components of a large-scale sonata structure.[51] Hence the first "movement"—dominated by a three-note cell reminiscent of the "Muß es sein?" motive from Beethoven's Op. 135 and a rhetorically profiled, almost Straussian melody (*Mit großem Schwung*)—functions simultaneously as an exposition; the slow "movement" dissolves into a developmental episode; and the "finale," initiated by the most rarefied of waltzes, concludes with a recapitulatory coda based on the main ideas of the first "movement." But the multidimensional form, ostensibly an agent of expansiveness, is compressed into the space of a mere two hundred bars.

For the Second Viennese School, highly compressed forms pointed the way toward "musical prose," the utopian syntax that Schoenberg, in "Brahms the Progressive" (1947), defined as "a direct and straightforward presentation of ideas, without any patchwork, without mere padding and empty repetitions."[52] Max Reger, who has garnered an undeserved reputation as a strict adherent of textbook forms, proved to be a key player in the cultivation of a "proselike" approach to musical syntax, especially in the chamber music of his later years.[53] The tendency toward musical prose is much in evidence in the C Major Violin Sonata, Op. 72 (1903), a work whose first performance in Munich was greeted by an outpouring of invective from the local press. But while Reger's detractors railed against what they took to be "complete perversity," "incurable sickness," and "nerve-killing unnaturalness," the composer himself claimed that "there is nothing *more simple and more lucid* than my Op. 72."[54]

How can we reconcile these diametrically opposing points of view? The critical incomprehension surrounding Reger's unquestionably difficult work probably emanated from two sources: first, many of its ideas teeter on the brink of atonality; second, and more significantly, these ideas frequently eschew the symmetries of periodic structure, exemplifying instead a rapidly developing, proselike syntax. Yet Reger's insistence on the lucidity of his composition is borne out by his employment of the multidimensional principle. The development section of the first movement begins with a tonally obfuscatory series of whole notes (B♭–G♭–C) in the piano. The ensuing music—murky arpeggios over a low B pedal, plus disconnected and almost inaudible asides from the violin—does little to dispel the mystery. Yet within about twenty measures the piano introduces an apparently unrelated melody that, unlike the immediately preceding passage, unfolds a clear if unconventional tonal scheme (moving initially from F to F♯ major), proceeds in regular four-bar phrases, and discloses a rich if conventional texture (a melody amplified in thirds supported by a slow-moving bass and an undulating inner voice). The remainder of the development is then devoted to a thoroughgoing elaboration of these markedly contrasting ideas. What we have, in other words, is a projection of sonata-form categories onto an individual section of a larger sonata-form movement: the enigmatic opening passage and the ensuing *cantabile* together comprise a miniature "exposition," while the elaboration that follows makes for a "development within a development." The application of formal categories at a "lower order of magnitude" thus saves Reger's musical prose from disintegrating into a mere sequence of disjointed utterances.

The threat of incoherence is even greater in the first movement of Reger's F♯ Minor String Quartet, Op. 121 (1911), whose rarefied textures and aphoristic themes intimate more than they divulge.[56] The lengthy and thematically differentiated first group (mm. 1–75) is indeed interpretable as a loose network of no less than eight motivic characters: a plaintive opening gesture (*a*) bearing more than a passing resemblance to the opening of Mozart's "Hoffmeister" Quartet, K. 499; a continuation featuring hemiolas and sigh gestures (*b*); a cryptic three-note motive (*c*) initially comprising the pitches A, F, and D♯, *pianississimo diminuendo* in all four instruments; a series of emphatic and obtrusive variants of the same (*d*); two lyrical ideas centered tonally on B♭ (*e* and *f*); and an *agitato* including a descending flurry of sixteenths (*g*) and a complementary chromatic ascent in syncopated quarter notes (*h*). But this apparently chaotic jumble of diverse ideas in fact takes on the outlines of a diminutive sonata-form movement, with *a, b,* and *c* serving as first group, *d* as transition, *e* and *f* as second group, *g* and *h* as development, and the truncated return of *a* as recapitulation. Too often brushed aside as a reactionary partisan of old-fashioned principles, Reger, at least in his later chamber music, proves to have been fully engaged in the critique of the modernist will to monumentality.

The Celebration of the Commonplace

The cultivation of expansive but thematically and tonally cohesive designs speaks clearly to the high seriousness pervading late nineteenth-century musical culture. But running alongside the "official" style of musical modernism were other renegade tendencies that called its dead earnestness and hyperexpressivity into question. The solemn utterance was often displaced by popularizing or downright trivial elements, just as the self-consciously cultured pose at times gave way to a deliberate antiacademicism; the structural dimension sometimes renounced the subtle art of transition in favor of striking juxtapositions associated with the montage principle; and finally, at the affective level, irony or parody often figured in lieu of gravity. All these "subversive" traits undoubtedly played a crucial role in the New Music of the early twentieth century, but interestingly enough, they began to assert themselves with some urgency in the chamber music of the preceding period. The dual presence of high seriousness and subversion in many works—like that of monumental breadth and extreme compression—further strengthens the supposition that *fin de siècle* chamber music embraces its own critique.

It is probably no accident that this critique began to take shape in Vienna, the city whose social system was rent by a tradition of semifeudal oppression, on the one hand, and on the other, an easygoing liberalism that, in Theodor Adorno's words, simply asked "whether a thing was good" but not what it might be good *for*.[56] The laissez-faire attitude of the bourgeoisie in turn contributed to a cultural climate in which the most extraordinary assaults on received opinion regarding manners, politics, and art were tolerated, and in some circles even encouraged. Johann Nestroy's social satires, popular in the 1850s and 1860s, represent an early manifestation of the impulse that would later inform Karl Kraus's ironic critique of language and Schoenberg's paradoxical rethinking of the Austro-German musical tradition.

Even the music of Anton Bruckner, whom history has painted as a naïve devotee of that tradition, bears the imprint of a refractory time and place. In a review of Bruckner's F Major String Quintet (1879/1884), Hugo Wolf (quoting Hans Sachs's *Flieder* monologue from *Die Meistersinger*) marveled over the fact that the work "sounded so old, and was yet so new," tracing this quality to the "strong, popular strain that emerges everywhere in his symphonic compositions, sometimes overtly, sometimes hidden."[57] Indeed, the "popular strain" in the F Major Quintet is at times so strong that it borders on the aesthetically questionable—consider, for example, the unabashed *Gemütlichkeit* of the second movement's trio section. In accordance with his high-minded aims as a symphonist and upholder of a venerable tradition, Bruckner places this easygoing ländler amidst a web of recurrent materials. The head motive of the trio at once points backward to a retransitional passage in the scherzo and forward to an important idea employed throughout the finale. This retransition, however, bears closer scrutiny, if only because it apparently consists of little more than the mechanical repetition of an inconsequential motive. The passage nicely exemplifies that quintessentially Viennese propensity for *Bandeln*, roughly translatable as "pottering" or "busy idleness." According to Adorno, the *Bandler* indulges in "activities with which to pass the time, to squander it, without any evident rational purpose, but also activities which are, absurdly, practical."[58] In the scherzo of his F Major Quintet, Bruckner demonstrates his fondness for activities of just this sort, and in so doing registers a quiet challenge to the teleological dynamism that had dominated mainstream Austro-German music for over a century.

Given Wolf's high regard for the popular element in Bruckner's music, it is little wonder that we should encounter a similar emphasis in his own. Then, too, both composers lived and worked in a cultural environment where the elegant waltzes of Johann Strauss, Jr. and the buoyant operettas of Franz von Suppé reigned supreme. But for Wolf, faith in the popular spirit went hand in hand with an outright disdain for academicism. (The modern composer, he once quipped, was most successful in scherzos and finales, where one "need only be a proficient contrapuntist and jumble the voices together topsy-turvy.")[59] In his "Italian" Serenade for string quartet (1887; version for chamber orchestra, 1892), Wolf's antiacademicism comes perilously close to an intentionally cultivated banality. Its main tune, an evocation of the jaunty but slight strains of a café orchestra, is characterized by three features: a cloying, sentimental chromaticism, the promise to unfold in square, four-bar phrases, and a mechanical accompaniment suggesting the strumming of a guitar. But all three features generate startling disturbances. The chromatic descent in the melody becomes a source for unusual, twisted harmonic effects later in the movement (see, for instance, the eerie counterlines in the restatement of the tune at mm. 240ff.); the symmetrical phrase structure is abrogated almost at once as the first violin sits obstinately on E for two measures longer than it should; and last, melody and accompaniment proceed oddly out of phase as the bass completes its stepwise descent to D a full four measures before the violin comes to a melodic cadence on the same pitch. While Bruckner's F Major Quintet lays bare the cracks in the "official" style, the tipsy opening of Wolf's "Italian" Serenade casts the popular manner itself in a critical light.

No aspect of the musical language was spared from the penetrating critique of style in which Viennese composers engaged at the *fin de siècle*.

This tendency was taken to its extremes in a work that, strictly speaking, stands outside the bounds of our period, Zemlinsky's Second String Quartet, Op. 15 (1914). Dedicated to Schoenberg, the quartet replaces the finely drawn transitions of that composer's *Verklärte Nacht* and D Minor String Quartet with a kaleidoscopic array of musical images: a recitative-like motto, hysterical Allegros, modally inflected *cantilene,* an archaic, expressionless chorale, a Mahlerian Adagio, a grotesque scherzo, and a serene apotheosis.[60] The montage technique manifests itself in the no fewer than twenty tempo changes of the quartet's second major section (a slow "movement" comprising introductory *cantabile,* chorale variations, and Adagio). But the most telling emblem of Zemlinsky's attempt to embed the imminent forces of disintegration into the very fabric of his music comes in the second chorale variation (rehearsal no. 24 in the Universal *Taschenpartitur*), where the violins are instructed to play "without regard for the slower tempo of the viola and cello" (see Example 9.3). Thus even the most fundamental premise of good ensemble playing—that individuals must coordinate their activities with those of the group—is subject to critique.

Although conceived beyond the immediate confines of the Viennese sphere, Reger's chamber music discloses a no less pronounced critical dimension. The String Quartet in A, Op. 54, No. 2 (1900) counts as one of the very few cases in his output that deviates from the customary four-movement form. But on reflection, the absence of a scherzo makes perfectly good sense, for in both the first and last movements the humorous tone is raised to an ironic pitch. The quartet opens (Allegro assai e bizzarro) with an unusually saucy idea whose persistently repeated Gs do little to stabilize the obliquely established A major tonic (see Example 9.4). A clear offense against good musical manners, the same indecorous gesture surfaces just five bars before the end of the entire work—hardly making for a grand moment of cyclic return, but rather for a bit of gentle mockery. Although a devoted student of the Austro-German tradition, Reger was obviously not reluctant to treat some of its basic tenets—at least those regarding the proper way to open and close a serious chamber work—as objects of parody.

Considered against this background, the antics of a self-proclaimed iconoclast such as Charles Ives are perhaps less radical than they at first appear. Many of his dozen or so works dating from the first decade of the twentieth century were actually conceived as "take-offs" or "stunts," to use Ives's own terms,[61] and among them are several notable contributions to the chamber repertory. In a brief account found in his *Memos,* for instance, Ives recalled the impetus for his Second String Quartet (1907–13): "After one of those Kneisel Quartet concerts . . . I started a string quartet score, half mad, half in fun, and half to try out, practice, and have some fun with making those men fiddlers get up and do something like men."[62] Aside from the aggressively gendered rhetoric and the fact that three halves do not make a whole, the quotation calls attention to the importance of the ludic element in Ives's approach to composition.

EXAMPLE 9.3.   Alexander Zemlinsky, String Quartet No. 2, Op. 15 (rehearsal no. 24).

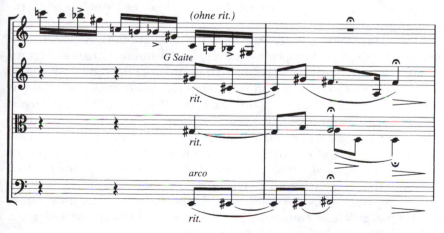

EXAMPLE 9.4.   Max Reger, String Quartet in A, Op. 54, No. 2, opening.

This element no doubt motivated Ives's use of the indication "Tsiaj" (for "This Scherzo is a joke") as a heading for the second movement of his Piano Trio (1904–5). The tautological title announces, and none too subtly, that if other scherzos do not live up to their genre designation, this one will. In a relatively short space, Ives calls up a welter of patriotic melodies, popular tunes, and children's songs, each more extravagantly treated than its predecessor. (Originally entitled "Medley on the Campus Fence" in the sketch for the trio, the movement was intended, again in Ives's words, to evoke the celebrations "at Mr. Yale's School for nice bad boys.")[63] The principal joke, however, resides in the handling of tonality. Indeed, the key of each tune is systematically and brutally denied: F♯ major chords grate against the uninflected G major of the first melody (mm. 15–42); oblivious to the C and A major tonalities of the second melody, the cello blithely repeats an ostinato in E♭ (mm. 43ff.); a G major tune introduced later by the piano (mm. 68–83) is surrounded by a cloud of chromatically irrational figuration.

The affront to musical propriety is less blatant but just as constitutive for the effect of the opening movement, "Autumn," of Ives's Second Sonata for Violin and Piano (1907–10). Like many of the composer's other works from this period, the movement is cast as a fantasy on a hymn tune—in this case, "Autumn" with the text, "Mighty God! While Angels Bless Thee"—but the tune and its derivatives trace an idiosyncratic course. The main body of the movement comprises a series of developmental parries on fragments of the hymn tune, a more complete presentation of which comes only at the movement's end. By according the chief point of tonal and thematic clarification a terminal position, the fantasy on "Mighty God" effectively turns the traditional theme-and-variations form on its head.[64] Ives may have employed "reverential" materials, but he took great delight in treating hallowed forms irreverently.

As Peter Burkholder has suggested, Ives's "take-offs" and "stunts" afforded the composer a release from academic strictures.[65] And although they were light years apart on many points, Ives and several of his European colleagues were no doubt at one on this: for all of them, humor, irony, and parody pointed the way toward an experimental freedom.[66] But there is more. The incursion of popular elements in Bruckner's Quintet tests the limits of the "official," high-serious style; Wolf's Serenade uncovers a troubling substrate even in the popular style; Reger's Op. 54 quartet exposes the cyclic return for what it is—an act of force imposed from without; Zemlinsky's Second Quartet demonstrates the viability of the montage as a structural mode. Each of these works provides a commentary, a critique on a received musical idea. And if anything, the critique gains in force precisely because it makes do without words, and because it resounds in the intimate spaces appropriate for chamber music.

"Air from Another Planet"

If there is a single chamber work that embodies but ultimately transcends the principal tendencies at the end of our period, that work is certainly Schoenberg's Second String Quartet in F♯ Minor, Op. 10. Composed between March 1907 and July 1908, the quartet came at a decisive turning point in Schoenberg's career, a fact that the composer himself was fond of emphasizing.[67] Like the other works either completed or begun during this period—the two Chamber Symphonies, Opp. 9 and 38, the ballads and songs Opp. 12 and 14, the chorus *Friede auf Erden*, Op. 13, the earlier settings from *Das Buch der hängenden Gärten*, Op. 15—the Second Quartet plays at the border of disparate worlds: tonality and atonality, late Romanticism and Expressionism, nineteenth-century modernism and twentieth-century modernity.[68] It earns its designation as the signature piece of the period if only because it articulates the transition from one realm to the other. That this transition should have been effected in the chamber idiom attests to the singular import of the genre.

The work's departure from the sprawling designs of the D Minor String Quartet and the First Chamber Symphony represents, as Schoenberg wrote, "one of the first symptoms that the period of greatly expanded forms" was coming to an end.[69] Apparently renouncing the single-movement, multidimensional forms of his previous instrumental works, Schoenberg opts in the Second Quartet for a clearly articulated four-movement structure. But we would be mistaken in interpreting this neo-classicizing feature as a submissive bow to tradition, for the quartet as a whole, and in its individual parts, engages far more in a pointed dialogue with the earlier practices it invokes.

On the surface, the opening movement of the quartet falls into a neatly contained sonata-allegro pattern. Yet as Catherine Dale rightly argues, it is difficult to ignore the movement's many departures from the tonal and thematic norms of this model.[70] In his own analytical notes on the movement, Schoenberg likewise stresses his "disinclination against traditional Durchführung or development" and his free handling of thematic order in the reprise.[71] Indeed, the differences of opinion among later commentators regarding the boundary between development and recapitulation may be taken as a measure both of Schoenberg's "disinclination against" and his liberal attitude toward the customary modes of ensuring structural coherence.[72] Not unexpectedly, Schoenberg frames his critique of tradition in terms actually derived from that tradition. The movement's "development" section commences in measure 90 with a melodic statement of the opening idea in its original key, F♯ minor, but couples this with an imitative statement of the same idea in D minor and a tonally ambiguous counterline in the lower voices. Thus, following one of the mature Brahms's favored approaches to sonata form, Schoenberg aims at a conflation of developmental and recapitulatory processes. Deciding on the precise limits of these processes is less important than recognizing what amounts to a powerful gesture of compression—and to be sure, the remainder of the movement is rich in such gestures. At the beginning of the coda, for example, Schoenberg combines the first pair of measures from a subordinate theme with its second pair (see Example 9.5), at the same time alluding, in the accompanying voices, to the quartal harmonies of another thematic idea from the exposition.

The desire to attain an utterly compact mode of expression lies behind the proselike, aphoristic syntax of the second movement. Schoenberg's references, in his description of this scherzolike movement, to "numerous quotations" of "thematic characters" is telling, for in only one famous instance is a well-known melody actually quoted.[73] The continual rotation and development of a complex of brief motivic snippets—obsti-

EXAMPLE 9.5.(a)   Schoenberg, String Quartet No. 2, Op. 10, mvt. 1: coda, mm. 196–97.

EXAMPLE 9.5.(b)   Schoenberg, String Quartet No. 2, Op. 10, mvt. 1: subordinate theme, mm. 43–46.

nately repeated Ds in the cello (mm. 1–4), scrambling eighths in the second violin (mm. 5–6), and skittish sigh figures in the first violin (mm. 7–8)—rather impart the quality of a *mélange* of quotations to the whole. Schoenberg's sketches and drafts, which document his constant reshuffling and recombination of these musical fragments, vividly attest to the importance of the montage principle for the compositional process itself.[74]

    In the finished movement, the effect produced by the kaleidoscopic play of motives is little short of amazing. No doubt the grotesquerie of the musical materials and their treatment contributed to the riotous behavior at the Viennese premiere of the quartet in December 1908, an event that, according to Schoenberg's account, "surpassed every previous and subsequent happening of this kind."[75] While the first movement was received without incident, large segments of the audience began to titter during the second, and their derision continued unabated until the coda of the finale. To be sure, scherzos are supposed to incite laughter, though of an inner, approbative sort. The scornful reaction generated by the second movement of Schoenberg's F♯ Minor Quartet reminds us of the ease with which the boundary between jollity and mockery can be abrogated. Yet Schoenberg, too, adopts an ambivalent stance on the question of boundaries when he interrupts the frantic progress of his scherzo's trio section to quote the popular Viennese tune "O, du lieber Augustin." This understandably celebrated gesture—an affront to the venerable quartet tradition if ever there were one—has been variously interpreted. For many writers, Schoenberg bids an ironic farewell ("alles ist hin" runs the text of the tune) to the world of tonal harmony with the D major singsong of a trifling melody. Pointing to the dissolution of the "Augustin" tune into a recall of chromatic material from the first movement, Walter Frisch views the entire passage as a statement on the proximity of atonality to tonality.[76] But Schoenberg's searing critique of a fundamental distinction in the realm of pitch organization assumes even greater force in that it is made through the agency of an inconsequential *Gassenhauer*. Both the combination of the popular tune with the sigh figure of measures 7–8 (a "tragicomic" gesture, according to Schoenberg)[77] and the tune's gradual turn toward the Expressionist idiom of the first movement occur at the interface between high seriousness and banality; Schoenberg's handling of "O, du lieber Augustin" thus demonstrates that the distance from one affect to the other may be a short one indeed. The critique of tonality, in other words, is embedded in a larger critique of the prententions of high art.

With the third and fourth movements—settings of extravagantly emotional poems by Stefan George, "Litanei" and "Entrückung"—Schoenberg departs radically from the quartet tradition by introducing the human voice. And what is more striking, he approaches the texts not as intimate lieder but rather as occasions for a passionate outpouring of music-dramatic rhetoric. To be sure, the justification for this treatment is easily discovered in the poems themselves. George's "Litanei," an intense plea for relief from sensual longing, recalls Amfortas's lament and prayer in the first and third acts respectively of Wagner's *Parsifal*. The penultimate line of the poem, "Töte das Sehnen, schliesse die Wunde!" (Kill [my] desire, close the wound!) hearkens specifically to the pained exhortations of the ailing Grail King.

Neither movement, Schoenberg maintained, could be subsumed under the heading of a "catalogued form."[78] On the contrary, each elaborates a dense web of motivic particles in the strings, over which the soprano soars with unfettered freedom: "The Leitmotif technique of Wagner has taught us how to vary such motifs and other phrases, so as to express every change of mood and character in a poem. Thematic unity and logic thus sustained, the finished product will not fail to satisfy a formalist's requirements."[79] Yet how are we to square this claim with the rigorously formalized theme-and-variations pattern of the third movement and the sonata-form outlines of the fourth? Schoenberg ascribed his employment of the variation form in "Litanei" to his fear that "the great dramatic emotionality of the poem" might lead him "to surpass the borderline of what should be admitted in chamber music.[80] Similarly, the sonata-form elements in the last movement might be viewed as a curb on the hyperexpressivity of the poem. But in both movements, the "canonical" form remains in the background as an abstract scaffolding; a flexible, processive approach to form determines the musical foreground.

In "Litanei" the soprano's entrance with a gracefully contoured "new" melody in measure 14 sounds like a true beginning even though it overlaps with the end of the first variation in the strings. This dialectic between subliminal form and surface event continues throughout the movement, which traces a progressive buildup to two climaxes (the first at "voll nur die qual" [rich only in pain], the second at "Töte das sehnen") before dissolving into an instrumental postlude. Some exceptions aside, the vocal line does not share in the dense play of motives—most of them transformed variants of ideas from the first movement—centered in the string parts. Schoenberg opts instead for a music-dramatic texture in which a web of leitmotives supports a freely intoned *cantilena*. The result is often stunning; witness the disembodied setting of "Leih deine kühle" (Lend [me] your coolness), *pianissimo* over a bewitching and highly differentiated string texture featuring harmonics and *sul ponticello* tremolos.

The shapes and textures of music drama likewise come to the fore in the setting of "Entrückung," a kind of Expressionist *Liebestod* in which the fleshly desires thematized in the previous poem are mystically but rapturously quelled. Indeed, the movement's pungent signature chord (D–A–G♯)—first employed to signal the otherworldly setting of the poem's opening line, "Ich fühle luft von anderem planeten" (I feel the air from another planet)—is easily interpreted as a latter-day response to (or a "taking back" of) Wagner's famed *Tristan* chord. Like the third movement, the fourth unfolds as a series of waves toward impending climaxes. But here the ultimate moment of release is consistently withheld to reflect the sufferer-poet's transcendent removal into a realm devoid of earthly longing. The point of recapitulation in the subliminal, sonata-form structure at measure 100 (which brings together the melody of "Ich fühle luft" and the chromatically charged chorale from mm. 51ff.) serves to defer the foreground climax until measures 110ff., where the "holy voice" of which the suffering poet has become only a "rumbling" is ecstatically represented through a combination of soaring *cantilena*, signature harmony, and the head motive of "Ich fühle luft" in the cello.

We know from Schoenberg's sketches that "Entrückung" was originally envisioned as the third movement of the F♯ Minor Quartet.[81] But both in structural and affective terms, the final sequence was the right one. In that "Litanei" draws largely on the material of the first movement, it functions as the development section in an all-embracing multidimensional form for which "Entrückung" serves as the apotheosis. The tortured subject of the former text finds peace in the sublime transport (*Entrückung*) thematized in the latter.

Although Schoenberg's Second String Quartet closes with a ruminative instrumental coda in which the tonal goal is a long-held F♯ major chord, only the naïve listener is left with the sense that the many contradictory issues raised in the work have been completely and magically resolved. On the contrary, the quartet is remarkable for the residual tensions is embodies: tensions between chamberlike intimacy and operatic effusiveness, atonality and lush, chromatic tonality, irony and high seriousness, rigorous background structure and music-dramatic excess, neo-Classical containment and expansive multidimensionality. In each case, the second term is held in check by the penetrating gaze of the first. If his D Minor Quartet was written "in accommodation to the faith of the time," Schoenberg's Second Quartet subjected the suppositions on which that faith was built to a penetrating critique. We can no longer speak of modernism; the twentieth-century modern is at hand.

Notes

1. Carl Dahlhaus, *Nineteenth-Century Music*, trans. J. Bradford Robinson (Berkeley, 1989), 330–35.

2. See ibid., 253–54, 336–38; Dahlhaus, *Schoenberg and the New Music*, trans. Derrick Puffett and Alfred Clayton (Cambridge, 1987), 96, 100; and Adorno, *Introduction to the Sociology of Music*, trans. E. B. Ashton (New York, 1976), 92. Cf. the similar account in Danuser, *Die Musik des 20. Jahrhunderts*, Neues Handbuch der Musikwissenschaft, ed. Carl Dahlhaus, vol. 7 (Laaber, 1984), 13–15.

3. See, e. g., *The New Grove*, s. v. "Chamber Music" by Michael Tilmouth, 4:117.

4. Dahlhaus, *Nineteenth-Century Music*, 338.

5. Carl Schorske, *Fin-de-siècle Vienna: Politics and Culture* (New York, 1981), 9.

6. Hugo Wolf, *The Music Criticism of Hugo Wolf*, trans. and ed. Henry Pleasants (New York, 1978), 10.

7. Heinrich Christoph Koch, *Musikalisches Lexikon* (Frankfurt, 1802), 821–22.

8. See Dahlhaus, *Nineteenth-Century Music*, 259–60.

9. Gustav Schilling, comp., *Encyclopädie der gesammten musikalischen Wissenschaften, oder Universal-Lexicon der Tonkunst* (Stuttgart, 1835–38) 4:39.

10. Tottmann's article, "Kammermusik," for Ersch and Gruber's *Allgemeine Encyclopädie der Wissenschaften und Künste* (Leipzig, 1882), is quoted in *Handwörterbuch der musikalischen Terminologie*, ed. Hans Heinrich Eggebrecht, s.v. "Kammermusik" by Erich Reimer, 12. On motivic density and developing variation as necessary conditions for an authentic chamber style, see Adorno, *Introduction to the Sociology of Music*, 85, 88–89; and Dahlhaus, *Nineteenth-Century Music*, 257.

11. Hugo Leichtentritt, "German and Austrian Chamber Music," in *Cobbett's Cyclopedic Survey of Chamber Music*, 2d ed. (London, 1963) 1:452.

12. See Paul Banks, "Fin-de-siècle Vienna: Politics and Modernism," in *The Late Romantic Era: From the Mid-Nineteenth Century to World War I*, ed. Jim Samson (Englewood Cliffs, NJ, 1991), 380.

13. See Stephen Walsh, *Bartók Chamber Music* (London, 1982), 14.

14. See Wolfgang Oberkogler, *Das Streichquartettschaffen in Wien von 1910 bis 1925* (Tutzing, 1982), 13.

15. Quoted in Joan Allen Smith, *Schoenberg and His Circle: A Viennese Portrait* (New York, 1981), 82.

16. For a listing of the society's programs, see Smith, *Schoenberg and His Circle*, 255–68.

17. Quoted from Walter Frisch, "The "Brahms Fog': On Analyzing Brahmsian Influence at the Fin de Siècle," in *Brahms and His World*, ed. Walter Frisch (Princeton, 1990), 82.

18. Again, according to Reger: "All truly intelligent and sensitive musicians . . . must acknowledge him [Brahms] as the greatest of living composers." Quoted from a letter of April 1894 in Frisch, "The 'Brahms Fog,'" in *Brahms and His World*, ed. Frisch, 81.

19. See "My Evolution" (1949), in Arnold Schoenberg, *Style and Idea*, ed. Leonard Stein, trans. Leo Black (Berkeley, 1975), 80.

20. "The 'Brahms Fog,'" in *Brahms and His World*, ed. Frisch, 91.

21. On this point, see Reinhard Gerlach, "War Schönberg von Dvořák beeinflußt: Zu Schönbergs Streichquartett D-dur," *Neue Zeitschrift für Musik* 133 (1972): 122–27, and Ulrich Thieme, *Studien zum Jugendwerk Arnold Schönbergs: Einflüsse und Wandlungen* (Regensburg, 1979), 114-15.

22. For a somewhat less sympathetic account of Zemlinsky's movement, see Frisch, "The 'Brahms Fog,'"in *Brahms and His World*, ed. Frisch, 86–88.

23. From a reminiscence published in *Musikblätter des Anbruch* (1922); quoted in *Brahms and His World*, ed. Frisch, 205.

24. For a detailed discussion of the role of Brahms's motive in Reger's Clarinet Quintet, see Roland Häfner, *Max Reger: Klarinettenquintett op. 146* (Munich, 1962), 11-14, 23-41. Häfner's attempts to locate the motive in the last three movements of Reger's work are intriguing but not always convincing. For a discussion of the relationship between Reger's quintet and the tradition embracing Mozart's K. 581 and Brahms's Op. 115, see Roman Brotbeck, *Zum Spätwerk Max Reger: Fünf Diskurse* (Wiesbaden, 1988), 37–63. Here, too, the author is perhaps overzealous in ferreting out thematic ties among the three compositions.

25. This distinction is a recurrent topos in Schoenberg's writings. See the following, all from Schoenberg, *Style and Idea:* "Twelve-tone Composition" (1923), 207–8; "Ornaments and Construction" (1923), 312; "National Music I and II" (1931), 170–71, 173–74; "Linear Counterpoint" (1931), 289–90; "New Music, Outmoded Music, Style and Idea" (1946), 115–18; "On Revient Toujours" (1948), 108–9; and "Bach" (1950), 397.

26. See Klaus-Jürgen Sachs, "Zur Konzeption des ersten Satzes aus dem Klaviertrio c-moll op. 101," in *Brahms-Analysen*, ed. Friedhelm Krummacher and Wolfram Steinbeck (Kassel, 1984).

27. See Dahlhaus, "Liszt, Schönberg und die große Form: Das Prinzip der Mehrsätzigkeit in der Einsätzigkeit," *Die Musikforschung* 41 (1988): 202–12, as well as idem, *Nineteenth-Century Music*, 366.

28. Alban Berg, "Why is Schönberg's Music So Hard to Understand?" trans. A Swarowsky and J. H. Lederer, *Music Review* 13 (1952): 190-96. See also Webern's untitled essay (1912) on Schoenberg's earlier string quartets, in Ursula von Rauchhaupt, ed., *Schoenberg, Berg, Webern: The String Quartets* (Hamburg, 1971), 16.

29. See Schoenberg's album notes to the Kolisch Quartet's recordings of his four string quartets (December 1936–January 1937), quoted in Fred Steiner, "A

History of the First Complete Recordings of the Schoenberg String Quartets,"
Journal of the Arnold Schoenberg Institute 2 (1978): 133.

30. According to Schumann's review of the first quartet in the cycle (*Neue Zeitschrift für Musik* 16 [1842]: 159–60), the Goethean superscriptions were added after the work was completed.

31. Frisch points out that Schoenberg's work on *Verklärte Nacht* was preceded by three attempts to draft large-scale programmatic compositions, the last a thirty-four-measure fragment for string sextet inspired by a poem by Gustav Falke. See Walter Frisch, *The Early Works of Arnold Schoenberg, 1893–1908* (Berkeley, 1993), 109.

32. "Analysis of the First String Quartet" (1936), quoted in *Schoenberg, Berg, Webern: The String Quartets,* ed. Rauchhaupt, 36.

33. Dahlhaus, *Schoenberg and the New Music,* 95–97. See also Christian Martin Schmidt, "Formprobleme in Schönbergs frühen Instrumentalwerken," in *Bericht über den 1. Kongreß der Internationalen Schönberg-Gesellschaft* (Vienna, 1978), 183, and Frisch, *Early Works of Arnold Schoenberg,* 113.

34. See "My Evolution," in Schoenberg, *Style and Idea,* 80. For a thorough discussion of thematic processes in Schoenberg's *Verklärte Nacht,* see Frisch, *Early Works of Schoenberg,* 116–22.

35. I borrow the term "expressive" from Robert Bailey, "The Structure of the *Ring* and its Evolution," *19th Century Music* 1 (1977): 51. In a series of analytical jottings written on a sleepless night in Madrid in 1932 ("Konstructives in der Verklärten Nacht"), Schoenberg spoke to the fundamental import of chromatic neighbor motion for the tonal planning of the sextet; see the commentary on this fascinating document in Frisch, *Early Works of Schoenberg,* 123–26.

36. See, e.g., the account of the work as a double sonata form in Swift, "1-XII-99," and the critique of this analysis in Frisch, *Early Works of Schoenberg,* 114–16.

37. "Analysis of the First String Quartet" (1936), in *Schoenberg, Berg, Webern: The String Quartets,* ed. Rauchhaupt, 36.

38. Schmidt, "Schönbergs 'Very Definite—but Private' Program zum Streichquartett Opus 7," in *Bericht über den 1. Kongreß der Internationalen Schönberg-Gesellschaft* (Vienna, 1978), 230-34.

39. Mark Benson, "Schoenberg's Private Program for the String Quartet in D minor, Op. 7," *Journal of Musicology* 11 (1993): 374–95.

40. Walsh, *Bartók Chamber Music,* 14. It is worth mentioning that while Bartók almost certainly knew *Verklärte Nacht* when he set to work on his First String Quartet, Schoenberg's D Minor Quartet came to be known in Hungary only after the Waldbauer-Kerpely Quartet took it up in 1911; see Halsey Stevens, *The Life and Music of Béla Bartók,* rev. ed. (London, 1964), 44.

41. Walsh, *Bartók Chamber Music,* 11.

42. See Elliott Antokoletz, *The Music of Béla Bartók: A Study of Tonality and Progression in Twentieth-Century Music* (Berkeley, 1984), 85–88.

43. See also Walsh, *Bartók Chamber Music,* 18.

44. See Antokoletz, *The Music of Béla Bartók,* 142–149 for a detailed discussion of the tonal organization of the quartet.

45. See Bruce Archibald, "Berg's Development as an Instrumental Composer," in *The Berg Companion,* ed. Douglas Jarman (Boston, 1989), 96–105.

46. Antony Beaumont, *Busoni the Composer* (Bloomington, IN, 1985), 53–54. In spite of the obvious reference to Beethoven's Op. 27 piano sonatas in its original title, Busoni's sonata has even closer affinities with the late E Major Piano Sonata,

Op. 109. For an illuminating comparison of the two works, both of which culminate in weighty, variation-form finales, see Albrecht Riethmüller, *Ferruccio Busonis Poetik* (Mainz, 1988), 43.

47. See Dahlhaus, "Liszt, Schönberg und die große Form," 202–4.

48. "Analysis of the First String Quartet" (1936), in *Schoenberg, Berg, Webern: The String Quartets*, ed. Rauchhaupt, 36.

49. Ibid., 39–42.

50. Dahlhaus, "Liszt, Schönberg und die große Form," 204–5, 208–9.

51. Webern's *homage à Schoenberg* takes an even more tangible form: an important figure first introduced in mm. 23–24 of the quartet conflates two gestures from *Verklärte Nacht* (mm. 79–80) and the D Minor String Quartet (mm. 8–9). For a detailed discussion of these and other relationships among the works, see Heinz-Klaus Metzger, "Über Anton Weberns Streichquartett 1905," *Musik-Konzepte,* special issue, *Anton Webern* (Munich, 1983), 85–92, and Reinhard Gerlach, *Musik und Jugendstil der Wiener Schule, 1900–1908* (Laaber, 1985), 167–70.

52. Schoenberg, *Style and Idea,* 415.

53. See, e. g., Rainer Cadenbach, *Max Reger und seine Zeit* (Laaber, 1991), 216, and Martin Möller, *Untersuchungen zur Satztechnik Max Regers: Studien an den Kopfsätzen der Kammermusikwerke* (Wiesbaden, 1984), 170. As Hermann Danuser has shown, Reger was probably the first composer to whose works the term "musical prose" was applied in an affirmative sense, and this long before Schoenberg's influential essay on Brahms. Already at the turn of the twentieth century, Reger's fondness for parenthetical asides, his freely shaped declamatory melodies, and his deliverance of the musical fabric into a perpetual state of transition were all subsumed under the rubric "musical prose." See Hermann Danuser, *Musikalische Prosa* (Regensburg, 1975), 119–24.

54. See Susanne Popp, "Zur musikalischen Prosa bei Reger und Schönberg," in *Reger-Studien I: Festschrift für Ottmar Schreiber,* ed. Günther Popp and Susanne Popp (Wiesbaden, 1978), 71-72.

55. On Reger's reliance on thematic "particles" as opposed to "themes" in this work, see Lothar Mattner, *Substanz und Akzidens: Analytische Studien an Streichquartettsätzen Max Regers* (Wiesbaden, 1985), 61-62.

56. See "Vienna" (1960), in Theodor W. Adorno, *Quasi una Fantasia: Essays on Modern Music,* trans. Rodney Livingstone (London, 1992), 206.

57. Review of 10 January 1886, in Wolf, *The Music Criticism of Hugo Wolf,* 179.

58. "Vienna" (1960), in Adorno, *Quasi una Fantasia,* 210.

59. Review of 8 February 1884, in Wolf, *The Music Criticism of Hugo Wolf,* 11.

60. On this point, cf. Horst Weber, *Alexander Zemlinsky* (Vienna, 1977), 108, and Werner Loll, *Zwischen Tradition und Avantgarde: Die Kammermusik Alexander Zemlinskys* (Kassel, 1990), 197.

61. J. Peter Burkholder, *Charles Ives: The Ideas behind the Music* (New Haven, CT, 1985), 89.

62. Quoted in H. Wiley Hitchcock, *Ives* (London, 1977), 61.

63. Burkholder, *Charles Ives,* 90.

64. For a more detailed discussion of this typically Ivesian procedure, see ibid., 87. See also idem, *All Made of Tunes: Charles Ives and the Uses of Musical Borrowing* (New Haven, CT, 1995), 174.

65. Burkholder, *Charles Ives,* 90–91.

66. For a provocative account of the affinities between Ives and Mahler, see Robert P. Morgan, "Ives and Mahler: Mutual Responses at the End of an Era," *19th*

Century Music 2 (1978): 72–81.

67. "Analysis of the Second Quartet" (1936), in *Schoenberg, Berg, Webern: The String Quartets,* ed. Rauchhaupt, 42.

68. For an excellent discussion of the kinship between the Second String Quartet and the other works from this period in Schoenberg's creative development (especially the first movement of the Second Chamber Symphony), see Frisch, *Early Works of Schoenberg,* 248–49.

69. "Analysis of the Second String Quartet," 42.

70. Catherine Dale, "Foreground Motif as a Determinant of Formal and Tonal Structure in the First Movement of Schönberg's Second String Quartet," *Music Review* 52 (1991): 52.

71. "Analysis of the Second String Quartet," 43.

72. Schoenberg located the beginning of the "recapitulation proper" at m. 146, where the main theme recurs in an F major/A minor context (see *Schoenberg, Berg, Webern: The String Quartets,* ed. Rauchhaupt, 44); several writers have taken the composer at his word (see Dale, "Foreground Motif as a Determinant of Formal and Tonal Structure," 52, and Frisch, *Early Works of Schoenberg,* 262). Others, however, have placed greater weight on the tonal return to F♯ minor and hence place the reprise at m. 159 (see Jim Samson, *Music in Transition: A Study of Tonal Expansion and Atonality, 1900–1920* [New York, 1977], 105).

73. "Analysis of the Second String Quartet" (1936), in *Schoenberg, Berg, Webern: The String Quartets,* ed. Rauchhaupt, 44.

74. See Frisch, *Early Works of Schoenberg,* 263–64.

75. Quoted in Steiner, "A History of the First Complete Recordings of the Schoenberg String Quartets," 133.

76. Frisch, *Early Works of Schoenberg,* 265–66. For a discussion of the "Augustin" tune as a motivic source for the entire movement (an intriguing but perhaps overstated claim), see Ernst Ludwig Waeltner, "O du lieber Augustin: Der Scherzo Satz im II. Streichquartett von Arnold Schönberg," in *Bericht über den 1. Kongreß der Internationalen Schönberg-Gesellschaft* (Vienna, 1978), 246–62.

77. "How One Becomes Lonely" (1937), in Schoenberg, *Style and Idea,* 48.

78. "Analysis of the Second String Quartet" (1936), 47. Webern made the same point in regard to the last movement in a brief, untitled essay on Schoenberg's string quartets dating from 1912; see *Schoenberg, Berg, Webern: The String Quartets,* ed. Rauchhaupt, 18.

79. "Analysis of the Second String Quartet" (1936), 47.

80. Ibid. For a detailed account of the strictness with which Schoenberg adhered to the variation technique, see Catherine Dale, "Schoenberg's Concept of Variation Form: A Paradigmatic Analysis of *Litanei* from the Second String Quartet, Op. 10," *Journal of the Royal Musical Association* 11 (1993): 94–120.

81. See Frisch, *Early Works of Schoenberg,* 267–68.

Bibliography

Adorno, Theodor W. *Introduction to the Sociology of Music.* Translated by E. B. Ashton. New York, 1976. (Orig. *Einleitung in die Musiksoziologie.* Frankfurt, 1962.)
———. *Quasi una Fantasia: Essays on Modern Music.* Translated by Rodney Livingstone. London, 1992.

Antokoletz, Elliott. *The Music of Béla Bartók: A Study of Tonality and Progression in Twentieth-Century Music.* Berkeley and Los Angeles, 1984.

Archibald, Bruce. "Berg's Development as an Instrumental Composer." In *The Berg Companion,* ed. Douglas Jarman, 91–122. Boston, 1989.

Beaumont, Antony. *Busoni the Composer.* Bloomington, IN, 1985.

Benson, Mark. "Schoenberg's Private Program for the String Quartet in D minor, Op. 7." *Journal of Musicology* 11 (1993): 374–95.

Berg, Alban. "Why is Schönberg's Music So Hard to Understand?" Translated by A. Swarowsky and J. H. Lederer. *Music Review* 13 (1952): 187–96. (Orig. "Warum ist Schönbergs Musik so schwer verständlich?" *Musikblätter des Anbruch,* 1924.)

Boestfleisch, Rainer. *Arnold Schönbergs frühe Kammermusik: Studien unter besonderer Berücksichtigung der ersten beiden Streichquartette.* Frankfurt am Main, 1990.

Brotbeck, Roman. *Zum Spätwerk Max Reger: Fünf Diskurse.* Wiesbaden, 1988.

Burkholder, J. Peter. *Charles Ives: The Ideas behind the Music.* New Haven, CT, 1985.

Cadenbach, Rainer. *Max Reger und seine Zeit.* Laaber, 1991.

Dahlhaus, Carl. "Liszt, Schönberg und die große Form: Das Prinzip der Mehrsätzigkeit in der Einsätzigkeit." *Die Musikforschung* 41 (1988): 202–12.

———. *Nineteenth-Century Music.* Translated by J. Bradford Robinson. Berkeley and Los Angeles, 1989. (Orig. *Die Musik des 19. Jahrhunderts.* Wiesbaden, 1980.)

———. *Schoenberg and the New Music.* Translated by Derrick Puffett and Alfred Clayton. Cambridge, 1987.

Dale, Catherine. "Foreground Motif as a Determinant of Formal and Tonal Structure in the First Movement of Schönberg's Second String Quartet." *Music Review* 52 (1991): 52–63.

———. "Schoenberg's Concept of Variation Form: A Paradigmatic Analysis of *Litanei* from the Second String Quartet, Op. 10." *Journal of the Royal Musical Association* 11 (1993): 94–120.

Danuser, Hermann. *Die Musik des 20. Jahrhunderts.* Vol. 7 of *Neues Handbuch der Musikwissenschaft,* edited by Carl Dahlhaus. Laaber, 1984.

———. *Musikalische Prosa.* Regensburg, 1975.

Frisch, Walter. *The Early Works of Arnold Schoenberg, 1893–1908.* Berkeley and Los Angeles, 1993.

———. "Thematic Form and the Genesis of Schoenberg's D-minor quartet, Opus 7." *Journal of the American Musicological Society* 41 (1988): 289–314.

———, ed. *Brahms and His World.* Princeton, NJ, 1990.

Gerlach, Reinhard. *Musik und Jugendstil der Wiener Schule, 1900–1908.* Laaber, 1985.

———. "War Schönberg von Dvořák beeinflußt: Zu Schönbergs Streichquartett D-dur." *Neue Zeitschrift für Musik* 133 (1972): 122–27.

Häfner, Roland. *Max Reger: Klarinettenquintett op. 146.* Munich, 1962.

Hitchcock, H. Wiley. *Ives.* London, 1977.

Ives, Charles. *Memos.* Edited by John Kirkpatrick. New York, [1972].

Koch, Heinrich Christoph. *Musikalisches Lexikon.* Frankfurt, 1802.

Leichtentritt, Hugo. "German and Austrian Chamber Music." In *Cobbett's Cyclopedic Survey of Chamber Music.* 2d ed., 444–51. London, 1963.

Loll, Werner. *Zwischen Tradition und Avantgarde: Die Kammermusik Alexander Zemlinskys.* Kassel, 1990.

Mattner, Lothar. *Substanz und Akzidens: Analytische Studien an Streichquartettsätzen*

Max Regers. Wiesbaden, 1985.

Metzger, Heinz-Klaus. "Über Anton Weberns Streichquartett 1905." *Musik-Konzepte,* special issue, *Anton Webern I* (1983): 76–111.

Möller, Martin. *Untersuchungen zur Satztechnik Max Regers: Studien an den Kopfsätzen der Kammermusikwerke.* Wiesbaden, 1984.

Popp, Susanne. "Zur musikalischen Prosa bei Reger und Schönberg." In *Reger-Studien I: Festschrift für Ottmar Schreiber,* edited by Günther Popp and Susanne Popp, 59–78. Wiesbaden, 1978.

Rauchhaupt, Ursula von, ed. *Schoenberg, Berg, Webern: The String Quartets.* Hamburg, 1971.

Riemann, Hugo. *Dictionary of Music.* Translated by J. S. Shedlock. 2 vols. 4th ed. London, 1908.

Riethmüller, Albrecht. *Ferruccio Busonis Poetik.* Mainz, 1988.

Sachs, Klaus-Jürgen. "Zur Konzeption des ersten Satzes aus dem Klaviertrio c-moll op. 101." In *Brahms-Analysen,* edited by Friedhelm Krummacher and Wolfram Steinbeck. Kassel, 1984.

Samson, Jim. *Music in Transition: A Study of Tonal Expansion and Atonality, 1900–1920.* New York, 1977.

———, ed. *The Late Romantic Era: From the Mid-Nineteenth Century to World War I.* Englewood Cliffs, NJ, 1991.

Schilling, Gustav, comp. *Encyclopädie der gesammten musikalischen Wissenschaften, oder Universal-Lexicon der Tonkunst.* 7 vols. Stuttgart, 1835–38.

Schmidt, Christian Martin. "Formprobleme in Schönbergs frühen Instrumentalwerken." In *Bericht über den 1. Kongreß der Internationalen Schönberg-Gesellschaft,* 180–86. Vienna, 1978.

———. "Schönbergs 'Very Definite—but Private' Program zum Streichquartett Opus 7." In *Bericht über den 1. Kongreß der Internationalen Schönberg-Gesellschaft,* 230–34. Vienna, 1978.

Schoenberg, Arnold. *Style and Idea.* Edited by Leonard Stein. Translated by Leo Black. Berkeley and Los Angeles, 1975.

Schorske, Carl E. *Fin-de-siècle Vienna: Politics and Culture.* New York, 1981.

Smith, Joan Allen. *Schoenberg and His Circle: A Viennese Portrait.* New York, 1986.

Steiner, Fred. "A History of the First Complete Recordings of the Schoenberg String Quartets." *Journal of the Arnold Schoenberg Institute* 2 (1978): 122–37.

Stevens, Halsey. *The Life and Music of Béla Bartók.* Rev. ed. London, 1964.

Swift, Richard. "1-XII-99: Tonal Relations in Schoenberg's *Verklärte Nacht.*" *19th Century Music* 1 (1977): 3–14.

Thieme, Ulrich. *Studien zum Jugendwerk Arnold Schönberg: Einflüsse und Wandlungen.* Regensburg, 1979.

Tilmouth, Michael. "Chamber Music." In *The New Grove Dictionary of Music and Musicians,* edited by Stanley Sadie, 4:113–18. London, 1980.

Waeltner, Ernst Ludwig. "O du lieber Augustin: Der Scherzo Satz im II. Streichquartett von Arnold Schönberg." In *Bericht über den 1. Kongreß der Internationalen Schönberg-Gesellschaft,* 246–62. Vienna, 1978.

Walsh, Stephen. *Bartók Chamber Music.* London, 1982.

Weber, Horst. *Alexander Zemlinsky.* Vienna, 1977.

Wolf, Hugo. *The Music Criticism of Hugo Wolf.* Translated and edited by Henry Pleasants. New York, 1978.

Index

Italics indicate detailed discussion or analysis of a work.